Training Guide: Administering Windows Server® 2012 R2

Orin Thomas

PUBLISHED BY
Microsoft Press
A Division of Microsoft Corporation
One Microsoft Way
Redmond, Washington 98052-6399

Library of Congress Control Number: 2014937581
ISBN: 978-0-7356-8469-0

Printed and bound in the United States of America.

4   16

Microsoft Press books are available through booksellers and distributors worldwide. If you need support related to this book, email Microsoft Press Book Support at mspinput@microsoft.com. Please tell us what you think of this book at http://www.microsoft.com/learning/booksurvey.

Microsoft and the trademarks listed at http://www.microsoft.com/en-us/legal/intellectualproperty/Trademarks/EN-US.aspx are trademarks of the Microsoft group of companies. All other marks are property of their respective owners.

The example companies, organizations, products, domain names, email addresses, logos, people, places, and events depicted herein are fictitious. No association with any real company, organization, product, domain name, email address, logo, person, place, or event is intended or should be inferred.

This book expresses the author's views and opinions. The information contained in this book is provided without any express, statutory, or implied warranties. Neither the authors, Microsoft Corporation, nor its resellers, or distributors will be held liable for any damages caused or alleged to be caused either directly or indirectly by this book.

Acquisitions Editor: Anne Hamilton
Developmental Editor: Karen Szall
Editorial Production: Troy Mott, Backstop Media LLC
Technical Reviewer: Telmo Sampaio
Copyeditor: Christina Rudloff
Indexer: Judy Hoer
Cover: Twist Creative • Seattle

Contents at a glance

Introduction   *xvii*

CHAPTER 1   Deploying and updating Windows Server 2012 R2   1

CHAPTER 2   Managing account policies and service accounts   65

CHAPTER 3   Configuring name resolution   123

CHAPTER 4   Administering Active Directory   181

CHAPTER 5   Managing Group Policy application and infrastructure   241

CHAPTER 6   Group Policy settings and preferences   281

CHAPTER 7   Administering network policies   345

CHAPTER 8   Administering remote access   417

CHAPTER 9   Managing file services   501

CHAPTER 10   Monitoring and auditing   591

Index   *659*

Contents

Introduction   xvii

Chapter 1: Deploying and updating Windows Server 2012 R2   1

Before you begin. 1

Lesson 1: Configuring and servicing Windows Server images. 1

    Understanding Windows images   2

    Configuring Windows images   3

    Servicing Windows images   4

    Lesson summary   10

    Lesson review   10

Lesson 2: Automatically deploying Windows Server images. 11

    Automating installation   12

    Configuring answer files   12

    Windows Deployment Services   14

    WDS requirements   15

    Managing images   17

    Configuring WDS   19

    Configuring transmissions   24

    Driver groups and packages   25

    Lesson summary   26

    Lesson review   26

Lesson 3: Servicing and updating deployed servers. 27

    Automated update deployment with WSUS   28

    New WSUS features   28

What do you think of this book? We want to hear from you!

Microsoft is interested in hearing your feedback so we can continually improve our
books and learning resources for you. To participate in a brief online survey, please visit:

www.microsoft.com/learning/booksurvey/

Deploy and manage WSUS................28

WSUS groups................33

WSUS policies................33

Deploying updates................35

Automatic approval rules................36

Lesson summary................38

Lesson review................38

Practice exercises 39

Exercise 1: Prepare update files................40

Exercise 2: Servicing a WIM image................42

Exercise 3: Deploy Windows Deployment Services................43

Exercise 4: Configure Windows Deployment Services................47

Exercise 5: Import driver package................52

Exercise 6: Deploy WSUS................54

Exercise 7: Configure WSUS................56

Exercise 8: WSUS groups and rules................58

Suggested practice exercises 60

Answers. 61

Lesson 1................61

Lesson 2................61

Lesson 3................62

Chapter 2: Managing account policies and service accounts   65

Before you begin. 65

Lesson 1: Implementing domain password and lockout policies. 65

Domain user password policies................66

Account lockout settings................70

Account management tasks................71

Lesson summary................76

Lesson review................76

Lesson 2: Using fine–grained password policies 77

Delegate password settings permissions................78

Fine–grained password policies................80

Lesson summary................85

      Lesson review   85

Lesson 3: Mastering Group Managed Service Accounts 87

      GMSAs   87

      Kerberos delegation   91

      Kerberos policies   92

      Service principal name management   94

      Lesson summary   94

      Lesson review   94

Practice exercises 95

      Exercise 1: Configure password and account lockout policies   96

      Exercise 2: Configure account lockout policies   101

      Exercise 3: Group Policy Modeling   104

      Exercise 4: Locate non-expiring passwords   107

      Exercise 5: Create fine–grained password policies   110

      Exercise 6: Prepare MEL-DC and ADL-DC   113

      Exercise 7: Create and configure GMSAs   114

Suggested practice exercises 116

Answers 117

      Lesson 1   117

      Lesson 2   118

      Lesson 3   119

Chapter 3: Configuring name resolution   **123**

Before you begin. 123

Lesson 1: Understanding DNS zones and forwarders 123

      DNS zone types   124

      Zone delegation   129

      Split DNS   131

      Forwarders and conditional forwarders   131

      Stub zones   134

      Lesson summary   136

      Lesson review   136

Lesson 2: Configuring WINS and managing GlobalNames zones 138

      WINS   138

GlobalNames zones 142

Peer Name Resolution Protocol (PNRP) 144

Lesson summary 145

Lesson review 146

Lesson 3: Understanding advanced DNS options.....................147

Resource records 147

Zone aging and scavenging 151

DNSSEC 153

Lesson summary 157

Lesson review 157

Practice exercises 158

Exercise 1: Manage DNS zones 159

Exercise 2: Configure partition-based replication 161

Exercise 3: DNS delegation and secondary zones 163

Exercise 4: Configure a secondary zone 168

Exercise 5: Single-label name resolution 171

Exercise 6: Configure and manage DNSSEC 173

Suggested practice exercises 176

Answers...177

Lesson 1 177

Lesson 2 178

Lesson 3 179

Chapter 4: Administering Active Directory — 181

Before you begin..181

Lesson 1: Managing domain controllers 181

Managing operations masters 182

Global Catalog servers 187

Universal group membership caching 189

Read-only domain controllers 190

Domain controller cloning 197

Lesson summary 198

Lesson review 199

Lesson 2: Maintaining domain controllers 200

    Active Directory database optimization   200

    Active Directory metadata cleanup   203

    Active Directory snapshots   204

    Lesson summary   206

    Lesson review   207

Lesson 3: Recovering Active Directory 208

    Active Directory Recycle Bin   208

    Active Directory backup   210

    Active Directory recovery   212

    Lesson summary   215

    Lesson review   216

Practice exercises 217

    Exercise 1: Domain controller installation   217

    Exercise 2: RODC deployment   225

    Exercise 3: Transfer operations master roles   230

    Exercise 4: Active Directory Recycle Bin   234

Suggested practice exercises 236

Answers. 237

    Lesson 1   237

    Lesson 2   238

    Lesson 3   239

Chapter 5: Managing Group Policy application and infrastructure 241

Before you begin. 241

Lesson 1: Maintaining Group Policy Object 241

    Managing Group Policy Objects   242

    Migrate Group Policy Objects   247

    Delegate GPO management   248

    Lesson summary   251

    Lesson review   252

Lesson 2: Managing Group Policy application. 253

    Policy processing precedence   253

Policy enforcement and blocking   254

Group Policy security filtering   255

Group Policy WMI filtering   257

Loopback processing   258

Group Policy caching   260

Force Group Policy update   261

Lesson summary   263

Lesson review   263

Practice exercises 265

Exercise 1: Prepare GPOs, security groups, and OUs   265

Exercise 2: Manage GPOs   268

Exercise 3: Manage Group Policy processing   271

Exercise 4: Group Policy inheritance and enforcement   274

Suggested practice exercises 277

Answers. 278

Lesson 1   278

Lesson 2   279

Chapter 6: Group Policy settings and preferences   281

Before you begin. 281

Lesson 1: Folder redirection, software installation, and scripts 281

Folder Redirection   282

Software installation   285

Scripts   291

Lesson summary   293

Lesson review   293

Lesson 2: Administrative templates 296

Administrative templates   296

Administrative template settings   297

Central store   297

ADMX Migrator   299

Filter property settings   300

Lesson summary   302

Lesson review   302

Lesson 3: Group Policy preferences................................303

    Group Policy preference settings   303

    Item-level targeting   305

    Mapping network drives   306

    Configuring printers   308

    Configuring power options   309

    Configuring the registry   314

    Internet options   314

    Additional settings   317

    Lesson summary   321

    Lesson review   322

Practice exercises 323

    Exercise 1: Prepare Folder Redirection and scripts   324

    Exercise 2: Configure Folder Redirection   325

    Exercise 3: Configure Group Policy scripts   329

    Exercise 4: Configure the central store and administrative template filtering   330

    Exercise 5: Configure Group Policy preferences   331

Suggested practice exercises 338

Answers...339

    Lesson 1   339

    Lesson 2   340

    Lesson 3   341

Chapter 7: Administering network policies   345

Before you begin...345

Lesson 1: Understanding Network Policy Server policies 345

    NPS deployment   346

    Connection request policies   350

    Client configuration   363

    IP filters   367

    Encryption   368

    IP settings   368

    Creating network policies   369

NPS templates   374

Lesson summary   375

Lesson review   375

Lesson 2: Understanding Network Access Protection
enforcement methods 376

DHCP enforcement   377

IPsec enforcement   380

802.1X enforcement   382

VPN enforcement   385

RD Gateway enforcement   387

Lesson summary   390

Lesson review   391

Lesson 3: Understanding Network Access Protection infrastructure 392

Windows Security Health Validator   392

System Health Validators and System Health Agents   395

Health policies   395

Health Registration Authorities   397

Remediation server groups   398

Lesson summary   399

Lesson review   399

Practice exercises 400

Exercise 1: Installing the DHCP role   401

Exercise 2: Deploying the NPS role   402

Exercise 3: Configuring Windows Security Health Validator   403

Exercise 4: Configuring a remediation server group   405

Exercise 5: Configuring client policies for DHCP enforcement   406

Exercise 6: Configuring NAP DHCP enforcement   408

Suggested practice exercises 412

Answers. 413

Lesson 1   413

Lesson 2   414

Lesson 3   415

Chapter 8: Administering remote access   417

Before you begin. 417

Lesson 1: Configuring RADIUS 417

    RADIUS servers   418

    RADIUS proxies   421

    RADIUS clients   426

    RADIUS accounting   429

    Lesson summary   433

    Lesson review   433

Lesson 2: Configuring VPN and routing. 434

    Deploy Routing and Remote Access   435

    Configure VPN settings   437

    Configure routing   446

    Network address translation (NAT)   448

    Web Application Proxy in pass-through mode   451

    Lesson summary   453

    Lesson review   453

Lesson 3: Configuring DirectAccess. 454

    Understanding DirectAccess   455

    DirectAccess infrastructure   455

    Configure DirectAccess   462

    Lesson summary   473

    Lesson review   474

Practice exercises 475

    Exercise 1: Configure a RADIUS server   475

    Exercise 2: Configure a remote RADIUS server group   477

    Exercise 3: Configure a RADIUS client   479

    Exercise 4: Set up RADIUS accounting   480

    Exercise 5: Install a VPN server   481

    Exercise 6: Configure a VPN server   482

    Exercise 7: Prepare for Web Application Proxy   483

    Exercise 8: Configure AD FS to support Web Application Proxy   489

Exercise 9: Deploy Web Application Proxy with pass-through
preauthentication   491

Suggested practice exercises 495

Answers. 496
    Lesson 1   496
    Lesson 2   497
    Lesson 3   498

Chapter 9: Managing file services   501

Before you begin. 501

Lesson 1: Configuring File Server Resource Manager 501
    Configuring quotas   502
    Configuring file screens   504
    Enabling file classification   505
    Configuring file management tasks   506
    Generating reports   507
    Lesson summary   509
    Lesson review   509

Lesson 2: Configuring a Distributed File System 511
    Understanding Distributed File System namespaces   511
    Understanding DFS replication   514
    Cloning the DFS Replication database   519
    Understanding DFSR and database recovery   520
    Lesson summary   520
    Lesson review   520

Lesson 3: Configuring file and disk encryption 522
    Configuring BitLocker   522
    Configuring Network Unlock   528
    Configuring Encrypting File System   530
    Using EFS with an enterprise CA   531
    Key and data recovery   532
    Lesson summary   533
    Lesson review   534

Practice exercises 535

Exercise 1: Install the File Server Resource Manager role
service and create a shared folder   536

Exercise 2: Configure file quotas   541

Exercise 3: Configure file screen   545

Exercise 4: Configure file expiration   549

Exercise 5: Configure storage reports   552

Exercise 6: Install DFS   555

Exercise 7: Create a DFS namespace and add a namespace server
558

Exercise 8: Configure DFS replication   560

Exercise 9: Install Enterprise CA   566

Exercise 10: Configure certificate templates   571

Exercise 11: Configure certificate enrollment   574

Exercise 12: Configure EFS-related Group Policies   578

Exercise 13: Configure BitLocker-related policies   582

Suggested practice exercises 584

Answers. 585

Lesson 1   585

Lesson 2   586

Lesson 3   588

Chapter 10: Monitoring and auditing   591

Before you begin. 591

Lesson 1: Monitoring servers 591

Configuring data collector sets   592

Managing alerts   597

Monitoring events with viewer   599

Configuring event subscriptions   603

Attaching event-driven tasks   606

Performing network monitoring   609

Lesson summary   612

Lesson review   613

Lesson 2: Advanced audit policies 614

    Configuring advanced auditing   614

    Using auditpol with auditing   619

    Lesson summary   619

    Lesson review   620

Practice exercises 621

    Exercise 1: Configure data collector sets   621

    Exercise 2: Collect data   626

    Exercise 3: Configure alerts   628

    Exercise 4: Prepare computers for event subscriptions   630

    Exercise 5: Configure event subscriptions   632

    Exercise 6: Configure network monitoring   636

    Exercise 7: Using Message Analyzer   638

    Exercise 8: Configure removable device auditing   641

    Exercise 9: Configure logon auditing   645

    Exercise 10: Configure expression-based audit policies   649

    Exercise 11: Configure folder auditing   652

Suggested practice exercises 654

Answers. 655

    Lesson 1   655

    Lesson 2   656

Index   659

What do you think of this book? We want to hear from you!

Microsoft is interested in hearing your feedback so we can continually improve our
books and learning resources for you. To participate in a brief online survey, please visit:

www.microsoft.com/learning/booksurvey/

Introduction

When Microsoft Learning puts together exam objectives for an exam, it doesn't randomly select pages from TechNet. Instead, in conjunction with subject matter experts and representatives of the product team, it puts together a list of tasks and areas of knowledge that represents what someone in a specific job role would do and need to know on a day-to-day, a weekly, or even a monthly basis.

Each exam maps to a different job role. The objectives for the 70-411 exam are a list of tasks and areas of knowledge that describe what an administrator of the Windows Server 2012 and Windows Server 2012 R2 operating systems with several years of on-the-job experience (managing other server operating systems as well as Windows Server 2012 and Windows Server 2012 R2) does and understands. The objectives don't cover everything that a Windows Server systems administrator would know, and there will be tasks and areas that will be relevant to one person's real world role and not another, but the exam objectives provide a reasonable approximation of that role.

This book covers the majority of the topics and skills that are the subject of the Microsoft certification exam 70-411. The idea behind this book is that by reading it, you can learn how to perform tasks you may need to perform on a day-to-day basis in your role as a Windows Server administrator. Using the exam objectives as a working definition of that role has the additional benefit of giving you a better understanding of the topics and tasks listed on the 70-411 exam objectives. This book will assist you in preparing for the exam, but it's not a complete exam preparation solution. If you are preparing for the exam, you should use additional study materials, such as practice tests and *Exam Ref 70-411: Administering Windows Server 2012 R2* (Microsoft Press, 2014) to help bolster your real world experience. For your reference, a mapping of the topics in this book to the exam objectives is included in the back of the book in the Objectives Map.

By using this training guide, you will learn how to do the following:

- Deploy, manage, and maintain servers
- Configure file and print services
- Configure network services and access
- Configure a network policy server infrastructure
- Configure and manage Active Directory
- Configure and manage Group Policy

System requirements

The following are the minimum system requirements your computer needs to meet to complete the practice exercises in this book. This book is designed assuming you will be using Hyper-V—either the client version available with some editions of Windows 8, Windows 8.1 or the version available in Windows Server 2012 or Windows Server 2012 R2. You can use other virtualization software instead, such as VirtualBox or VMWare Workstation, but the practice setup instructions assume that you are using Hyper-V.

Hardware and software requirements

This section presents the hardware requirements for Hyper-V and the software requirements.

Virtualization hardware requirements

If you choose to use virtualization software, you need only one physical computer to perform the exercises in this book. That physical host computer must meet the following minimum hardware requirements:

- x64-based processor that includes both hardware-assisted virtualization (AMD-V or Intel VT) and hardware data execution protection. (On AMD systems, the data execution protection feature is called the No Execute or NX bit. On Intel systems, this feature is called the Execute Disable or XD bit.) These features must also be enabled in the BIOS. (Note: You can run Windows Virtual PC without Intel-VT or AMD-V.) If you want to use Hyper-V on Windows 8 or Windows 8.1, you need a processor that supports Second Level Address Translation (SLAT).
- 8 GB of RAM (more is recommended).
- 80 GB of available hard disk space.
- Internet connectivity.

Software requirements

The following software is required to complete the practice exercises:

- Windows Server 2012 R2 evaluation. You can download an evaluation edition of Windows Server 2012 R2 in iso format from the Windows Server and Cloud Platform website at *http://www.microsoft.com/server*.

Virtual Machine setup instructions

The instructions for building the virtual machine environment that allow you to perform the exercises in this book are located here.

This set of exercises contains abbreviated instructions for setting up the SYD-DC, MEL-DC, ADL-DC, and CBR-DC computers used in the practice exercises in all chapters of this training guide. To perform these exercises, first install Windows Server 2012 R2 Standard edition using the default configuration, setting the administrator password to **Pa$$w0rd**.

Exercise 1: SYD-DC to function as a Windows Server 2012 R2 domain controller

1. Log on to the first computer on which you have installed Windows Server 2012 R2 using the Administrator account and the password **Pa$$w0rd**.

2. Open an elevated PowerShell prompt and issue the following commands:

   ```
   New-NetIPAddress -InterfaceAlias Ethernet -IPAddress 10.10.10.10 -PrefixLength 24
   Rename-Computer SYD-DC
   Restart-Computer
   ```

3. Restart the computer and log back on using the Administrator account.

4. Open an elevated PowerShell prompt and issue the following command:

   ```
   Install-WindowsFeature AD-Domain-Services -IncludeManagementTools
   ```

5. Open the Server Manager console. Click the Refresh icon.

6. Click on the Notifications icon and then click Promote This Server to Domain Controller.

7. On the Deployment Configuration page, choose Add a New Forest. Enter **Contoso.com** as the root domain name and then click Next.

8. On the Domain Controller Options page, configure the following settings and then click Next:

   - Forest Functional Level: **Windows Server 2012 R2**
   - Domain Functional Level: **Windows Server 2012 R2**
   - Domain Name System (DNS) Server: **Enabled**
   - Global Catalog: **Enabled**
   - DSRM Password: **Pa$$w0rd**

9. On the DNS Options page, click Next.

10. On the Additional Options page, click Next.

11. Accept the default settings for the Database, Log Files, and SYSVOL locations and click Next.

12. On the Review Options page, click Next.

13. On the Prerequisites Check page, click Install.

14. The computer will restart automatically.

Exercise 2: Prepare Active Directory Domain Server (AD DS)

1. Log on to server SYD-DC using the Administrator account.

2. Using Active Directory Users and Computers, create a user account named don_funk in the Users container and assign the account the password **Pa$$w0rd**. Configure the password to never expire. Add this user account to the Enterprise Admins, Domain Admins, and Schema Admins groups.

3. Open the DNS console and create a primary IPv4 Reverse Lookup Zone for the subnet 10.10.10.x. Ensure that the zone is stored within AD DS and is replicated to all DNS servers running on domain controllers in the forest and allows only secure dynamic updates.

4. Open an elevated PowerShell prompt and issue the following command:

```
Set-DNSClientServerAddress -InterfaceAlias Ethernet -ServerAddresses 10.10.10.10
```

Exercise 3: Prepare ADL-DC

1. Ensure that computer SYD-DC is turned on and connected to the network or virtual network to which the second computer is connected.

2. Log on to the second computer on which you have installed Windows Server 2012 R2 using the Administrator account and the password **Pa$$w0rd**.

3. Open an elevated PowerShell prompt and issue the following commands:

```
New-NetIPAddress -InterfaceAlias Ethernet -IPAddress 10.10.10.20 -PrefixLength 24
Set-DNSClientServerAddress -InterfaceAlias Ethernet -ServerAddresses 10.10.10.10
Rename-Computer ADL-DC
Restart-Computer
```

4. After the computer restarts, log on again using the Administrator account.

5. Shut down the computer.

Exercise 4: Prepare CBR-DC

1. Ensure that computer SYD-DC is turned on and connected to the network or virtual network to which the second computer is connected.

2. Log on to the third computer on which you have installed Windows Server 2012 R2 using the Administrator account and the password **Pa$$w0rd**.

3. Open an elevated PowerShell prompt and issue the following commands:

```
New-NetIPAddress -InterfaceAlias Ethernet -IPAddress 10.10.10.30 -PrefixLength 24
Set-DNSClientServerAddress -InterfaceAlias Ethernet -ServerAddresses 10.10.10.10
Rename-Computer CBR-DC
Restart-Computer
```

4. Restart the computer and then log on again using the Administrator account.

5. Shut down the computer.

Exercise 5: Prepare MEL-DC

1. Ensure that computer SYD-DC is turned on and connected to the network or virtual network to which the second computer is connected.

2. Log on to the third computer on which you have installed Windows Server 2012 R2 using the Administrator account and the password **Pa$$w0rd**.

3. Open an elevated PowerShell prompt and issue the following commands:

```
New-NetIPAddress -InterfaceAlias Ethernet -IPAddress 10.10.10.40 -PrefixLength 24
Set-DNSClientServerAddress -InterfaceAlias Ethernet -ServerAddresses 10.10.10.10
Rename-Computer MEL-DC
Restart-Computer
```

4. Restart the computer and then log on again using the Administrator account.

5. Shut down the computer.

Exercise 6: Checkpoint all virtual machines

1. Checkpoint all virtual machines. This is the state that they need to be in prior to performing exercises. Checkpoints were termed snapshots in prior versions of Hyper-V.

Acknowledgments

I'd like to thank the following people for their dedication and help in getting this book written: Karen Szall , Troy Mott, Telmo Sampaio and Christina Rudloff.

Errata, updates, & book support

We've made every effort to ensure the accuracy of this book. You can access updates to this book—in the form of a list of submitted errata and their related corrections—at:

http://aka.ms/TG411R2

If you discover an error that is not already listed, please submit it to us at the same page.

If you need additional support, email Microsoft Press Book Support at mspinput@ microsoft.com.

Please note that product support for Microsoft software and hardware is not offered through the previous addresses. For help with Microsoft software or hardware, go to *http:// support.microsoft.com*.

We want to hear from you

At Microsoft Press, your satisfaction is our top priority, and your feedback our most valuable asset. Please tell us what you think of this book at:

http://aka.ms/tellpress

The survey is short, and we read every one of your comments and ideas. Thanks in advance for your input!

Stay in touch

Let's keep the conversation going! We're on Twitter: *http://twitter.com/MicrosoftPress*.

CHAPTER 1

Deploying and updating Windows Server 2012 R2

Deploying and servicing Windows Server 2012 and Windows Server 2012 R2 is a routine task that you will perform in your career as a systems administrator. Deploying the operating system is something you generally do once per server, especially now that it's easier to restore a system image from backup, than it is to deploy from scratch. Servicing includes keeping your deployment images and your deployed services up to date. In your job role, you're likely to spend a lot more time on these tasks than you will on deployment. In this chapter, you'll learn about configuring and servicing Windows Server 2012 and Windows Server 2012 R2 images, about the tools included with Windows Server that enable you to automate its deployment, and about the technologies that are available to automate the process of keeping deployed servers up to date with hotfixes and software updates.

Lessons in this chapter:

- Lesson 1: Configuring and servicing Windows Server images **1**
- Lesson 2: Automatically deploying Windows Server images **11**
- Lesson 3: Servicing and updating deployed servers **27**

Before you begin

To complete the practice exercises in this chapter, you must set up the lab of virtual machines, as described in the Introduction. You should take a checkpoint (formerly known as a snapshot) of each virtual machine prior to performing the practice exercises. You can revert the virtual machines to their original state once you have completed the exercises.

Lesson 1: Configuring and servicing Windows Server images

Although you can install Windows Server 2012 from the installation media, most organizations that deploy the server operating system use custom images. By using custom images, systems administrators can deploy operating systems so that they require a minimum of post-installation configuration. In this lesson, you will learn about Windows images, the steps that you can take to configure these images, and the processes involved in servicing those images.

> **After this lesson, you will be able to:**
> - Understand Windows images.
> - Configure Windows images.
> - Service Windows images.
>
> **Estimated lesson time: 45 minutes**

Understanding Windows images

In earlier versions of the Windows Server operating system, such as Windows NT 4.0 and Windows Server 2003, all of the files needed to install the operating system were located in a special i386 directory on the installation media. With Windows images, the entire operating system—as well as associated drivers, updates, and applications—is stored within a single file, known as an image file. During installation, this image is applied to the target volume. Windows images use the Windows Imaging (WIM) file format and have the following benefits:

- **Multiple deployment methods**   You can use a variety of ways to deploy Windows images. You can deploy .wim files using a traditional DVD-ROM, from a bootable USB drive, from a network share, or through specialized deployment technologies such as Windows Deployment Services (WDS) or Microsoft System Center 2012 Configuration Manager.
- **Editable**   You can mount an image and edit it, enabling, disabling, or removing operating system roles and features as necessary.
- **Updatable**   You can update an image without having to perform an operating system image capture. In previous versions of Windows, you had to perform a deployment, apply updates, and then capture a new image. If you wanted to update that image, you'd have to start from scratch.

The Windows Server 2012 installation media contain two .wim files in the Sources directory: Boot.wim and Install.wim. Boot.wim is used by the installation media to load the preinstallation environment that you use to deploy Windows Server 2012. Install.wim stores one or more operating system images. For example, as Figure 1-1 shows, the Install.wim file available with the evaluation version of Windows Server 2012 contains four different editions of Windows Server 2012.

> *MORE INFO*   **WINDOWS SERVER 2012 R2**
>
> This book uses the evaluation version that you can download from the Microsoft website at *http://technet.microsoft.com/en-US/evalcenter/dn205286.aspx*.

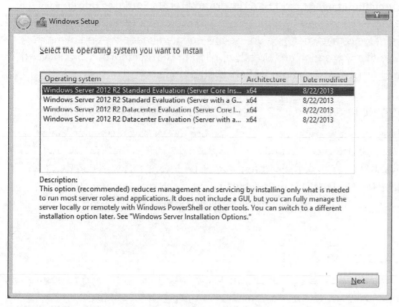

FIGURE 1-1 Operating systems included in the evaluation Install.wim file

---

MORE INFO   **WINDOWS IMAGING (WIM) FILE FORMAT**

To learn more about the Windows Imaging (WIM) file format, consult the following Microsoft white paper at *http://www.microsoft.com/en-us/download/details.aspx?id=13096*

Configuring Windows images

Although you can deploy Windows Server 2012 and Windows Server 2012 R2 straight off the installation media, in enterprise environments you will want to make modifications to the image. The Deployment Image Servicing and Management (DISM) tool is a command-line tool that you can use to manage images in an offline state. The advantage of performing offline modifications to images is that you don't need to install an operating system and then perform a capture to make changes.

You can use *Dism.exe* to perform the following tasks:

- Enable or disable roles and features
- List roles and features
- Add, remove, and list software updates
- Add, remove, and list software drivers
- Add, remove, and list software packages in .appx format to a Windows image

For example, you can take the Install.wim file from the Windows Server installation media and use Dism.exe to mount that image, add new drivers and recent software updates to that image, and save those changes—all without having to perform a Windows Server 2012 deployment. The advantage is that when you do use this updated image for deployment, the drivers and updates that you added are already applied to the image. You don't have to install them as part of your post-installation configuration routine.

REAL WORLD **FINDING DRIVERS**

Rather than searching vendor websites in vain, you can use the Microsoft Update Catalog (*http://catalog.update.microsoft.com*) to find and download driver files that you can add to WIM images. This site stores all of the certified hardware drivers, software updates, and hotfixes published by Microsoft. Once you download drivers and software updates, you can add them to your existing installation images by using Dism.exe.

Servicing Windows images

As a systems administrator responsible for deploying Windows Server, you need to ensure that your deployment images are kept up to date. The latest software updates must be applied to the image, and any new device drivers for commonly used server hardware should be included.

The main goals of an image servicing strategy are the following:

- Ensure that the latest software updates and hotfixes are applied to the image before the image is deployed to new servers.
- Ensure that the latest drivers are applied to the image before the image is deployed to new servers.

If you don't take these steps, you'll have to wait until after you've deployed the operating system before you can apply updates and drivers, which consumes a significant amount of time. If your images are up to date, you won't have to pause between deploying Windows Server, and waiting for it to contact Microsoft Update or the local Windows Server Update Services (WSUS) server before you can move on to the next step (for example, deploying a server application such as Microsoft Exchange 2013, Microsoft SharePoint 2013, or Microsoft SQL Server 2012).

REAL WORLD **LOCATING UPDATE FILES**

Instead of searching through TechNet to locate specific update files, the Microsoft Update Catalog (*http://catalog.update.microsoft.com*) contains all of the software update and hotfix files published by Microsoft. You can inject these updates into an operating system image by using Dism.exe.

Using Dism.exe to service images

The Dism.exe command-line utility is included with the Windows Server 2012 operating system. You can use the Dism.exe utility to service the current operating system in an online state or perform offline servicing of a Windows image. This lesson is concerned with performing maintenance of installation images, so it covers only that aspect of Dism.exe functionality.

Servicing images with Dism.exe involves performing the following general steps:

1. Mount the image so that it can be modified.

2. Service the image.

3. Commit or discard the changes made to the image.

Mounting images

By mounting an image, you can make changes to that image. When you *mount an image*, you link it to a folder. You can use File Explorer, Windows PowerShell, or Cmd.exe to navigate the structure of this folder and interact with it as you would any other folder located on the file system. Once the image is mounted, you can also use Dism.exe to perform servicing tasks, such as adding and removing drivers and updates.

A single WIM file can contain multiple operating system images. Each operating system image is assigned an index number, which you need to know before you can use Dism.exe to mount the image. You locate this using the /Get-wiminfo switch. For example, if you have an image named Install.wim located in the C:\Images folder, you can use the following command to get a list of the operating system images it contains.

```
Dism.exe /get-wiminfo /wimfile:c:\images\install.wim
```

Figure 1-2 shows the result of this command and lists the images contained in Windows Server 2012. The Standard Edition of Windows Server 2012 R2 is assigned index identity 2, the Server Core version of the Standard Edition is listed as index identity 1, the Server Core version of the Datacenter Edition is assigned index identity 3, and the version of the Datacenter Edition that installs the GUI components is assigned index identity 4.

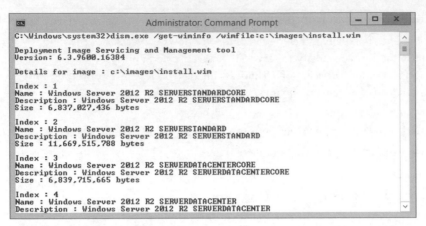

FIGURE 1-2 List of images in a .wim file

Once you have determined which operating system image you want to service, use the /Mount-image switch with the Dism.exe command to mount that image. For example, to mount the Standard Edition of Windows Server 2012 R2 from the Install.wim file that is available with the Evaluation Edition in the C:\Mount folder, issue this command.

```
Dism.exe /mount-image /imagefile:c:\images\install.wim /index:2 /mountdir:c:\mount
```

Adding drivers and updates to images

Once you have mounted an image, you can start to service that image. When servicing images used to deploy Windows Server, the most common tasks are adding device drivers and software updates to the image. You can use the /Add-Driver switch with the Dism.exe command to add a driver to a mounted image. When using the switch by itself, you need to specify the location of the driver's .inf file. Rather than adding a driver at a time, you can use the /Recurse option to have all drivers located in a folder and its subfolders added to an image. For example, to add all of the drivers located in and under the C:\Drivers folder to the image mounted in the C:\Mount folder, use the following command.

```
Dism.exe /image:c:\mount /Add-Driver /driver:c:\drivers\ /recurse
```

You can use the /Get-Driver option to list all drivers that have been added to the image and the /Remove-Driver option to remove a driver from an image. You can remove only the drivers that you or someone else has added to an image. You can't remove any of the drivers that were present on the image when it was published by Microsoft. You might choose to remove an existing driver if the driver you added in the past has since been updated.

> **MORE INFO** **ADDING DRIVERS TO IMAGES**
>
> You can learn more about adding drivers to images by consulting the following TechNet article at *http://technet.microsoft.com/en-us/library/hh824971.aspx*.

You can use Dism.exe with the /Add-Package switch to add packages that contain updates or packages in .cab or .msu format. Software updates are available from the Microsoft Update Catalog website in .msu format. For example, if you download an update from the Microsoft Update Catalog website named Security Update For Windows Server 2012 R2 (KB2893294) to the C:\Updates folder on a computer, and you mounted a WIM image of the Windows Server 2012 R2 operating system in the C:\Mount folder, you could apply the update to the image by using this command.

```
Dism.exe /image:c:\mount /Add-Package /PackagePath:"c:\updates\Security Update for
Windows Server 2012 R2 (KB2893294)"
```

> **REAL WORLD** **DRIVERSTORE FOLDER**
>
> You can download drivers from the Microsoft Update Catalog website. You can also use the C:\Windows\system32\driverstore directory from another deployment of Windows Server 2012, Windows Server 2012 R2, Windows 8, or Windows 8.1 on the x64 platform. Copy this folder to a USB drive and store it separately because it contains all of the drivers that have been downloaded for the current hardware.

The updates in this folder in .msu format are then applied to the mounted image, as shown in Figure 1-3. You can use the /Get-Package option to list the updates and packages that were already added to the image.

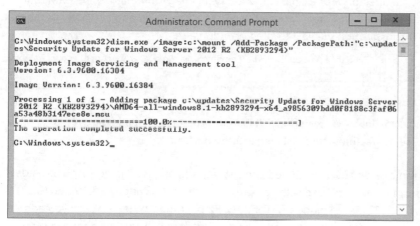

FIGURE 1-3 Adding updates to the image

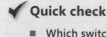 **Quick check**

- Which switch do you use with Dism.exe to add updates to a mounted image?

Quick check answer

- You use the /Add-Package switch with Dism.exe to add updates to a mounted image.

Adding features and app packages

You can determine which features are available in a mounted operating system image by using the /Get-Features switch. For example, to learn which features are available on the image mounted in the C:\Mount folder, use this command.

```
Dism.exe /image:c:\mount /Get-Features
```

You can enable or disable a specific feature using the /Enable-Feature switch. For example, to enable the NetFx3ServerFeatures feature, which enables the .NET Framework 3.5 server features in an image, use this command.

```
Dism.exe /image:c:\mount /Enable-Feature /all /FeatureName:NetFx3ServerFeatures
```

Some features on the Windows Server image are in a state in which they are listed as having their payload removed, which means that the installation files for that feature are not included on the image. If you install a feature that had its payload removed when the operating system was deployed, the operating system can download the files from the Microsoft update servers on the Internet. You can also specify the location of the installation files. The installation files for the features that have had their payload removed in Windows Server are located in the \Sources\sxs folder of the volume in which the installation media is located.

You can add these payload-removed features to an image by using Dism.exe and specifying the source directory. For example, to modify an image mounted in the C:\Mount folder so that the Microsoft .NET Framework 3.5 features are installed and available, issue this command when the installation media is located on volume D.

```
Dism.exe /image:c:\mount /Enable-Feature /all /FeatureName:NetFx3 /Source:d:\sources\sxs
```

> **NOTE INSTALLING .NET FRAMEWORK 3.5 FEATURES**
>
> Before you can install the .NET Framework 3.5 features, you must first add the .NET Framework 3.5 server features (NetFx3ServerFeatures) payload.

You can add, remove, and list provisioned app packages to an install image. App packages are located in .appx files and are used with computers running the Windows 8, Windows 8.1, Windows Server 2012, and Windows Server 2012 R2 operating systems. When you add a provisioned app package to an install image, the application will be installed for all users. You use the /Add-ProvisionedAppxPackage, /Get-ProvisionedAppxPackage, and /Remove-ProvisionedAppxPackage switches with the Dism.exe command to accomplish these goals.

> **REAL WORLD .NET FRAMEWORK 3.5**
>
> A lot of current software needs the .NET Framework 3.5 components. Rather than searching for the installation media, adding the payload files is one of the things that I first change when customizing Install.wim.

Committing an image

When you finish servicing an image, you can save your changes using the /Unmount-Wim switch with the /Commit option. You can discard changes using the /Discard option. For example, to make changes and then *commit the image* mounted in the C:\Mount folder, use this command.

```
Dism.exe /Unmount-Wim /MountDir:c:\mount /commit
```

Once you have committed the changes, the .wim file that you originally mounted is updated with these modifications. You can then import this .wim file into WDS, or use it with bootable USB installation media to deploy Windows Server 2012 or Windows Server 2012 R2 with these updates already applied.

Build and capture

The *build and capture* process is commonly used with client operating systems and less commonly with server operating systems. When you perform a build and capture, you deploy an operating system; provision that operating system with updates, applications, and drivers; and then capture that operating system for deployment. Build and capture is used less often with server operating systems because they rarely require the same sort of application deployment that is required for client operating systems.

If your deployment strategy does involve the deployment and capture of Windows Server 2012 and Windows Server 2012 R2, you need to remember that you'll need to generalize the image prior to capture, removing any configuration information that is specific to the installation. You can perform this task using the Sysprep.exe utility. Sysprep.exe is included with Windows Server 2012 and Windows Server 2012 R2, and has the dialog box shown in Figure 1-4. When you use Sysprep.exe to prepare the image, you can configure the image to return to the system Out-of-Box Experience (OOBE). This is the same experience you get when Windows Server boots for the first time, though in this case all of the updates, applications, and drivers included on the captured image will be included on the newly deployed image.

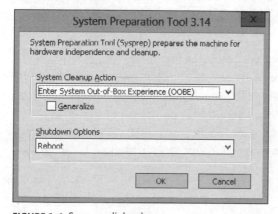

FIGURE 1-4 Sysprep dialog box

With previous versions of the Windows Server operating system, you would use a utility known as ImageX.exe to capture and apply images. To perform these tasks, you would boot a prepared server into a special Windows Preinstallation Environment (Windows PE) that included these tools. You would then use the ImageX.exe tool to capture the prepared operating system in .wim format, saving it on a separate volume or on a network share. This image capture and deployment functionality is now present in the Dism.exe command-line utility. You can use Dism.exe with the /Capture-Image switch to capture an image and the /Apply-Image switch to write an existing image to a volume.

Another capture option is to build a virtual machine, run Sysprep.exe to prepare the installation, shut down, and then import the .vhd or .vhdx file into WDS. WDS in Windows Server 2012 R2 supports importing and managing images in .vhd or .vhdx format using the console. Images in this format can be deployed from WDS to "bare metal" or to virtual machines in the same way that images in .wim format are.

> **MORE INFO** **CAPTURE AND APPLY IMAGES**
>
> To learn more about capturing and applying images using Dism.exe, consult the following TechNet article at *http://technet.microsoft.com/en-us/library/hh825258.aspx*.

Lesson summary

- Install.wim, located in the \Sources folder of the Windows Server 2012 installation media, stores the Windows Server 2012 operating system images.
- You can use Dism.exe to add and remove drivers and software updates from installation images.
- You must mount an installation image before you can modify it.
- You must commit your changes when dismounting an installation image to have those changes saved.
- Use Sysprep.exe to prepare an image for capture.

Lesson review

Answer the following questions to test your knowledge of the information in this lesson. You can find the answers to these questions and explanations of why each answer choice is correct or incorrect in the "Answers" section at the end of this chapter.

1. You want to configure an existing Windows Server 2012 deployment image with several recently released software updates that are in .msu format without performing a build and capture. Which of the following commands can you use to accomplish this goal? (Choose all that apply.)

   A. ImageX.exe

   B. Dism.exe

C. Sysprep.exe

D. Diskpart.exe

2. Which of the following switches do you use with the Dism.exe utility if you want to add software updates in .msu format to a mounted image? (Choose all that apply.)

A. /Add-Driver

B. /Enable-Feature

C. /Add-Package

D. /Add-ProvisionedAppxPackage

3. Which of the following steps must you take before you can modify an existing offline installation image?

A. Commit the image.

B. Capture the image.

C. Mount the image.

D. Discard the image.

Lesson 2: Automatically deploying Windows Server images

Deploying a server operating system requires that the systems administrator answer a few brief questions, but those questions are spaced out across the operating system deployment process. An administrator who can automate this process doesn't need to spend time shepherding the server operating system deployment, but instead can go on to perform unrelated tasks. Automating operating system deployment also has the benefit of ensuring that configuration steps are performed in a consistent manner. Automating the process minimizes the chance that a careless mistake will result in the operating system deployment process needing to be restarted from the beginning. In this lesson, you learn about WDS, understand different image types used with automated operating system deployment technologies, and learn how to create answer files so that operating system deployment can be deployed without requiring direct administrator attention.

After this lesson, you will be able to:

- Create answer files.
- Manage Windows Deployment Services (WDS).
- Deploy the discover, boot, and install images.

Estimated lesson time: 45 minutes

Automating installation

When performing an operating system installation, you spend far more time watching process bars than you do inputting configuration information. If you *automate* server operating system deployment, you can minimize the amount of time you have to spend watching the operating system install. Automating the process also minimizes the chance of configuration mistakes that might occur when bored administrators get distracted during the deployment process.

There are two different ways to automate server operating system deployment:

- **Answer files** You can start an operating system deployment and provide an answer file. The installation process uses the answer file to answer all necessary questions. A complex answer file can perform post–installation configuration tasks. The drawback of answer files is that they take time to configure properly. Once you get them working, though, they'll save you many hours.

- **Centralized deployment** Rather than installing operating systems from a DVD or USB stick, you can use centralized deployment to perform simultaneous installations of the same operating system on multiple computers. Centralized deployment can even be used with answer files.

When considering your operating system deployment strategy, remember what you learned about image servicing in Lesson 1. Keeping your deployment images up to date means that when you automatically deploy Windows Server, the deployed operating system will have the latest software updates and drivers.

Configuring answer files

With *answer files,* you can automate the process of deploying Windows Server. Instead of having to manually select specific installation options and perform post–installation configuration actions such as joining a newly deployed server to an AD DS domain, you can automate the process with answer files. During setup, the Windows Server looks for a file on local and attached media named Autounattend.xml. If this file is present, Windows Server automatically uses the settings contained in the file to configure the new server deployment.

As its name suggests, Autounattend.xml uses the XML file format. Although it is certainly possible for you to manually edit this XML file using a text editor such as Notepad, this process is complicated, and you are likely to make errors that cause the file to not work. The Windows System Image Manager (known as *Windows SIM*) is a GUI-based tool that you can use to create an answer file. When using the tool, you must specify the image for which you want to create an answer file. Windows SIM then creates a catalog file for all the options that you can configure. After you configure all the settings that you want automated during installation and post-installation configuration, you can have the tool output an answer file using correct XML syntax. Windows SIM is included with the Windows Assessment and Deployment Kit (*Windows ADK*), which you can download from the Microsoft website.

To create an answer file using Windows SIM, perform the following steps:

1. Download and install Windows ADK from the Microsoft website using the installation defaults.

2. Copy the file \Sources\install.wim from the Windows Server installation media to a temporary directory on the computer on which you have installed Windows ADK.

3. Open Windows SIM from the Start screen.

4. On the Windows SIM interface, click File, and then click Select Windows Image. Open the file Install.wim.

5. Select an operating system image on the install image for which you wish to create an answer file.

6. When prompted to create a catalog file, click Yes.

7. Click File, and click New Answer File.

8. Use Windows SIM to select each component that you want to configure. Figure 1-5 shows how you can configure installation to join the Contoso.com domain.

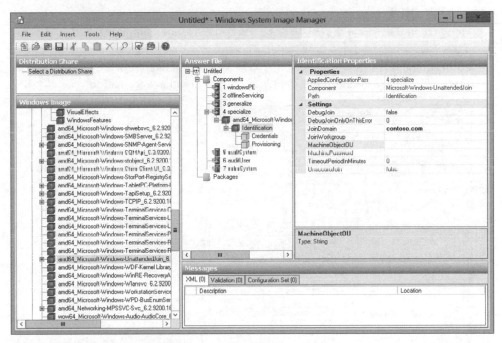

FIGURE 1-5 Configuring an answer file

MORE INFO WINDOWS SIM

You can learn more about Windows SIM by visiting the following TechNet website at *http://technet.microsoft.com/en-us/library/hh824929.aspx.*

Windows Deployment Services

WDS is a server role that you can deploy on computers running Windows Server. WDS enables you to deploy operating systems, including but not limited to Windows 8, Windows 8.1, Windows Server 2012, and Windows Server 2012 R2, to computers over the network. WDS sends these operating systems across the network using *multicast transmissions*, which means that multiple computers receive the same operating system image while minimizing the use of network bandwidth. When you use multicast transmissions, the same amount of traffic crosses the network independently of whether you are deploying Windows Server to 1 computer or 50.

Deploying Windows Server through WDS involves performing the following steps:

1. An operating system deployment transmission is prepared on the WDS server.

2. The media access control (MAC) addresses of Pre-boot Execution Environment (PXE)–compliant network adapters are made available to the WDS server.

3. The computers that are targets of the transmission boot using their PXE–compliant network adapters.

4. These computers locate the WDS server and begin the operating system setup process. If the WDS server has been provisioned with an answer file, as shown in Figure 1-6, the setup completes automatically. If the WDS server has not been provisioned with an answer file, an administrator must enter setup configuration information.

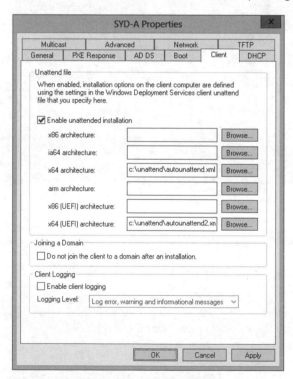

FIGURE 1-6 Configuring unattended files

WDS requirements

WDS clients need a PXE–compliant network adapter, which is rarely a problem because almost all modern network adapters are PXE–compliant. You can also use WDS to deploy Windows Server 2012 or Windows Server 2012 R2 to virtual machines running under Hyper-V. The trick to doing this is to use a legacy rather than a synthetic network adapter when creating the virtual machine as a Generation 1 virtual machine. This isn't necessary when using Generation 2 virtual machines, as the Generation 2 virtual machine network adapters support PXE booting.

If you have a computer that does not have a PXE–compliant network adapter, you can configure a special type of boot image known as a *discover image*. A discover image boots an environment, loading special drivers to enable the network adapter to interact with the WDS server. You create the boot image by adding the appropriate network adapter drivers associated with the computer that can't PXE boot to the Boot.wim file from the Windows Server installation media.

WDS has the following requirements:

- A Windows Server DNS server must be present on the local area network (LAN). This is implied by the domain membership.
- An authorized Dynamic Host Configuration Protocol (DHCP) server must be present on the network. You can host WDS and DHCP on the same computer as long as you configure the options shown in Figure 1-7.

With Windows Server, you can deploy WDS on a server that is not a member of an AD DS domain. This is a feature new to Windows Server 2012. You can't deploy WDS on a server running Windows Server 2008 or Windows Server 2008 R2 unless that server is a member of an AD DS domain.

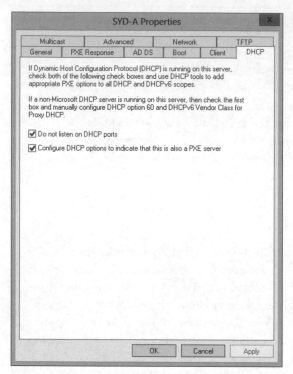

FIGURE 1-7 WDS and DHCP colocation settings

If you install WDS from the Add Roles And Features Wizard, you can configure these settings automatically. Although the WDS server does not require a static IP address, it is good practice to ensure that infrastructure roles such as WDS always use a consistent network address. You can install WDS on computers running the Server Core version of Windows Server. To install WDS on a computer running the Server Core version of Windows Server, import the ServerManager Windows PowerShell module using the following Windows PowerShell command.

```
Import-module ServerManager
```

And then install the role using the following command.

```
Install-WindowsFeature -IncludeAllSubFeature WDS
```

When installing WDS on Server Core, you have to specify the location of the source files or ensure that the server has a connection to the Internet, which enables them to be downloaded automatically. Although it is possible to manage WDS from Windows PowerShell, most administrators will use the graphical WDS Remote Server Administration Tools (RSAT) from a computer running Windows 8, Windows 8.1, Windows Server 2012, or Windows Server 2012 R2 with the graphical tools to perform this task. You can use Windows PowerShell to install the role on computers running the version of Windows Server 2012 or Windows Server 2012 R2 that includes the graphical tools. When using Windows PowerShell to install

WDS on a version of Windows Server 2012 that includes the graphical tools, also use the -IncludeManagementTools switch. To install WDS using the Add Roles And Features Wizard, select the Windows Deployment Services role, as shown in Figure 1-8.

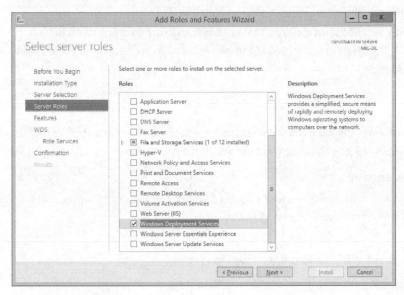

FIGURE 1-8 Install WDS role

MORE INFO **WDS OVERVIEW**

You can learn more about deploying WDS by consulting the following TechNet website at *http://technet.microsoft.com/en-us/library/hh831764.aspx.*

Managing images

Images contain either entire operating systems or a version of a special stripped-down operating system known as Windows PE. Windows PE functions as a type of boot disk, enabling a basic environment to be loaded from which more complex maintenance and installation tasks can be performed. WDS uses four image types: *boot image*, *install image*, *discover image*, and *capture image*.

- **Boot image** A special image that enables the computer to boot and begin installing the operating system using the install image. A default boot image, named Boot.wim, is located in the sources folder of the Windows Server installation media.

- **Install image** The main type of image discussed in this chapter. Contains the operating system as well as any other included components, such as software updates and additional applications. A default install image, named Install.wim, is present in the sources folder of the Windows Server installation media. Install images can be in .vhd or .vhdx format, though you can only manage install images using the WDS console in

Windows Server 2012 R2. You can only manage .vhd and .vhdx install images with WDS in Windows Server 2012 from the command line.

- **Discover image**   This special image is for computers that cannot PXE boot to load appropriate network drivers to begin a session with a WDS server.
- **Capture image**   A special image type that enables a prepared computer to be booted so that its operating system state can be captured as an install image. You add capture images as boot images in WDS.

✓ **Quick check**

- What type of image do you modify if you want to include support for a specific network adapter so it is present after Windows Server is first installed?

Quick check answer

- You modify an install image to include support for a specific network adapter so it is present after Windows Server is first installed.

To import an image into WDS, perform the following steps:

1. Open the Windows Deployment Services console.
2. Click Install Images. From the Action menu, click Add Install Image.
3. Choose whether to create a new image group, or to use an existing image group.
4. Specify the location of the image file.
5. On the Available Images page of the Add Image Wizard, shown in Figure 1-9, select the operating system images that you want to add. When the image or images are added, click Next, and then click Finish.

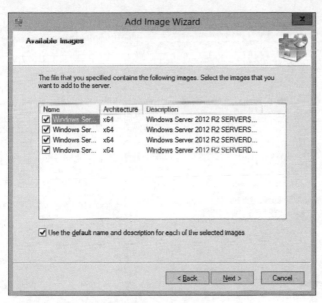

FIGURE 1-9 Select images to add to WDS

Configuring WDS

The installation defaults for WDS are suitable when you deploy the role in small environments. If you are deploying WDS in larger environments and do not choose to implement System Center 2012 R2 Virtual Machine Manager for server operating system deployments, you might want to configure the options discussed in the following sections, which are available by editing the properties of the WDS server in the Windows Deployment Services console.

PXE response settings

With PXE response settings, you can configure how the WDS server responds to computers. As Figure 1-10 shows, you can configure WDS not to respond to any client computers (this effectively disables WDS), to respond to known client computers, or to respond to all computers but require an administrator to manually approve an unknown computer. Known computers are ones that have *prestaged accounts* in Active Directory. You can prestage computers if you know the MAC address of the network interface card (NIC) that the computer uses. Vendors often supply a list of MAC addresses associated with computers when you purchase those computers, and you can use this list to prestage computer accounts.

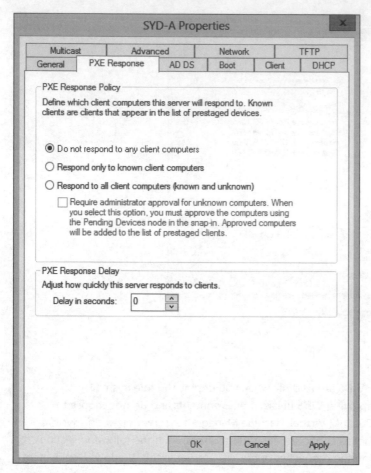

FIGURE 1-10 PXE Response settings

You use the PXE Response Delay setting when you have more than one WDS server in an environment. You can use this setting to ensure that clients receive transmissions from one WDS server over another, with the server configured with the lowest PXE response delay having priority over other WDS servers with higher delay settings.

Client naming policy

The client naming policy enables you to configure how computers installed from WDS will be named if you aren't using deployment options that perform the action. You can also use the settings on this tab, shown in Figure 1-11, to configure domain membership and organizational unit (OU) options for the computer account.

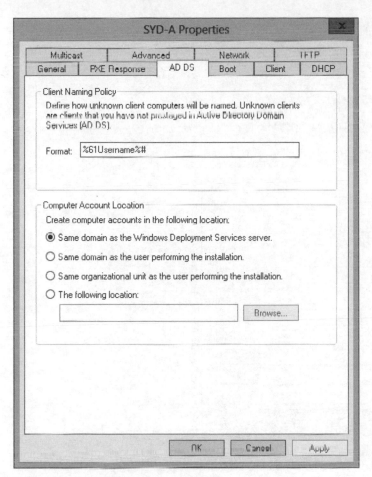

FIGURE 1-11 Client Naming Policy settings

WDS boot options

On the Boot options tab of the WDS server's properties dialog box, shown in Figure 1-12, you can configure how clients that PXE boot interact with the WDS server. You can also configure a default boot image for each architecture supported by WDS. By default, once a client has connected to a WDS server, someone must press the F12 key to continue deploying the operating system. In environments in which you are performing a large number of simultaneous deployments, requiring this level of manual intervention might substantially delay the deployment.

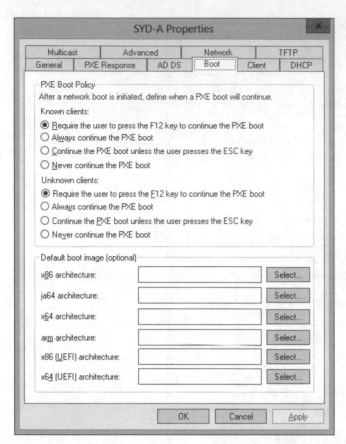

FIGURE 1-12 Boot options

Multicast options

The default settings of WDS have all computers that join the *multicast transmission* receiving the installation image at the same speed. If you frequently deploy operating systems, you are aware that sometimes there are 1 or 2 computers that have network adapters that slow a transmission that should take only 15 minutes into one that takes half a day. You can configure the transfer settings on the Multicast tab, shown in Figure 1-13, so that clients are partitioned into separate sessions depending on how fast they can consume the multicast transmission. You still have those slow computers taking a long time to receive the image, but the other computers connected to the transmission can complete the deployment more quickly.

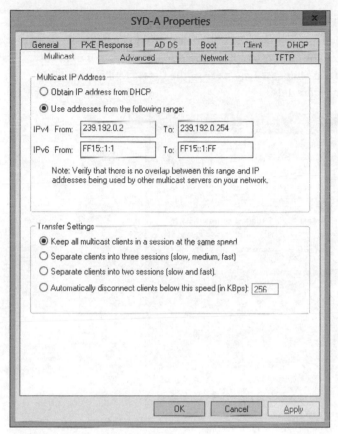

FIGURE 1-13 WDS multicast options

Other options

Although you are less likely to need them, you can configure other options on the following tabs:

- **Advanced tab** You can configure WDS to use a specific domain controller and global catalog (GC) server. You can also configure whether WDS is authorized in DHCP. DHCP authorization occurs automatically when you install the WDS role.

- **Network tab** You can specify a User Datagram Protocol (UDP) port policy to limit when UDP ports are used with transmissions. You can also configure a network profile to specify the speed of the network, minimizing the chance that WDS transmissions will slow the network down.

- **TFTP tab** You can specify maximum block size and Trivial File Transfer Protocol (TFTP) window size.

Configuring transmissions

You use WDS transmissions to set WDS to transfer the operating system image to PXE clients. When configuring a WDS transmission, you need to decide what type of multicast transmission you will perform on the Multicast Type page of the Create Multicast Transmission Wizard, as shown in Figure 1-14.

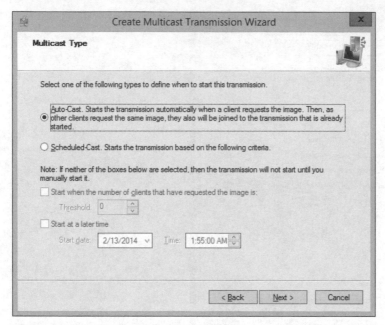

FIGURE 1-14 Multicast type

The difference between these options is as follows:

- **Auto-Cast**   A transmission starts whenever a client requests the image. If another client requests the same image, the client will join the existing transmission, caching data from the current transfer, and then retrieving data that was transmitted before the client joined the transmission. This is the best option to use when you are performing one-off deployments.

- **Scheduled-Cast**   You choose either to start the transmission when a specified number of clients have joined, or at a particular date and time. This is the best option to use when you are deploying the same operating system image to a large number of computers.

To configure a WDS transmission, perform the following steps:

1. Open the Windows Deployment Services console, expand the WDS server from which you want to perform the deployment and click Multicast Transmissions. On the Action menu, click Create Multicast Transmission.

2. Provide a name for the multicast transmission.

3. On the Image Selection page, specify which operating system image you want to deploy using the transmission.

4. On the Multicast Type page, specify whether you will use Auto-Cast or Scheduled-Cast. If you choose Scheduled-Cast, select the number of clients, or the transmission start time.

REAL WORLD **VIRTUAL MACHINE TEMPLATES**

As more infrastructure moves to private and public clouds, you will increasingly deploy servers from virtual machine templates, such as those that you can configure using the VMM component of System Center 2012 R2, rather than performing a traditional installation from an image. Although configuring virtual machine templates is beyond the scope of the 70-411 exam and this book, in the real world you'll probably be deploying virtualized servers from templates more often than you will Windows Server from WDS.

Driver groups and packages

You can stage device drivers on a WDS server by importing the device driver as a *package*. A driver package contains the extracted driver files. You can import the driver package into WDS by locating the driver's .inf file. When using the WDS console, you can either import individual driver packages, or all of the drivers in a set of folders.

On the WDS console, you can organize drivers into driver groups. A driver package can be a member of more than one *group,* and deleting a driver group does not delete the associated driver packages. Figure 1-15 shows a collection of driver packages in a group. You can use driver groups with filters to limit which driver packages are available to WDS clients.

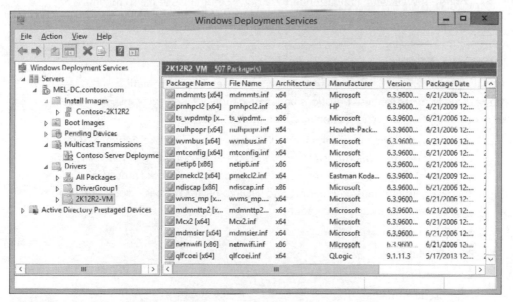

FIGURE 1-15 Driver groups and packages

Lesson summary

- Unless you are booting from a discover image, computers must be able to PXE boot to receive an operating system image from a WDS server.
- With boot images, computers with PXE-compliant network cards can load a preinstallation environment over the network from which it is possible to then load a minimal operating system.
- Install images contain the operating system as well as additional components, such as software updates and applications.
- Discover images are used with computers that do not have PXE-compliant network cards. Capture images are used when you want to capture a prepared operating system.
- Multicast transmissions enable the same installation image to be transmitted to multiple computers at the same time.
- If a WDS server also hosts the DHCP server role, it is necessary to configure the server to listen on a separate port and to configure DHCP option tag 60 for all scopes.
- You use Windows SIM to create unattended Windows Setup answer files. You can configure WDS with an unattended Windows Setup answer file to minimize the amount of interaction you need to perform when deploying Windows Server.

Lesson review

Answer the following questions to test your knowledge of the information in this lesson. You can find the answers to these questions and explanations of why each answer choice is correct or incorrect in the "Answers" section at the end of this chapter.

1. You are in the process of configuring WDS so you can use it to deploy a number of computers that will run the Windows Server 2012 operating system. All of the computers in your organization have PXE–compliant network cards. Which of the following images must you import into WDS to perform a basic operating system deployment? (Choose all that apply.)

   A. Boot image

   B. Install image

   C. Capture image

   D. Discover image

2. You have just used Windows PowerShell to add the WDS role to a computer in the Melbourne branch office running the Windows Server 2012 operating system. The computer already functioned as a domain controller, DHCP server, and DNS server. You attempt to perform a test deployment of a Windows Server 2012 install image, but the PXE network card on the test server cannot connect to WDS. Which of the following strategies should you pursue to resolve this problem? (Choose all that apply.)

   A. Configure WDS not to listen on DHCP ports.

   B. Configure WDS not to listen on DNS ports.

   C. Configure DHCP options to support WDS.

   D. Authorize the WDS server in AD.

3. At the moment, WDS does not respond to client computers. You want to configure WDS so it responds to all clients, but an administrator must manually approve deployments to any computers with unrecognized MAC addresses. Which of the following settings must you configure to accomplish this goal? (Choose two. Each answer forms part of a complete solution.)

   A. Do Not Respond To Any Client Computers

   B. Require Administrator Approval For Unknown Computers

   C. Respond Only To Known Client Computers

   D. Respond To All Client Computers (Known And Unknown)

Lesson 3: Servicing and updating deployed servers

Windows Server Update Services (WSUS) 4.0 is a role that is built into Windows Server 2012 and Windows Server 2012 R2. WSUS functions as a local mirror of the Microsoft Update servers on the Internet. Organizations that have deployed WSUS can use Group Policy to configure client and server operating systems to check for available updates against a local WSUS server instead of checking against the Microsoft Update servers on the Internet. The primary benefits to you as an administrator in deploying WSUS, is that you can minimize the amount of update traffic that goes across your organization's Internet connection and take control of which updates are approved for deployment to computers in your organization.

> **After this lesson, you will be able to:**
> - Deploy Windows Server Update Services.
> - Use Windows Server Update Services to manage updates.
>
> **Estimated lesson time: 45 minutes**

Automated update deployment with WSUS

WSUS, and before it, Software Update Services (SUS), has been available as free add-ins for Windows Server operating systems for more than a decade. WSUS 4.0 is the version of WSUS released with Windows Server 2012 and Windows Server 2012 R2. Unlike previous versions of the Windows Server operating system, in which you needed to download WSUS separately or install a special update to make the role available, WSUS 4.0 can be deployed directly as a server role.

Because it has been available free of charge for so long, WSUS is widely deployed with Microsoft, registering more than 1 million WSUS servers regularly synchronizing against the Microsoft Update servers on the Internet. Although there are more sophisticated update deployment solutions available from Microsoft and third-party vendors, WSUS is the most commonly used update deployment solution besides Windows Update.

New WSUS features

Administrators who have used WSUS 3.0 Service Pack 2 (SP2), which can be deployed on servers running Windows Server 2003, Windows Server 2003 R2, Windows Server 2008, and Windows Server 2008 R2, will find WSUS 4.0 very familiar. The big changes between WSUS 3.0 SP2 and WSUS 4.0 are as follows:

- **Integrated Administration console** WSUS 3.0 SP2 had a console that was separate from the Server Manager console. The WSUS 4.0 console is integrated into the Windows Server 2012 and Windows Server 2012 R2 Server Manager console.

- **Supports Server Core** You can install WSUS 4.0 on computers running the Windows Server 2012 and Windows Server 2012 R2 operating system deployed with the Server Core installation option. This applies only to Windows Server 2012 and Windows Server 2012 R2. You can't install WSUS 4.0 on computers running Windows Server 2008 R2 installed with the Server Core installation option.

- **Windows PowerShell support** WSUS 4.0 includes Windows PowerShell support for several commonly performed administrative functions.

Deploy and manage WSUS

You can install WSUS 4.0 as a role on Windows Server 2012 and Windows Server 2012 R2 in both the Server Core and full administrative interface configurations. The advantage of deploying WSUS on Server Core installations is that these deployments require fewer updates. If you do deploy WSUS on a Server Core deployment, you need to ensure that you install the WSUS RSAT components on another computer, either running Windows 8, Windows 8.1, Windows Server 2012, or Windows Server 2012 R2, to perform WSUS administration tasks. Although WSUS 4.0 does include Windows PowerShell support, not all WSUS functionality has been replicated in Windows PowerShell.

When you install WSUS, you can choose between using a local Windows Internal Database (WID) or a SQL Server instance. The advantage of using a SQL Server instance is that it's easier to back up and you can run more complex reports. The majority of WSUS deployments use the built-in WID database. When you install WSUS 4.0 on Windows Server 2012 or Windows Server 2012 R2, all prerequisite components are also installed.

Products, security classifications, and languages

During setup, you are asked to choose which update you want to download based on product name, security classification, and languages. Although you can choose to download updates for all product categories for all classifications in all languages, you'll minimize the amount of configuration required later if you download updates only for products used on your organizational network.

> **REAL WORLD**   **YOU STILL NEED TO APPROVE THE UPDATES**
>
> Remember that you need to choose whether to approve updates. If you aren't selective, you'll have to spend a lot of time dealing with updates that aren't relevant to the computers you are responsible for managing.

When WSUS synchronizes, it may update the list of available product names to reflect newly released software. If your organization deploys a new product, if it retires an old product, or if you simply want to alter which updates are synchronized, you can do this in the Products And Classifications dialog box, available through Options on the Update Services console, and shown in Figure 1-16.

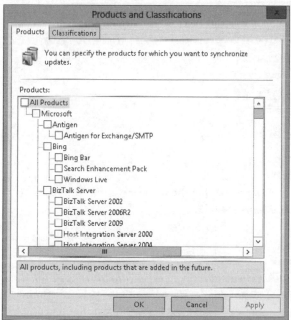

FIGURE 1-16 Products and classifications

Autonomous and replica modes

In large organizations there are likely to be multiple WSUS servers because even if a single WSUS server can support about 25,000 clients, it's better to have a local WSUS server at each large site, rather than having clients pull updates and approvals across wide area network (WAN) links. Instead of administrators performing the same approvals on each WSUS server in the organization, you can configure a WSUS server as a *replica* of another server. When you configure a WSUS server as a replica, as shown in Figure 1-17, the downstream server copies all update approvals, settings, computers, and groups from its parent. You can configure the Update Source settings, as well as specify information that enables WSUS to use a proxy server, through the Update Source And Proxy Server item in Options, on the Update Services console.

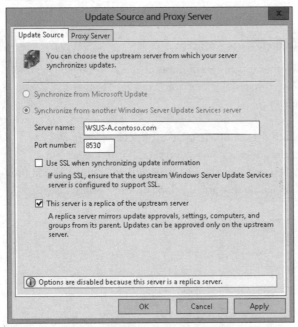

FIGURE 1-17 WSUS server as a replica

MORE INFO **WSUS TOPOLOGIES**

You can learn more about WSUS topologies by consulting the following TechNet website at *http://technet.microsoft.com/en-us/library/hh852344.aspx*.

Update files

One of the benefits of deploying WSUS is that clients on the local network download their updates from the WSUS server rather than downloading updates from the Microsoft Update servers on the Internet. You can configure update storage location settings using the Update

Files And Languages item on the Options area of the Update Services console. You can configure the following options, which are shown in Figure 1-18:

- **Store Update Files Locally On This Server** When you choose this option, you can choose whether to download files only after they have been approved; download express installation files, which install more quickly on clients; or download files from Microsoft Update. With the last option, you can configure a server as a replica server, but have update files downloaded from Microsoft Update rather than the upstream replica server.

- **Don't Store Update Files Locally; Computers Install From Microsoft Update** When you configure this option, clients use WSUS for update approvals, but retrieve the updates from the Microsoft Update servers on the Internet. This option is most appropriate when you are providing update approvals to clients located outside of the organizational network.

FIGURE 1-18 Update file location

Windows PowerShell cmdlets

WSUS 4.0 includes Windows PowerShell support. Although you can use Windows PowerShell to perform a certain number of management tasks on a preconfigured WSUS server, you are more likely to perform WSUS administration tasks using the Update Services console. The Windows PowerShell commands available with WSUS are as follows:

- **Add-WsusComputer** Adds a computer to a target WSUS group.
- **Approve-WsusUpdate** Approves a specific update for deployment.

- **Deny-WsusUpdate**   Denies an update for deployment.
- **Get-WsusClassification**   Enables you to view all WSUS classifications.
- **Get-WsusComputer**   Enables you to filter computers known to the WSUS server by operating system, name, update installation status, and other criteria.
- **Get-WsusProduct**   Lists all available products that are available to WSUS.
- **Get-WsusServer**   Provides information about the WSUS server.
- **Invoke-WsusServerCleanup**   Cleans up WSUS, including removing superseded updates.
- **Set-WsusClassification**   Enables or disables synchronization of a specific category of updates.
- **Set-WsusProduct**   Enables or disables synchronization of a specific product's updates.
- **Set-WsusServerSynchronization**   Enables you to configure the WSUS server synchronization schedule.

WSUS security roles

In large organizations, you are more likely to separate the roles of server administrator and update administrator. When you install WSUS, two local security groups are created. By adding users to these groups, you grant users the permission to perform the tasks assigned with these roles. The roles are as follows:

- **WSUS Administrators**   Users who are added to the local WSUS Administrators group can perform any WSUS administration task. These tasks include approving updates, managing computer groups, configuring automatic approval rules, and modifying the WSUS server's update source.
- **WSUS Reporters**   Users who are members of this role can run reports on the WSUS server. These reports detail the update compliance status on the basis of update and computer. For example, a user who is a member of this group can run a WSUS report and determine which computers are missing a specific critical update.

✔ **Quick check**
- You want WSUS servers in branch office locations to use the same approval settings as the WSUS server in your organization's head office. How do you configure the branch office WSUS servers to accomplish this goal?

Quick check answer
- You can configure the branch office WSUS servers as replicas of the WSUS server in your organization's head office. When you do this, branch office servers will use the same approval settings as the upstream server.

WSUS groups

You can use WSUS groups to organize computers for the purpose of deploying updates. For example, you might have a WSUS group for servers in Sydney and another WSUS group for servers in Melbourne. A computer can be a member of multiple WSUS groups, and WSUS groups can exist in parent-child relationships. For example, the Australia WSUS group might have both the Melbourne and Sydney WSUS groups as members. Updates approved for the Australia group are automatically approved for members of the Melbourne and Sydney groups unless overridden.

You can assign computers to WSUS groups manually or through Group Policy. Computers can be assigned to WSUS groups through Group Policy only if the computer groups already exist on the WSUS server. To assign a computer manually, the computer must have already reported to the WSUS server. Computers that have reported to the WSUS server, but have not been assigned to a group, will be members of the Unassigned Computers group.

An administrator must create WSUS groups. To create a WSUS group, perform the following steps:

1. Open the Update Services console.
2. Click the group you want to have as the parent group. The Computers/All Computers group is the parent group for all groups.
3. From the Action menu, click Add Computer Group.
4. Specify the computer group name, and click Add.

> **REAL WORLD** **SIMPLE NAMES**
>
> Keep the computer group names simple because you have to also use them with Group Policy when using client-side targeting.

WSUS policies

You can configure most WSUS client options through Group Policy. Many of these policies are related to the experience that users of client operating systems have when updates are installed and are not directly applicable to updating server operating systems. Windows Update policies are located in the Computer Configuration\Policies\Administrative Templates\Windows Components\Windows Update node of a standard GPO, as shown in Figure 1-19.

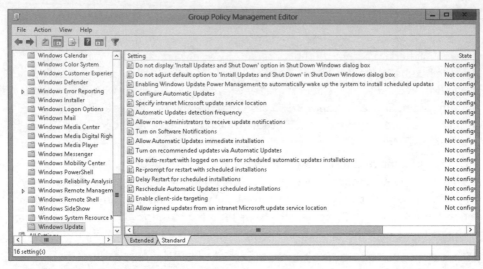

FIGURE 1-19 Windows Update–related policies

The most important policies from the perspective of the server administrator are as follows:

- **Configure Automatic Updates** You can enable automatic updating, specify a day for update installations, and a time for update installation to occur. It's usually not a good idea to have this one policy to apply to all servers in your organization. Having all servers install and reboot at the same time can cause substantial disruptions.

- **Specify Intranet Microsoft Update Service Location** You can specify the location of the WSUS server and the statistics server. (The statistics server receives information on successful update installation and is usually the same as the WSUS server.)

- **Automatic Update Detection Frequency** Determines how often the computer checks for updates.

- **Enable Client-Side Targeting** Use this policy to specify which WSUS groups computers should be a member of. If names do not match, computers will end up in the Unassigned Computers group.

REAL WORLD **MIGRATING TO SYSTEM CENTER 2012 CONFIGURATION MANAGER**

If your organization shifts to using System Center 2012 Configuration Manager, Windows Intune, or another product to manage software updates, remember to remove any existing WSUS-related policies. If you don't do this, it might cause conflicts that lead to computers not receiving updates in a timely manner.

Deploying updates

When you deploy updates, you decide whether to deploy the update, to which computer groups you deploy the update, and what deadline should apply to the deployment. You can deploy an update multiple times to different groups, so you can deploy an update to a test group and then, if no issues arise with the update, deploy the update more generally. To deploy an update, perform the following steps:

1. Open the Update Services console and select the Updates\All Updates node. You can also choose to select a child node, such as Critical Updates, if you want to view only available critical updates.

2. Set the Approval setting to Unapproved and the Status to Any, as shown in Figure 1-20, and click Refresh. All unapproved updates are then listed.

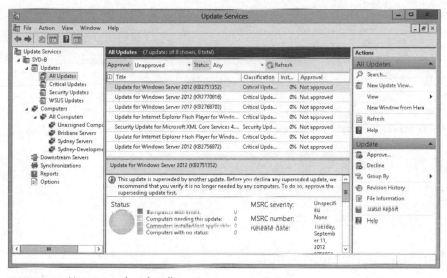

FIGURE 1-20 Unapproved update list

3. Click an update, or click multiple updates, if you want to select more than one update; then, click Approve on the Actions pane.

4. In the Approve Updates dialog box, select which computer groups the update is approved for. Figure 1-21 shows updates approved for the Sydney-Development-Servers group. You can choose between the following settings:

   - **Approved For Install**   Approves the update.
   - **Approved For Removal**   Removes a previously deployed update.
   - **Not Approved**   Does not approve the update.
   - **Keep Existing Approvals**   Inherits the approval from the parent group.
   - **Deadline**   Specifies an update deployment deadline.

FIGURE 1-21 Approve updates for installation

Prior to deploying updates, you should perform a synchronization, which will ensure that the WSUS server is to be up to date before choosing whether to deploy updates.

> **MORE INFO DEPLOYING UPDATES WITH WSUS**
>
> To learn more about deploying updates with WSUS, consult the following TechNet webpage at *http://technet.microsoft.com/en-us/library/hh852348.aspx.*

Automatic approval rules

Automatic approval rules enable specifically categorized updates to be automatically approved. For example, you might choose to automatically approve critical updates for the Sydney-Development-Servers WSUS group, as shown in Figure 1-22.

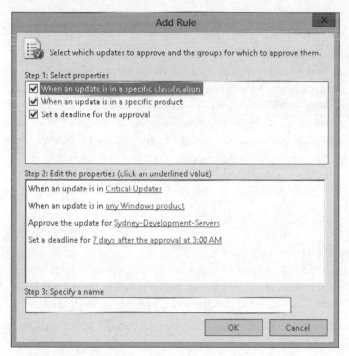

FIGURE 1-22 Automatic approval rules

To configure an automatic approval rule, perform the following steps:

1. Open the Update Services console. You can do this from the Tools menu of Server Manager, or by right-clicking the server in a server group and clicking Windows Server Update Services.

2. On the Update Services console, click Options and then click Automatic Approvals.

3. In the Automatic Approvals dialog box, click New Rule.

4. In the Add Rule dialog box, choose the following rule options:

   - **When An Update Is In A Specific Classification**   You can choose that the rule applies when an update matches a specific classification or number of classifications. Update classifications include Critical Updates, Definition Updates, Drivers, Feature Packs, Security Updates, Service Packs, Tools, Update Rollups, and Updates. Microsoft includes classifications for each software update when it publishes the update.

   - **When An Update Is For A Specific Product**   You can specify products, either by category, such as Exchange, or by specific product, such as Exchange Server 2013.

   - **Approve The Update For A Specific Computer Group**   The update can be approved for selected computer groups.

   - **Set An Approval Deadline**   Sets an installation deadline for the update based on the time and date the update was first approved.

Lesson summary

- Install WSUS in autonomous mode if you want to have an administrator manage updates for computers that report to the WSUS server. Install WSUS in replica mode if you want to have other WSUS servers inherit another WSUS server's configuration.

- Create computer groups using the WSUS console and then use Group Policy to assign computers to these groups.

- Create automatic deployment rules to automatically approve updates to WSUS clients. Use automatic deployment rules for computers only where you will not be testing updates prior to deploying them.

- Use the WSUS Administrators local group to grant users the ability to manage WSUS update deployments.

- Use Windows Intune to manage update deployment to computers that are outside of the perimeter network.

- Use System Center 2012 Configuration Manager to deploy updates to third-party products.

Lesson review

Answer the following questions to test your knowledge of the information in this lesson. You can find the answers to these questions and explanations of why each answer choice is correct or incorrect in the "Answers" section at the end of this chapter.

1. You are in the process of configuring WSUS 4.0 to manage software updates for computers in your organization. You have created a WSUS computer group named Sydney-Servers. You want all servers that have computer accounts in the Sydney-Servers OU to be automatically added to this computer group. Which of the following group policies would you configure to assign the servers in the Sydney-Servers OU to the Sydney-Servers WSUS computer group? (Choose all that apply.)

A. Configure Automatic Updates

B. Enable Client-Side Targeting

C. Delay Restart For Scheduled Installations

D. Specify An Intranet Microsoft Update Service Location

2. Your organization has a single WSUS server named SYDNEY-WSUS. You want to ensure that all software updates marked as Security and Critical for Windows Server 2012 R2 are automatically deployed to a group of computers in the Sydney office that are part of the development environment. The deployment of these updates should not require explicit administrator approval. (Choose three. Each answer forms part of a complete solution.)

A. Create a local security group on SYDNEY-WSUS named UpdateTest.

B. Create a WSUS group on SYDNEY-WSUS named UpdateTest.

C. Add all computers that are part of the development environment to UpdateTest.

D. Create an automatic approval rule for Critical and Security updates for the UpdateTest group.

3. You are in the process of configuring WSUS servers in the Melbourne and Perth branch offices. You have already configured a WSUS server in the Sydney head office. You want to have a consistent set of update approvals across the organization, but have each branch office server retrieve updates from the Microsoft Update servers on the Internet. Clients in each branch office should retrieve updates from their local WSUS server. Which of the following settings should you configure? (Choose all that apply.)

A. Configure the Sydney server as a replica of the Melbourne and Perth servers.

B. Configure the Melbourne and Perth servers to store update files locally. Enable the Download files from Microsoft Update; do not download from upstream server option.

C. Configure the Melbourne and Perth servers to not store update files locally

D. Configure the Melbourne and Perth servers as replicas of the Sydney WSUS server.

Practice exercises

The goal of this section is to provide you with hands-on practice with the following:

- Configuring Windows images
- Configuring Windows Deployment Services
- Deploying and configuring WSUS

To perform the exercises in this section, you need access to an evaluation version of Windows Server 2012 R2. You should also have access to virtual machines SYD-DC, MEL-DC, and CBR-DC, the setup instructions for which are described in the Introduction. You should ensure that you have a checkpoint of these virtual machines that you can revert to at the end of the practice exercises.

Exercise 1: Prepare update files

In this exercise, you download a software update from the Internet. To complete this exercise, perform the following steps:

1. In Hyper-V Manager, right-click SYD-DC, and click Settings.
2. In the Settings For SYD-DC dialog box, shown in Figure 1-23, click Add Hardware, click Network Adapter, and click Add.

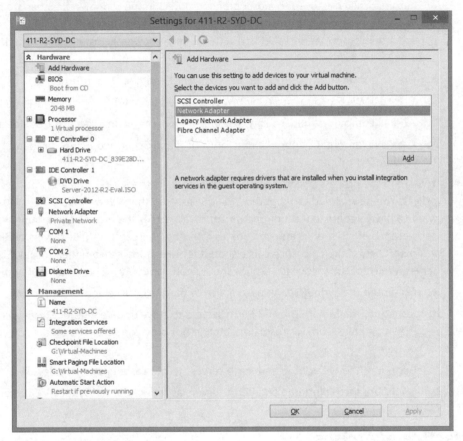

FIGURE 1-23 Add network adapter

3. In the Settings For DC dialog box, select the new network adapter.
4. On the Virtual Switch drop-down menu, click the arrow, and select a virtual switch that is connected to an external network adapter.
5. Ensure that you have connected the Windows Server 2012 R2 evaluation edition ISO to the DVD drive connected to IDE Controller 1.
6. Click OK to close the Settings for the SYD-DC dialog box.
7. On Hyper-V Manager, right-click SYD-DC, and click Start.

8. Sign on as Contoso\Don_Funk with the password **Pa$$w0rd.**

9. On the Server Manager console, click the Local Server node.

10. Click the text next to IE Enhanced Security Configuration.

11. In the Internet Explorer Enhanced Security Configuration dialog box, shown in Figure 1-24, ensure that the Administrators setting is configured to Off, and then click OK.

FIGURE 1-24 Configuring Internet Explorer Enhanced Security Configuration (IE ESC)

12. Click File Explorer on the taskbar.

13. Double-click Local Disk (C:).

14. On the title bar of the Local Disk (C:) window, click the New Folder icon.

15. Name the folder **Updates.**

16. Repeat step 13 and 14 twice. Name the new folders **Images** and **Mount**.

17. Copy the file D:\Sources\Install.wim to C:\images.

18. Open Internet Explorer from the Start screen.

19. On the Internet Explorer dialog box, click Ask Me Later.

20. In the address bar, type **http://catalog.update.microsoft.com**

21. When prompted, install the Microsoft Update Catalog add-in. You will need to click Yes on a User Account Control dialog box, to click Install to install the update, and to click Run Control to run the add-in.

22. In the Search box, type **KB2893294,** and click Search.

23. Click Add next to Security Update For Windows Server 2012 R2 (KB2893294). Ensure that you have selected the update for Windows Server 2012 R2 and not the preview.

24. Click View Basket. On the Updates In Your Basket page, shown in Figure 1-25, click Download.

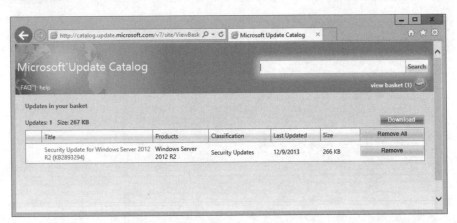

FIGURE 1-25 Microsoft Update Catalog

25. On the Download Options page, navigate to C:\Updates, click OK, and click Continue. When the update completes downloading, click Close.

Exercise 2: Servicing a WIM image

In this exercise, you service a Windows Server 2012 R2 installation image, injecting an update and deploying payload files. To complete this exercise, perform the following steps:

1. On SYD-DC, open an elevated command prompt by right clicking on the Start item and clicking Command Prompt (Admin). Click Yes when prompted on the User Account Control dialog box.

2. Execute the following command to identify the index number of the Standard Server installation.

```
Dism.exe /get-wiminfo /wimfile:c:\images\install.wim
```

3. Execute the following command to mount the Standard Edition server image located in Install.wim using the C:\Mount folder.

```
Dism.exe /mount-image /imagefile:c:\images\install.wim /index:2 /mountdir:c:\mount
```

4. Execute the following command to apply the software update you downloaded from the Microsoft Update Catalog webpage.

```
Dism.exe /image:c:\mount /Add-Package /PackagePath:"c:\updates\Security Update for
Windows Server 2012 R2 (KB2893294)"
```

5. Execute the following command to enable the .NET Framework 3.5 features using the mounted installation media as the source location.

```
Dism.exe /image:c:\mount /Enable-Feature /all /FeatureName:NetFx3 /Source:d:\
sources\sxs
```

6. Execute the following command to dismount and commit the modified image.

```
Dism.exe /Unmount-Wim /MountDir:c:\mount /commit
```

7. Keep SYD-DC running because you will use it in Exercise 2 and Exercise 3. Do not revert the virtual machine until you complete all practice exercises.

Exercise 3: Deploy Windows Deployment Services

In this exercise, you deploy WDS. To complete this exercise, perform the following steps:

1. Sign on to server MEL-DC as Administrator with the password **Pa$$w0rd**.

2. Open the Windows PowerShell prompt, and type the following command to join the contoso.com domain.

```
Add-Computer -DomainName contoso.com
```

3. In the Windows PowerShell Credentials dialog box, shown in Figure 1-26, type **don_ funk@contoso.com** and **Pa$$w0rd,** and click OK.

FIGURE 1-26 PowerShell credentials

4. Type the following command into the Windows PowerShell prompt to restart the computer.

```
Restart-Computer
```

5. Sign on to server MEL-DC as Contoso\don_funk with the password **Pa$$w0rd**.

6. Connect the Windows Server 2012 R2 installation media to the emulated DVD drive of MEL-DC.

7. On the Server Manager console, launch the Add Roles And Features Wizard from the Manage menu.

8. On the Before You Begin page of the Add Roles And Features Wizard, click Next.

9. On the Select Installation Type page, click Role-based or Feature-based installation, and click Next.

10. On the Select Destination Server page, click MEL-DC.contoso.com, and click Next.

11. On the Select Server Roles page, click DHCP Server. When prompted to add additional features, click Add Features.

12. On the Select Server Roles page, click Windows Deployment Services. When prompted, click Add Features. Verify that the Add Roles And Features Wizard appears similar to Figure 1-27, and click Next.

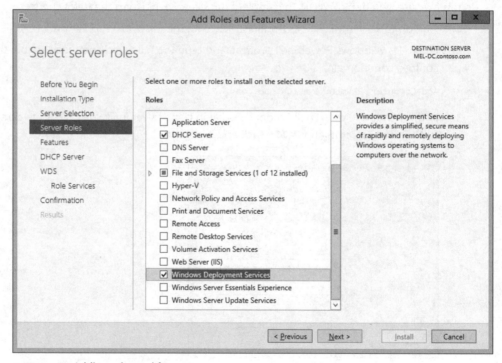

FIGURE 1-27 Adding roles and features

13. On the Features page, click Next.

14. On the DHCP Server page, click Next.

15. On the WDS page, click Next.

16. On the Select Role Services page, verify that Deployment Server and Transport Server are selected, as shown in Figure 1-28, and click Next.

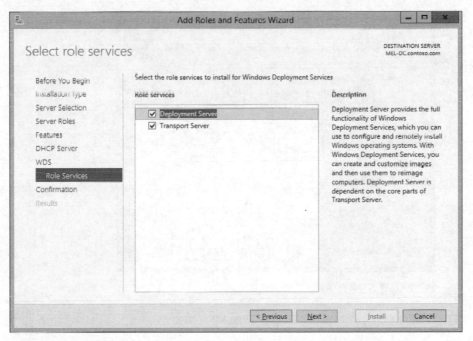

FIGURE 1-28 Adding the WDS Role Services

17. On the Confirmation page, click Install.

18. When the installation completes, click Close to close the Add Roles And Features Wizard. Refresh Server Manager Console.

19. On the Tools menu, click DHCP.

20. On the DHCP console, click Mel-dc.contoso.com.

21. On the Action menu, click Authorize.

22. On the DHCP console, click IPv4. On the Action menu, click New Scope. This will start the New Scope Wizard. Click Next.

23. On the Scope Name page, type the name **WDS Scope,** and click Next.

24. On the IP Address Range page, shown in Figure 1-29, enter the following settings and click Next:

- Start IP Address: **10.10.10.100**
- End IP address: **10.10.10.200**
- Length: **24**
- Subnet Mask: **255.255.255.0**

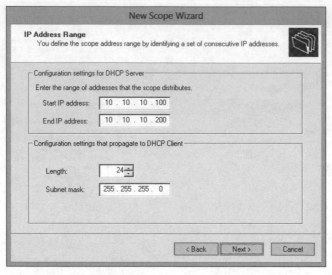

FIGURE 1-29 Creating a DHCP scope

25. On the Add Exclusions And Delay page, click Next.

26. On the Lease Duration page, click Next.

27. On the Configure DHCP Options page, click Yes, I Want To Configure These Options Now, and click Next.

28. On the Router (Default Gateway) page, click Next.

29. On the Domain Name And DNS Servers page, verify that 10.10.10.10 is present, as shown in Figure 1-30, and then click Next.

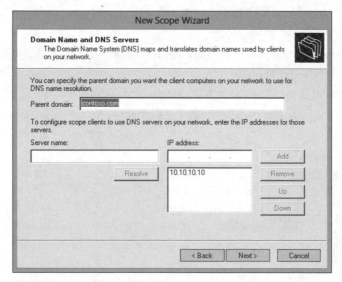

FIGURE 1-30 Configuring DHCP options

30. On the WINS Servers page, click Next.

31. On the Activate Scope page, click Yes, I Want To Activate This Scope Now, and click Next.

32. On the Completing The New Scope Wizard page, click Finish.

33. Close the DHCP console.

Exercise 4: Configure Windows Deployment Services

In this exercise, you configure WDS and import installation and boot images. To complete this exercise, perform the following steps:

1. Open the Windows Deployment Services console from the Tools menu in Server Manager.

2. Expand Servers. Click MEL-DC.contoso.com. On the Action menu, click Configure Server. This will launch the Windows Deployment Services Configuration Wizard. Click Next.

3. On the Install Options page, shown in Figure 1-31, click Integrated With Active Directory, and then click Next.

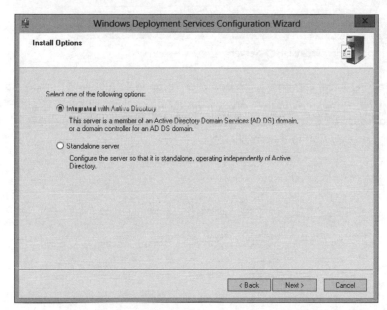

FIGURE 1-31 Configuring WDS

4. On the Remote Installation Folder Location page, verify that C:\RemoteInstall is selected, and click Next.

5. In the System Volume Warning dialog box, click Yes.

6. In the Proxy DHCP Server dialog box, shown in Figure 1-32, verify that Do Not Listen On DHCP And DHCPv6 Ports, and Configure DHCP Options For Proxy DHCP are selected; then click Next.

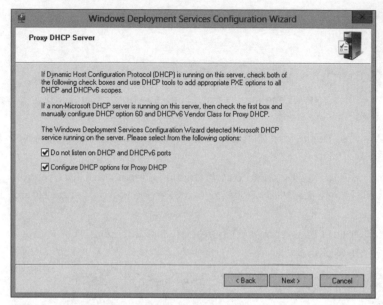

FIGURE 1-32 Configuring Proxy DHCP Server

7. In the PXE Server Initial Settings dialog box, click Respond To All Client Computers (Known And Unknown) and Require Administrator Approval For Unknown Computers as shown in Figure 1-33, and click Next. Click Finish to complete the Windows Deployment Services Configuration Wizard.

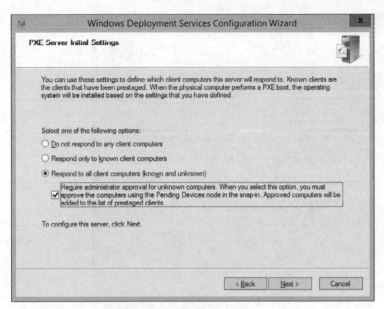

FIGURE 1-33 Configuring PXE Server Initial Settings

8. On the Windows Deployment Services console, click MEL-DC.contoso.com. On the Action menu, click All Tasks, and click Start.

9. In the Server dialog box, click OK.

10. Click Install Images. On the Action menu, click Add Install Image.

11. On the Image Group page of the Add Image Wizard, type the name **Contoso-2K12R2** next to Create An Image Group; then click Next.

12. On the Image File page, type the location **\\syd-dc\c$\images\install.wim**, as shown in Figure 1-34, and click Next.

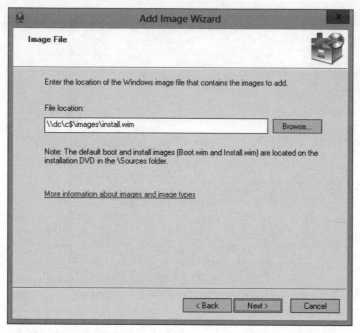

FIGURE 1-34 Adding image

13. In the Available Images dialog box, ensure that all four images are selected, and click Next.

14. On the Summary page, click Next. When the images are imported, click Finish.

15. On the Windows Deployment Services console, click Boot Images. On the Action menu, click Add Boot Image.

16. In the Image File location dialog box, shown in Figure 1-35, type **d:\sources\boot. wim** and click Next.

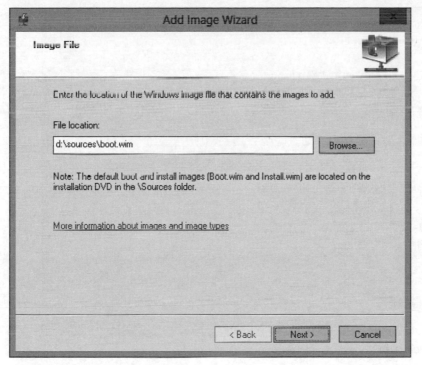

FIGURE 1-35 Adding boot image

17. On the Image Metadata page, accept the default image name and description, and click Next.

18. On the Summary page, click Next. Click Finish to close the Add Image Wizard.

19. Click Multicast Transmissions. On the Action menu, click Create Multicast Transmission.

20. On the Transmission Name page of the Create Multicast Transmission Wizard dialog box, type **Contoso Server Deployment** and click Next.

21. On the Image Selection page, shown in Figure 1-36, select Contoso-2K12R2, and click Next.

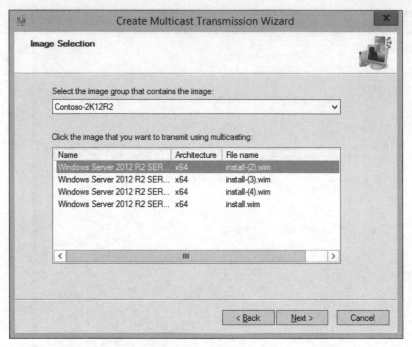

FIGURE 1-36 Creating a multicast transmission

22. On the Multicast Type page, click Auto-Cast, and click Next.

23. On the Operation Complete page, click Finish.

Exercise 5: Import driver package

In this exercise, you import a driver package into WDS. To complete this exercise, perform the following steps:

1. On the WDS console, right-click on the Drivers node, and click Add Driver Package.

2. On the Driver Package Location page of the Add Driver Package Wizard, click Select All Driver Packages From A Folder, and enter the address c:\windows\system32\driverstore as shown in Figure 1-37, and click Next.

FIGURE 1-37 Import driver packages

3. On the Available Driver Packages, ensure that all packages are selected as shown in Figure 1-38, and click Next.

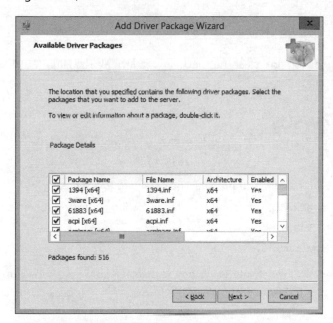

FIGURE 1-38 List of available driver packages

4. On the Summary page, click Next.

5. On the Task Progress page, click Next.

6. On the Failed Package page, click Next.

7. On the Driver Groups page, click Create A New Driver Group Named, and type **2K12R2-VM** as shown in Figure 1-39, and then click Next.

FIGURE 1-39 List of available driver packages

8. On the Task Complete dialog box, clear the check next to Modify The Filters For This Group Now, and click Finish.

Exercise 6: Deploy WSUS

In this exercise, you deploy the WSUS server role on ADL-DC. To complete this exercise, perform the following steps:

1. Sign on to server ADL-DC as Administrator with the password **Pa$$w0rd**.

2. Open the Windows PowerShell prompt and type the following command to join the contoso.com domain.

   ```
   Add-Computer -DomainName contoso.com
   ```

3. In the Windows PowerShell Credentials dialog box, shown in Figure 1-40, type **don_funk@contoso.com** and **Pa$$w0rd,** and click OK.

FIGURE 1-40 PowerShell credentials

4. Type the following command into the Windows PowerShell prompt to shut down the computer.

   Stop-Computer

5. In Hyper-V Manager, right-click ADL-DC, and click Settings.

6. In the Settings For ADL-DC dialog box, click Network Adapter, and click Add.

7. In the Settings For ADL-DC dialog box, select the new network adapter.

8. On the Virtual Switch: drop down menu, click the arrow and select a virtual switch that is connected to an external network adapter.

9. Click OK to close the Settings For ADL-DC dialog box.

10. Start ADL-DC.

11. Sign on to server ADL-DC with the Contoso\don_funk account.

12. Click File Explorer on the taskbar and then double-click Local Disk (C:).

13. Click the New Folder item on the title bar. Name the new folder **Updates**.

14. On the Manage menu of the Server Manager console, click Add Roles And Features.

15. On the Before You Begin page of the Add Roles And Features Wizard, click Next.

16. On the Select Installation Type page, click Role-based or Feature-based Installation, and click Next.

17. On the Select Destination Server page, click ADL-DC.contoso.com, and click Next.

18. On the Select Server Roles page, click Windows Server Update Services.

19. In the Add Roles And Features Wizard pop-up dialog box, click Add Features. Click Next.

20. On the Features page, click Next two times.

21. On the Select Role Services page, shown in Figure 1-41, select both WID Database and WSUS Services, and click Next.

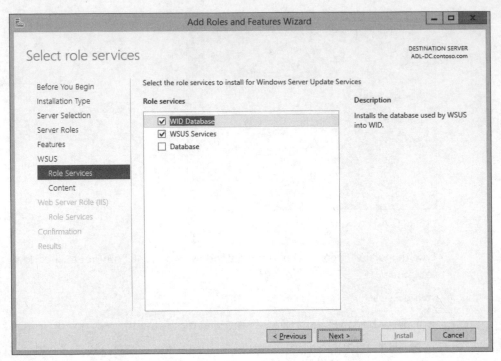

FIGURE 1-41 Adding WSUS roles

22. On the Content Location Selection page, type the address **c:\updates,** and click Next.

23. On the Web Server Role (IIS) page, click Next twice.

24. On the Confirm Installation Selections page, click Install.

25. When the installation completes, close the Add Roles And Features Wizard.

Exercise 7: Configure WSUS

In this exercise, you configure the WSUS server role on ADL-DC. To complete this exercise, perform the following steps:

1. From the Tools menu on the Server Manager console, open the Windows Server Update Services console.

2. In the Complete WSUS Installation dialog box, shown in Figure 1-41, click Run. After the post–installation configuration completes, click Close.

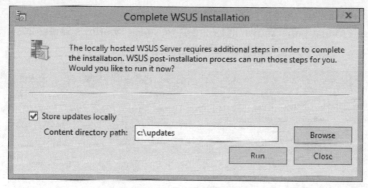

FIGURE 1-42 Complete WSUS Installation dialog box

3. On the Before You Begin page of the Windows Server Update Services Configuration Wizard, click Next.

4. On the Microsoft Update Improvement Program page, click Next.

5. On the Choose Upstream Server page, click Synchronize From Microsoft Update, as shown in Figure 1-43, and click Next.

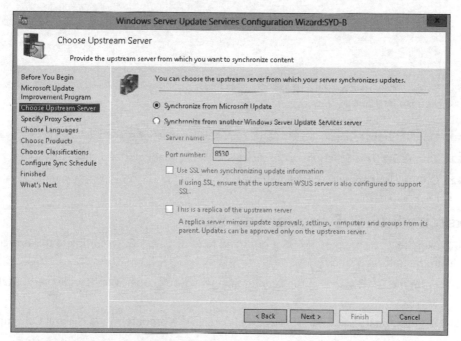

FIGURE 1-43 Choosing the upstream server

6. On the Specify Proxy Server page, click Next.

7. On the Connect To Upstream Server page, click Start Connecting. This operation may take several minutes to complete. When the operation completes, click Next.

8. On the Choose Languages page, click Next.

9. On the Choose Product page, shown in Figure 1-44, select Windows Server 2012 R2, and click Next.

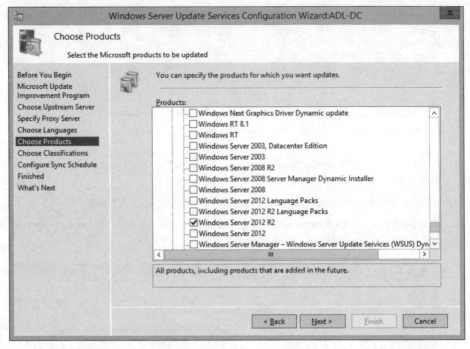

FIGURE 1-44 Choosing products

10. On the Choose Classifications page, click All Classifications, and click Next.

11. On the Set Sync Schedule page, click Synchronize Manually, and click Next.

12. On the Finished page, click Finish.

Exercise 8: WSUS groups and rules

In this exercise, you configure WSUS groups and rules on ADL-DC. To complete this exercise, perform the following steps:

1. From the Tools menu on the Server Manager console, open Windows Server Update Services.

2. On the Update Services console, expand ADL-DC\Computers, and click All Computers.

3. In the Actions pane, click Add Computer Group.

4. In the Add Computer Group dialog box, shown in Figure 1-45, type **Sydney Servers,** and click Add.

FIGURE 1-45 Add Computer Group dialog box

5. Repeat steps 3 and 4 to add the Brisbane Servers computer group.

6. Click Options, and then click Automatic Approvals.

7. In the Automatic Approvals dialog box, click New Rule.

8. In the Add Rule dialog box, shown in Figure 1-46, select the following options and then click OK:

   - When An Update Is In A Specific Classification: **Critical Updates**
   - When An Update Is In A Specific Product: **Windows Server 2012 R2**
   - Approve The Update For: **Sydney Servers**
   - Name: **Sydney Servers Critical Updates**

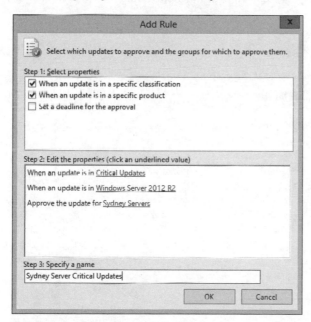

FIGURE 1-46 Adding an approval rule

Suggested practice exercises

The following additional practice exercises are designed to give you more opportunities to practice what you've learned and to help you successfully master the lessons presented in this chapter.

- **Exercise 1**   Use the Microsoft Update Catalog and the Dism.exe command-line utility to locate Windows Server 2012 R2 device drivers and add them to the Datacenter Edition image of Windows Server 2012.

- **Exercise 2**   Use WDS to perform a PXE deployment of Windows Server 2012 R2 to a virtual machine that does not have an operating system installed.

- **Exercise 3**   Create WSUS groups for development Exchange and SQL Servers. Configure automatic deployment rules to automatically approve critical updates for Exchange and SQL Server for the Exchange and SQL groups, respectively.

REAL WORLD   **AUTOMATIC UPDATES TO DEVELOPMENT SERVERS**

You should always test updates before applying them to servers in production environments. Some organizations have updates automatically deployed to servers in development environments and then check to see whether any issues arise that might prevent those updates from being deployed to production servers.

Answers

This section contains the answers to the lesson review questions in this chapter.

Lesson 1

1. **Correct answer: B**

   A. **Incorrect.** You can use ImageX.exe to mount, capture, and apply images. You can't use ImageX.exe to apply software updates in .msu format to an existing image.

   B. **Correct.** You can use Dism.exe to apply software updates in .msu format to an existing image.

   C. **Incorrect.** The Syspep.exe utility enables you to prepare an image for capture. You can't use this utility to apply software updates to an existing image.

   D. **Incorrect.** You use the Diskpart.exe utility to modify disks and volumes. You can't use this utility to apply software updates in .msu format to an existing image.

2. **Correct answer: C**

   A. **Incorrect.** You use the /Add-Driver switch when you want to add drivers to a mounted image.

   B. **Incorrect.** You use the /Enable-Feature switch when you want to enable an operating system feature.

   C. **Correct.** You use the /Add-Package switch when you want to add software updates in .msu format to a mounted operating system image.

   D. **Incorrect.** You use the /Add-ProvisionedAppxPackage when you want to add an application package in .appx format to a mounted operating system image.

3. **Correct answer: C**

   A. **Incorrect.** You commit an image only after you have made modifications to the image.

   B. **Incorrect.** You capture an image when you've deployed a new operating system and you want to write the changes to that operating system.

   C. **Correct.** You must mount an offline installation image before you can modify the image.

   D. **Incorrect.** You discard an image only if you do not want to save the changes that you made to an image.

Lesson 2

1. **Correct answers: A and B**

   A. **Correct.** The boot images enable computers to PXE boot.

B. **Correct.** The install image provides computers with the Windows Server 2012 operating system.

C. **Incorrect.** Capture images are used to create install images. You don't need to be able to create install images to perform basic operating system deployment because they are included with the installation media.

D. **Incorrect.** Discover images are used with computers that can't perform a PXE boot and can't acquire a boot image.

2. **Correct answers: A and C**

A. **Correct.** By default, WDS and DHCP use the same port. When colocating these services, ensure that WDS is configured to use a different port.

B. **Incorrect.** An incorrectly configured WDS server can listen on the same port as a DHCP server, but it can't listen on the port used by a DNS server unless substantial modifications are made to the configuration.

C. **Correct.** Configuring DHCP options sets option tag 60 to DHCP scopes that enables clients to determine the appropriate port to use for WDS transmissions.

D. **Incorrect.** By default, WDS does not need to be authorized. You can enable authorization as a requirement for WDS, but this is not a default setting.

3. **Correct answers: B and D**

A. **Incorrect.** You want the WDS server to respond to client computers, so you should not choose this setting.

B. **Correct.** You want an administrator to manually approve deployments. To accomplish this, you must configure this setting.

C. **Incorrect.** If you select this option, WDS automatically rejects connections from computers with unknown MAC addresses.

D. **Correct.** This option needs to be selected with the Require Administrator Approval For Unknown Computers option. After it is selected, known computers will receive images from WDS, and unknown computers will be able to receive images from WDS after approval.

Lesson 3

1. **Correct answer: B**

A. **Incorrect.** This policy enables you to configure whether a computer will receive automatic updates. This policy cannot be used to assign a computer to a WSUS computer group.

B. **Correct.** This policy enables you to specify the name of the WSUS group in which the computer should be a member.

C. Incorrect. This policy enables you to set a period of time between when updates are installed and any necessary restarts occur. This policy can't be used to assign a computer to a WSUS computer group.

D. Incorrect. You use this policy to specify the location of the WSUS server. This policy can't be used to assign a computer to a WSUS computer group.

2. **Correct answers: B, C, and D**

A. Incorrect. WSUS computer groups are separate from local security groups. You need to create a WSUS group on SYDNEY-WSUS.

B. Correct. You need to create a WSUS group if you want to target specific computers with an automatic approval rule.

C. Correct. By adding the computers to the UpdateTest group, you can target these computers with an automatic approval rule.

D. Correct. Creating an automatic approval rule for the UpdateTest group enables you to have critical and security updates automatically approved to computers that are members of this group.

3. **Correct answers: B and D**

A. Incorrect. You want to have the Melbourne and Perth servers as replicas of the Sydney server.

B. Correct. You want the Melbourne and Perth servers to retrieve updates from Microsoft Update and then have clients in those branch offices retrieve updates from those local servers.

C. Incorrect. You need to configure the Melbourne and Perth servers to store update files locally. If they don't do this, clients in these branch offices will retrieve updates from the Microsoft Update servers on the Internet.

D. Correct. Replicas take approval information and update metadata from upstream servers, which enables the approvals from the Sydney office to flow down to the Melbourne and Perth offices. Although the approvals flow down, these replicas can still retrieve the actual update files from the Microsoft Update servers.

CHAPTER 2

Managing account policies and service accounts

I f you don't force users to update their passwords, they are likely to keep the same ones indefinitely. The longer a person uses the same password, however, the more likely it is that other people will learn it and be able to gain access to that user's account. Password policies enable you to ensure that users update their passwords on a regular basis. Account lockout policies enable you to specify what happens when a user enters an incorrect password in succession. They give you the option of locking accounts out for a limited or indefinite amount of time. In this chapter, you learn about password and account lockout policies, as well as fine–grained password policies and Group Managed Service Accounts (GMSAs). By implementing appropriate policies, you ensure that account passwords in your organization are managed in a secure and efficient manner.

Lessons in this chapter:

- Lesson 1: Implementing domain password and lockout policies **65**
- Lesson 2: Using fine–grained password policies **77**
- Lesson 3: Mastering Group Managed Service Accounts **87**

Before you begin

To complete the practice exercises in this chapter, you need to have deployed computers SYD-DC, MEL-DC, and ADL-DC, as described in the Introduction using the evaluation edition of Windows Server 2012 R2.

Lesson 1: Implementing domain password and lockout policies

Although some organizations use smart cards and biometrics for authentication, the majority of organizations use passwords consisting of alphanumeric characters and symbols as a way to verify a user's identity. The properties of these passwords and the way those properties are enforced have a direct relationship on how effective those passwords are as a security mechanism. You use password policies to specify the properties of the passwords used in your environment. These policies include how long those passwords are, how often users have to change their passwords, how many previous passwords are remembered by Active Directory, and whether a user account is locked after the user enters an incorrect password a specific number of times.

> **After this lesson, you will be able to:**
>
> - Configure domain user password policy.
> - Configure local user password policy.
> - Configure account lockout settings.
>
> **Estimated lesson time: 60 minutes**

Domain user password policies

Most of the accounts used in your organization will be domain-based rather than local accounts. Except for the occasional local account, users, services, and computers authenticate against Active Directory Domain Services (AD DS). By using password policies, administrators can specify the rules for allowable passwords. They determine how long and how complicated passwords must be, as well as how often they must be changed, how often they can be changed, and whether previously used passwords can be used again.

Unless you take special steps, the properties of passwords used with domain accounts are determined through domain-based password policies. You configure password policies by editing Group Policy Objects (GPOs) linked at the domain level. This fact is important, and although you can set password policies at GPOs linked at the organizational unit (OU) and site level, these policies have no effect on the properties of user passwords.

 Remember that you can have only one set of domain password policies configured through Group Policy. The GPO order at the domain level determines the domain password policy. In Figure 2-1, the password policy settings in the default domain policy would override any password policies configured in other GPOs. The exceptions to the rule about one password policy per domain is *fine–grained password policies*, which are not configured directly through Group Policy and are covered in Lesson 2, "Using fine–grained password policies."

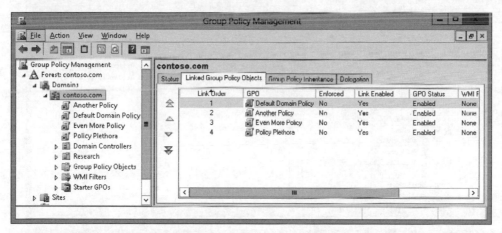

FIGURE 2-1 Multiple GPOs linked to domain

REAL WORLD **DEFAULT DOMAIN POLICY**

Most organizations configure password policy using the Default Domain Policy GPO. Although you can link other policies at the domain level, using the Default Domain Policy GPO simplifies the process of locating and making changes to a domain password policy.

Password policies are located in the Computer Configuration\Policies\Windows Settings\ Security Settings\Account Policies node of a GPO, as shown in Figure 2-2. Although most administrators think of password policy and account lockout policy as parts of the same whole, they are actually separate. Windows Server 2012 and Windows Server 2012 R2 ship with a default password policy, but account lockout policy is not enabled. This part of the lesson focuses on the policies related to password settings, with account lockout policy covered later.

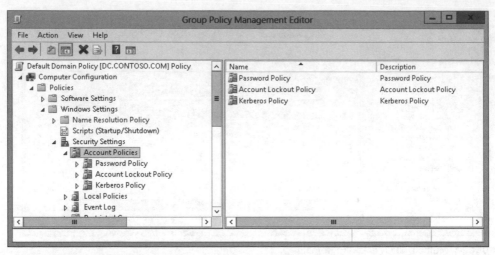

FIGURE 2-2 Password policy location

✔ **Quick check**
- At which level of Active Directory do you apply password policies through Group Policy?

Quick check answer
- Password policies are applied at the domain level. Policies applied at the site and OU level are ignored when password policy is determined.

Password policy items

The following list shows five main password policies that you are likely to use when configuring a password policy for your organization—and one that you probably won't use. These password policies are the following (and shown in Figure 2-3):

- **Enforce password history** This policy means that the configured number of previously used passwords is stored within Active Directory. It stops users from using the same set of small passwords. The default and maximum value is 24 remembered passwords.

- **Maximum password age** This policy specifies the maximum length of time that can elapse before a password must be changed. The default value is 42 days. You can set it to 999 days. Setting the value to 0 days means that there is no maximum password age.

- **Minimum password age** You use this policy to restrict users from changing their password instantly. This policy exists because some users spend a couple of minutes repeatedly changing their password until they have exhausted the password history and return to using their original password. Users can change their password after the specified period has elapsed. The default value is 1 day.

- **Minimum password length** This policy sets the minimum number of characters in a password. Longer passwords are more secure than shorter ones. Windows Server 2012 and Windows Server 2012 R2 support passwords up to 128 characters long when changed using GUI tools, and 256 when modified using Windows PowerShell.

- **Password must meet complexity requirements** This policy ensures that passwords use a mix of numerals, symbols, and uppercase and lowercase alphabet characters. When enabled, it also stops users from using their account name in the password.

REAL WORLD **PASS PHRASES**

People often forget that they can use the space character in passwords and that passwords can be up to 128 characters long. Using sentences rather than short, complex, hard-to-remember strings of characters enables passwords to be both memorable and secure.

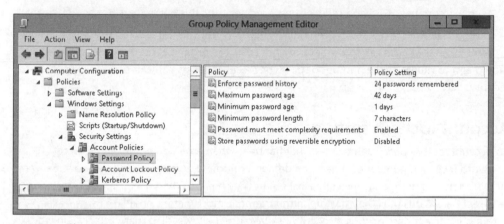

FIGURE 2-3 Five password policies to use

REAL WORLD **THE STORE PASSWORDS USING REVERSIBLE ENCRYPTION POLICY NOT NEEDED**

You are unlikely to need the Store Passwords Using Reversible Encryption policy, shown in Figure 2-3. This policy has been available in most previous versions of the Windows Server operating system. It provides backward compatibility for applications that could not access passwords stored in Active Directory using the native method of encryption. Unless your organization is running some software that was written back when Windows NT 4.0 was the Windows Server operating system, you probably won't need to enable this policy.

Establishing balanced password policies

Password policies require balance, and a password policy that is too strict can be as detrimental as one that is not strict enough. For example, some organizations that implement strict password policies find that users write complicated passwords down because they can't remember them. By increasing the severity of their password policies, the IT department may prompt users to behave in a way that makes the organization less secure.

When considering password policies, keep the following in mind:

- Users dislike changing their password. Many want to log on and get to work rather than coming up with a new password to remember that also meets the requirements of the password policy.

- Users are more likely to forget a new password than one they have been using for some time. Users who constantly forget passwords tend to do things that decrease security such as writing those passwords on notes taped to their monitors.

- If you increase the minimum password length, forcing users to use pass phrases, you can also increase the maximum time before the password expires. Increasing password length increases security by making the password less guessable. Although increasing maximum password age reduces password security, this decrease is not as significant as the improvement achieved by increasing password length.

Remember that each call to the service desk costs the organization money and time. You should aim to minimize the number of password reset requests without decreasing password security.

Account lockout settings

 An *account lockout policy* determines what happens when a person enters an incorrect password a certain number of times. The default Windows Server 2012 and Windows Server 2012 R2 settings do not have account lockout policy configured, so users can keep entering incorrect passwords until they give up in frustration. Unfortunately, enabling users to keep entering incorrect passwords is a security risk because it allows "dictionary attacks," in which an automated system keeps entering passwords from a list until it locates the correct one. Account lockout policies are shown in Figure 2-4.

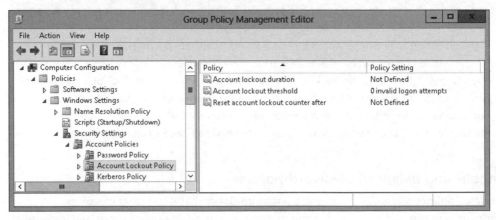

FIGURE 2-4 Account Lockout Policy

These policies enable you to do the following:

- **Account Lockout Duration**   Use this policy to specify how long an account is locked out. When enabled, this setting defaults to 30 minutes. If you set this policy to 0, the account is locked out until someone with the appropriate privileges can unlock it.

- **Account Lockout Threshold**   Use this policy to specify the number of invalid logon attempts that trigger an account lockout. When enabled, the default value is 5, but you can set it to 999. The number of invalid logons must occur within the period specified in the Reset Account Lockout Counter After policy. A value of 0 will mean that account lockout will not be triggered.

- **Reset Account Lockout Counter After**   Use this policy to specify the amount of time in which the number of invalid logon attempts must occur. When enabled, this policy defaults to a value of 30 minutes. If the defaults are used and a user enters an incorrect password three times in 30 minutes, the account is locked out for 30 minutes. If a user enters an incorrect password three times in 31 minutes, however, the account is not locked out.

REAL WORLD   **ACCOUNT LOCKOUT**

You have to consider balance when configuring lockout policies. How many failed attempts suggest that users won't remember their password? For the average user, a lockout of 30 minutes is functionally equivalent to a lockout that never expires. Even if you explain to users a thousand times that they have to wait 30 minutes and try again, they will still ring the help desk within moments of being locked out. Consider a 1-minute lockout and mention it using the logon disclaimer Group Policy item. It enables you to protect against dictionary attacks and probably minimize calls to the service desk.

Account management tasks

Having a set of account policies in place is only the first step in a comprehensive account management strategy. Administrators must regularly check the status of user accounts to determine how well account policies are functioning, as well as locate any accounts in which there is suspicious activity.

Accounts with non-expiring passwords

You can configure an account so that the password never expires. When you do this, the user associated with the account never has to change the password. Password policies don't override accounts that have been explicitly configured so that their passwords do not expire. Configuring the Password Never Expires setting, as shown in Figure 2-5, exempts an account from any password-expiration policies.

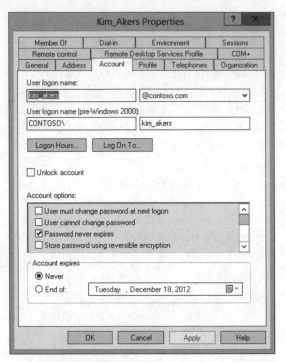

FIGURE 2-5 Password Never Expires setting

To configure an account so that password policies apply, you need to remove the Password Never Expires option. You should also force the user to change the password at the next logon as if the password were configured not to expire because it is reasonable to assume that the user hasn't changed it recently. You can figure out which accounts have been configured not to expire using the Active Directory Administrative Center, and performing a query to find all accounts that have been configured with no expiration date, as shown in Figure 2-6.

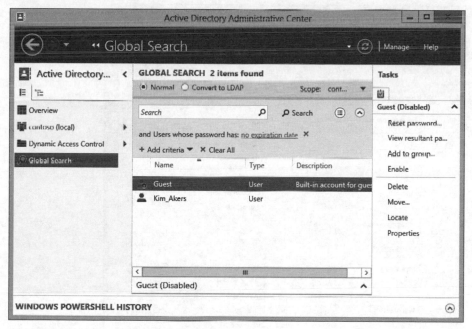

FIGURE 2-6 Locate accounts with no password expiration

You can then modify the properties of these accounts by selecting them all and checking the Password Never Expires option in the Multiple User Account properties dialog box, as shown in Figure 2-7. This dialog box is available when you view the properties of multiple selected accounts in the Active Directory Administrative Center. When performing this task, you should also force users to change their passwords on their next logon, which ensures that password policies apply in the future.

> **REAL WORLD** **ADMINISTRATOR PASSWORDS**
>
> Many systems administrators have the bad habit of configuring their passwords not to expire simply because they realize how annoying it is to have to change passwords constantly. Given that systems administrator accounts are usually the most powerful in the organization, it is a bad idea to enable them to exempt themselves from an organizational password policy. If anything, systems administrators should be subject to more stringent password policies than ordinary users.

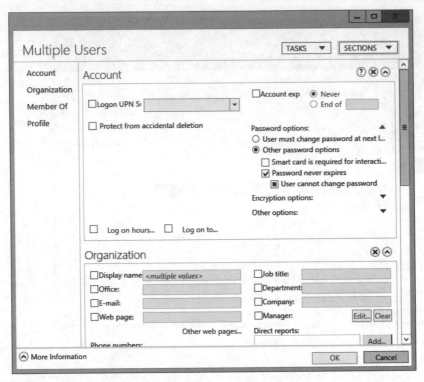

FIGURE 2-7 Multiple account properties

Locked-out accounts

As you learned earlier, the length of time an account is locked out depends on account lockout policies. Many organizations that permanently lock out accounts when a user enters incorrect passwords in succession wait for the locked-out user to ring the service desk to request a password reset. Although most users contact the service desk quickly when their user account is locked out, there are situations in which this does not occur, such as when someone attempts to gain access to a coworker's account while that coworker is on leave. You can use the Active Directory Administrative Center Global Search option, shown in Figure 2-8, to locate users with enabled, but locked-out accounts. You should further investigate locked accounts when the user associated with the account has not contacted the service desk.

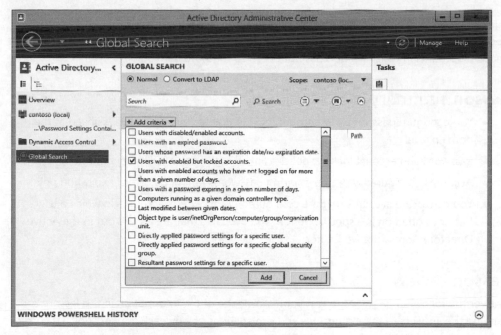

FIGURE 2-8 Locate locked-out user accounts

Inactive accounts

Although the IT department is often notified when a person new to the organization needs a new user account, the IT department is not always notified when people leave the organization. As a result, most organizations have a number of *inactive user accounts* that are associated with people no longer directly associated with the organization. There can be good reasons for the inactivity; for example, a person may be on maternity or long service leave. As an administrator, you should frequently search for accounts in which the user has not signed on for a good length of time. You can disable user accounts associated with users who have temporarily departed the organization. This gives you the option of reenabling the account when the user returns. You can later remove user accounts associated with users who have left the organization.

> **REAL WORLD** **DISABLE OR DELETE?**
>
> Disabling an account allows you to reactivate the account if it is necessary to access resources to which the departed user had access. Some organizations have a special "Disabled User Accounts" OU to store these accounts. Deleting an account is a more permanent option. Although it is possible to recover deleted items if backups are available, it gets increasingly difficult once the tombstone lifetime expires.

You can locate inactive accounts by using the Global Search function in the Active Directory Administrative Center to search for users with enabled accounts who have not signed on for more than a given number of days. The value you choose here will depend upon the nature of your environment, but you should definitely investigate any active enabled accounts in which a logon has not occurred for more than 50 days.

Lesson summary

- You configure password and account lockout policies by editing GPOs linked at the domain level.
- Password and account lockout policies linked at the site or OU level have no effect.
- Accounts configured with non-expiring passwords ignore password expiration policy.
- You can locate accounts that are configured not to expire, accounts in which a user has not signed on in a specific period, and accounts that are locked out in the Active Directory Administrative Center.

Lesson review

Answer the following questions to test your knowledge of the information in this lesson. You can find the answers to these questions and explanations of why each answer choice is correct or incorrect in the "Answers" section at the end of this chapter.

1. You want to ensure that users can't have a password shorter than 10 characters and must keep any new password for a week. Which of the following Group Policy items should you configure to accomplish this goal? (Choose all that apply.)
   A. Enforce Password History
   B. Minimum Password Length
   C. Minimum Password Age
   D. Maximum Password Age

2. You want to ensure that users change their passwords every 4 weeks and don't use any of their 10 previous passwords. Which of the following policies should you configure to accomplish this goal? (Choose all that apply.)
   A. Maximum Password Age
   B. Minimum Password Age
   C. Minimum Password Length
   D. Enforce Password History

3. You want to ensure that users cannot use part of their user name as part of their password. Which of the following policies must you configure to accomplish this goal? (Choose all that apply.)
   A. Minimum Password Age
   B. Passwords Must Meet Complexity Requirements
   C. Enforce Password History

D. Minimum Password Length

4. You want to ensure that users who enter five incorrect passwords in succession in a 2-hour period have their account locked out. Five incorrect passwords in succession entered in a 125-minute period should not trigger an account lockout. Which of the following Group Policy items must you configure to accomplish this goal? (Choose all that apply.)

   A. Password Policy\Minimum Password Length

   B. Account Lockout Policy\Account Lockout Duration

   C. Account Lockout Policy\Account Lockout Threshold

   D. Account Lockout Policy\Reset Account Lockout Counter After

5. Your organization has a single AD DS domain forest, and its domain name is contoso. internal. There is one site named Melbourne. All user accounts are located in a special OU named User_Accounts. All computer accounts are located in a special OU named Computer_Accounts. You want to apply a password and account lockout policy to all user accounts in the domain. Which of the following steps should you take to accomplish that goal? (Choose all that apply.)

   A. Apply a GPO with a password and an account lockout policy to the User_Accounts OU.

   B. Apply a GPO with a password and an account lockout policy to the Computer_Accounts OU.

   C. Apply a GPO with a password and an account lockout policy to the Melbourne site.

   D. Configure the password and account lockout policies in the contoso.internal Default Domain GPO.

Lesson 2: Using fine–grained password policies

With fine–grained password policies, you can configure password policies on the group or even the individual user level. Without fine–grained password policies, a single password policy applies to all user accounts in the organization. Fine–grained password policies provide administrators with flexibility, enabling them to subject sensitive accounts to more stringent password policies than regular user accounts. Any setting that can be configured through password or account lockout policy in an Active Directory GPO can be configured. Fine–grained password policies can be applied to global security groups or individual user accounts.

Delegate password settings permissions

People tend to be good at remembering passwords that they have used for a long time. They tend not to be so good at remembering new passwords, especially if those passwords contain a mix of numbers, letters, and symbols. Users who frequently have to change their passwords are more likely to end up forgetting those passwords. If an account lockout policy is enforced, users are more likely to end up calling the service desk to get their password reset. The stricter an organization's password policy is, the more time the service desk has to spend untangling users from forgotten passwords.

Instead of having users call the service desk to have their password reset, you can delegate the ability to reset user passwords to someone in the user's own department, such as an administrative assistant or office manager. Taking this step can increase security because someone in the user's own department can more easily verify the user's identity than a service desk technician can. It also shifts work away from the service desk, which enables service desk technicians to concentrate on other tasks.

> *REAL WORLD* **INCREASED SECURITY**
>
> Having someone who directly knows the user, be responsible for resetting a password, minimizes the likelihood of a successful social engineering attack. In organizations without a policy that verifies a caller's identity before resetting a password, it is possible for a nefarious third party to call the service desk, claiming to be a user and getting a password reset. If the person with the ability to reset passwords actually knows the user in question, this type of attack is less likely to succeed.

The default Active Directory settings give members of the Account Operators, Domain Admins, or Enterprise Admins Active Directory groups the right to change user passwords. You can delegate the ability to manage password settings on a per-OU basis through the delegation of a control wizard. When you do this, you move user accounts into specific OUs that match your administrative requirements. For example, you can move all user accounts of people who work in the research department to the Research OU, and then delegate the right to reset passwords and force password change at the next logon to the research department's departmental manager. You can also delegate the ability to manage password settings at the domain level, though most organizations do this by adding users to the Account Operators, Domain Admins, or Enterprise Admins groups.

To delegate the right to reset passwords and force password changes at the next logon, run the Delegation Of Control Wizard. You can access this wizard by right-clicking an OU in Active Directory Users And Computers and then clicking Delegate Control. You should be careful to select only the Reset User Passwords And Force Password Change At Next Logon task, as shown in Figure 2-9, not grant non-IT department users the right to perform other tasks.

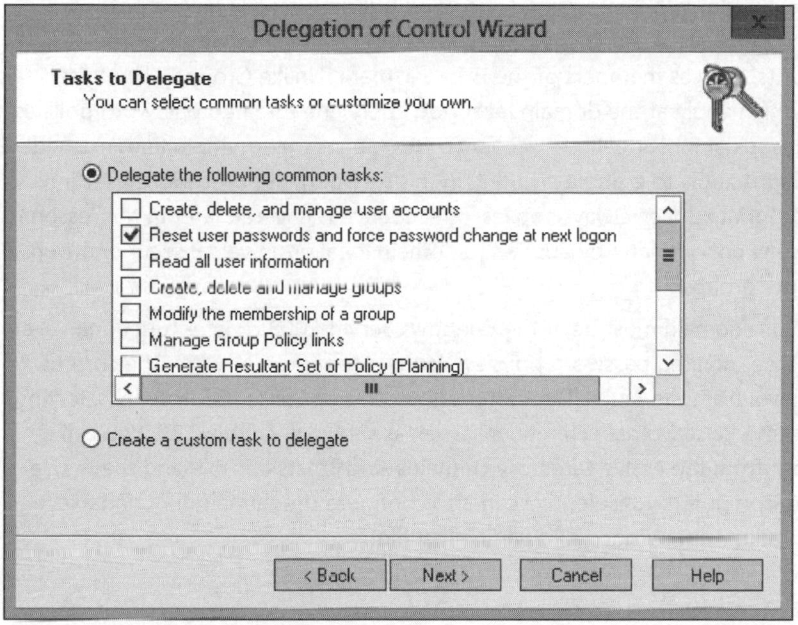

FIGURE 2-9 Delegate password reset

MORE INFO **DELEGATING ADMINISTRATION OF ACCOUNT OUS**

To learn more about delegating administration of account OUs, consult the following TechNet article at *http://technet.microsoft.com/en-us/library/cc771454(WS.10).aspx*.

Larger organizations should consider providing a self–service password reset portal. Self–service password reset portals enable users to reset their Active Directory user account passwords after performing a series of tasks that verify their identity. This process provides users with a quick method of resetting forgotten passwords and reduces the number of password reset requests for service desk technicians. You can implement self–service password reset with Microsoft Forefront Identity Manager 2010 R2, which integrates with Active Directory Domain Services to enable this functionality.

Fine–grained password policies

Fine–grained password policies enable you to have separate password policies within a single domain. For example, with fine–grained password policies you can have a password policy that applies to general users and have a stricter set of policies that apply to users with sensitive accounts, such as members of the IT department. Unlike Group Policy-based password policies, which apply at the domain level, you apply fine–grained password policies to global security groups or individual user accounts. This means that multiple fine–grained password policies might apply to a single account. In this situation, use precedence settings to ensure that the appropriate policy always applies. (Precedence is covered later in this lesson.) Fine–grained password policies can't be applied to domain local or universal security groups, only to global security groups.

The Active Directory domain must be at the Windows Server 2008 or later functional level before you can use fine–grained password policies. You can configure or verify the current domain functional level from the Active Directory Administrative Center Console by selecting the domain and clicking Raise Domain Functional Level, as shown in Figure 2-10. You can also perform this task from the Active Directory Domains And Trusts console and the Active Directory Users And Computers console. You can also configure the domain functional level using the Set-ADDomainMode Windows PowerShell cmdlet.

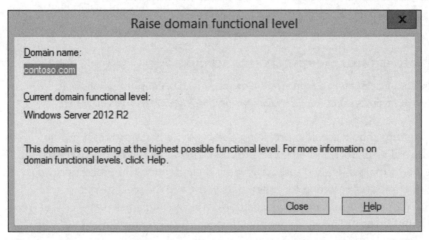

FIGURE 2-10 Domain functional level

For example, to raise the domain functional level of the contoso.com domain to Windows Server 2008 from the Windows Server 2003 functional level, issue the following command.

```
Set-ADDomainMode -Identity contoso.com -DomainMode 3
```

You should plan modifications to domain functional levels carefully. You can't lower the domain functional level once it has been set, and the domain functional level determines which operating systems you can use to host Active Directory domain controllers. You'll learn more about domain functional levels in Chapter 4, "Administering Active Directory."

REAL WORLD **MUCH EASIER**

In previous versions of the Windows Server operating system, you had to perform a complicated set of steps using ADSIEdit to configure fine-grained password policies. Although many administrators appreciated the functionality that fine-grained password policies offered, many considered the configuration process too cumbersome to implement in their own environment. By simplifying the process of configuring fine-grained password policies, Microsoft makes them far more likely to be adopted by systems administrators who want to leverage this functionality.

Managing fine-grained password policies

You create and manage fine-grained password policies through the Active Directory Administrative Center. To create a new Password Settings Object (PSO), open the Active Directory Administrative Center and navigate to the Password Settings Container (PSC), which is located in the System Container of the domain, as shown in Figure 2-11. From the Tasks menu, click New, and then click Password Settings. The PSC enables you to view the precedence of PSOs. Password settings with lower precedence values override password settings with higher precedence values. When you apply PSOs to the user and the groups that the user belongs to, the group based PSOs will be ignored and only the PSOs that apply to the user's account will be checked for precedence.

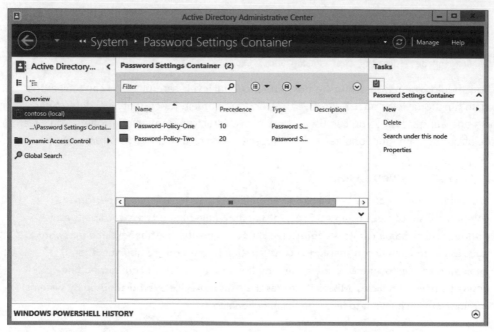

FIGURE 2-11 Password Settings Container

> ✔ **Quick check**
>
> ■ PSO Alpha has a precedence value of 100. PSO Beta has a precedence value of 10. A
>   user account is a member of groups to which both PSO Alpha and Beta apply. Which
>   PSO settings apply to the user account?
>
> **Quick check answer**
>
> ■ The settings in PSO Beta apply to the user account because the value of 10 overrides
>   the value of 100.

Configuring Password Settings Objects

A *Password Settings Object* (PSO), shown in Figure 2-12, contains settings for both password
policy and account lockout policy. A PSO applies to the groups and users specified in the
Directly Applies To area. If a PSO applies to a user account, either directly or indirectly
through group membership, that PSO overrides the existing password and account lockout
policies configured at the domain level.

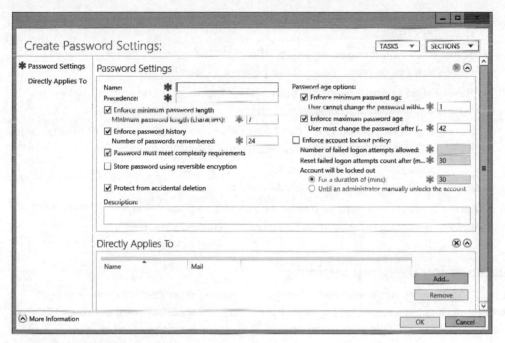

FIGURE 2-12 Password Settings Object

PSOs contain the following options:

- **Name** Enables you to configure a name for the PSO.
- **Precedence** When multiple PSOs apply to an account, the PSO with the lowest precedence value has priority.
- **Enforce Minimum Password Length** Minimum password length that can be used by users subject to the policy.
- **Enforce Password History** The number of passwords remembered by Active Directory. Remembered passwords can't be reused.
- **Password Must Meet Complexity Requirements** A password must contain a mix of numbers, symbols, and uppercase and lowercase letters.
- **Store Password Using Reversible Encryption** Provides backward compatibility with older software and is rarely used in Windows Server 2012 environments.
- **Protect From Accidental Deletion** The user account can't be accidentally deleted. Although this setting is not available in Group Policy password or account lockout settings, you can edit an object directly to configure it.
- **Enforce Minimum Password Age** The minimum length of time users must have a password before they are eligible to change it.
- **Enforce Maximum Password Age** The maximum number of days that users can go without changing their password.

- **Enforce Account Lockout Policy**   You can configure the following three policies with this policy enabled:

- **Number Of Failed Logon Attempts Allowed**   The number of incorrect password entries that can be made in succession before a lockout is triggered.

- **Reset Failed Logon Attempts Count After**   The period of time in which the incorrect password entries must be made.

- **Account Will Be Locked Out**   Can be set either to a specific number of minutes or to a setting for which the administrator must manually unlock the account.

> *MORE INFO*   **FINE–GRAINED PASSWORD POLICIES**
>
> To learn more about fine–grained password policies, consult the following TechNet article at *http://technet.microsoft.com/en-us/library/jj574144.aspx#BKMK_FGPP*.

Determining password settings

If your organization uses a number of fine–grained password policies, it might be difficult to determine, at a glance, which password policy applies to a particular user because PSOs can be applied to multiple groups and users, and users can be members of multiple groups. Rather than work everything out manually, the Active Directory Administrative Center's Global Search function provides the following criteria to determine which fine–grained password policy applies to a specific user or group:

- **Directly Applied Password Settings For A Specific User**   You can determine which PSOs directly apply to a specific user account. PSOs that apply to security groups of which the user account is a member are not listed.

- **Directly Applied Password Settings For A Specific Global Security Group**   You can determine which PSOs directly apply to a specific security group.

- **Resultant Password Settings For A Specific User**   You can determine which PSO applies to a specific user account based upon directly applied PSOs as well as PSOs that apply indirectly through group membership. The results of this query are shown in Figure 2-13.

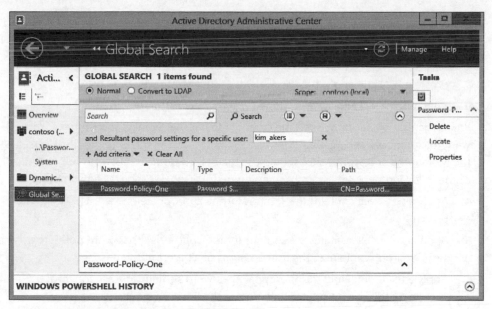

FIGURE 2-13 Resultant set of password policies

Lesson summary

- You delegate the ability to reset passwords using the Delegation Of Control Wizard. You can perform this task at the domain or OU level.
- You can create and manage PSOs by using the Active Directory Administrative Center
- PSOs can apply to global security groups or individual user accounts.
- PSOs enable you to apply all password and account policy settings available in Group Policy. You can also protect accounts from deletion.
- PSOs with lower numerical precedence numbers override PSOs with higher numerical precedence numbers.
- You can use the Active Directory Administrative Center to determine which PSO has precedence when multiple PSOs apply directly and indirectly to an account.

Lesson review

Answer the following questions to test your knowledge of the information in this lesson. You can find the answers to these questions and explanations of why each answer choice is correct or incorrect in the "Answers" section at the end of this chapter.

1. You want to configure a separate password policy for members of the systems administration team. The user accounts of all members of the systems administration team are located in the Systems_Administration OU. Which of the following steps can you take to accomplish this goal? (Choose all that apply.)

A. Create a security group named Systems_Administrators. Place all the user accounts of the systems administration team in this security group.

B. Create a PSO and apply it to the Systems_Administration OU.

C. Create a PSO and apply it to the Systems_Administrators security group.

D. Configure a GPO and apply it to the Systems_Administration OU.

2. Your organization has three sites: the cities of Melbourne, Sydney, and Brisbane. You want to configure a separate password policy for all users in the Brisbane site. Users in the Melbourne and Sydney sites should use the default domain password policy. Which of the following steps can you take to accomplish this goal? (Choose all that apply.)

A. Apply a GPO that contains the settings for the appropriate password policy to the Brisbane site.

B. Apply a GPO that contains the settings for the appropriate password policy to a security group containing the user accounts of all users at the Brisbane site.

C. Apply a PSO containing the appropriate password settings to a security group containing the user accounts of all users at the Brisbane site.

D. Apply a PSO to the Brisbane site.

3. Which of the following tools can you use to configure fine-grained password policies? (Choose all that apply.)

A. Group Policy Management Console

B. Active Directory Administrative Center

C. Active Directory Users And Computers

D. Active Directory Sites And Services

4. Rooslan and Oksana are part of the IT department, and all members of the department have user accounts that are members of the IT_Staff security group. All user accounts for members of the IT department are stored in the IT_Dept OU. You want members of the IT department to be subjected to a separate password policy from the rest of the organization. Rooslan and Oksana in turn need to be subject to a password policy that is different from both the organizational password policy and the password policy applied to the rest of the IT department. No policies are currently in place. Which of the following steps should you take to accomplish this goal? (Choose all that apply.)

A. Edit the Default Domain Policy and configure the password policy for the organization.

B. Create a PSO that applies to the IT_Staff security group, which reflects the password policy that must be applied to the IT department. Assign this PSO a precedence of 20.

C. Create a PSO that reflects the password policy that should apply to Oksana and Rooslan and apply it to their user accounts. Assign this PSO a precedence of 30.

D. Create a PSO that reflects the password policy that should apply to Oksana and Rooslan and apply it to their user accounts. Assign this PSO a precedence of 10.

5. Which of the following domain functional levels are the minimum at which fine-grained password policies are supported? (Choose all that apply.)

   A. Windows Server 2003

   B. Windows Server 2008

   C. Windows Server 2008 R2

   D. Windows Server 2012

Lesson 3: Mastering Group Managed Service Accounts

 A *Group Managed Service Account* (GMSA) is a special account type that you can use with services on computers running Windows Server 2012 and Windows Server 2012 R2. When you use a GMSA, the password of the account is automatically updated on a regular basis. When you use GMSAs, you don't have to manually update the account password in Active Directory or any services configured to use the GMSA.

> **After this lesson, you will be able to:**
> - Create GMSAs.
> - Install GMSAs.
> - Perform Kerberos delegation.
>
> **Estimated lesson time: 45 minutes**

Password policies require users to change their passwords periodically as a method of increasing security because the longer the same password is used, the more likely it is that an unauthorized person may learn it. Service accounts are a special type of account that gives a service an identity, and many systems administrators don't want to deal with them. Like user accounts, service accounts have passwords; and like other accounts, the passwords of service accounts should be changed on a regular basis.

GMSAs

Managed Service Accounts were introduced with Windows Server 2008 R2. These accounts functioned in a manner similar to GMSAs except that you could not use a single Managed Service Account across multiple servers. If you wanted to use Managed Service Accounts for the same service on two different servers, you needed to create two separate Managed Service Accounts, one for each server. If an administrator wanted to use the same Managed Service Account across multiple servers, something required for many applications that require high availability, they needed to configure a user account to perform this role.

GMSAs enable you to use the same Managed Service Account across multiple servers. You can use GMSAs only on computers running the Windows Server 2012 and later operating systems. GMSAs used with computers running Windows Server 2008 R2 must function as non-GMSAs and are limited to being installed on a single server.

GMSAs are stored in the Managed Service Account Container. This container is visible by default in Active Directory Administrative Center, as shown in Figure 2-14, and is visible if you enabled the Advanced Features view option in Active Directory Users And Computers.

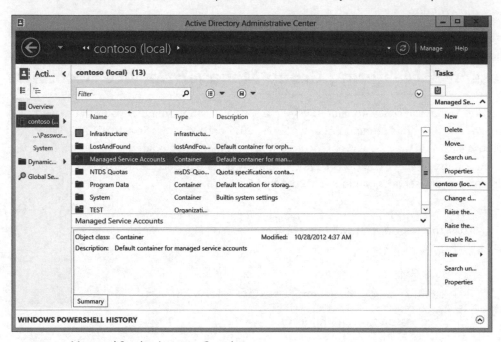

FIGURE 2-14 Managed Service Accounts Container

GMSA requirements

GMSAs require that .NET Framework 3.5.x is installed on the local server. You can use GMSAs without extending the Active Directory Schema if the domain is running at the Windows Server 2008 R2 or higher functional level. If the domain is not running at this functional level and is instead running at the Windows Server 2003 or Windows Server 2008 levels, you can extend the schema so that it supports GMSAs. To use GMSAs, at least one domain controller in the domain must be running Windows Server 2012 or later.

Before creating the first GMSA in an organization, it is necessary to create a key distribution services root key with the Add-KDSRootKey cmdlet. You can do this with the following command.

```
Add-KdsRootKey -EffectiveImmediately
```

With some versions of PowerShell, the created key becomes operational only 10 hours after the command is issued. If you want to use GMSAs immediately, you must configure the time to be 10 hours prior to the current time by using the following command.

```
Add-KdsRootKey -EffectiveTime ((get-date).addhours(-10))
```

Creating GMSAs

After you create the *key distribution services root key*, you can then create GMSAs using the New-ADServiceAccount cmdlet. For example, to create a new GMSA named GMSA-Alpha using the Windows Server 2012 domain controller SYD-DC.contoso.com, execute this command.

```
New-ADServiceAccount -Name GMSA-Alpha -DNSHostname SYD-DC.contoso.com
```

You can configure the computers that use the GMSA by using the Set-ADServiceAccount cmdlet. When you specify accounts, use their Security Account Manager (SAM) names. For example, to configure the GMSAs GMSA-Alpha to be used by servers MEL-DC and ADL-DC, issue this command.

```
Set-ADServiceAccount -Identity GMSA-Alpha -PrincipalsAllowedToRetrieveManagedPassword
MEL-DC$, ADL-DC$
```

Rather than specifying individual server accounts, you can also specify group names. Any computers that are members of this security group can use the GMSA. For example, to create a new GMSA named GMSA-Beta that can be used by computers that are members of the GMSA-Beta-Group, issue this command.

```
New-ADServiceAccount -Name GMSA-Beta -PrincipalsAllowedToRetrieveManagedPassword GMSA-
Beta-Group -DNSHostname SYD-DC.contoso.com
```

After the GMSA is created, you need to install it on each server before you can use it with services. You do this with the Install-ADServiceAccount cmdlet. This cmdlet is located in the Active Directory Windows PowerShell module, which you can add to a computer by installing the Remote Server Administration Tools (RSAT). For example, to install the GMSA GMSA-Alpha on the local server, execute this command.

```
Install-ADServiceAccount -Identity GMSA-Alpha
```

After the GMSA is created, you can configure a service to use the account. You do this by editing the properties of the service, clicking Browse on the Log On tab, and selecting the service account from the Entire Directory location, as shown in Figure 2-15. Although accounts that aren't installed on the server are visible, you can use only accounts that have been installed on the server with the service.

> **MORE INFO** **GROUP MANAGED SERVICE ACCOUNTS**
>
> You can find out more about GMSAs at *http://technet.microsoft.com/en-us/library/hh831782.aspx*.

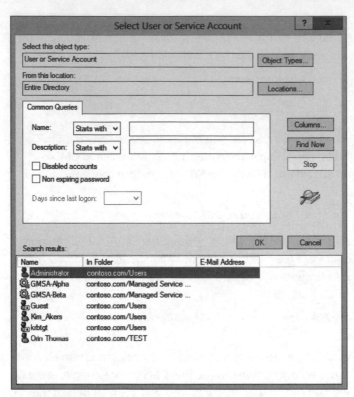

FIGURE 2-15 Select service account

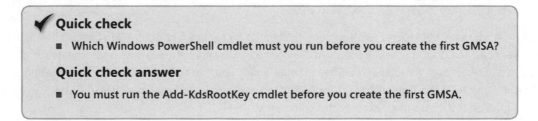

✔ **Quick check**

- Which Windows PowerShell cmdlet must you run before you create the first GMSA?

Quick check answer

- You must run the Add-KdsRootKey cmdlet before you create the first GMSA.

Virtual accounts

A *virtual account* is a local version of a Managed Service Account that is used for local services running on the host computer. Virtual accounts can access resources on the network using the computer's identity when the computer is a member of the domain. Virtual accounts are supported only on computers running Windows Server 2008 R2, Windows 7, Windows Server 2012, Windows Server 2012 R2, Windows 8, and Windows 8.1. You don't need to run any special Windows PowerShell cmdlets to create the virtual service account, or configure a service to use that account. You just need to know the name of the service, which you can learn by using the Get-Service cmdlet. To configure a service to use a virtual service account, perform the following steps:

1. Open the Services console and edit the properties of the service that you want to configure to use the virtual service account.

2. On the Log On tab, click This Account

3. In the This Account text box, type the service name as **NT Service\servicename**. Figure 2-16 shows the configuration of the Windows Update service with its associated service name. You should configure the service with a blank password when installing it. The operating system configures the service with a managed password when you restart the service.

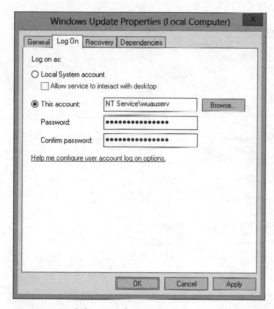

FIGURE 2-16 Select service account

> **MORE INFO   VIRTUAL ACCOUNTS**
>
> You can find out more about virtual accounts at *http://technet.microsoft.com/en-us/library/dd548356(v=ws.10).aspx*.

Kerberos delegation

Kerberos constrained delegation restricts how and where application services can act on a user's behalf. You can configure accounts so that they can be used only for specific tasks. For example, Figure 2-17 shows configuring delegation of the account for computer SYD-B, for delegation through Kerberos, for the time service on computer SYD-A. Windows Server 2012 and Windows Server 2012 R2 enable constrained delegation to be performed where the front-end service and the resource service are located in separate domains. You can configure Kerberos delegation using the Set-ADComputer, Set-ADServiceAccount, and Set-ADUser cmdlets with the PrincipalsAllowedToDelegateAccount parameter.

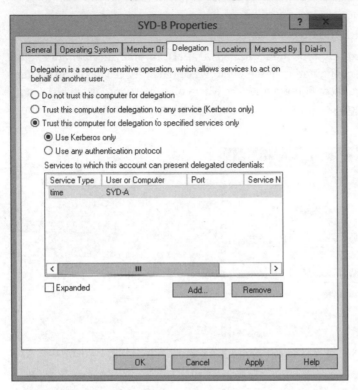

FIGURE 2-17 Kerberos delegation

> **MORE INFO   KERBEROS CONSTRAINED DELEGATION**
>
> You can find out more about Kerberos delegation at *http://technet.microsoft.com/en-us/ library/jj553400.aspx*.

Kerberos policies

Kerberos policies determine how the service and user tickets are used in the Authentication function in an Active Directory domain. Like password and account lockout policy, Kerberos policy is applied at the domain level. Kerberos policies applied at the site and organizational level have no effect on Kerberos policy. Kerberos policies are located in the Computer Configuration\Policies\Windows Settings\Security Settings\Account Policies node, as shown in Figure 2-18.

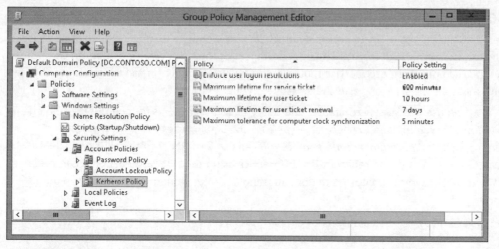

FIGURE 2-18 Kerberos policies

Windows Server 2012 and Windows Server 2012 R2 enable you to configure the following Kerberos policies:

- **Enforce User Logon Restrictions** Ensures that Kerberos checks every request for a session ticket, also known as a service ticket.

- **Maximum Lifetime For Service Ticket** Configures the maximum lifetime of a service ticket, which is also known as a session ticket. The default value for this policy is 10 hours. The value of this policy must be less than or equal to the value specified in the Maximum Lifetime For User Ticket policy.

- **Maximum Lifetime For User Ticket** Determines the maximum lifetime of a user ticket, also known as a Ticket Granting Ticket (TGT). The default value of this policy is 10 hours.

- **Maximum Lifetime For User Ticket Renewal** Specifies the maximum TGT renewal period. The default is 7 days.

- **Maximum Tolerance For Computer Clock Synchronization** Specifies how much drift there can be in domain controller clocks before ticket errors occur. The default setting is 5 minutes.

MORE INFO **KERBEROS POLICY**

You can find out more about Kerberos policy at *http://technet.microsoft.com/en-us/library/ cc961968.aspx*.

Service principal name management

Kerberos clients use a *service principal name* (SPN) to identify a unique instance of a service on a given computer. If there are multiple instances of the same service hosted on computers in a domain or forest, each service requires a unique SPN. Service instances can be configured with multiple SPNs, as long as those SPNs are unique.

You can use the SetSPN command-line utility to configure SPNs for computers running Windows Server 2012 and Windows Server 2012 R2. SetSPN uses this syntax: *setspn serviceclass/host:portnumber servicename*. You can use **SetSPN /?** to see a list of all SPN switches. For example, to register the HTTP service using the standard port on a computer named MEL-DC in the contoso.com domain using a GMSA named SYD-SRVC, issue this command.

```
Setpspn -s http/MEL-DC.contoso.com CONTOSO\SYD-SRVC
```

> **MORE INFO** **SERVICE PRINCIPAL NAMES**
>
> You can find out more about SPNs at *http://social.technet.microsoft.com/wiki/contents/ articles/717.service-principal-names-spns-setspn-syntax-setspn-exe.aspx*.

Lesson summary

- You must create a key distribution services key before you can create GMSAs.
- You use the New-ADServiceAccount cmdlet to create a new GMSA.
- You use the Set-AdServiceAccount cmdlet to configure a new GMSA.
- You use the Install-ADServiceAccount cmdlet to install an account on a new computer.
- Kerberos constrained delegation enables you to configure what services and accounts can be used for when delegated using Kerberos.

Lesson review

Answer the following questions to test your knowledge of the information in this lesson. You can find the answers to these questions and explanations of why each answer choice is correct or incorrect in the "Answers" section at the end of this chapter.

1. Which of the following operating systems supports virtual service accounts?

   A. Windows Server 2008

   B. Windows Server 2012

   C. Windows Server 2008 R2

   D. Windows Server 2003 R2

2. You want to deploy GMSAs in your new Windows Server 2012 R2 environment. Which of the following Windows PowerShell cmdlets must you run first?

    A. New-AdServiceAccount

    B. Install ADServiceAccount

    C. Set-ADServiceAccount

    D. Add-KdsRootKey

3. You want to configure an existing GMSA to be used by additional computers. Which of the following Windows PowerShell cmdlets do you use to accomplish this goal?

    A. Install-ADServiceAccount

    B. Add-KdsRootKey

    C. New-AdServiceAccount

    D. Set-ADServiceAccount

4. You want to use a particular GMSA on a computer running the Windows Server 2012 operating system. You have created and configured the GMSA in Active Directory. Which of the following commands must you run on the computer before you can configure a service to use the account?

    A. Set-ADServiceAccount

    B. Add-KdsRootKey

    C. Install-ADServiceAccount

    D. New-AdServiceAccount

5. Which of the following policies should you configure at the domain level to ensure that the clocks of domain controllers must be synchronized within 2 minutes of one another for Kerberos to function correctly?

    A. Maximum Lifetime Of A Service Ticket

    B. Maximum Lifetime For User Ticket Renewal

    C. Maximum Tolerance For Computer Clock Synchronization

    D. Maximum Lifetime For User Ticket

Practice exercises

The goal of this section is to provide you with hands-on practice with the following:

- Configure password and account lockout policies
- Create fine–grained password policies
- Create and configure GMSAs

To perform the exercises in this section, you need access to an evaluation version of Windows Server 2012Windows Server 2012 R2. You should also have access to virtual machines SYD-DC, MEL-DC, CBR-DC, and ADL-DC, the setup instructions for which are described in the Introduction. You should ensure that you have a snapshot checkpoint of these virtual machines that you can revert to at the end of the practice exercises. You should revert the virtual machines to this initial state prior to beginning these exercises.

Exercise 1: Configure password and account lockout policies

In this exercise, you configure the password policy and account lockout policy in an AD DS domain. You also use Active Directory Administrative Center to locate accounts that are configured with passwords that never expire. To complete this exercise, perform the following steps:

1. Sign on to SYD-DC as Contoso\Administrator.
2. From the Tools menu of the Server menu, click Group Policy Management.
3. On the Group Policy Management Console (GPMC), expand the Forest: Contoso.com, Domains, contoso.com\Group Policy Objects node and click Default Domain Policy, as shown in Figure 2-19.

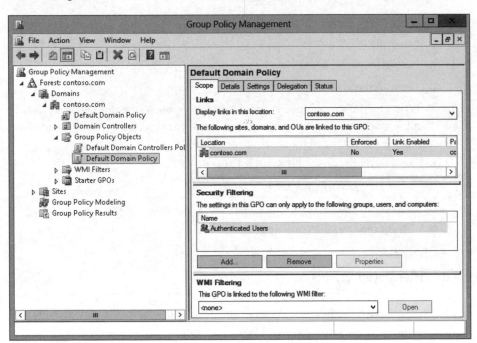

FIGURE 2-19 Default Domain Policy

4. On the Action menu, click Edit.
5. In the Group Policy Management Editor, expand the Computer Configuration\Policies\ Windows Settings\Security Settings\Account Policies\Password Policy node.
6. Right-click Enforce Password History, and click Properties.

7. In the Enforce Password History Properties dialog box, ensure that Define This Policy Setting is enabled, set the Keep Password History For setting to 20 Passwords Remembered (as shown in Figure 2-20), and click OK.

FIGURE 2-20 Password history

8. Click the Maximum Password Age policy. On the Action menu, click Properties

9. In the Maximum Password Age Properties dialog box, ensure that Define This Policy Setting is enabled. Set the Password Will Expire In Value to 88 days, as shown in Figure 2-21, and click OK.

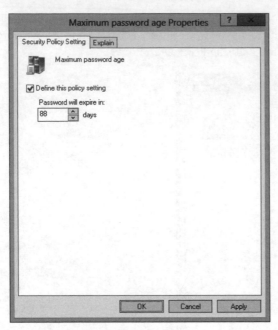

FIGURE 2-21 Maximum Password Age

10. Click the Minimum Password Age policy. On the Action menu, click Properties.

11. In the Minimum Password Age Properties dialog box, ensure that Define This Policy Setting is selected. Configure the Password Can Be Changed After value to 12 days, as shown in Figure 2-22, and click OK.

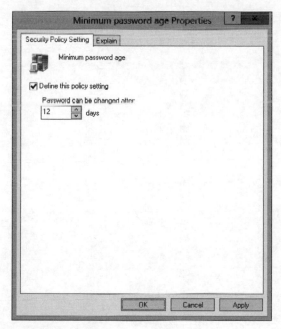

FIGURE 2-22 Minimum Password Age

12. In the Group Policy Management Editor, click Minimum Password Length. On the Action menu, click Properties.

13. In the Minimum Password Length Properties dialog box, ensure that Define This Policy Setting check box is selected. Set the Password Must Be At Least to 10 characters, as shown in Figure 2-23, and then click OK.

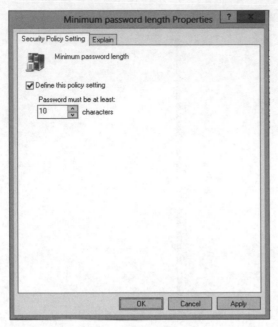

FIGURE 2-23 Minimum Password Length

14. In the Group Policy Management Editor, click the Password Must Meet Complexity Requirements policy. On the Action menu, click Properties.

15. In the Password Must Meet Complexity Requirements Properties dialog box, ensure that Define This Policy Setting check box is selected. Ensure that the policy setting is configured as Enabled, as shown in Figure 2-24, and then click OK.

FIGURE 2-24 Password must meet complexity requirements

16. Close the Group Policy Management Editor.

Exercise 2: Configure account lockout policies

In this exercise, you configure account lockout policy in an AD DS domain. To complete this exercise, perform the following steps:

1. In the GPMC, expand the Forest: Contoso.com, Domains, Contoso.com\Group Policy objects node, and click Default Domain Policy.

2. On the Action menu, click Edit.

3. In the Group Policy Management Editor, expand the Computer Configuration\Policies\ Windows Settings\Security Settings\Account Policies\Account Lockout Policy node.

4. Click the Account Lockout Duration policy. On the Action menu, click Properties.

5. In the Account Location Duration Properties dialog box, click Define This Policy Setting. Configure the number of minutes to 120, as shown in Figure 2-25, and then click OK.

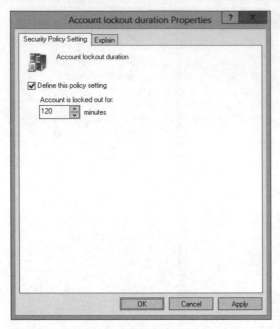

FIGURE 2-25 Account Lockout Duration

6. In the Suggested Value Changes dialog box, shown in Figure 2-26, click OK.

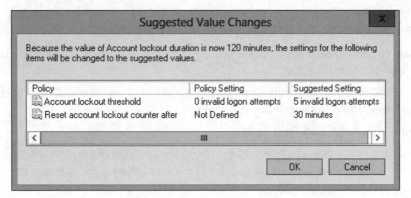

FIGURE 2-26 Suggested Value Changes

7. Click the Account Lockout Threshold policy. On the Action menu, click Properties.

8. In the Account Lockout Threshold Properties dialog box, ensure that the Define This Policy Setting check box is selected. Set the Account Will Lock Out After value to 3 Invalid Logon Attempts, as shown in Figure 2-27, and click OK.

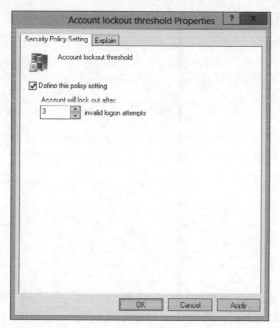

FIGURE 2-27 Account Lockout Threshold

9. In the Group Policy Management Editor, click Reset Account Lockout Counter After. On the Action menu, click Properties.

10. In the Reset Account Lockout Counter After Properties dialog box, ensure that Define This Policy Setting is selected. Set the Reset Account Lockout Counter After value to 2400 minutes, as shown in Figure 2-28, and click OK.

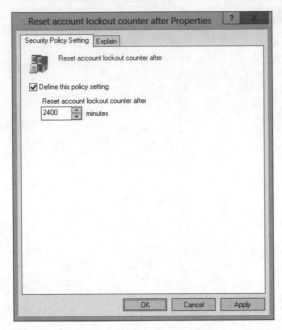

FIGURE 2-28 Reset account lockout counter

11. In the Suggested Value Changes dialog box, click OK.

12. Close the Group Policy Management Editor.

13. Configure the following account lockout policy settings:

   - Account Lockout Duration: 2400 minutes
   - Account Lockout Threshold: 3 invalid logon attempts
   - Reset Account Lockout Counter After: 2400 minutes

Exercise 3: Group Policy Modeling

In this exercise, you use the Active Directory Administrative Center to locate accounts that are configured with passwords that never expire. To complete this exercise, perform the following steps:

1. In the GPMC, expand the Forest: Contoso.com, and click Group Policy Modeling.

2. On the Action menu, click the Group Policy Modeling Wizard.

3. On the Welcome To The Group Policy Modeling Wizard page, click Next.

4. On the Domain Controller Selection page, click This Domain Controller and click SYD-DC.contoso.com, as shown in Figure 2-29. Click Next.

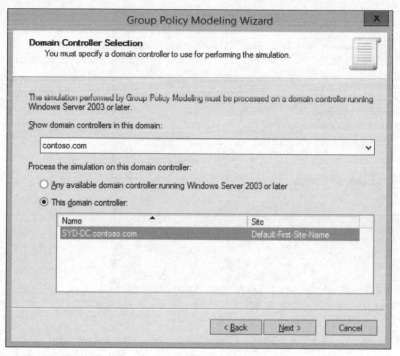

FIGURE 2-29 Domain Controller Selection

5. On the User And Computer Selection page of the Group Policy Modeling Wizard, click Browse next to Container in the User Information area.

6. In the Choose User Container dialog box, expand Contoso, click Users, and click OK.

7. On the User And Computer Selection page of the Group Policy Modeling Wizard, click Browse next to Container in the Computer Information area.

8. In the Choose Computer Container dialog box, expand Contoso, click Computers, and click OK.

9. Verify that the User And Computer Selection page matches Figure 2-30 and then click Next.

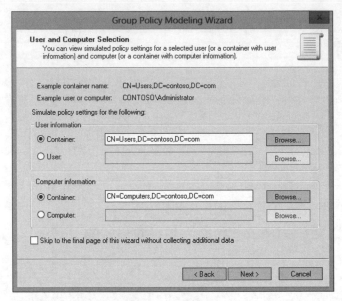

FIGURE 2-30 User And Computer Selection

10. On the Advanced Simulation Options page, click Next.

11. On the User Security Groups page, shown in Figure 2-31, click Authenticated Users, and then click Next.

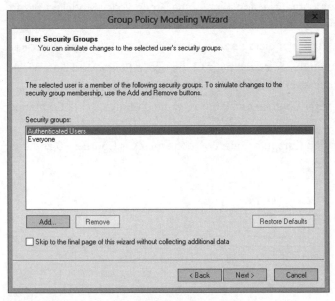

FIGURE 2-31 User Security Groups selection

12. On the Computer Security Groups page, click Next.

13. On the WMI Filters For Users page, click Next.

14. On the WMI Filters For Computers page, click Next.

15. On the Summary Of Selections page, click Next.

16. On the Completing The Group Policy Modeling Wizard page, click Finish.

17. In the Internet Explorer dialog box, click Add.

18. In the Trusted Sites dialog box, click Add, and then click Close.

19. Click Contoso, and then click the Details page.

20. Click Show next to Security Settings.

21. Click Show next to Account Policies/Password Policy, and click show next to Account Policies/Account Lockout Policy.

22. Verify that the settings displayed match those shown in Figure 2-32.

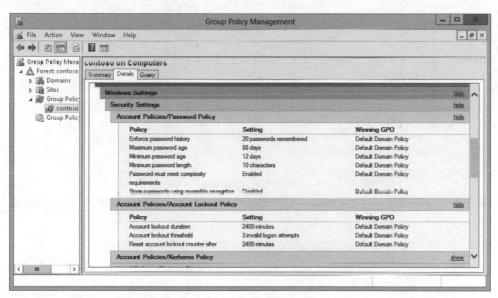

FIGURE 2-32 Verify policy configuration

23. Close the GPMC.

Exercise 4: Locate non-expiring passwords

In this exercise, you use Active Directory Administrative Center to locate accounts that are configured with passwords that never expire. To complete this exercise, perform the following steps:

1. In Server Manager, click Active Directory Users And Computers on the Tools menu.

2. In Active Directory Users And Computers, click the Users container. Click the Action menu, click New, and click User.

3. In the New Object – User dialog box, type the following details, as shown in Figure 2-33, and then click Next:

- First Name: **Test**
- Last Name: **User**
- Full Name: **Test User**
- User Logon Name: **Test_User**

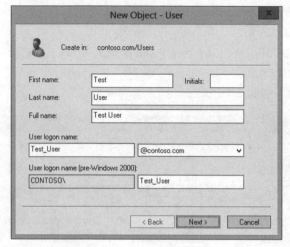

FIGURE 2-33 Creating a new user

4. In the New Object-User dialog box, type the password **Pa$$w0rd** twice. Remove the selection next to User Must Change Password At Next Logon. Select the Password Never Expires option, as shown in Figure 2-34, and click Next.

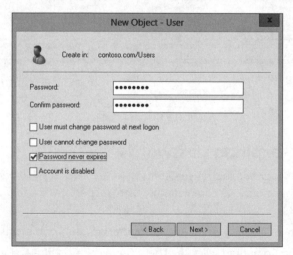

FIGURE 2-34 Password Never Expires option

5. In the New Object – User dialog box, click Finish.

6. In the Active Directory Domain Services dialog box, shown in Figure 2-35, review the message that explains why the password cannot be set, and click OK.

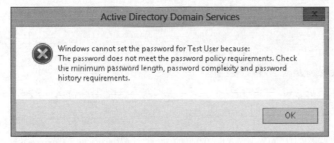

Active Directory Domain Services

Windows cannot set the password for Test User because:
The password does not meet the password policy requirements. Check the minimum password length, password complexity and password history requirements.

OK

FIGURE 2-35 Password configuration error

7. Click Back. Type the following password twice: **Pa$$w0rd!!**, click Next, and click Finish.

8. Close Active Directory Users And Computers.

9. From the Tools menu, click Active Directory Administrative Center.

10. In the Active Directory Administrative Center, click Global Search.

11. Click the down arrow, and click Add Criteria.

12. Click Users Whose Password Has An Expiration Date/No Expiration Date, and click Add.

13. Click Search. Verify that the result of the query matches that shown in Figure 2-36 and that Test User is listed as a user with a non-expiring password.

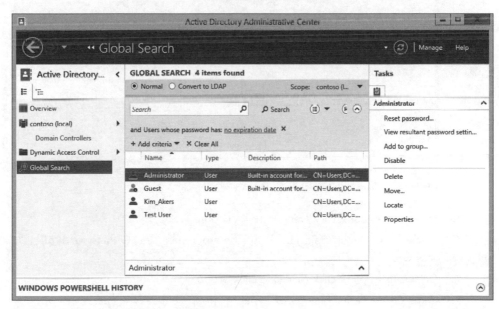

FIGURE 2-36 Password expiration search

14. Close the Active Directory Administrative Center.

Exercise 5: Create fine–grained password policies

In this exercise, you create two different fine–grained password policies that apply to different security groups. To complete this exercise, perform the following steps:

1. In the Server Manager, click Active Directory Administrative Center from the Tools menu.

2. Click Contoso (Local) and then double-click Users.

3. On the Tasks pane, click New, and click User.

4. In the Create User dialog box, type the following details, as shown in Figure 2-37, and then click OK.

   - Full Name: **Gabe Frost**
   - User SamAccountName: **contoso\Gabe_Frost**
   - Password: **Pa$$w0rd!!**
   - Confirm Password: **Pa$$w0rd!!**

FIGURE 2-37 Creating user Gabe Frost

5. On the Tasks pane, click New, and click Group.

6. In the Create Group dialog box, type the group name as **FG_PasswordPolicyOne** and click OK.

7. On the Tasks pane, click New, and click Group.

8. In the Create Group dialog box, type the group name as **FG_PasswordPolicyTwo**, as shown in Figure 2-38, and click OK.

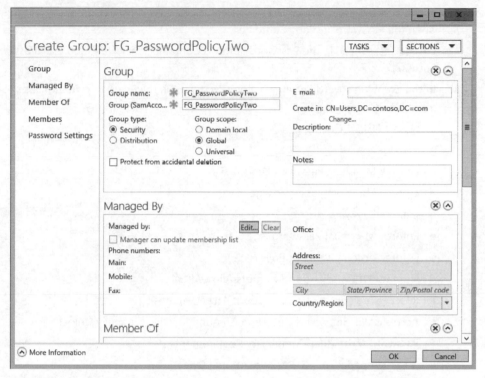

FIGURE 2-38 Create Security Group

9. In the Active Directory Administrative Center, right-click Don Funk, and click Add To Group.

10. In the Select Groups dialog box, type **FG_PasswordPolicyOne; FG_PasswordPolicyTwo**, as shown in Figure 2-39, click Check Names, and click OK.

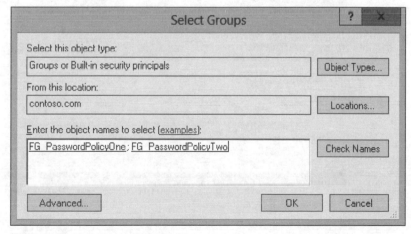

FIGURE 2-39 Adding to Security Group

11. In the Active Directory Administrative Center, open the System Container, and then open the Password Settings Container.

12. On the Tasks menu in the Password Settings Container, click New, and click Password Settings.

13. In the Create Password Settings dialog box, type the following information, as shown in Figure 2-40, and click OK.

- Name: **FGPW_One**
- Precedence: **10**
- Enforce Minimum Password Length: **5**
- Enforce Minimum Password Age: **5**
- Enforce Password History: **10**
- Enforce Maximum Password Age: **21**
- Enforce Account Lockout Policy
- Number Of Failed Logon Attempts Allowed: **3**
- Reset Failed Logon Attempts Count After (Minutes): **45**
- Account Will Be Locked Out: Until An Administrator Manually Unlocks The Account
- Password Must Meet Complexity Requirements
- Directly Applies To: **FG_PasswordPolicyOne**

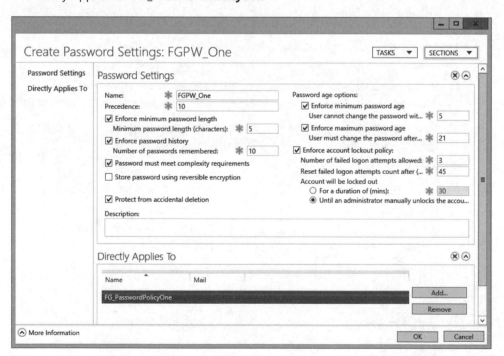

FIGURE 2-40 Creating a fine–grained password policy

14. On the Tasks menu in the Password Settings Container, click New, and click Password Settings.

15. In the Create Password Settings dialog box, type the following information and click OK:
    - Name: **FGPW_Two**
    - Precedence: **20**
    - Enforce Minimum Password Length: **10**
    - Enforce Minimum Password Age: **14**
    - Enforce Password History: **15**
    - Enforce Maximum Password Age: **30**
    - Enforce Account Lockout Policy
    - Number Of Failed Logon Attempts Allowed: **2**
    - Reset Failed Logon Attempts Count After (Minutes): **60**
    - Account Will Be Locked Out: Until An Administrator Manually Unlocks The Account
    - Password Must Meet Complexity Requirements
    - Directly Applies To: **FG_PasswordPolicyTwo**

16. In the Active Directory Administrative Center, navigate to the Users Container and click Gabe Frost.

17. On the Tasks pane, click View Resultant Password Settings.

Exercise 6: Prepare MEL-DC and ADL-DC

In this exercise, you prepare MEL-DC and ADL-DC for exercise 7. To complete this exercise, perform the following steps:

1. Start MEL-DC and sign in using the Administrator account with the password **Pa$$w0rd**.

2. Open the Windows PowerShell prompt and type the following commands.

   ```
   Add-Computer -DomainName contoso.com
   ```

3. In the Windows PowerShell Credentials dialog box type **don_funk@contoso.com** and **Pa$$w0rd,** and click OK.

4. Type the following command in the Windows PowerShell prompt to restart the computer.

   ```
   Restart-Computer
   ```

5. Start ADL-DC and sign in using the Administrator account with the password **Pa$$w0rd**.

6. Open the Windows PowerShell prompt and type the following commands.

   ```
   Add-Computer -DomainName contoso.com
   ```

7. In the Windows PowerShell Credentials dialog box, type **don_funk@contoso.com** and **Pa$$w0rd,** and click OK.

8. Type the following command in the Windows PowerShell prompt to restart the computer.

```
Restart-Computer
```

Exercise 7: Create and configure GMSAs

In this exercise, you create and configure two GMSAs. To complete this exercise, perform the following steps:

1. On SYD-DC, click Windows PowerShell on the task bar.

2. Execute the following command to create a new key distribution services root key that you can use right after creating it, not 10 hours later.

```
Add-KdsRootKey -EffectiveTime ((get-date).addhours(-10))
```

3. Execute the following commands to create two new GMSAs named GMSA-Alpha and GMSA-Beta so that they can be used on servers MEL-DC and ADL-DC.

```
New-ADServiceAccount -Name GMSA-Alpha -PrincipalsAllowedToRetrieveManagedPassword
MEL-DC$, ADL-DC$ -DNSHostname SYD-DC.contoso.com

New-ADServiceAccount -Name GMSA-Beta -PrincipalsAllowedToRetrieveManagedPassword
MEL-DC$, ADL-DC$ -DNSHostname SYD-DC.contoso.com
```

4. Sign on to server MEL-DC with the Contoso\Administrator account.

5. In Windows PowerShell, execute the following command to install the account GMSA-Alpha.

```
Install-WindowsFeature RSAT-AD-PowerShell

Install-ADServiceAccount -Identity GMSA-Alpha
```

6. Open the Search charm and type **Services**. Click Services.

7. Right-click the Windows Update service, and click Properties.

8. On the Log On tab, select This Account, and click Browse.

9. Click Locations, click Entire Directory, and click OK.

10. Type the name **Contoso\GMSA-Alpha**, click Check Names, and click OK.

11. In the Windows Update Properties (Local Computer) dialog box shown in Figure 2-41, click OK.

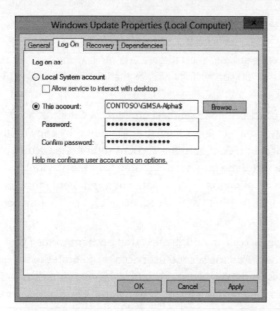

FIGURE 2-41 Configure Group Managed Service Account

12. Repeat steps 4 through 11 to install and use GMSA-Beta as the service account for the Windows Update service on ADL-DC.

Suggested practice exercises

The following additional practice exercises are designed to give you more opportunities to practice what you've learned and to help you successfully master the lessons presented in this chapter.

- **Exercise 1**   After configuring password policy and account lockout policies and enabling Group Policy to update, create a new administrator account by copying the built-in domain administrator account. Configure the account so that the account password must be changed the next time the user associated with the account signs on. Sign off and then sign on using the newly created account. Verify that the password length policy was applied. Verify that the account lockout policy functions by entering an incorrect password four times.

- **Exercise 2**   Create two new user accounts. Add the first user account to the FG_PasswordPolicyOne security group. Add the second user account to both the FG_PasswordPolicyOne and FG_PasswordPolicyTwo security groups. Verify that password policy precedence was configured by testing minimum password length and account lockout thresholds.

- **Exercise 3**   Create a security group named GMSA-Gamma-Group. Create a new Group Managed Service Account named GMSA-Gamma. Configure the Group Managed Service Account to be used by computers that are members of the GMSA-Gamma group.

Answers

This section contains the answers to the lesson review questions in this chapter.

Lesson 1

1. **Correct answers: B and C**

    A. **Incorrect**. You configure the Enforce Password History policy when you want to ensure that users do not use an earlier password.

    B. **Correct**. You configure the Minimum Password Length policy when you want to ensure that users use a password that has a minimum number of characters.

    C. **Correct**. You configure the Minimum Password Age policy when you want to ensure that users use a password for a minimum length of time.

    D. **Incorrect**. You configure the Maximum Password Age policy when you want to limit the maximum amount of time that a person can have the same password.

2. **Correct answers: A and D**

    A. **Correct**. You configure the Maximum Password Age policy when you want to limit the maximum amount of time that a person can have the same password.

    B. **Incorrect**. You configure the Minimum Password Age policy when you want to ensure that users use a password for a minimum length of time.

    C. **Incorrect**. You configure the Minimum Password Length policy when you want to ensure that users use a password that has a minimum number of characters.

    D. **Correct**. You configure the Enforce Password History policy when you want to ensure that users do not use an earlier password.

3. **Correct answer: B**

    A. **Incorrect**. You configure the Minimum Password Age policy when you want to ensure that users use a password for a minimum length of time.

    B. **Correct**. You configure the Passwords Must Meet Complexity Requirements policy to ensure that users must use passwords that contain a combination of numbers, symbols, and uppercase and lowercase characters. This policy also blocks users from using passwords that contain their names.

    C. **Incorrect**. You configure the Enforce Password History policy when you want to ensure that users do not use an earlier password.

    D. **Incorrect**. You configure the Minimum Password Length policy when you want to ensure that users use a password that has a minimum number of characters.

4. **Correct answers: C and D**

    A. **Incorrect**. This policy determines the minimum length of a password, not the number of incorrectly entered passwords and period of time that will configure a lockout.

B. **Incorrect**. This policy determines how long an account is locked out. You don't need to configure this policy to accomplish the specifics of your goal. You must configure the other two policies to accomplish the specifics of your goal.

C. **Correct**. This policy determines the number of incorrect passwords entered in succession to trigger a lockout.

D. **Correct**. This policy determines the period in which the number of incorrect passwords must be entered in succession.

5. **Correct answer: D**

A. **Incorrect**. You can apply GPO–based password policies only at the domain level.

B. **Incorrect**. You can apply GPO–based password policies only at the domain level.

C. **Incorrect**. You can apply GPO–based password policies only at the domain level.

D. **Correct**. You can apply GPO–based password policies only at the domain level.

Lesson 2

1. **Correct answers: A and C**

A. **Correct**. You can apply fine–grained password policies to security groups or user accounts. You need to collect the accounts of the system administrators together before you can apply fine–grained password policies to those accounts.

B. **Incorrect**. You can't apply PSOs to OUs. You can apply PSOs only to user accounts and security groups.

C. **Correct**. You can apply PSOs to user accounts or security groups.

D. **Incorrect**. Although Group Policy can be applied at the OU level, password policy can be applied through Group Policy only at the domain level.

2. **Correct answer: C**

A. **Incorrect**. Group Policy-applied password settings can be applied only at the domain level.

B. **Incorrect**. GPOs can't be applied to security groups.

C. **Correct**. You can create a security group that contains the user accounts of all users at the Brisbane site and then apply a PSO containing a custom password policy to this security group.

D. **Incorrect**. You can't apply PSOs to sites. You can apply PSOs only to security accounts or security groups.

3. **Correct answer: B**

A. **Incorrect**. The GPMC enables you to manage GPOs. You need the Active Directory Administrative Center to manage fine–grained password policies.

B. **Correct**. You can manage fine–grained password policies using the Active Directory Administrative Center.

    C. **Incorrect**. You can use Active Directory Users and Computers to manage user accounts and OUs. You can't use Active Directory Users and Computers to manage fine-grained password policies.

    D. **Incorrect**. You can use Active Directory Sites And Services to manage Active Directory sites and site links. You can't use Active Directory Sites And Services to manage password policies.

4. **Correct answers: A, B, and D**

    A. **Correct**. You must configure a policy at the domain level for all users in the organization.

    B. **Correct**. You must create a fine-grained password policy and apply it to the IT_ Staff security group. These users then have a different password policy from other users in the domain.

    C. **Incorrect**. PSOs assigned with a lower numerical value override PSOs assigned with a higher numerical value. A value of 30 means that Rooslan and Oksana are subject to the PSO applied to the IT_Staff security group.

    D. **Correct**. You must assign the PSO that applies to Rooslan and Oksana a lower numerical precedence than the one used with the PSO applied to the IT_Staff security group. Assigning a precedence of 10 means that this PSO overrides the one that applies to these accounts through the membership of the IT_Staff group.

5. **Correct answer: B**

    A. **Incorrect**. Fine-grained password policies are supported at the Windows Server 2008 domain functional level.

    B. **Correct**. Fine-grained password policies are supported at the Windows Server 2008 domain functional level.

    C. **Incorrect**. Fine-grained password policies are supported at the Windows Server 2008 domain functional level.

    D. **Incorrect**. Fine-grained password policies are supported at the Windows Server 2008 domain functional level.

Lesson 3

1. **Correct answers: B and C**

    A. **Incorrect**. Windows Server 2008 does not support virtual service accounts.

    B. **Correct**. Windows Server 2012 does support virtual service accounts.

    C. **Correct**. Windows Server 2008 R2 does support virtual service accounts.

    D. **Incorrect**. Windows Server 2008 does not support virtual service accounts.

2. **Correct answer: D**
    A. **Incorrect**. Use this cmdlet to create a new Group Managed Service Account. You must create the key distribution services key before you can create Group Managed Service Accounts.
    B. **Incorrect**. Use this cmdlet to install a Group Managed Service Account on a computer after it is created. You must create the key distribution services key before you can create group Managed Service Accounts.
    C. **Incorrect**. This cmdlet configures the properties of a Group Managed Service Account. You must create the key distribution services key before you can create G Group Managed Service Accounts.
    D. **Correct**. You must create the key distribution services key before you can create Group Managed Service Accounts.

3. **Correct answer: D**
    A. **Incorrect**. Use this cmdlet to install a Group Managed Service Account on a computer after it is created. You must use the Set-ADServiceAccount cmdlet to configure an existing Group Managed Service Account so that it can be used by additional computers.
    B. **Incorrect**. You use this cmdlet to create the key distribution services key before you can create Group Managed Service Accounts.
    C. **Incorrect**. This cmdlet is used to create a new Group Managed Service Account. You must use the Set-ADServiceAccount cmdlet to configure an existing Group Managed Service Account so that it can be used by additional computers.
    D. **Correct**. You use the Set-ADServiceAccount cmdlet to configure an existing Group Managed Service Account so that it can be used by additional computers.

4. **Correct answer: C**
    A. **Incorrect**. You use the Set-ADServiceAccount cmdlet to configure an existing Group Managed Service Account so that it can be used by additional computers. You must use the Install-ADServiceAccount cmdlet before you can use a Group Managed Service Account on a computer.
    B. **Incorrect**. You use this cmdlet to create the key distribution services key before you can create Group Managed Service Accounts. You must use the Install-ADServiceAccount cmdlet before you can use a Group Managed Service Account on a computer.
    C. **Correct**. Use this cmdlet to install a Group Managed Service Account on a computer after it is created. You must use the Install-ADServiceAccount cmdlet before you can use a Group Managed Service Account on a computer.
    D. **Incorrect**. This cmdlet is used to create a new Group Managed Service Account.

5. **Correct answer: C**

   A. **Incorrect**. This policy determines maximum service ticket lifetime and is not related to domain controller clock drift.

   B. **Incorrect**. This policy determines user ticket renewal lifetime and is not related to domain controller clock drift.

   C. **Correct**. This policy defines how much drift there can be in computer clock synchronization between domain controllers before service and user ticket errors occur.

   D. **Incorrect**. This policy specifies the maximum validity of a user ticket and is not related to domain controller clock drift.

CHAPTER 3

Configuring name resolution

Name resolution involves translating human readable names, most commonly fully qualified domain names (FQDNs), into IP addresses. Most name resolution on Windows networks occurs through DNS. Although it is possible to use third-party DNS solutions with Active Directory, it's simpler to deploy the built-in DNS Server role. This role can be installed on computers running the full GUI or Server Core installation of Windows Server 2012, or Windows Server 2012 R2. Windows Server 2012 and Windows Server 2012 R2 also support single-label name resolution with the Windows Internet Name Service (WINS) role. For organizations that are tired of maintaining WINS servers, it is possible to transition to using GlobalNames zones with DNS. Windows Server 2012 and Windows Server 2012 R2 also support the Peer Name Resolution Protocol (PNRP), which is a peer-to-peer IPv6 name resolution protocol that does not require a centralized name resolution server infrastructure.

Lessons in this chapter:

- Lesson 1: Understanding DNS zones and forwarders **123**
- Lesson 2: Configuring WINS and managing GlobalNames zones **138**
- Lesson 3: Understanding advanced DNS options **147**

Before you begin

To complete the practice exercises in this chapter:

- You need to have deployed computers SYD-DC, MEL-DC, and ADL-DC as described in the Introduction, using the evaluation edition of Windows Server 2012 R2.

Lesson 1: Understanding DNS zones and forwarders

Windows Server 2012 DNS supports several different types of DNS zones. The difference between DNS zone types comes down to the nature of that collection of records, whether that collection is updatable, and how that collection will replicate to other DNS servers. Part of the 70-411 exam involves being able to choose the correct zone type to resolve a specific problem and knowing what steps you need to take to configure that zone to meet your organization's needs. Forwarders are a method of redirecting DNS queries to specific servers. You use them to improve DNS performance or allow connections to specific DNS zones that might otherwise not be directly accessible.

DNS zone types

The DNS Server service in Windows Server 2012 supports several zone types, each of which is appropriate for a different set of circumstances. To pass the 70-411 exam, you'll need to know the difference among primary, secondary, and stub zones. You'll also need to know the difference between a zone that is Active Directory integrated and one that is not. You will also need to have an understanding of the different replication scopes that are available for each type of DNS zone.

Active Directory integrated zones

Active Directory integrated zones can be replicated to all domain controllers in a domain, all domain controllers in a forest, or all domain controllers enrolled in a specific Active Directory partition. You can create an Active Directory integrated zone only on a writable domain controller. You can configure primary and stub zones as Active Directory integrated zones. Domain controllers with DNS servers that host Active Directory integrated zones can process updates to those zones.

You make a zone Active Directory integrated by selecting the Store The Zone In Active Directory option on the Zone Type page of the New Zone Wizard, as shown in Figure 3-1.

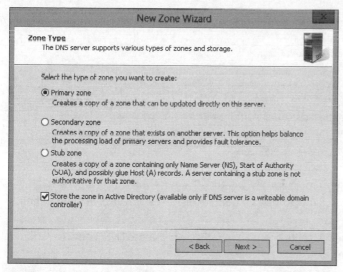

FIGURE 3-1 Configuring the Primary Zone to be Active Directory integrated

When you choose to make a zone Active Directory integrated, you get the option of configuring a replication scope, as shown in Figure 3-2. You can configure the zone to be replicated so that it will be present on all domain controllers in the domain, in the forest, or within the scope of a custom Active Directory partition. You can also choose the option of replicating for Windows 2000 compatibility.

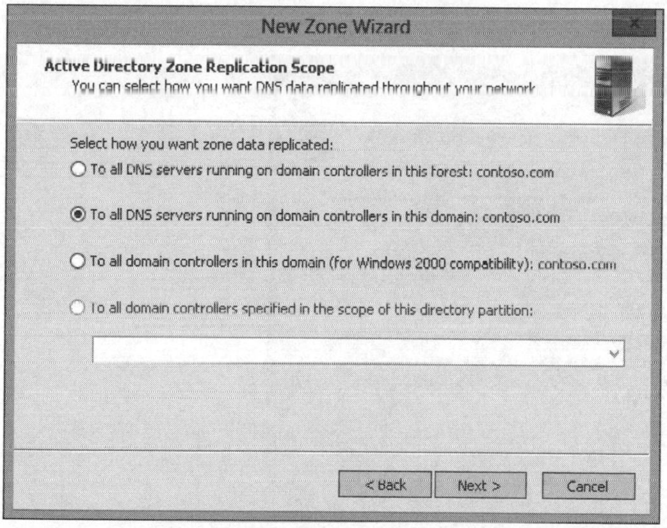

FIGURE 3-2 Replication scope

Using custom directory partitions allows you to replicate to some (but not all) domain controllers. You can select this option only if there is an existing application directory partition. You can use the Add-DNSServerDirectoryPartition cmdlet to create a directory partition. For example, to create a DNS Server directory partition called Tasmania, execute this command:

```
Add-DNSServerDirectoryPartition -Name Tasmania
```

> **MORE INFO** **CREATING APPLICATION DIRECTORY PARTITIONS**
>
> You can learn more about creating custom partitions to manage the scope of DNS replication by consulting the following MSDN article at *http://msdn.microsoft.com/en-us/library/windows/desktop/ms675765(v=vs.85).aspx*.

When creating a DNS zone, you must specify whether the zone will support *dynamic updates*. Dynamic updates allow clients to update DNS records. This is useful in environments in which clients change IP addresses on a regular basis. When a client gets a new IP address, it can update the record associated with its host name in the appropriate DNS zone. As Figure 3-3 shows, there are three options:

- **Allow Only Secure Dynamic Updates** You can use this option only with Active Directory integrated zones. Only authenticated clients can update DNS records.
- **Allow Both Nonsecure And Secure Dynamic Updates** With this option, any client can update a record. Although this option is convenient, it is also insecure because any client can update the DNS zone, potentially redirecting clients that trust the quality of the information stored on the DNS server.
- **Do Not Allow Dynamic Updates** When you choose this option, all DNS updates must be performed manually. This option is very secure, but it is also labor-intensive.

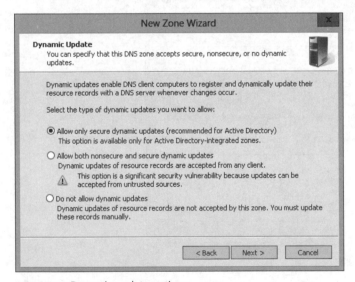

FIGURE 3-3 Dynamic update options

An Active Directory integrated zone can replicate to a read-only domain controller (RODC), but this zone is read-only and cannot process updates to the zone, as is the case with a traditional writable domain controller. An RODC will forward any zone update traffic directed at it, to a writable domain controller.

You can create an Active Directory integrated primary zone by using the Add-DnsServerPrimaryZone cmdlet with the ReplicationScope parameter. For example, to create the Active Directory integrated zone cpandl.com to replicate to all domain controllers in the forest, issue this command.

```
Add-DnsServerPrimaryZone -Name cpandl.com -ReplicationScope Forest
```

When you first install Active Directory, the installation process ensures that the DNS zone associated with the root domain is automatically configured as an Active Directory integrated zone and is replicated to all domain controllers in the forest.

Primary and secondary zones

In traditional DNS implementations, a single server hosting a *primary zone* processes all zone updates, and a collection of secondary servers replicates zone data from the primary zone. One drawback to this model is that a failure of the primary server means that no zone updates can occur until the primary zone is restored.

Windows Server 2012 supports two types of primary zones: Active Directory integrated zones and standard primary zones. Active Directory integrated zones can be hosted only on computers that also function as domain controllers. Computers running Windows Server 2012 that are not domain controllers can host standard primary zones. When you create a primary zone on a computer that is not a domain controller, the wizard does not enable you to specify a replication scope for the zone.

A *secondary zone* is a read-only copy of a primary zone. Secondary zones cannot process updates. They can only retrieve updates from a primary zone. Secondary zones cannot be Active Directory integrated zones, but you can configure a secondary zone of a zone that is an Active Directory integrated primary zone. Prior to configuring a secondary zone, you need to configure the primary zone that it will replicate from to enable transfers to that zone. You can do this on the Zone Transfers tab of the zone properties, as shown in Figure 3-4. Secondary zones work best when the primary zone they replicate from does not update frequently. If the primary zone is frequently updated, it is possible that the secondary zone may have out-of-date records.

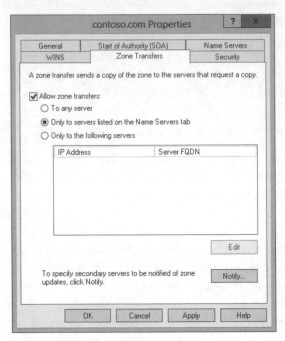

FIGURE 3-4 Using the Zone Transfers tab to configure replication scope

Reverse lookup zones

Reverse lookup zones translate IP addresses into FQDNs. You can create IPv4 or IPv6 reverse lookup zones, and reverse lookup zones can be configured as Active Directory integrated zones. You can configure reverse lookup zones as standard primary, secondary, or stub zones. The domain controller promotion process automatically creates a reverse lookup zone based on the IP address of the first domain controller promoted in the organization.

Reverse lookup zones are dependent on the network ID of the IP address range they represent. IPv4 reverse lookup zones can represent only /8, /16, or /24 (the old Class A, Class B, and Class C) networks. You can't create a single reverse lookup zone for IP subnets that don't fit into these categories, and the smallest reverse lookup zone you can create is for subnet mask /24 (255.255.255.0).

You can create a reverse lookup zone by performing the following steps:

1. In the DNS Manager Console, right-click Reverse Lookup Zones, and click New Zone.

2. On the Zone Type page, select the type of reverse lookup zone that you want to create. You can create a primary or a stub zone that can be Active Directory integrated if you are managing a DNS server on a domain controller, or create a secondary zone if the reverse lookup zone is being replicated from an existing primary reverse lookup zone.

3. If you have chosen to make the lookup zone Active Directory integrated, you'll need to choose the zone replication scope.

4. On the Reverse Lookup Zone Name page, choose between IPv4 and IPv6 Reverse Lookup Zone.

5. You can configure the reverse lookup zone either on the basis of choosing Network ID or Reverse Lookup Zone Name, as shown in Figure 3-5. The name is automatically generated when you provide the ID.

6. You can then choose whether to enable secure dynamic updates, enable nonsecure and secure dynamic updates, or not enable dynamic updates.

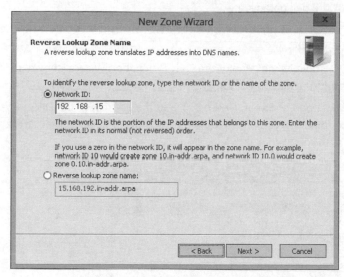

FIGURE 3-5 Configuring reverse lookup zones adding the Network ID

REAL WORLD **REVERSE LOOKUP ZONES**

Few applications actually require that you configure reverse lookup zones. In most organizations, the only reverse lookup zone will be the one automatically created when Active Directory is installed. One of the few times when reverse lookup zones seemed necessary is when configuring Simple Mail Transfer Protocol (SMTP) gateways because some anti-spam checks perform a reverse IP address lookup to verify the identity of the SMTP gateway. The difficulty is that often the IP address of the SMTP gateway, being a public address, belongs to the Internet service provider (ISP). This means that creating the reverse lookup zone entry is often beyond your direct control as a systems administrator.

Zone delegation

 Zone delegations function as pointers to the next DNS layer down in the DNS hierarchy. For example, if your organization uses the contoso.com DNS zone and you want to create a separate australia.contoso.com DNS zone, you can perform a *zone delegation* so that the

DNS servers for the contoso.com DNS zone would point to the DNS servers for the australia. contoso.com DNS zone. When you create a new child domain in an Active Directory forest, zone delegation occurs automatically. When you are performing a manual delegation, create the delegated zone on the target DNS server prior to performing the delegation from the parent zone.

You can configure a zone delegation by performing the following steps:

1. Create the primary zone, either standard or Active Directory integrated, on the DNS server that will host the delegated zone.

2. In the DNS Manager Console, right-click the zone that you want to create a delegation for, and click New Delegation.

3. On the Delegated Domain Name page of the New Delegation Wizard, shown in Figure 3-6, enter the name of the delegated domain.

4. On the Name Servers page, shown in Figure 3-6, add the address of the DNS server that hosts the zone for which you are creating a delegation. The wizard will check that the DNS server is authoritative for the delegated zone.

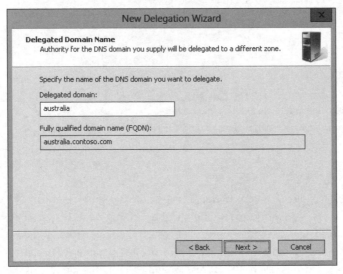

FIGURE 3-6 Adding zone delegation

You can create delegations using the Add-DnsServerZoneDelegation cmdlet. Although you can delegate several levels, remember that the maximum length of a FQDN is 255 bytes, and the maximum length of a FQDN for an Active Directory Domain Services domain controller is 155 bytes.

MORE INFO **ZONE DELEGATION**

You can learn more about DNS zone delegation by consulting the following TechNet article at *http://technet.microsoft.com/en-us/library/cc771640.aspx*.

Split DNS

Split DNS, sometimes named "split-brain DNS", enables organizations to use the same namespace for internal and external hosts, but enables those organizations to ensure that external hosts can't resolve internal names. For example, an organization might want to enable internal users to resolve the addresses *www.tailspintoys.com* and *aus-fs1.tailspintoys.com*, but enable external users to resolve only *www.tailspintoys.com*.

> **REAL WORLD** **SPLIT DNS**
>
> Many organizations don't bother hosting the publicly resolvable zone associated with their organization, but instead have it hosted on their ISP's DNS servers.

To implement split DNS, create two zones on different name servers for the same DNS zone. For example, you can configure split DNS in the following way:

- Contoso.com is an Active Directory integrated primary zone replicated to all domain controllers on your organization's internal network. Internal clients would run queries against these DNS servers for the contoso.com zone.
- Contoso.com is a standard primary zone hosted on a computer running Windows Server 2012 that is not a member of a domain and is located on your organization's perimeter network. External clients would run queries against this DNS server for the contoso.com zone.

You can configure the standard primary zone hosted on the computer on the perimeter network to accept only manual updates. You can then manually populate the zone with those records that external hosts should be able to resolve, such as the address of web servers and mail gateways.

> **Quick check**
>
> - In which circumstances are you unable to create an Active Directory integrated primary zone on a computer running Windows Server 2012 with the DNS Server role installed?
>
> **Quick check answer**
>
> - You can't create an Active Directory integrated primary zone if the Windows Server 2012 computer hosting the DNS Server service is not a domain controller.

Forwarders and conditional forwarders

Forwarders and conditional forwarders enable your DNS server to forward traffic to specific DNS servers when a lookup request cannot be handled locally. If you don't configure a forwarder, or if a configured forwarder can't be contacted, the DNS Server service will forward the request to a DNS root server, and the request will be resolved normally.

Forwarders

You are likely to use a DNS forwarder, rather than have your DNS server just use the root server when you want to have a specific DNS server on the Internet handle your organization's DNS resolution traffic. You are most likely to configure your organization's ISP's DNS server as a forwarder. When you do this, the ISP's DNS server performs all the query work, returning the result to your organization's DNS server that returns the result of the query back to the original requesting client.

You configure forwarders on a per-DNS server level. You can configure a forwarder using the DNS Manager, by editing the properties of a DNS server and then editing the list of forwarders on the Forwarders tab, as shown in Figure 3-7.

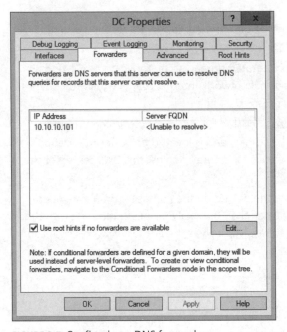

FIGURE 3-7 Configuring a DNS forwarder

You can create a DNS forwarder using the Add-DnsServerForwarder cmdlet. For example, to create a DNS forwarder for a DNS server with IP address 10.10.10.111, issue this command.

```
Add-DnsServerForwarder 10.10.10.111
```

You can't create a forwarder on one DNS server and then have it replicate to all other DNS servers in the forest or the domain, although this is possible with conditional forwarders and stub zones.

Conditional forwarders

Conditional forwarders forward address requests from only specific domains, rather than all requests that can't be resolved by the DNS server. When configured, a conditional forwarder takes precedence over a forwarder. Conditional forwarders are useful when your organization has a trust relationship or partnership with another organization. You can configure a conditional forwarder that directs all traffic to host names within that organization instead of them having to be resolved by the standard DNS-resolution process.

To create a conditional forwarder, perform the following steps:

1. Open DNS Manager.

2. Expand the DNS server on which you want to create the conditional forwarder. Since conditional forwarders can be replicated to all DNS servers in a forest or domain, you have to create the forwarder only once.

3. Right-click Conditional Forwards, and choose New Conditional Forwarder.

4. Enter the DNS domain name of the zone for the forwarder. For example, if you want all traffic for hosts in the wingtiptoys.com zone to be forwarded to specific DNS servers, type **wingtiptoys.com** as the DNS domain name.

5. Enter the IP address or addresses of the DNS server to which you want to forward DNS traffic.

6. Select whether the conditional forwarder will be stored within Active Directory. Choose whether to replicate the forwarder to all servers in the forest or in the domain, as shown in Figure 3-8.

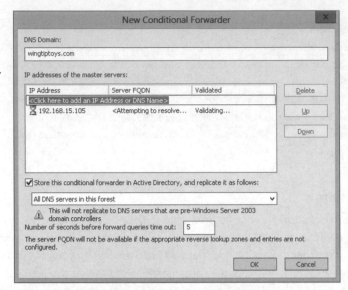

FIGURE 3-8 Configuring conditional forwarders

You can create conditional forwarders using the Add-DnsServerConditionalForwarderZone PowerShell cmdlet. For example, to create a conditional forwarder for the DNS domain tailspintoys.com that forwards DNS queries to the server at IP address 10.10.10.102 and replicates that conditional forwarder to all DNS servers within the Active Directory forest, issue this command.

```
Add-DnsServerConditionalForwarderZone -MasterServers 10.10.10.102 -Name tailspintoys.com
-ReplicationScope Forest
```

Stub zones

A *stub zone* is a special zone that stores authoritative name server records for a target zone. Stub zones have an advantage over forwarders when the address of a target zone's authoritative DNS server changes on a regular basis. Stub zones are often used to host the records for authoritative DNS servers in delegated zones. Using stub zones in this way ensures that delegated zone information is up to date. If you create the stub zone on a writable domain controller, as shown in Figure 3-9, it can be stored with Active Directory and replicated to other DCs in the domain or forest.

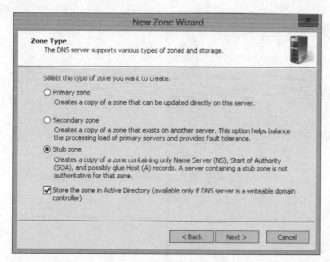

FIGURE 3-9 Creating a stub zone

You can create a stub zone by performing the following steps:

1. In DNS Manager, right-click Forward Lookup Zones and click New Zone.

2. On the Zone Type page of the New Zone Wizard, select Stub Zone, as shown in Figure 3-9.

3. If you chose the Store The Zone In Active Directory option, you see the Active Directory Zone Replication Scope page. Choose whether to replicate the stub zone to all domain controllers in the forest, in the domain, or to all domain controllers enrolled in a specific directory partition.

4. Provide the stub zone with the name of the target DNS zone.

5. On the Master DNS Servers page, shown in Figure 3-10, provide the address of an authoritative DNS name server for the zone. Choose the Use The Above Servers To Create A Local List Of Master Servers option to generate a list of all authoritative name servers in the target DNS zone.

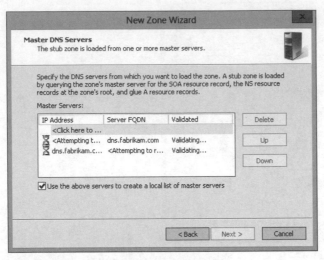

FIGURE 3-10 List of stub zone master DNS servers

You can add a stub zone using the Add-DnsServerStubZone cmdlet. For example, to add a DNS stub zone for the fabrikam.com zone using the DNS server at 10.10.10.222 that replicates to all DNS servers in the forest, execute this command.

```
Add-DnsServerStubZone –MasterServers 10.10.10.222 –Name fabrikam.com –ReplicationScope
Forest –LoadExisting
```

Lesson summary

- Primary and stub zones can be configured as Active Directory integrated zones.
- Active Directory integrated zones can be replicated to all domain controllers in a domain, in the forest, or that have a specific DNS application partition.
- Reverse lookup zones translate IP addresses into FQDNs.
- Reverse lookup zones can be Active Directory integrated zones.
- Secondary zones are read-only.
- Conditional forwarders forward all traffic for a particular zone to a particular DNS server.
- Forwarders forward all traffic not handled by conditional forwarders to a specific DNS server.

Lesson review

Answer the following questions to test your knowledge of the information in this lesson. You can find the answers to these questions and explanations of why each answer choice is correct or incorrect in the "Answers" section at the end of this chapter.

1. You want to create a new DNS zone. Only computers that are members of the domain should be able to update the zone. You should not have to perform zone updates manually. Which of the following steps should you take to accomplish this goal? (Choose all that apply.)

    A. Configure the contoso.com zone as an Active Directory integrated primary.

    B. Configure the contoso.com zone as a standard primary zone.

    C. Configure the zone to enable only secure dynamic updates.

    D. Configure the zone to not enable dynamic updates.

2. Which of the following network IDs is associated with the reverse lookup zone 15.168.192.in-addr.arpa?

    A. 192.168.15.0 /16

    B. 15.168.192.0 /24

    C. 192.168.15.0 /24

    D. 15.168.192.0 /24

3. You want to create a delegation for the zone australia.fabrikam.com. This zone will be hosted on a DNS server with the IP address 10.100.10.10. The DNS server that is authoritative for the zone fabrikam.com is hosted on a computer with the IP address 10.10.10.10. Which of the following steps must you take first? (Choose all that apply.)

    A. Create the zone australia.fabrikam.com on the computer that hosts the DNS server with the IP address 10.10.10.10.

    B. Create the zone australia.fabrikam.com on the computer that hosts the DNS server with the IP address 10.100.10.10.

    C. Create the delegation using the zone fabrikam.com on the computer that hosts the DNS server with the IP address 10.100.10.10.

    D. Create the delegation using the zone fabrikam.com on the computer that hosts the DNS server with the IP address 10.10.10.10.

4. A partner organization frequently alters the IP addresses of its authoritative name servers. Clients in the partner DNS zone also change their DNS records frequently. You want to enable clients in your organizational network to be able to quickly resolve addresses in the partner's DNS zone without worrying that your own DNS server is hosting stale DNS records. Which of the following should you create on your local DNS server to accomplish this goal? (Choose all that apply.)

    A. Secondary zone

    B. Conditional forwarder

    C. Forwarder

    D. Stub zone

5. You want to have all DNS requests for nonlocal addresses go to your ISP's DNS server, except those for hosts located in the margiestravel.com zone. Any requests for hosts

located in the margiestravel.com zone should automatically be forwarded to a DNS server with a specific IP address. Which of the following should you configure to accomplish this goal? (Choose all that apply.)

A. Stub zone

B. Forwarder

C. Conditional forwarder

D. Secondary zone

Lesson 2: Configuring WINS and managing GlobalNames zones

Both WINS and GlobalNames zones provide single-label name resolution solutions. Single-label name resolution solutions are often required because custom code and scripts, some dating back to the days when Windows NT 4.0 was the server operating system of choice, don't use the DNS FQDNs. In this lesson, you learn how to provide an appropriate single-label name resolution solution for your organizational network.

> **After this lesson, you will be able to:**
> - Configure WINS.
> - Manage GlobalNames zones.
> - Understand Peer Name Resolution Protocol (PNRP).
>
> **Estimated lesson time: 45 minutes**

WINS

WINS is an older name resolution technology that resolves NetBIOS names to IP addresses. WINS was primarily used on networks running Windows NT 4.0 and has been declining in utilization ever since. Other than small changes to make WINS less vulnerable to malicious attacks, the functionality of WINS has not changed substantially since the release of Windows Server 2003 almost a decade ago. Windows Server 2012 still includes the WINS role because a large number of organizations have need for *single-label name resolution* functionality. Single-label name resolution is required when a host is referred to on the network with a single name, such as Windows Server Update Services (WSUS), rather than an FQDN such as wsus.contoso.internal. Depending on how DNS is configured, some clients can use their DNS host suffix to locate hosts on the basis of a single label. You can also integrate DNS with WINS.

To install and configure the WINS role on a computer running Windows Server 2012, perform the following steps:

1. From Server Manager, use the Manage menu to launch the Add Roles And Features Wizard.

2. Select the WINS Server feature, as shown in Figure 3-11.

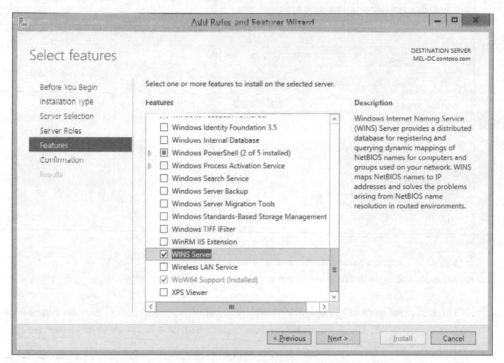

FIGURE 3-11 Adding the WINS Server feature of the Add Roles And Features Wizard

To install WINS using Windows PowerShell, use the following command.

```
Install-WindowsFeature WINS
```

Unless the routers are specially configured, NetBIOS traffic doesn't cross subnet boundaries. This means that unless you take specific steps, the WINS database will not be populated with address entries by hosts on remote networks. WINS does support the creation of static address entries, and you can use it to manually populate the WINS database with the addresses of important hosts that must be resolvable using single-label names. Client computers must know the address of a WINS server to utilize it for single-label name resolution. You can configure a client with the address of a WINS server by configuring DHCP option 044. You can also configure the address of a WINS server by editing the TCP/IPv4 properties on a specific network adapter, as shown in Figure 3-12.

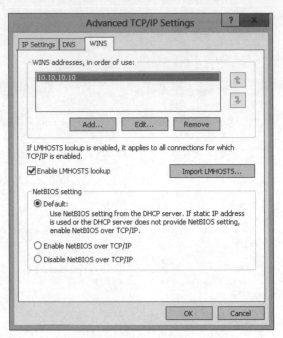

FIGURE 3-12 Adding a WINS server address

You can configure WINS servers on different subnets as replication partners. When you do this, these WINS servers exchange address data with one another. WINS uses two types of partners in replication:

- **Push partner** A WINS server that notifies a pull partner that the WINS database has been updated. The pull partner will respond with a replication request, and database changes will be replicated. Push replication occurs only when a certain number of updates to the database have occurred.

- **Pull partner** Waits for notification that the database has been updated and then replicates database changes.

To replicate database entries bidirectionally, each server must be a *push partner* and a *pull partner*. You configure replication on a per-WINS server basis using the Replication Partner Properties dialog box, as shown in Figure 3-13. This dialog box enables you to configure the push and pull replication intervals. On the General tab of this dialog box, you can configure WINS so that it replicates only with known partners. On small networks, you can enable automatic partner configuration. When you do this, WINS automatically detects other WINS servers. You should not use this on larger networks because of the increase in traffic.

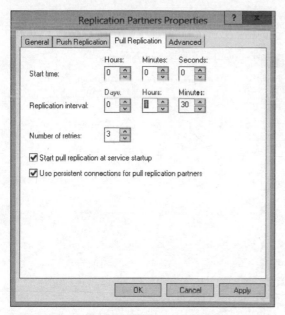

FIGURE 3-13 Configuring WINS replication properties

You can configure a replication partner by performing the following steps:

1. In the WINS console, right-click Replication Partners, and click New Replication Partner.

2. Enter the name or IP address of the server that you want to add as a replication partner in the New Replication Partner dialog box, shown in Figure 3-14.

FIGURE 3-14 Replication partner properties

> **MORE INFO**   **WINS**
>
> To learn more about WINS, consult the following TechNet article at *http://technet.microsoft.com/en-us/library/hh831671.aspx*.

You can integrate WINS with DNS by configuring WINS forward lookup. You can do this on the WINS tab of the zone properties in DNS Manager, as shown in Figure 3-15. When you do this, the DNS server will check with the WINS server if it can't find a record for a single-label name within the zone queried.

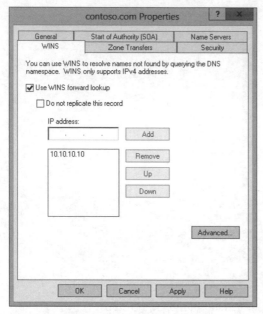

FIGURE 3-15 WINS integration properties

> ✓ **Quick check**
>
> ■ You want to ensure that a WINS server retrieves all updates made on a remote WINS server every two hours. What should you configure to accomplish this goal?
>
> **Quick check answer**
>
> ■ You configure the pull replication interval to ensure that a WINS server retrieves all updates made on a remote server every two hours.

GlobalNames zones

GlobalNames zones are a single-label name resolution replacement that can utilize existing DNS infrastructure. GlobalNames zones can function as a single-label name resolution replacement for WINS, enabling organizations to retire their existing WINS servers. You can use the GlobalNames zone as long as your organization's DNS servers are running Windows Server 2008, Windows Server 2008 R2, or Windows Server 2012.

Your organization should consider deploying GlobalNames zones instead of WINS in the following situations:

- Your organization is transitioning to IPv6. WINS does not support IPv6, and you need to support single-label name resolution.

- Single-label name resolution is limited to a small number of hosts that rarely change. GlobalNames zones must be updated manually.

- You have a large number of suffix search lists because of a complex naming strategy or disjoined namespace.

Entries in the GlobalNames zones must be populated manually. GlobalNames zones entries are alias (CNAME) records to existing DNS A or AAAA records. The existing DNS A and AAAA records can be dynamically updated, which flow on to records in the GlobalNames zone.

To deploy a GlobalNames zone in a forest, perform the following steps:

1. On a domain controller configured as a DNS server, create a new Active Directory integrated forward lookup zone that is configured to replicate to every domain controller in the forest using the New Zone Wizard.

2. On the Zone Name page, type the name **GlobalNames** as the zone name, as shown in Figure 3-16. You can also accomplish the same task by running the following Windows PowerShell command.

```
Add-DnsServerPrimaryZone –Name GlobalNames –ReplicationScope Forest
```

3. Activate the GlobalNames zone on each authoritative DNS server hosted on a domain controller in the forest by executing the following Windows PowerShell command (where DNSServerName is the name of the domain controller hosting DNS).

```
Set-DnsServerGlobalNameZone –ComputerName DNSServerName –Enable $True
```

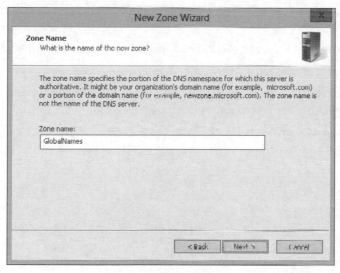

FIGURE 3-16 Adding a GlobalNames zone

To populate the GlobalNames zone, create alias (CNAME) records in the zone that point to A or AAAA records in existing zones. You will learn more about DNS host records in Lesson 3: "Understanding advanced DNS options".

> **MORE INFO   GLOBALNAMES ZONES**
>
> To learn more about GlobalNames zones, consult the following TechNet article at *http://technet.microsoft.com/en-us/library/cc731744.aspx*.

Peer Name Resolution Protocol (PNRP)

Peer Name Resolution Protocol (PNRP) provides IPv6 with a peer-to-peer name resolution. Devices connected to the Internet that are assigned an IPv6 address can publish their peer name/address combination to peers. This includes both FQDN and single-label names. Other devices query peers to learn IPv6 addressing information. For example, imagine that there are computers named Sydney, Melbourne, Canberra, Adelaide, Brisbane, Hobart, and Perth. Computer Sydney needs to know the IPv6 address of Perth. Sydney is near Canberra, Melbourne, and Brisbane. Sydney will query Canberra, Melbourne, and Brisbane in turn to determine whether any of them knows the IPv6 address of Perth. Rather than using a central server such as DNS or WINS, PNRP uses the information that each computer knows about every other computer to determine address information. PNRP has the following properties:

- Does not require centralized infrastructure. Servers are required only for bootstrapping.
- Can scale to billions of names and is fault-tolerant. Multiple computers can host copies of the same PNRP record.
- Names are updated in real time, and PNRP is designed to not return stale addresses.
- Can be used to name services rather than just computers.
- Names can be published in a secure or insecure manner. When published in a secure manner, PNRP uses public key cryptography to validate records.
- Installed as a feature, as shown in Figure 3-17.

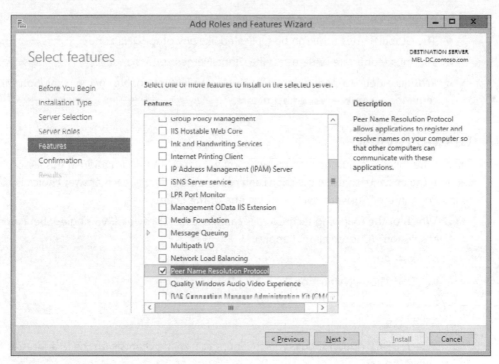

FIGURE 3-17 PNRP feature

PNRP peer groups are termed *clouds*. When installed, PNRP can use the following clouds:

- **Global cloud** Uses the global IPv6 address scope and represents all computers and devices connected to the Internet. There is a single global cloud.

- **Link-local cloud** All addresses in the link-local IPv6 address scope. It roughly corresponds to the local subnet. An organization can have multiple link-local clouds.

> *MORE INFO* **PEER NAME RESOLUTION PROTOCOL (PNRP)**
>
> To learn more about PNRP, consult the following TechNet article at *http://technet.microsoft.com/en-us/library/cc732919.aspx*.

Lesson summary

- WINS provides single-label name resolution based on a NetBIOS name.
- You can create static WINS mappings or enable mappings to be generated automatically.
- WINS does not support IPv6.
- A GlobalNames zone is a special DNS zone type that enables single-label name resolution.

- GlobalNames zones support IPv4 and IPv6.
- The GlobalNames zone can be replicated like any other DNS zone.
- You must configure updates for the GlobalNames zone manually.
- PNRP is a peer-to-peer name resolution protocol that enables name resolution without requiring a name server infrastructure.

Lesson review

Answer the following questions to test your knowledge of the information in this lesson. You can find the answers to these questions and explanations of why each answer choice is correct or incorrect in the "Answers" section at the end of this chapter.

1. Which of the following technologies can you use to provide IPv6 single-label name resolution? (Choose all that apply.)

   A. DHCP

   B. DNS GlobalNames zone

   C. WINS

   D. PNRP

2. Which DHCP option should you configure to provide clients with the IP address of a WINS server?

   A. 006

   B. 044

   C. 004

   D. 015

3. You want to provide single-label name resolution on your organization's network without deploying WINS. You must be able to update these records manually. Which of the following technologies should you use to accomplish this goal?

   A. Reverse lookup zone

   B. Stub zone

   C. Secondary zone

   D. GlobalNames zone

4. Which of the following technologies enable you to provide name resolution on a local area network without having to deploy a centralized server? (Choose all that apply.)

   A. DNS

   B. WINS

   C. PNRP

   D. DHCP

5. You have created and enabled a GlobalNames zone on a domain controller in your organization. You have configured the zone to replicate to all domain controllers in the forest. You want to enable the GlobalNames zone on another domain controller that hosts the DNS Server service. Which of the following Windows PowerShell cmdlets would you use to accomplish this goal? (Choose all that apply.)

   A. Set-DnsServer

   B. Set-DnsServerConditionalForwarderZone

   C. Set-DnsServerGlobalNameZone

   D. Set-DNSServerForwarder

Lesson 3: Understanding advanced DNS options

Once DNS has been deployed on your network, you'll probably want to look further into what you can do to keep it running in a fast and secure manner. Until recently, there was no way for DNS clients to determine whether a resource record returned by a DNS server was valid. It was entirely possible that the DNS server responding to the record request had been hijacked by a third-party attacker and was redirecting clients to malicious sites instead of their intended destination. Domain Name System Security Extensions (DNSSEC) is a technology that leverages public key cryptography to enable supported DNS clients to be certain that the DNS record returned by a DNS server is valid. Aging and scavenging enables administrators to reduce the chance that stale resource records will clog up DNS zones.

After this lesson, you will be able to:

- Manage resource records.
- Configure zone scavenging.
- Manage round robin DNS.
- Use DNS security.

Estimated lesson time: 30 minutes

Resource records

DNS supports a large number of resource records. The most basic resource record maps an FQDN to an IP address. More complex resource records provide information about the location of services, such as SMTP servers and domain controllers. You can create 26 different types of resource records in a DNS zone using DNS Manager. In this section, you'll learn about the most commonly used resource record types.

Host records

Host records are the most common form of record. They map FQDNs to IP addresses. There are two types of host record. The first is an A record, which is used to map FQDNs to IPv4 addresses. The second type are AAAA records, which are used to map FQDNs to IPv6 addresses. You can add a new host record to a zone by right-clicking the zone in DNS Manager and then clicking New Host (A or AAAA). This will open the New Host dialog box, shown in Figure 3-18. You have the option of also creating a pointer (PTR) resource record in the appropriate reverse lookup zone, if one exists. You can add host records with the Add-DnsServerResourceRecordA cmdlet. You can add AAAA records with the Add-DnsServerResourceRecordAAAA cmdlet.

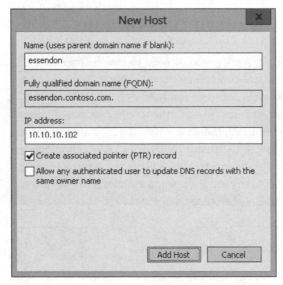

FIGURE 3-18 Adding a new host record

Alias (CNAME)

An alias, or *CNAME* record enables you to provide an alternate name when there is an existing host record. You can create as many aliases for a particular record as you need to. You can create a new alias in a zone by right-clicking the zone in DNS Manager and clicking New Alias (CNAME). This will open the New Resource Record dialog box, shown in Figure 3-19. When you create an alias, you must point the alias to an existing host record. You can use the Browse button to navigate to the target host record or enter it manually. You can add an alias record to a zone from Windows PowerShell by using the Add-DnsServerResourceRecordCName cmdlet.

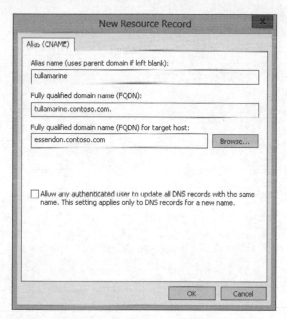

FIGURE 3-19 Adding a new CNAME record

Mail exchanger

Mail exchanger (MX) records are used to locate mail gateways. For example, when a remote mail gateway wants to forward an email message to an email address associated with your organization's DNS zone, it will perform an MX lookup to determine the location of the mail gateway. Once that determination has been made, the remote mail gateway will contact the local gateway and transmit the message. MX records must map to existing host records. You can create an MX record by right-clicking the zone in DNS Manager, clicking New Mail Exchanger (MX), and entering information in the New Resource Record dialog box, shown in Figure 3-20. The Mail Server Priority field is available to allow for the existence of more than one MX record in a zone. This is often used when organizations have multiple mail gateways. This is done so that if an organization's primary mail gateway fails, remote mail servers will forward message traffic to other mail gateways. You can add MX records using the Add-DnsServerResourceRecordMX PowerShell cmdlet.

FIGURE 3-20 Adding a new MX record

Pointer record

Pointer (PTR) records enable you to connect IP addresses to FQDNs. PTR records are hosted in reverse lookup zones. When you create a host record, a PTR record is automatically created by default if an appropriate reverse lookup zone exists. To create a PTR record, right-click the reverse lookup zone in DNS Manager, click New Pointer (PTR), and in the New Resource Record dialog box, shown in Figure 3-21, enter the PTR record information. You can create a PTR record from Windows PowerShell by using the Add-DnsServerResourceRecordPtr cmdlet.

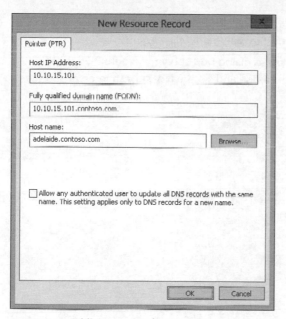

FIGURE 3-21 Adding a new pointer record

> **MORE INFO   RESOURCE RECORDS**
>
> To learn more about resource records, consult the following TechNet article at
> http://technet.microsoft.com/en-us/library/cc730624.aspx.

Zone aging and scavenging

Aging and *scavenging* provide a technique to reduce the incidence of stale resource records
in a primary DNS zone. Stale records are records that are out of date or no longer relevant. If
your organization has zones that relate to users of portable computers, such as laptops and
tablets, those zones may end up accumulating stale resource records. This can lead to the
following problems:

- DNS queries return stale rather than relevant results.
- Large zones can cause DNS server performance problems.
- Stale records may present DNS names being reassigned to different devices.

To resolve these problems, you can configure the DNS Server service to do the following:

- Time stamp resource records that are dynamically added to primary zones. This occurs
  when you enable aging and scavenging.
- Age resource records based on a refresh time period.
- Scavenge resource records that are still present beyond the refresh period.

To configure aging and scavenging on a zone, perform the following steps:

1. In DNS Manager, right-click the zone and click Properties.

2. On the General tab of the Zone Properties dialog box, click Aging.

3. In the Zone Aging/Scavenging Properties dialog box, shown in Figure 3-22, enable the Scavenge Stale Resource Records option and set the No-Refresh Interval and the Refresh Interval.

FIGURE 3-22 Zone aging/scavenging properties

Once configured, aging and scavenging will occur automatically. It is also possible to trigger scavenging by right-clicking the DNS server in DNS Manager and then clicking Scavenge Stale Resource Records. You should be aware that statically created records may not have a creation data and therefore will not be removed by the scavenging process. You can configure aging and scavenging using the Set-DnsServerScavenging cmdlet. For example, to enable scavenging of stale resource records on all zones on a DNS server and to set the No-Refresh and Refresh Intervals to 10 days, issue this command.

```
Set-DnsServerScavenging –ApplyOnAllZones –RefreshInterval 10.0:0:0 –ScavengingInterval
10.0:0:0 –ScavengingState $True
```

MORE INFO **AGING AND SCAVENGING**

To learn more about zone aging and scavenging, consult the following TechNet article at *http://technet.microsoft.com/en-us/library/cc771677.aspx.*

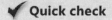

Quick check

- What type of record do you create in a reverse lookup zone if you want to map an IP address to an FQDN?

Quick check answer

- You create a PTR record if you want to map an IP address to an FQDN.

DNSSEC

Domain Name System Security Extensions (DNSSEC) adds security to DNS by enabling DNS servers to validate the responses given by other DNS servers. *DNSSEC* enables digital signatures to be used with DNS zones. When the DNS resolver issues a query for a record in a signed zone, the authoritative DNS server provides both the record and a digital signature that enables validation of that record.

To sign a zone, perform the following steps:

1. Right-click the zone in DNS manager, click DNSSEC, and then click Sign The Zone.

2. On the Signing Options page, shown in Figure 3-23, select Use Default Settings To Sign The Zone.

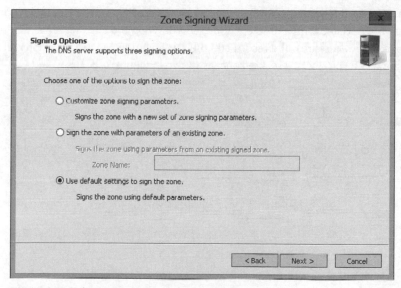

FIGURE 3-23 Using zone signing default settings

When you configure DNSSEC, three new resource records are used, as shown in Figure 3-24.

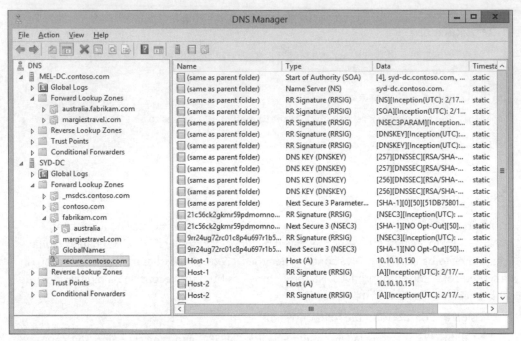

FIGURE 3-24 Zone configured with DNSSEC

These records have the following properties:

- **Resource Record Signature (RRSIG) record** This record is stored within the zone, and each is associated with a different zone record. When the DNS server is queried for a zone record, it returns the record and the associated RRSIG record. RRSIG records are visible when you query a secure zone, as shown in Figure 3-25.

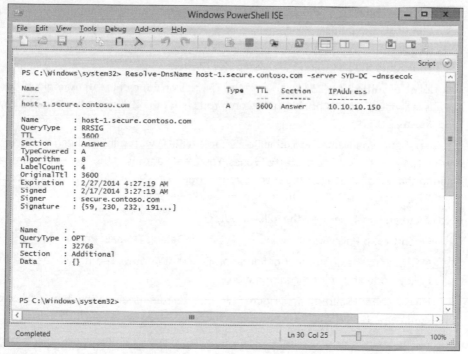

FIGURE 3-25 Displaying RRSIG record

- **DNSKEY** This is a public key resource record that enables the validation of RRSIG records.

- **Next Secure (NSEC/NSEC3) record** This record is used as proof that a record does not exist. For example, if a query is looking for ftp.contoso.com, the contoso.com zone is configured with DNSSEC. If there is no record for ftp.contoso.com, the NSEC record will be returned, informing the host making the query that no such record exists. NSEC3 are an advanced record that provide increased security over NSEC records but serve the same general purpose.

In addition to the special resource records, a DNSSEC implementation has the following components:

- **Trust anchor** This is a special public key associated with a zone. Trust anchors enable a DNS server to validate DNSKEY resource records. If you deploy DNSSEC on a DNS server hosted on a domain controller, the trust anchors can be stored in the Active Directory forest directory partition. This replicates the trust anchor to all DNS servers hosted on domain controllers in the forest.

- **DNSSEC Key Master** A special DNS server that you use to generate and manage signing keys for a DNSSEC-protected zone. Any computer running Windows Server 2012 that hosts a primary zone, whether standard or integrated, can function as a DNSSEC Key Master. A single computer can function as a DNSSEC Key Master for multiple zones. The DNSSEC Key Master role can be transferred to another DNS server that hosts the primary zone.

- **Key Signing Key (KSK)**   You use the KSK to sign all DNSKEY records at the zone root. You create the KSK using the DNSSEC Key Master.

- **Zone Signing Key (ZSK)**   You use the ZSK to sign zone data. An example of this is individual records hosted in the zone. You create the ZSK using the DNSSEC Key Master.

You configure the Name Resolution Policy Table (NRPT) with rules to determine how clients interact with DNSSEC-protected zones. You create entries in the table. An example is requiring that all queries against a specific zone require DNSSEC validation. You can configure the NRPT using Group Policy or through Windows PowerShell.

To create an NRPT, perform the following steps:

1. Open Group Policy Management and edit the Default Domain Policy.

2. Navigate to the Computer Configuration\Policies\Windows Settings\Name Resolution Policy node and enter the information.

3. Fill out the rule information. Figure 3-26 shows a rule requiring that the secure.contoso.com zone use DNSSEC.

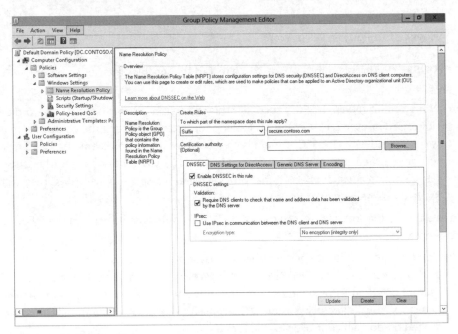

FIGURE 3-26 NRPT policy

MORE INFO **DNSSEC**

To learn more about DNSSEC, consult the following TechNet article at *http://technet. microsoft.com/en-us/library/jj200221.aspx*.

Lesson summary

- A and AAAA records map FQDNs to IP addresses.
- PTR records map IP addresses to FQDNs.
- CNAME records enable you to create aliases for FQDNs.
- MX records are used to provide information about the location of mail servers.
- Scavenging and aging enable you to minimize the amount of stale resource records in a DNS zone.
- Scavenging and aging can only scavenge dynamically generated resource records.
- DNSSEC uses public key cryptography to sign DNS zones and resource records.
- When a query occurs against a DNSSEC signed zone, both the requested record and a key to validate the records are provided.

Lesson review

Answer the following questions to test your knowledge of the information in this lesson. You can find the answers to these questions and explanations of why each answer choice is correct or incorrect in the "Answers" section at the end of this chapter.

1. What type of resource record do you create if you want to have a different name associated with an existing FQDN?

   A. A record

   B. MX record

   C. PTR record

   D. CNAME record

2. You have just deployed a server that will function as an SMTP gateway on your organization's perimeter network. This server has been assigned an FQDN, and an entry exists pointing to the server in the reverse lookup zone associated with the server's public IP address. Which type of resource record should you create if you want to ensure that the mail servers of external organizations can recognize this server as your organization's external mail gateway?

   A. CNAME record

   B. PTR record

   C. MX record

   D. A record

3. Which of the following Windows PowerShell cmdlets should you use to create a host record that maps an FQDN with an IPv6 address?

   A. Add-DnsServerResourceRecordCName

   B. Add-DnsServerResourceRecordAAAA

   C. Add-DnsServerResourceRecordMX

   D. Add-DnsServerResourceRecordPtr

4. Which of the following can you enable to reduce the number of stale resource records in a zone?

   A. Secure dynamic updates

   B. Aging and scavenging

   C. DNSSEC

   D. Zone transfers

5. You want to ensure that clients can validate the authenticity of DNS records in several primary zones that are hosted on DNS servers in your organization. Which of the following should you enable to accomplish this goal? (Choose all that apply.)

   A. DNSSEC

   B. Zone transfers

   C. Aging and scavenging

   D. Secure dynamic updates

Practice exercises

The goal of this section is to provide you with hands-on practice with the following:

- Managing DNS zones
- Single-label name resolution
- Configuring and managing DNSSEC

To perform the exercises in this section, you need access to an evaluation version of Windows Server 2012 R2. You should also have access to virtual machines SYD-DC, MEL-DC, CBR-DC, and ADL-DC, the setup instructions for which are described in the Introduction. You should ensure that you have a checkpoint of these virtual machines that you can revert to at the end of the practice exercises. You should revert the virtual machines to this initial state prior to beginning these exercises.

Exercise 1: Manage DNS zones

In this exercise, you create a new Active Directory integrated zone, configure this zone to replicate to all domain controllers in the forest, and configure the zone to accept only secure dynamic updates. To complete this exercise, perform the following steps:

1. Sign on to SYD-DC as Contoso\don_funk.

2. In Server Manager, click the Tools menu, and click DNS.

3. In the DNS Manager Console, expand SYD-DC, and click Forward Lookup Zones, as shown in Figure 3-27.

FIGURE 3-27 Forward Lookup Zones

4. In the Action menu, click New Zone.

5. On the first page of the New Zone Wizard, click Next.

6. On the Zone Type page, click Primary Zone and ensure that Store The Zone In Active Directory is selected, as shown in Figure 3-28, and click Next.

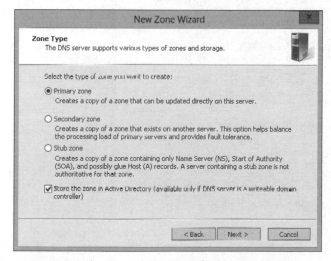

FIGURE 3-28 Active Directory integrated primary zone

7. In the Active Directory Zone Replication Scope page, click To All DNS Servers Running On Domain Controllers In This Forest: Contoso.com, as shown in Figure 3-29, and click Next.

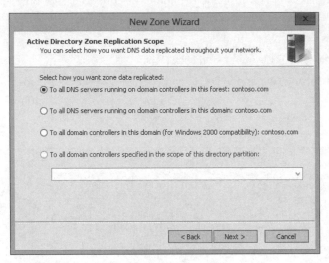

FIGURE 3-29 Zone replication scope

8. On the Zone Name page, type **fabrikam.com** and click Next.

9. On the Dynamic Update page, click Allow Only Secure Dynamic Updates, as shown in Figure 3-30, and click Next.

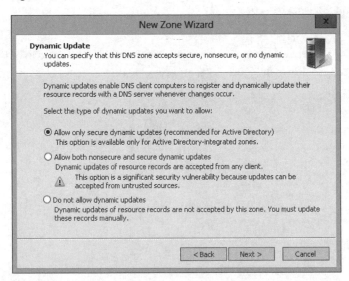

FIGURE 3-30 Configuring secure dynamic updates

10. Click Finish to complete the New Zone Wizard.

Exercise 2: Configure partition-based replication

In this exercise, you create a new Active Directory DNS partition and then create a new Active Directory integrated zone that replicates to DNS servers enrolled in this partition. To complete this exercise, perform the following steps:

1. On SYD-DC, right-click the Windows PowerShell prompt, and click Run As Administrator.

2. Execute the following command to create a new Active Directory DNS partition named Tasmania:

   ```
   Add-DNSServerDirectoryPartition -Name Tasmania
   ```

3. Close the Windows PowerShell window.

4. In the DNS Manager console, click Forward Lookup Zones.

5. In the Action menu, click New Zone.

6. On the Welcome page of the New Zone Wizard, click Next.

7. In the Zone Type page, click Primary Zone, verify that Store The Zone In Active Directory is selected, and click Next.

8. In the Active Directory Zone Replication Scope page, click To All Domain Controllers Specified In The Scope Of This Directory Partition and click Tasmania, as shown in Figure 3-31, and click Next.

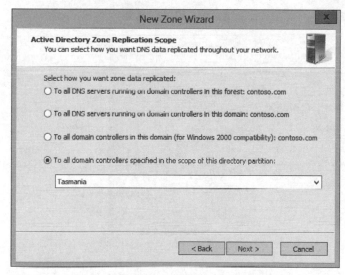

FIGURE 3-31 Replicating to a specific directory partition

9. In the Zone Name Wizard page, type **margiestravel.com**, as shown in Figure 3-32, and click Next.

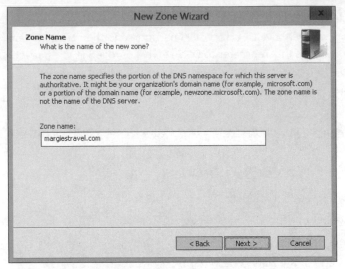

FIGURE 3-32 Providing a zone name

10. In the Dynamic Update page, click Do Not Allow Dynamic Updates, as shown in Figure 3-33, and click Next.

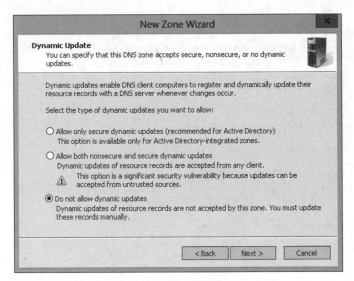

FIGURE 3-33 Do Not Allow Dynamic Updates

11. Click Finish to complete the New Zone Wizard.

Exercise 3: DNS delegation and secondary zones

In this exercise, you install the DNS role and perform a zone delegation. To complete this exercise, perform the following steps:

1. Start MEL DC, and sign in using the Administrator account with the password **Pa$$w0rd**.

2. Open the Windows PowerShell prompt and type the following commands.

   ```
   Add-Computer -DomainName contoso.com
   ```

3. In the Windows PowerShell Credentials dialog box type **don_funk@contoso.com** and **Pa$$w0rd,** and click OK.

4. Type the following command in the Windows PowerShell prompt to restart the computer.

   ```
   Restart-Computer
   ```

5. Ensure that you are signed on to SYD-DC as Contoso\don_funk.

6. In Server Manager on SYD-DC, click All Servers.

7. In the Manage menu, click Add Servers.

8. In the Name box, type **MEL-DC** and click Find Now.

9. In the Add Servers dialog box, click MEL-DC, and click the arrow button, as shown in Figure 3-34, and click OK.

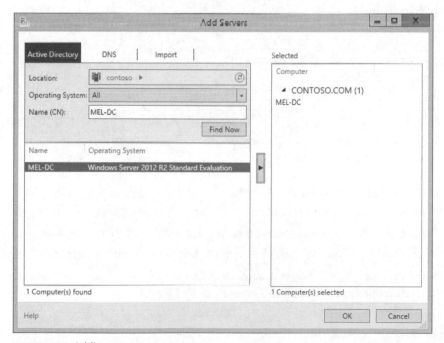

FIGURE 3-34 Adding servers to a group

10. In the All Servers area of Server Manager on SYD-DC, click MEL-DC. From the Manage menu, click Add Roles And Features.

11. In the Before You Begin page of the Add Roles And Features Wizard, click Next.

12. In the Installation Type page, click Role-Based Or Feature-Based Installation, and click Next.

13. In the Select Destination Server page, click MEL-DC.contoso.com, and click Next.

14. In the Select Server Roles page, click DNS Server. In the Add Roles And Features Wizard pop-up list, click Add Features.

15. Verify that the Add Roles And Features Wizard appears the same as shown in Figure 3-35 and click Next.

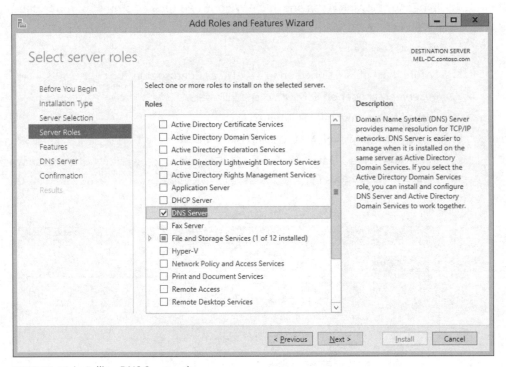

FIGURE 3-35 Installing DNS Server role

16. In the Select Features page, click Next.

17. In the DNS Server page, click Next.

18. In the Confirm Installation Selections page, click Install, and then click Close.

19. In DNS Manager console, click DNS. In the Action menu, click Connect To DNS Server.

20. In the Connect To DNS Server dialog box, click The Following Computer: and type **MEL-DC.contoso.com**, as shown in Figure 3-36. Click OK.

FIGURE 3-36 Connecting to a DNS server

21. In the DNS Manager Console, click Forward Lookup Zones under MEL-DC.contoso.com, as shown in Figure 3-37.

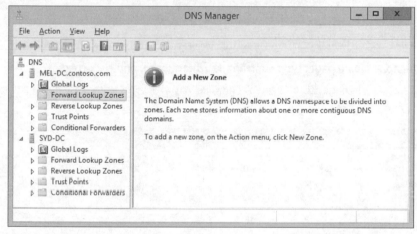

FIGURE 3-37 Connecting to two DNS servers

22. Click Action, and click New Zone.

23. In the Welcome page of the New Zone Wizard, click Next.

24. In the Zone Type page of the New Zone Wizard, click Primary Zone. Note (as shown in Figure 3-38) that the option to store the zone in Active Directory is not present because MEL-DC is not an Active Directory domain controller. Click Next.

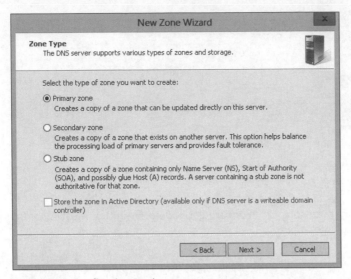

FIGURE 3-38 Configuring a primary zone

25. In the Zone Name page, type **australia.fabrikam.com,** and click Next.

26. In the Zone File page, click Create A New File With This File Name, as shown in Figure 3-39, and click Next.

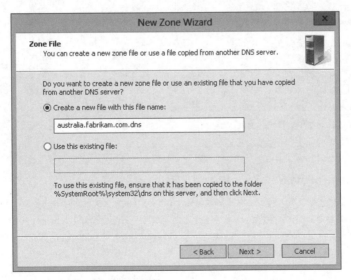

FIGURE 3-39 Creating a zone file

27. In the Dynamic Update page, click Do Not Allow Dynamic Updates, and click Next.

28. In the Completion page, click Finish.

29. In the DNS Manager Console, expand SYD-DC\Forward Lookup Zones and click Fabrikam.com.

30. In the Action menu, click New Delegation.

31. In the Welcome page of the New Delegation Wizard, click Next.

32. In the Delegated Domain Name page, type **australia**, as shown in Figure 3-40, and click Next.

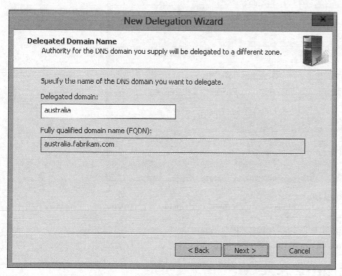

FIGURE 3-40 Configuring a delegated domain

33. In the Name Servers page, click Add.

34. In the New Name Server Record dialog box, type **MEL DC.contoso.com** and click Resolve. Click OK.

35. Verify that the Name Servers page of the New Delegation Wizard matches Figure 3-41 and then click Next.

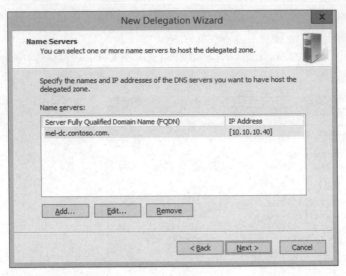

FIGURE 3-41 Delegated name server

36. Click Finish to close the New Delegation Wizard.

Exercise 4: Configure a secondary zone

In this exercise, you configure a DNS server to host the secondary zone copy of a DNS zone. To complete this exercise, perform the following steps:

1. On SYD-DC, in DNS Manager, click Margiestravel.com.

2. In the Action menu, click Properties.

3. On the Zone Transfers tab, click Allow Zone Transfers, and click Only To The Following Servers.

4. Click Edit. In the Allow Zone Transfers dialog box, click the text <Click Here To Add An IP Address Or DNS Name>, type **MEL-DC.contoso.com**, and press Enter.

5. Click No Such Host Is Known, and click Delete. Even though an error symbol is present, click OK.

6. Verify that the Zone Transfers tab matches Figure 3-42, and click OK.

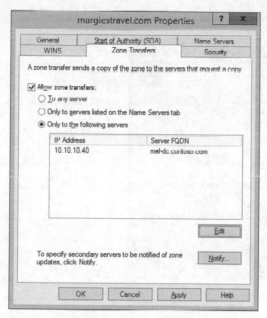

FIGURE 3-42 Configuring zone transfers

7. In the DNS Manager Console, click Forward Lookup Zones under MEL-DC.contoso.com, as shown in Figure 3-43.

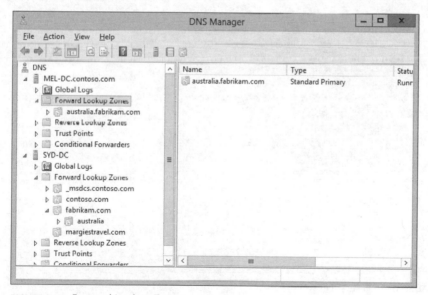

FIGURE 3-43 Forward Lookup Zones

8. In the Action menu, click New Zone.

9. In the Welcome page of the New Zone Wizard, click Next.

10. In the Zone Type page, click Secondary Zone, as shown in Figure 3-44, and click Next.

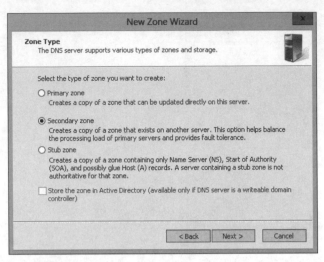

FIGURE 3-44 Secondary zone

11. In the Zone Name page, type **margiestravel.com** and click Next.

12. In the Master DNS Servers page, type **SYD-DC.contoso.com**, press Enter, and click Next (as shown in Figure 3-45).

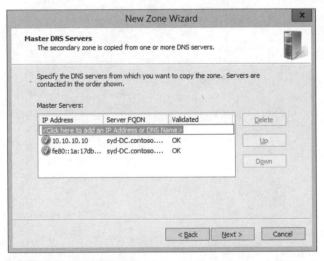

FIGURE 3-45 Master DNS Servers

13. Click Finish and verify that margiestravel.com is listed as a secondary zone on MEL-DC. contoso.com, as shown in Figure 3-46.

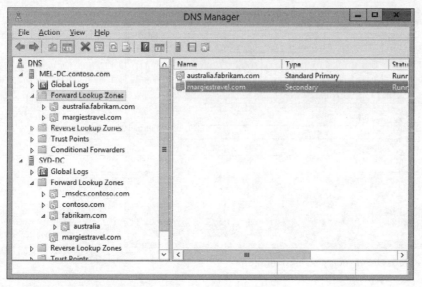

FIGURE 3-46 Secondary zone configured

Exercise 5: Single-label name resolution

In this exercise, you configure single-label name resolution. To complete this exercise, perform the following steps:

1. In the DNS Manager, click Forward Lookup Zones under SYD-DC.

2. Click the Action Menu, and click New Zone.

3. In the Welcome page of the New Zone Wizard, click Next.

4. In the Zone Type page, click Primary Zone, ensure that Store The Zone In Active Directory is selected, and click Next.

5. In the Active Directory Zone Replication Scope page, click To All DNS Servers Running On Domain Controllers In This Forest: Contoso.com and click Next.

6. In the Zone Name page, type **GlobalNames**, as shown in Figure 3-47, and click Next.

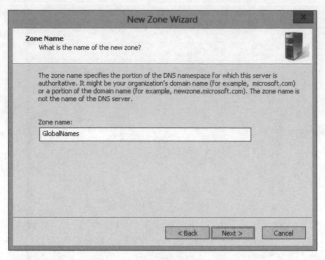

FIGURE 3-47 Secondary zone configured

7. In the Dynamic Update page, click Do Not Allow Dynamic Updates, and click Next.

8. In the Completing The New Zone Wizard page, click Finish.

9. Right-click the Windows PowerShell icon on the taskbar, and click Run As Administrator.

10. Issue the following command to enable the GlobalNames zone on SYD-DC.

    ```
    Set-DnsServerGlobalNameZone -ComputerName SYD-DC -Enable $True
    ```

11. Switch to DNS Manager.

12. Click the GlobalNames zone. In the Action menu, click New Alias (CNAME).

13. In the New Resource Record dialog box, configure the following information, as shown in Figure 3-48, and click OK.

    - Alias Name (Uses Parent Domain If Left Blank): **Wollongong**
    - Fully Qualified Domain Name (FQDN) For Target Host: **MEL-DC.contoso.com**

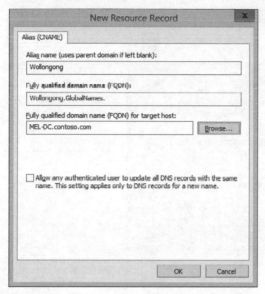

FIGURE 3-48 Record in GlobalNames zone

14. In the Windows PowerShell prompt, type the following to verify single name resolution.

```
nslookup Wollongong
```

Exercise 6: Configure and manage DNSSEC

In this exercise, you configure and manage DNSSEC. To complete this exercise, perform the following steps:

1. In DNS Manager, click Forward Lookup Zones under SYD-DC.

2. In the Action menu, click New Zone.

3. In the Welcome page of the New Zone Wizard, click Next.

4. In the Zone Type page, click Primary Zone, enable the Store The Zone In Active Directory option, and click Next.

5. In the Active Directory Zone Replication Scope page, click To All DNS Servers Running On Domain Controllers In This Forest: Contoso.com.

6. In the Zone Name page, type the zone name as **secure.contoso.com**, as shown in Figure 3-49, and click Next.

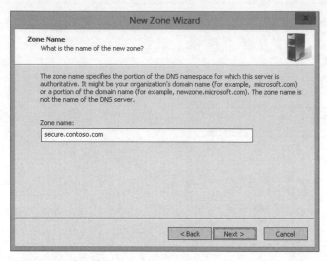

FIGURE 3-49 Creating a new zone

7. In the Dynamic Update page, click Allow Only Secure Dynamic Updates, and click Next.

8. In the Completing The New Zone Wizard page, click Finish.

9. In the DNS Manager, click Secure.contoso.com under Forward Lookup Zones.

10. In the Action menu, click New Host (A Or AAAA).

11. In the New Host dialog box, configure the following details, as shown in Figure 3-50, and then click Add Host.

    ■ Name: **Host-1**

    ■ IP Address: **10.10.10.150**

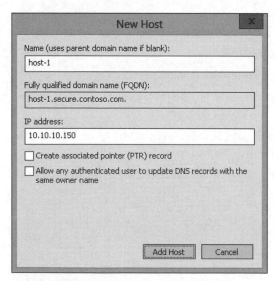

FIGURE 3-50 Creating a new host

12. In the New Host dialog box, configure the following details, click Add Host, and click Done:

   ■ Name: **Host-2**

   ■ IP Address: **10.10.10.151**

13. Run the following Windows PowerShell command to verify that no RRSIG record is present.

```
Resolve-DNSname host-1.secure.contoso.com -server SYD-DC -dnssecok
```

14. In DNS Manager, click Secure.contoso.com.

15. From the Action menu, click DNSSEC and click Sign The Zone.

16. In the DNS Security Extensions (DNSSEC) page of the Zone Signing Wizard, click Next.

17. In the Signing Options page, click Use Default Settings To Sign The Zone, as shown in Figure 3-51, and click Next.

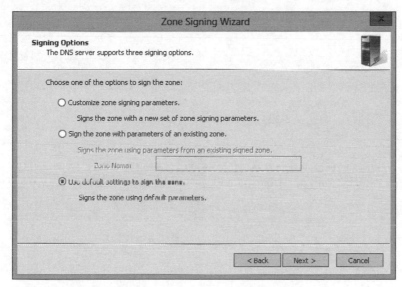

FIGURE 3-51 Sign DNS Zone

18. In the DNS Security Extensions page, click Next.

19. In the Signing The Zone page, click Finish.

20. Click Secure.contoso.com and from the Action menu, click Refresh.

21. View the contents of the Secure.contoso.com zone in DNS Manager to verify the presence of the new DNSKEY, RRSIG, and NSEC3 records.

22. Rerun the Windows PowerShell command from step 13 and note the presence of the RRSIG record.

Suggested practice exercises

The following additional practice exercises are designed to give you more opportunities to practice what you've learned and to help you successfully master the lessons presented in this chapter.

- **Exercise 1**   Configure a primary zone on MEL-DC. Configure a secondary zone of the primary zone on SYD-DC. Create host records in the primary zone on MEL-DC and verify that they replicate to the secondary zone on SYD-DC.

- **Exercise 2**   Install Peer Name Resolution Protocol on SYD-DC, MEL-DC, and ADL-DC. Use PNRP to resolve the IPv6 address of each server.

- **Exercise 3**   Use Windows PowerShell to create A, CNAME, PTR, and MX records in the secure.contoso.com zone created in Exercise 3.

Answers

This section contains the answers to the lesson review questions in this chapter.

Lesson 1

1. **Correct answers: A and C**

   A. **Correct**. Configuring the zone as Active Directory integrated primary enables you to configure the zone to accept only secure dynamic updates.

   B. **Incorrect**. You cannot configure a standard primary zone so that it will accept only secure dynamic updates. A standard primary zone can be configured to accept both secure and insecure dynamic updates.

   C. **Correct**. Configuring this setting ensures that only computers that are members of the domain can update the zone.

   D. **Incorrect**. If you do not configure the zone to allow dynamic updates, you have to perform zone updates manually.

2. **Correct answer: C**

   A. **Incorrect**. This network ID would be associated with the 168.192.in-addr.arpa zone.

   B. **Incorrect**. This network ID would be associated with the 192.186.15.in-addr.arpa zone.

   C. **Correct**. Zone names use octets in reverse. The zero is dropped from the zone name.

   D. **Incorrect**. This network ID would be associated with the 15.168.192.0.in-addr.apra zone.

3. **Correct answer: B**

   A. **Incorrect**. You should not create the target zone on the computer on which you are going to perform the delegation, unless that computer will host that zone. In this situation, the target zone will be hosted on the computer with IP address 10.100.10.10.

   B. **Correct**. You must create the target zone on the server that will host that zone prior to performing the delegation.

   C. **Incorrect**. You must create the target zone before you perform a delegation.

   D. **Incorrect**. You must create the target zone before you perform a delegation.

4. **Correct answer: D**

   A. **Incorrect**. Although configuring a secondary zone will provide a local copy of the partner organization's zone, a better approach is to use a stub zone because the zone updates frequently. This way, clients on your organizational network can quickly locate the authoritative name servers in the partner zone and resolve addresses in that zone accurately.

    B. **Incorrect**. Conditional forwarders use static entries for authoritative servers in the target zone. Because the authoritative servers in the target zone often change, a conditional forwarder is quickly out of date.

    C. **Incorrect**. Forwarders are used to forward all queries, rather than queries to a specific zone.

    D. **Correct**. The best approach is to use a stub zone. This way, clients on your organizational network can quickly locate the authoritative name servers in the partner zone and resolve addresses in that zone accurately.

5. **Correct answers: B and C**

    A. **Incorrect**. A stub zone replicates authoritative name server information from a target zone. In this situation, you simply want to forward traffic for hosts in a specific zone to a specific DNS server.

    B. **Correct**. You need to configure a forwarder that will forward traffic to your ISP's DNS server.

    C. **Correct**. A conditional forwarder will forward all traffic to the margiestravel.com DNS zone, to a DNS server at a specific address.

    D. **Incorrect**. You want to forward client request traffic either to your ISP's DNS server or to the margiestravel.com DNS server. Hosting a secondary zone of the margiestravel.com DNS zone does not accomplish this goal.

Lesson 2

1. **Correct answer: B and D**

    A. **Incorrect**. DHCP provides network address information to clients, but can't be used to provide IPv6 single-label name resolution.

    B. **Correct**. GlobalNames zones can be used to provide single-label name resolution for IPv6.

    C. **Incorrect**. WINS does not support IPv6.

    D. **Correct**. PNRP provides single-label name resolution for IPv6.

2. **Correct answer: B**

    A. **Incorrect**. DNS option 005 is used to provide clients with the address of DNS servers.

    B. **Correct**. DNS option 044 is used to provide clients with the address of WINS servers.

    C. **Incorrect**. Option 004 is used to provide clients with the address of time servers.

    D. **Incorrect**. Option 015 is used to provide clients with their DNS domain name.

3. **Correct answer: D**

   A. **Incorrect**. Reverse lookup zones are used to translate IP addresses into FQDNs. They can't be used for single-label name resolution.

   B. **Incorrect**. Stub zones are used to store the addresses of authoritative name servers. They can't be used for single-label name resolution.

   C. **Incorrect**. Secondary zones are read-only replicas of primary zones, although it is possible to create a secondary zone of a GlobalNames zone.

   D. **Correct**. GlobalNames zones allow you to provide single-label name resolution without deploying WINS. You can manually update a GlobalNames zone.

4. **Correct answer: C**

   A. **Incorrect**. DNS requires the deployment of a centralized server to respond to DNS lookup requests.

   B. **Incorrect**. WINS requires the deployment of a centralized server to respond to WINS lookup requests.

   C. **Correct**. PNRP provides IPv6 name resolution without requiring the deployment of a centralized server.

   D. **Incorrect**. DHCP provides IP address information. It can't be used to resolve name resolution queries.

5. **Correct answer: C**

   A. **Incorrect**. Although Set-DnsServer can be used to configure the properties of a DNS server, it can't be used to enable GlobalNames zone.

   B. **Incorrect**. You use this cmdlet to configure DNS conditional forwarders.

   C. **Correct**. You use the Set-DnsServerGlobalNameZone cmdlet to enable GlobalNames zones once they are created.

   D. **Incorrect**. You use this cmdlet to configure a DNS server forwarder.

Lesson 3

1. **Correct answer: D**

   A. **Incorrect**. A records are associated with IP addresses. In this case, you want to associate a new name with an existing FQDN.

   B. **Incorrect**. MX records are used to provide MX information.

   C. **Incorrect**. PTR records are used to associate IP addresses with FQDNs.

   D. **Correct**. A CNAME record, also known as an alias record, allows you to provide an alternate name that points to an existing A record

2. **Correct answer: C**

   A. **Incorrect**. You don't need to create an alias record; you need to create an MX record to allow the mail servers of external organizations to locate your organization's mail gateway.

   B. **Incorrect**. A PTR record already exists in this scenario.

   C. **Correct**. MX records are used by mail gateways to determine the address of remote mail gateways during message delivery.

   D. **Incorrect**. An A record already exists for this host.

3. **Correct answer: B**

   A. **Incorrect**. You use the Add-DnsServerResourceRecordCName cmdlet to add an alias rather than an AAAA record.

   B. **Correct**. You use the Add-DnsServerResourceRecordAAAA cmdlet to create an AAAA record. AAAA records map FQDNs to IPv6 addresses.

   C. **Incorrect**. You use the Add-DnsServerResourceRecordMX cmdlet to add MX records to a DNS zone.

   D. **Incorrect**. You use the Add-DNSSErverResourceRecordPtr cmdlet to add a pointer record. A pointer record has already been configured for this host.

4. **Correct answer: B**

   A. **Incorrect**. Secure dynamic updates ensure that only authorized hosts can update records in a DNS zone. They do not reduce the number of stale resource records.

   B. **Correct**. By time stamping records, aging and scavenging ensures that stale resource records are removed from a zone in a timely manner.

   C. **Incorrect**. You use DNSSEC to validate the authenticity of DNS records.

   D. **Incorrect**. You configure zone transfers to authorize which servers can perform zone transfers of a DNS zone.

5. **Correct answer: A**

   A. **Correct**. You can use DNSSEC to validate the authenticity of DNS records.

   B. **Incorrect**. You configure zone transfers to authorize which servers can perform zone transfers of a DNS zone.

   C. **Incorrect**. Aging and scavenging ensures that stale resource records are removed from a zone in a timely manner. You can't use aging and scavenging to validate the authenticity of records.

   D. **Incorrect**. Secure dynamic updates ensure that only authorized hosts can update records in a DNS zone. This technology does not allow a client to determine the authenticity of the results of a DNS query.

Administering Active Directory

There is more to managing Active Directory than deploying domain controllers. It's important for administrators of Windows Server 2012 and Windows Server 2012 R2 domains to be familiar with the function and placement of flexible single-master roles, read-only domain controllers, and Global Catalog servers. It's also important for systems administrators to be able to defragment and optimize the Active Directory Domain Services (AD DS) database and perform efficient backup and recovery operations.

Lessons in this chapter:

- Lesson 1: Managing domain controllers **181**
- Lesson 2: Maintaining domain controllers **200**
- Lesson 3: Recovering Active Directory **208**

Before you begin

To complete the practice exercises in this chapter:

- You need to have deployed computers SYD-DC, MEL-DC, and ADL-DC, as described in the Introduction, using the evaluation edition of Windows Server 2012 R2.

Lesson 1: Managing domain controllers

In this lesson, you will learn about the flexible single master operations roles, the functionality and deployment strategies for Global Catalog servers, and management of read-only domain controllers. You'll also learn about the conditions under which you can clone a virtualized domain controller.

After this lesson, you will be able to:

- Manage operations master roles.
- Deploy Global Catalog servers.
- Utilize universal group membership caching.
- Manage read-only domain controllers.
- Implement domain controller cloning.

Estimated lesson time: 45 minutes

Managing operations masters

There are five *operations masters* in a single domain Active Directory forest. Two of these operations masters are unique to the forest. There can only be one instance of each of these operations masters in the forest. Three operations masters are present in each domain in the forest. You can determine the location of the forest-level operations masters by running the Get-ADForest cmdlet. You can determine the location of the domain-level operations masters by running the Get-ADDomain cmdlet. You can also determine the location of the domain-level operations masters by right-clicking the domain in Active Directory Users And Computers and then clicking Operations Masters. This process displays the Operations Masters dialog box, shown in Figure 4-1. Both cmdlets are part of the Active Directory Windows PowerShell module, which is invoked automatically when run on a Windows Server 2012 or Windows Server 2012 R2 domain controller.

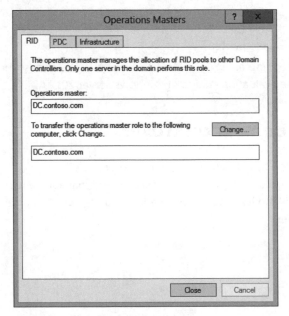

FIGURE 4-1 Domain operations masters

Schema master

The domain controller that hosts the *schema master* role is responsible for processing updates to the Active Directory schema. This forest-level operations master is present on a domain controller in the forest root domain. Some products that need to update the Active Directory Schema, such as Microsoft Exchange, must run that process in the same site as the schema master. Other products that need to update the schema may need to run on the computer that hosts the schema master.

You can locate the schema master using the Active Directory Schema snap-in for the Microsoft Management Console (MMC). This snap-in is available only if you register the schmmgmt.dll by running the following command from an elevated command prompt.

```
Regsvr32.exe Schmmgmt.dll
```

MORE INFO **ACTIVE DIRECTORY SCHEMA SNAP-IN**

You can learn more about deploying the Active Directory Schema snap-in at *http://technet. microsoft.com/en-us/library/cc737499(v=WS.10).aspx*.

After the Active Directory Schema snap-in has been added, you can open the Change Schema Master dialog box, shown in Figure 4-2, by right-clicking Active Directory Schema, and then clicking Operations Master. You can also use this dialog box to transfer the schema master role to another computer.

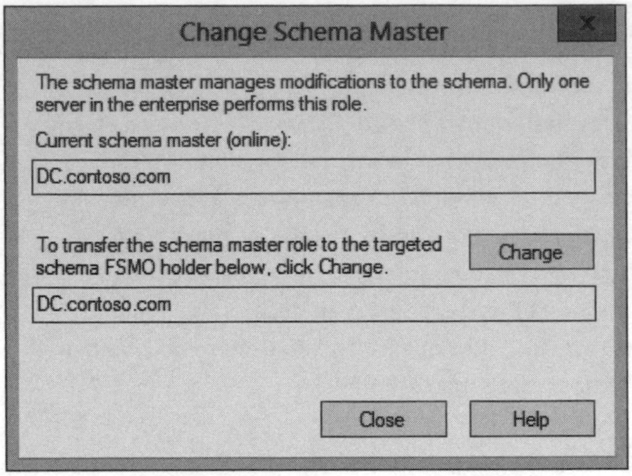

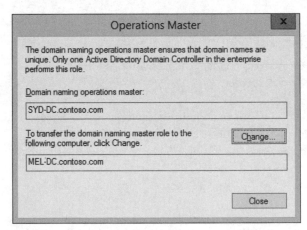

FIGURE 4-2 Schema master

Domain naming master

 The *domain naming master* is a forest-level operations master role, meaning that there is only one domain controller that holds this role in an Active Directory forest. The domain naming master is responsible for managing the addition and removal of domains and application partitions in the forest. The computer that hosts this role is also responsible for handling references to domains in forests that have a trust relationship with the source forest. You can move the domain naming master role using the Operations Master dialog box, available through the Active Directory Domains And Trusts console, and shown in Figure 4-3.

FIGURE 4-3 Domain naming master

PDC emulator

The *PDC emulator* is a domain-based role that manages the following:

- **Changing domain account passwords** The PDC emulator ensures that password changes replicate to other domain controllers as soon as possible.

- **Time synchronization across domain members** As PDC emulators within child domains in a forest perform time synchronization against the PDC emulator in the root domain, you should ensure that you configure the PDC emulator in the root domain to perform time synchronization against a trusted external time source. Doing this ensures that all computers in the forest keep correct time.

- **Group Policy changes** The PDC emulator ensures that there are no conflicts in the event that the same Group Policy Object (GPO) is being edited by two or more different people at the same time.

- **Domain master browser** The PDC emulator provides clients with a list of workgroups and domains when the client is browsing the network.

You can move the PDC emulator to another domain controller using the Operations Masters dialog box, which is available by right-clicking the target domain in Active Directory Users And Computers. This dialog box is shown in Figure 4-4.

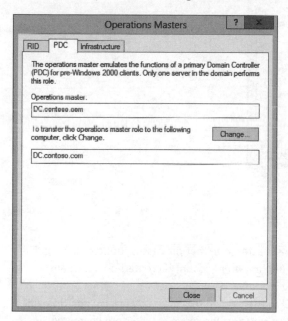

FIGURE 4-4 Locating the PDC emulator

Infrastructure master

The domain controller that holds the *infrastructure master* role keeps track of changes made in other domains in the forest, and their impact on objects in the local domain. There is a domain controller hosting the infrastructure master role in each domain in a forest. Unless each domain controller in a domain also holds the Global Catalog server role for performance reasons, you should avoid placing the infrastructure master role on a domain controller that also functions as a Global Catalog server. You can move the infrastructure master to another domain controller using the Operations Masters dialog box, which is available by right-clicking the target domain in Active Directory Users And Computers. This dialog box is shown in Figure 4-5.

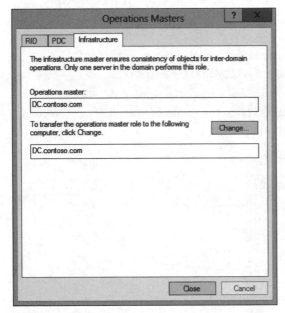

FIGURE 4-5 Locating the infrastructure master

RID master

The *RID master* is a domain-level operations master role that processes requests for relative identifiers (RIDs). Whenever a user, group, or computer account is created on a domain controller, that object is assigned a security identifier (SID). SIDs consist of both a domain SID and a unique RID generated by the RID master. When moving objects between domains using tools including movetree.exe, you must perform the move on the domain controller that holds the RID master role for the source domain. You can move the RID master to another domain controller using the Operations Masters dialog box, which is available by right-clicking the target domain in Active Directory Users And Computers. RID masters provide domain controllers with blocks of RIDs. Domain controllers will be unable to create user, group, or computer accounts if they exhaust their assigned block of RIDs and are unable to procure more from a RID master.

Seizing operations master roles

If a domain controller that is hosting an operations master role fails, you might not be able to transfer that role to another domain controller using the methods outlined earlier. If you can't transfer an operations master role using the previously mentioned tools, you can seize the operations master role by using the Force parameter with the Move-ADDirectoryServerOpera tionMasterRole cmdlet. This is also known as seizing the operations master role. For example, to seize the RID master, infrastructure master, and domain naming master roles and place them on server MEL DC, use the following command.

```
Move-ADDirectoryServerOperationMasterRole –Identity MEL-DC –OperationMasterRole
DomainNamingMaster,InfrastructureMAster,RIDMaster –Force
```

You can also seize operations master roles using the ntdsutil.exe utility, although this operation is significantly more complex than using the Move-ADDirectoryServerOperatio nMasterRole cmdlet. Using Windows PowerShell is the recommended way to manage the placement of operations master roles on Windows Server 2012 and Windows Server 2012 R2.

> **MORE INFO**   **USING NTDSUTIL.EXE TO SEIZE OPERATIONS MASTER ROLES**
>
> You can learn more about using NTDSutil.exe to seize operations master roles at *http://support.microsoft.com/kb/255504*.

 Quick check

- Which operations master role is responsible for processing account password changes in a domain?

Quick check answer

- The PDC emulator role is responsible for processing account password changes in a domain.

Global Catalog servers

Global Catalog servers contain partial information about all objects in all domains in a forest and are often used to provide information on universal group membership in forests that have multiple domains. When a local domain controller authenticates users, it uses the Global Catalog server to determine whether the user account it is authenticating is a member of any universal groups. Global Catalog servers are extremely important in environments in which you have deployed products such as Microsoft Exchange.

The first domain controller in a new domain is a Global Catalog server by default. You can configure a domain controller to be a Global Catalog server in the Domain Controller Options page of the Active Directory Domain Services Configuration Wizard, as shown in Figure 4-6. Both a traditionally deployed and a read-only domain controller can function as a Global Catalog server.

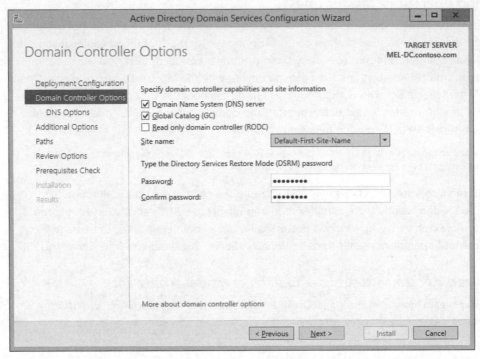

FIGURE 4-6 Installing a new domain controller as a Global Catalog server

You can convert an existing domain controller so that it functions as a Global Catalog server or remove the Global Catalog role from a domain controller in the NTDS Settings Properties dialog box. To access this dialog box, you have to open the Active Directory Sites And Services console, locate the site the domain controller is in, select the domain controller, and then edit the properties of the NTDS Settings item. This dialog box is shown in Figure 4-7.

FIGURE 4-7 Configuring a domain controller to function as a Global Catalog server

Consider the following when choosing to deploy Global Catalog servers:

- For optimal performance, make every domain controller a Global Catalog server in a single domain forest.

- In multidomain forests, deploy at least one Global Catalog server to each site that has more than 100 users.

The drawback to deploying Global Catalog servers in multidomain environments (and the reason why this role isn't enabled by default) is replication. In multidomain forests in which universal groups are in use, Global Catalog servers can be responsible for a substantial amount of replication traffic across branch-office wide area network (WAN) links. If a site has fewer than 100 users, you can enable universal group membership caching to achieve a similar result without the bandwidth utilization that deploying a Global Catalog server incurs.

Universal group membership caching

Universal group membership caching (UGMC) performs a function similar to the one that a Global Catalog server performs. UGMC is suitable for small sites that don't have enough users to justify deploying a Global Catalog server. You enable UGMC at the site level instead of at the Global Catalog server level by configuring NTDS Site Settings properties, as shown in Figure 4-8.

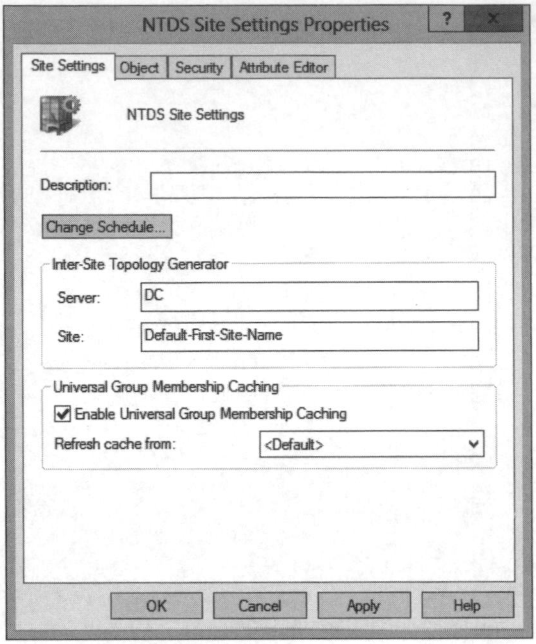

FIGURE 4-8 Enabling UGMC

Read-only domain controllers

A *read-only domain controller* (RODC) is a special type of domain controller that stores the passwords of only some users, but not all. You deploy a RODC when you are concerned about the physical security of a domain controller. For example, suppose that you need to have a domain controller at a branch office site, but the branch office site doesn't have a special secure locked server room, and the local servers instead sit in a cabinet in the same room that holds the shared printer, photocopier, and fax machine.

If a domain controller is stolen, the best security practice is to change all the passwords of all accounts in the domain. It's theoretically possible (although exceptionally unlikely) that the person who stole the domain controller isn't looking for some computer hardware to sell off at the pub, but is instead a master hacker who can extract user name and password data from the Active Directory database. Although having someone extract the password of Sam in sales may not seem like much of a security risk, if the password of Anna the systems administrator is cracked, the organization has an even bigger security problem.

RODCs store only a select set of user account passwords. If someone misappropriates the branch office domain controller, you can quickly ascertain which user accounts have passwords that are potentially vulnerable. You can then reset these passwords without having to worry about having to reset every password of every account in the domain. If you choose to deploy an RODC at a site, you should deploy RODCs only at that site. There is no point deploying an RODC next to a typical domain controller because you have concerns about the security of the location, and then hoping that anyone who wants to steal a computer from the site chooses the one that doesn't have local copies of all domain account passwords.

RODCs have the following requirements:

- Forest functional level must be set to Windows Server 2003 or higher.

- If the forest is not running at the Windows Server 2012 or higher functional level, it must be prepared for RODC deployment. You can do this by running the command adprep/rodcprep using a user account that is a member of the Enterprise Admins group. Adprep.exe is located in the Support\Adprep folder of the Windows Server 2012 and Windows Server 2012 R2 installation media.

- A domain controller running Windows Server 2008 or higher must be present in any domain in which you want to deploy an RODC.

To deploy an RODC, perform the following steps:

1. Run the Add Roles And Features Wizard, and add the Active Directory Domain Services role and all features required to support that role to the computer that will function as the RODC.

2. Run the Active Directory Domain Services Configuration Wizard, and choose to add a domain controller to an existing domain, as shown in Figure 4-9. RODCs require that an existing writable domain controller be present in a domain and can't be the first domain controller in a domain.

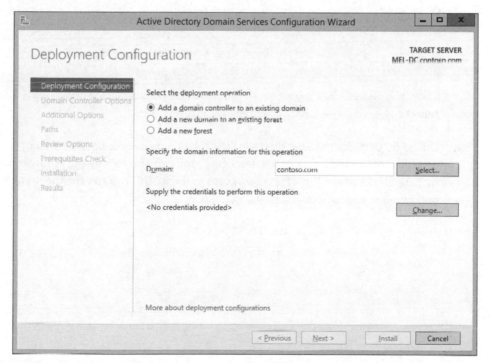

FIGURE 4-9 Adding a domain controller to an existing domain

3. On the Domain Controller Options page, you need to select the Read Only Domain Controller (RODC) option, choose the site that the domain controller will be located in, and enter a Directory Services Restore Mode (DSRM) password, as shown in Figure 4-10. You can also configure the RODC as a DNS server. When you do this, the DNS server does not process updates, but instead passes updates to a writable domain controller for processing.

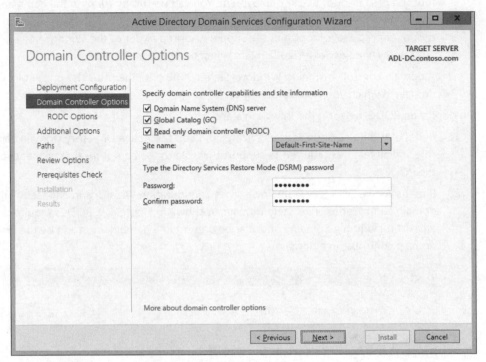

FIGURE 4-10 Configure a domain controller as an RODC

4. On the RODC Options page, shown in Figure 4-11, you can configure the list of accounts that can replicate to the new RODC. You can also modify the list of accounts that are blocked from replicating passwords to the RODC. You can change these options after you have deployed the RODC.

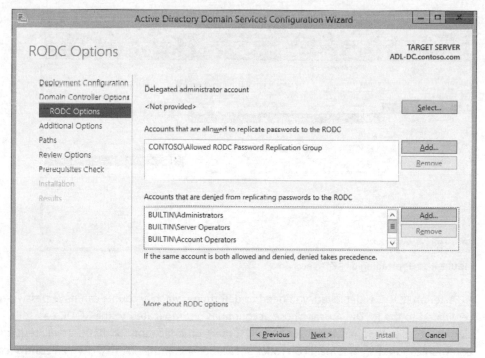

FIGURE 4-11 RODC options

5. The rest of the options in the Active Directory Domain Services Configuration Wizard are the same as those presented when you deploy a typical domain controller. When you complete the wizard, the computer that will host the RODC role restarts.

You can create a prestaged RODC computer account by clicking Pre-create A Read-Only Domain Controller Account in the Active Directory Administrative Center, as shown in Figure 4-12, or by using the Add-ADDSReadOnlyDomainControllerAccount cmdlet. For example, to create a prestaged account for an RODC named Sydney-RODC in the Sydney site of the Contoso domain, execute the following command.

```
Add-ADDSReadOnlyDomainControllerAccount -DomainControllerAccountName Sydney-RODC -
DomainName Contoso -SiteName Sydney
```

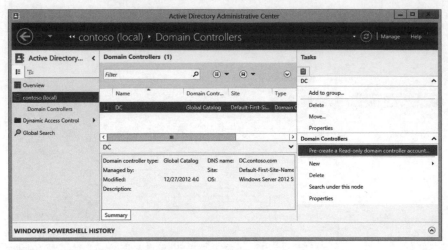

FIGURE 4-12 Prestaging an RODC account

After an RODC is deployed, you need to determine which accounts can have passwords replicated to the RODC. A user whose account has not replicated to the RODC can still sign on at a site that has only RODCs; it's just that authentication for that user will require communication with a domain controller at another site. If the link to a domain controller that stores the password is down, any user who doesn't have a password replicated to the RODC and who needs to be authenticated by the RODC can't sign on.

By default, accounts located in the Allowed RODC Password Replication Group domain-based security can replicate to the RODC. Accounts that are in the following groups are blocked from replicating to the RODC:

- BUILTIN\Administrators
- BUILTIN\Server Operators
- BUILTIN\Backup Operators
- BUILTIN\Account Operators
- DOMAIN\Denied RODC Password Replication Group

Accounts that are members of any denied security group do not replicate to the RODC, even if they are members of a group that has been explicitly allowed. You can configure which accounts are blocked and allowed to have password data replicated to an RODC by editing the properties of each RODC and selecting the password replication policy, as shown in Figure 4-13.

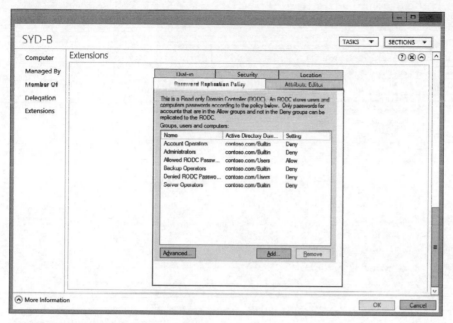

FIGURE 4-13 Password replication policy

You can use the Advanced Password Replication Policy dialog box, shown in Figure 4-14, to determine which passwords have been replicated to the RODC. You can use this dialog box if someone steals the RODC and you want to assess which accounts might be compromised. You can use the Prepopulate Passwords option to replicate the passwords of all users who are subject to the Password Replication Policy. You can use the Resultant Policy tab to calculate whether a particular user account password will be replicated to the RODC.

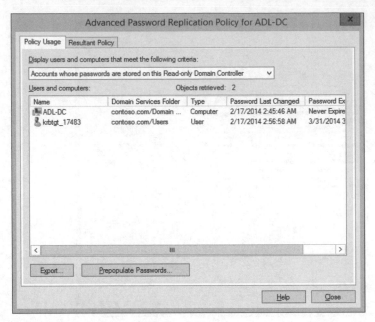

FIGURE 4-14 Passwords on RODC

Deploying a domain controller as an RODC is only the first step in ensuring that a branch office domain controller is secure. If you are concerned about security, ensure that you configured the computer hosting the RODC with BitLocker. An RODC deployed as a virtual machine on a Hyper-V host that uses BitLocker to encrypt the hard drive and protect the boot environment is extremely difficult for an attacker to compromise. Even so, if the BitLocker-protected computer hosting the RODC virtual machine is stolen from the branch office, you should still change the passwords of all user accounts that may have been affected.

REAL WORLD **VERY SPECIFIC USAGE SCENARIOS**

RODCs have a very specific usage scenario. You put them in locations in which you can't guarantee the physical security of the domain controller. If you have confidence in the security of a branch office location, you're better off deploying a traditional domain controller. In the future, you might also choose to use Microsoft Azure Active Directory as an alternative to deploying domain controllers at locations in which physical security is questionable.

A user must normally be a member of a group such as the Domain Admins group to perform administration tasks on a domain controller. Since RODCs are designed to be deployed in locations remote from your organization's head office, you can delegate administration of RODCs so that it's possible for a user to sign on and perform administrative tasks without having to make them a member of a group that has extensive privileges in the domain. You can do this on the Managed By tab of the RODC's computer account properties, as shown in Figure 4-15.

MORE INFO **DEPLOYING RODCS**

You can learn more about deploying RODCs at *http://technet.microsoft.com/en-us/library/jj574152.aspx.*

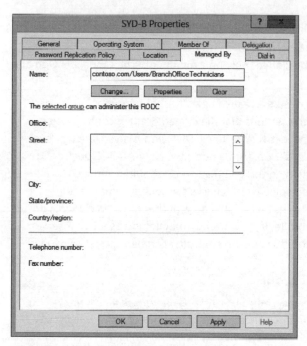

FIGURE 4-15 Branch office technicians

✔ **Quick check**

- What console can you use to configure a domain controller as a Global Catalog server or enable UGMC at a site?

Quick check answer

- You use the Active Directory Sites And Services console to configure a domain controller as a Global Catalog server or enable UGMC at a site.

Domain controller cloning

Domain controller cloning is a new feature in Windows Server 2012 and later that enables you to create copies of virtualized domain controllers under specific conditions. These conditions are as follows:

- The hypervisor supports VM-GenerationID. VM-GenerationID is a special 128-bit cryptographically random integer that uniquely identifies a snapshot. Hyper-V 3.0, which is the version available with Windows Server 2012, supports VM-GenerationID. Some third-party hypervisor solutions also support this feature. VM-GenerationID is also supported with the version of Hyper-V available in Windows Server 2012 R2.

- The domain controller must be running Windows Server 2012 or Windows Server 2012 R2
- The PDC emulator operations master role must be online, available, and held by a computer running Windows Server 2012 or Windows Server 2012 R2
- The domain controller that will be cloned must be a member of the Cloneable Domain Controllers security group.

After these conditions are met, you need to create a new XML configuration file named DCCloneConfig.xml. This file stores all the settings that the cloned domain controller has when it boots, including computer name, network settings, DNS, and Active Directory site name. You can generate the DCCloneConfig.xml file by using the New-ADDCCloneConfig Windows PowerShell cmdlet. Prior to running this command, you should run the Get-ADDCCloningExcludedApplicationsList cmdlet, which checks the source computer to determine whether it is running any services that might cause problems when cloned. For example, you can't clone a domain controller if it is currently functioning as a DHCP server, and you'll have to remove this role before the domain controller can be successfully cloned.

> **MORE INFO**   **DOMAIN CONTROLLER CLONING**
>
> You can learn more about cloning domain controllers at *http://blogs.technet.com/b/ askpfeplat/archive/2012/10/01/virtual-domain-controller-cloning-in-windows-server-2012. aspx.*

Lesson summary

- There are five operations masters. Schema master controls updates to the schema. The domain-naming master manages additions and removals of domains in the forest. The PDC emulator master processes password changes and manages time synchronization. The infrastructure master keeps track of changes made in other domains that affect objects in the local domain. The RID master processes requests for relative IDs.
- Global Catalog servers assist with determining the universal group membership of user accounts in multiple-domain forests.
- You can control password replication to RODCs by configuring the RODC Password Replication Policy.
- Cloning domain controllers requires that the virtualization platform supports VM-GenerationID, the domain controller must be running Windows Server 2012 or later, and the PDC emulator must be online and also running Windows Server 2012 or later.
- The source domain controller must be a member of the Cloneable Domain Controllers security group.

Lesson review

Answer the following questions to test your knowledge of the information in this lesson. You can find the answers to these questions and explanations of why each answer choice is correct or incorrect in the "Answers" section at the end of this chapter.

1. You want to create a copy of a virtualized domain controller. Which of the following conditions must be met before you can accomplish this goal? (Choose all that apply.)

   A. The hypervisor must support VM-GenerationID.

   B. The source domain controller must be a member of the Cloneable Domain Controllers security group.

   C. The schema master must be online and running the Windows Server 2012 or Windows Server 2012 R2 operating system.

   D. The PDC emulator must be online and running the Windows Server 2012 or Windows Server 2012 R2 operating system.

2. Which operations master is responsible for ensuring that clocks are set consistently across members of a domain?

   A. Infrastructure master

   B. PDC emulator

   C. RID master

   D. Domain naming master

   E. Schema master

3. You need to make updates to the Active Directory schema. Which operations master must be online for you to accomplish this goal?

   A. Infrastructure master

   B. PDC emulator

   C. RID master

   D. Domain naming master

   E. Schema master

4. Which infrastructure master generates pools of unique relative identifiers to ensure that domain SIDs are unique? (Choose all that apply.)

   A. Infrastructure master

   B. PDC emulator

   C. RID master

   D. Domain naming master

   E. Schema master

5. You want to add several new application partitions in the forest. Which operations master must be available to complete this task? (Choose all that apply.)

   A. Infrastructure master

   B. PDC emulator

   C. RID master

   D. Domain naming master

   E. Schema master

Lesson 2: Maintaining domain controllers

Ensuring that domain controllers perform as well as they can is an important part of a systems administrator's job. Having poorly performing domain controllers means extended logon times for users, and the longer it takes users to sign on, the less happy they are. You can take the following steps to ensure that Active Directory is functioning efficiently: Defragment the database, check the integrity of the file that hosts the database, and perform a semantic analysis to check the logical integrity of the database. In this lesson, you will learn how to accomplish these tasks. You will also learn how to perform metadata cleanup, and how to create and view database snapshots.

> **After this lesson, you will be able to:**
> - Implement Active Directory database optimization.
> - Implement Active Directory metadata cleanup.
> - Implement Active Directory snapshots.
>
> **Estimated lesson time: 25 minutes**

Active Directory database optimization

There are several steps you can take to optimize your Active Directory database, including defragmenting the database, performing a file integrity check, and performing a semantic integrity check. When you defragment the Active Directory database, a new copy of the database file, Ntds.dit, is created. You can defragment the Active Directory database or perform other operations only if the database is offline. You can take the Active Directory database offline by stopping the AD DS service, which you can do from the Update Services console or by issuing the following command from an elevated Windows PowerShell prompt.

```
Stop-Service NTDS -force
```

You use the ntdsutil.exe utility to perform the fragmentation, as shown in Figure 4-16. Issue the following command.

```
ntdsutil.exe "activate instance ntds" files "compact to c:\\" quit quit
```

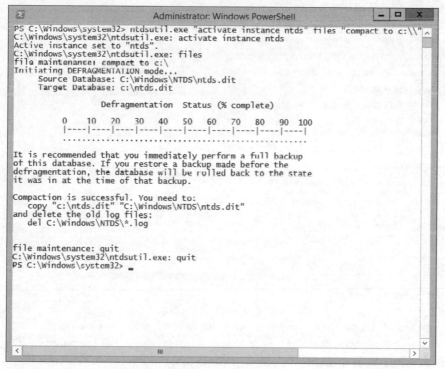

```
                    Administrator: Windows PowerShell                    _  □  x
PS C:\Windows\system32> ntdsutil.exe "activate instance ntds" files "compact to c:\\"
C:\Windows\system32\ntdsutil.exe: activate instance ntds
Active instance set to "ntds".
C:\Windows\system32\ntdsutil.exe: files
file maintenance: compact to c:\
Initiating DEFRAGMENTATION mode...
    Source Database: C:\Windows\NTDS\ntds.dit
    Target Database: c:\ntds.dit

              Defragmentation  Status (% complete)

      0    10   20   30   40   50   60   70   80   90   100
      |----|----|----|----|----|----|----|----|----|----|
      ...................................................

It is recommended that you immediately perform a full backup
of this database. If you restore a backup made before the
defragmentation, the database will be rolled back to the state
it was in at the time of that backup.

Compaction is successful. You need to:
    copy "c:\ntds.dit" "C:\Windows\NTDS\ntds.dit"
and delete the old log files:
    del C:\Windows\NTDS\*.log


file maintenance: quit
C:\Windows\system32\ntdsutil.exe: quit
PS C:\Windows\system32> _
```

FIGURE 4-16 Defragmenting the Active Directory database

After the defragmentation has completed, copy the defragmented database over the original located in C:\windows\NTDS\ntds.dit and delete all log files in the C:\windows\NTDS folder.

You can check the integrity of the file that stores the database using the ntdsutil.exe command, as shown in Figure 4-17. You can perform this check by issuing the following command from an elevated prompt when the AD DS service is stopped.

```
ntdsutil.exe "activate instance ntds" files integrity quit quit
```

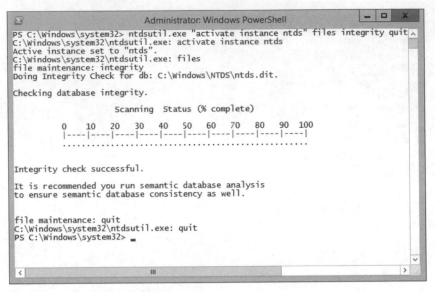

FIGURE 4-17 Database integrity check

To verify that the AD DS database is internally consistent, you can run a semantic consistency check. The semantic check, shown in Figure 4-18, can also repair the database if problems are detected. You can perform a semantic check using ntdsutil.exe by issuing the following command.

```
ntdsutil.exe "activate instance ntds" "semantic database analysis" "verbose on" "go
fixup" quit quit
```

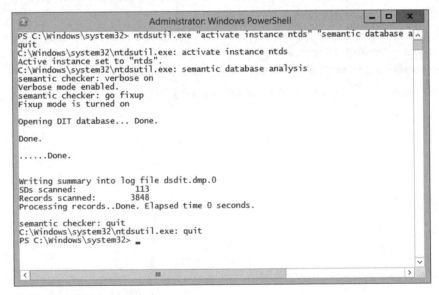

FIGURE 4-18 Semantic analysis

Active Directory metadata cleanup

The graceful way to remove a domain controller is to run the Active Directory Domain Services Configuration Wizard to remove AD DS, as shown in Figure 4-19. You can also remove the domain controller gracefully by using the Uninstall-ADDSDomainController cmdlet. When you do this, the domain controller is removed, all references to the domain controller in Active Directory are also removed, and any operations master roles that the domain controller hosted are transferred to other domain controllers in the domain.

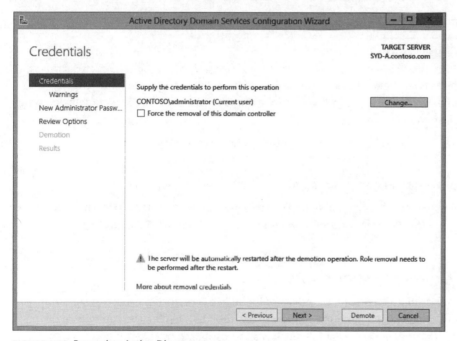

FIGURE 4-19 Removing Active Directory

 Active Directory *metadata cleanup* is necessary if a domain controller has been forcibly removed from Active Directory. Here's an example: An existing domain controller catches fire or is accidentally thrown out of a window by a systems administrator having a bad day. When this happens, references to the domain controller within Active Directory remain. These references, especially if the domain controller hosted operations master roles, can cause problems if not removed. Metadata cleanup is the process of removing these references.

If you use the Active Directory Users And Computers or Active Directory Sites And Services console to delete the computer account of a domain controller, the metadata associated with the domain controller are cleaned up. The console will prompt you, as shown in Figure 4-20, when you try to delete the account of a domain controller that can't be contacted. You confirm that you can't contact the domain controller. When you do this, metadata cleanup occurs automatically.

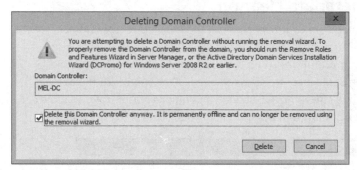

FIGURE 4-20 Deleting the domain controller

To remove server metadata using ntdsutil, issue the following command, where <ServerName> is the distinguished name of the domain controller whose metadata you want to remove from Active Directory.

```
Ntdsutil "metadata cleanup" "remove selected server <ServerName>"
```

> **MORE INFO** **ACTIVE DIRECTORY METADATA CLEANUP**
>
> To learn more about cleaning up Active Directory metadata, consult the following TechNet webpage at *http://technet.microsoft.com/en-us/library/cc816907(WS.10).aspx*.

Active Directory snapshots

 You can use ntdsutil.exe to create *snapshots* of the Active Directory database. A snapshot is a point-in-time copy of the database. You can use tools to examine the contents of the database, as it existed at that point in time. It is also possible to transfer objects from the snapshot of the Active Directory database back into the version currently used with your domain's domain controllers. The AD DS service must be running to create a snapshot.

To create a snapshot, execute the following command.

```
Ntdsutil snapshot "Activate Instance NTDS" create quit quit
```

Each snapshot is identified by a GUID. You can create a scheduled task to create snapshots on a regular basis. You can view a list of all current snapshots on a domain controller by running the following command.

```
Ntdsutil snapshot "list all" quit quit
```

To mount a snapshot, make a note of the GUID of the snapshot that you want to mount and then issue the following command.

```
Ntdsutil "activate instance ntds" snapshot "mount {GUID}" quit quit
```

> **NOTE MOUNTING SNAPSHOTS**
>
> When mounting snapshots, you must use the {} braces with the GUID. You can also use the snapshot number associated with the GUID when mounting the snapshot with the ntdsutil. exe command. This number is always an odd number.

When the snapshot mounts, take a note of the path associated with the snapshot. You use this path when mounting the snapshot with dsamain. For example, to use dsamain with the snapshot mounted as c:\$SNAP_201212291630_VOLUMEc$\, issue this command:

```
Dsamain /dbpath 'c:\$SNAP_201212291630_VOLUMEC$\Windows\NTDS\ntds.dit' /ldapport 50000
```

You can choose to mount the snapshot using any available TCP port number; 50000 is just easy to remember. Leave the Windows PowerShell windows open when performing this action. After the snapshot is mounted, you can access it using Active Directory Users And Computers. To do this, perform the following steps:

1. Open Active Directory Users And Computers.
2. Right-click the root node, and click Change Domain Controller.
3. In the Change Directory Server dialog box, shown in Figure 4-21, enter the name of the domain controller and the port, and click OK. You can then view the contents of the snapshot using Active Directory Users And Computers in the same way that you would the contents of the current directory.

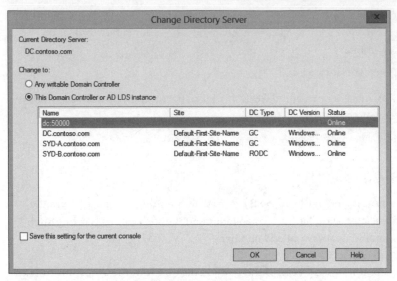

FIGURE 4-21 Connecting to a snapshot

You can dismount the snapshot by using Ctrl+C to close dsamain, and then executing the following command to dismount the snapshot.

```
Ntdsutil.exe "activate instance ntds" snapshot "unmount {GUID}" quit quit
```

Lesson summary

- The default location of the Active Directory database file is C:\Windows\NTDS\ntds.dit.
- You can defragment the Active Directory database file using ntdsutil.exe. You can perform this operation only if the AD DS service has stopped.
- You can check the integrity of the file that hosts the Active Directory database by using the ntdsutil.exe command. You can perform this operation only if the AD DS service has stopped.
- You can check the integrity of the semantic metadata of the database using ntdsutil. exe, which checks whether the database is internally consistent. Ntdsutil.exe can also repair any problems that arise during this check.
- You can perform metadata cleanup if a domain controller is forcibly removed from Active Directory by using Active Directory Users And Computers, or by using the Uninstall-ADDSDomainController cmdlet. You can also perform metadata cleanup using the ntdsutil.exe cmdlet.
- You can use the ntdsutil.exe cmdlet to take snapshots of Active Directory. You must take snapshots while the AD DS database is online.
- You use the dsamain command-line utility to mount Active Directory snapshots. You can navigate the mounted snapshot using Active Directory Users And Computers.

Lesson review

Answer the following questions to test your knowledge of the information in this lesson. You can find the answers to these questions and explanations of why each answer choice is correct or Incorrect In the "Answers" section at the end of this chapter.

1. Which of the following commands should you use to mount a snapshot of the AD DS database where {GUID} is the GUID associated with the snapshot?

   A. Ntdsutil.exe "activate instance ntds" snapshot "unmount {GUID}" quit quit

   B. Ntdsutil "activate instance ntds" snapshot "mount {GUID}" quit quit

   C. Ntdsutil snapshot "Activate Instance NTDS" create quit quit

   D. Ntdsutil.exe "activate instance ntds" "semantic database analysis" "verbose on" "go fixup" quit quit

2. Which of the following commands should you use to defragment the file that hosts the AD DS database?

   A. Ntdsutil.exe "activate instance ntds" files integrity quit quit

   B. Ntdsutil.exe "activate instance ntds" files "compact to c:\\" quit quit

   C. Ntdsutil.exe "activate instance ntds" snapshot "unmount {GUID}" quit quit

   D. Ntdsutil "activate instance ntds" snapshot "mount {GUID}" quit quit

3. Which of the following commands should you use to take a snapshot of the AD DS database?

   A. Ntdsutil snapshot "Activate Instance NTDS" create quit quit

   B. Ntdsutil.exe "activate instance ntds" "semantic database analysis" "verbose on" "go fixup" quit quit

   C. Ntdsutil.exe "activate instance ntds" files integrity quit quit

   D. Ntdsutil.exe "activate instance ntds" files "compact to c:\\" quit quit

4. Which of the following commands should you use to form a check of the integrity of the file that hosts the AD DS database?

   A. Ntdsutil.exe "activate instance ntds" "semantic database analysis" "verbose on" "go fixup" quit quit

   B. Ntdsutil.exe "activate instance ntds" files "compact to c:\\" quit quit

   C. Ntdsutil.exe "activate instance ntds" files integrity quit quit

   D. Ntdsutil "activate instance ntds" snapshot "mount {GUID}" quit quit

5. Which of the following commands should you use to check the logical integrity of the AD DS database?

   A. Ntdsutil snapshot "Activate Instance NTDS" create quit quit

   B. Ntdsutil.exe "activate instance ntds" files integrity quit quit

   C. Ntdsutil "activate instance ntds" snapshot "mount {GUID}" quit quit

   D. Ntdsutil.exe "activate instance ntds" "semantic database analysis" "verbose on" "go fixup" quit quit

Lesson 3: Recovering Active Directory

In this lesson, you'll learn how to configure the new tool to manage the Active Directory Recycle Bin and how you can use this tool to recover deleted objects.

> **After this lesson, you will be able to:**
> - Implement Active Directory Recycle Bin.
> - Implement Active Directory backup.
> - Implement Active Directory recovery.
>
> **Estimated lesson time: 45 minutes**

Active Directory Recycle Bin

The *Active Directory Recycle Bin* enables you to restore deleted Active Directory objects without the complexity of rebooting a domain controller computer into DSRM. Although the Active Directory Recycle Bin was available in Windows Server 2008 R2, the interface was command line only. This meant that performing an object restoration using the Active Directory Recycle Bin was as complicated as using DSRM. Combined with the necessity of upgrading the forest to the Windows Server 2008 R2 functional level, many administrators simply did not believe that the benefits outweighed the drawbacks, and did not bother with the technology.

The Active Directory Recycle Bin in Windows Server 2012 and Windows Server 2012 R2 provides a graphic interface, which makes it relatively straightforward for administrators to restore deleted items. The Active Directory Recycle Bin has the advantage that all link-valued and non-link-valued attributes of Active Directory deleted objects are stored with the object. This means that restored objects will retain attributes such as group membership and permissions that they had prior to deletion. You enable the Active Directory Recycle Bin on a forest-wide basis. Enabling the Active Directory Recycle Bin is a one-way operation, and after you enable Active Directory Recycle Bin, you can't disable it.

To enable Active Directory Recycle Bin, perform the following steps:

1. Ensure that the forest functional level is set to Windows Server 2008 R2 or higher.
2. In the Active Directory Administrative Center, select the root domain, and then click Enable Recycle Bin in the Tasks pane. You see the Enable Recycle Bin Confirmation dialog box shown in Figure 4-22.

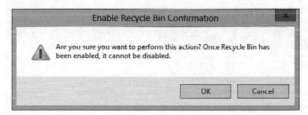

FIGURE 4-22 Enabling the Active Directory Recycle Bin

3. After you click OK, the Active Directory Recycle Bin is enabled in all domains in the forest.

You can use the Active Directory Recycle Bin only to restore objects that have been deleted since the Active Directory Recycle Bin was enabled. If there are objects that you need to restore that were deleted prior to enabling the Active Directory Recycle Bin, you have to use DSRM to accomplish this goal.

When you enable the Active Directory Recycle Bin using the default values, deleted objects can be recovered using the Active Directory Recycle Bin for 180 days. You can modify this value by changing the value of the msDS-deletedObjectLifetime attribute. You can modify the value of the msDS-deletedObjectLifetime attribute using the Set-ADObject cmdlet or the ldp.exe utility, as shown in Figure 4-23.

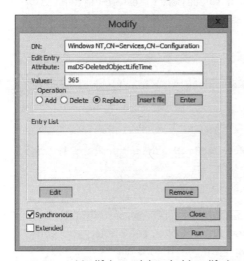

FIGURE 4-23 Modifying a deleted object lifetime

To recover items from the Active Directory Recycle Bin, perform the following steps:

1. Open Active Directory Administrative Center.
2. Navigate to the Deleted Objects container.
3. Select the object that you want to restore; in the Tasks pane, shown in Figure 4-24, click Restore if you want to restore it to its original location in Active Directory, or click Restore To if you want to restore it to an alternate location.

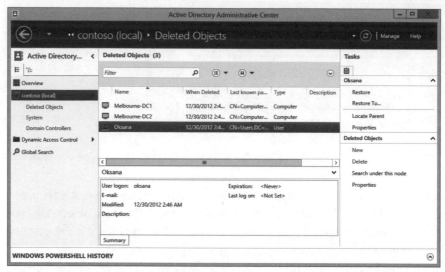

FIGURE 4-24 Recovering an item from the Active Directory Recycle Bin

With the Active Directory Recycle Bin, it isn't possible to restore child objects if a parent object is deleted. For example, you can't restore a single user account if the organizational unit (OU) that hosts the user account is also deleted. It is necessary to restore the deleted OU and then restore the deleted user account.

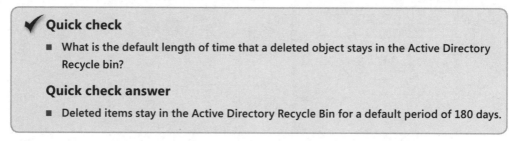

✔ **Quick check**

- What is the default length of time that a deleted object stays in the Active Directory Recycle bin?

Quick check answer

- Deleted items stay in the Active Directory Recycle Bin for a default period of 180 days.

Active Directory backup

Active Directory is backed up when you perform a backup of the server's system state. This occurs when you back up all critical volumes on a domain controller. The primary tool you use for backing up this data is Windows Server Backup, which is not installed by default on computers running Windows Server 2012 or Windows Server 2012 R2. You can install Windows Server Backup as a feature using the Add Roles And Features Wizard, as shown in Figure 4-25.

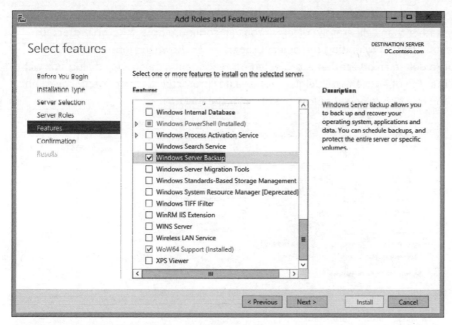

FIGURE 4-25 Installing Windows Server Backup

After Windows Server Backup is installed, you can perform a full server backup, as shown in Figure 4-26, to back up the AD DS database.

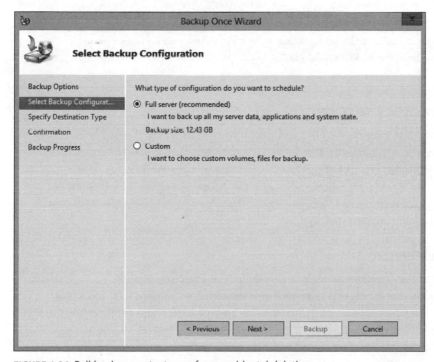

FIGURE 4-26 Full backup protects you from accidental deletion

The majority of restore operations occur because Active Directory objects were accidentally (rather than deliberately) deleted. You can configure objects to be protected from accidental deletion by editing the object properties, as shown in Figure 4-27. When you attempt to delete an object that is protected from accidental deletion, a dialog box will inform you that the object can't be deleted because it is protected from accidental deletion. This protection must be removed before the object is deleted.

FIGURE 4-27 Protecting from accidental deletion

Active Directory recovery

The simplest way to recover deleted Active Directory objects is to use the Active Directory Recycle Bin. In some environments, the Active Directory Recycle Bin may not be enabled for business reasons; for example, if the forest is still operating at the Windows Server 2003 or Windows Server 2008 forest functional level. If the Active Directory Recycle Bin is not available, and you need to recover a deleted object, you'll need to restart the computer in DSRM and perform an authoritative restore.

Authoritative restore

You use an *authoritative restore* to recover deleted Active Directory objects. You can perform an authoritative restore for objects that were deleted within the value of the tombstone lifetime setting. The default value of the tombstone lifetime is 180 days for forests set to the Windows Server 2003, Windows Server 2008, Windows Server 2008 R2, Windows Server 2012, and Windows Server 2012 R2 functional level. You can modify this attribute by using ADSIEdit or by using the Set-ADObject Windows PowerShell cmdlet. Where possible, you should perform an authoritative restore on a server that also holds the Global Catalog role.

You restore from a backup that holds the items that were deleted. You then mark those items as authoritative before replication can occur. When you mark an object for authoritative restore, the version number of the object is incremented higher than the version that applies to the deleted object. This higher version means that the restored object overwrites the deleted object, which will have a lower version number.

You can use authoritative restore to restore the following objects:

- Objects in domain directory partitions. These objects must be restored on any domain controller in the domain.

- Objects in application directory partitions. These objects need to be restored on domain controllers that host that specific application directory partition. If the application directory partition is deleted entirely, the restoration must occur on the computer that holds the domain-naming master operations master role.

- Objects in configuration directory partitions. These objects can be restored on any domain controller in the forest.

You perform an authoritative restore from DSRM, which is a special mode in which you can start a domain controller. To start a domain controller in DSRM, run msconfig.exe, select the Boot tab, and choose the Safe Boot option with Active Directory Repair, as shown in Figure 4-28. You will need the DRSM password to enter DSRM. It is set during the installation of the domain controller, but you can reset it using the following command:

```
Ntdsutil.exe "Set DSRM Password" "Reset Password on server NULL" quit quit
```

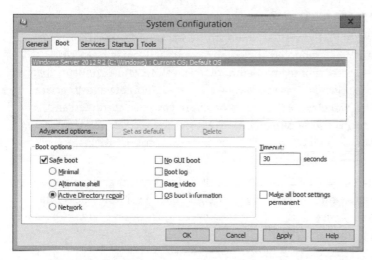

FIGURE 4-28 Booting into DSRM mode

To perform an authoritative restore, perform the following steps:

1. Locate the most recent system state backup for the domain controller on which you want to perform the restore.

2. Restart the domain controller in DSRM mode and enter the DSRM password.

3. Use Windows Server Backup to restore the system state data.

4. Use the ntdsutil.exe command with the "authoritative restore" option to restore the item. For example, to restore the object Neptune from the OU Planets in the domain contoso.com, issue the following command.

   ```
   Ntdsutil.exe "authoritative restore" "restore object
   cn=Neptune,ou=Planets,dc=contoso,dc=com" quit quit
   ```

5. If you need to restore an OU and all objects underneath it, you can use the "restore subtree" option. For example, to restore all objects in the Planets OU of the contoso.com domain, issue the following command.

   ```
   Ntdsutil.exe "authoritative restore" "restore subtree
   OU=Planets,dc=contoso,dc=com" quit quit
   ```

6. Restart the domain controller. The changes will replicate, restoring the deleted items.

> **MORE INFO**   **AUTHORITATIVE RESTORE**
>
> Although this article refers to Windows Server 2008 R2, the advice it contains also applies to Windows Server 2012 and Windows Server 2012 R2. You can find it at *http://technet. microsoft.com/en-us/library/cc816878(WS.10).aspx.*

Non-authoritative restore

When you perform a non-authoritative restore, you restore a backup of Active Directory that's in a good known state. When rebooted, the domain controller contacts replication partners and overwrites the contents of the non-authoritative restore with all updates that have occurred to the database since the backup was taken. Non-authoritative restores are appropriate when the Active Directory database on a database has been corrupted and needs to be recovered. You don't use a non-authoritative restore to recover deleted items, as any deleted items that are restored when performing the non-authoritative restore will be overwritten when changes replicate from other domain controllers.

Performing a full system recovery on a domain controller functions in a similar way to performing a non-authoritative restore. When the recovered domain controller boots, all changes that have occurred in Active Directory since the backup was taken overwrite existing information in the database.

Other methods of recovering deleted items

Although the recommended way of ensuring that deleted Active Directory objects are recoverable is to enable the Active Directory Recycle Bin or to perform an authoritative restore using DSRM, you can also use tombstone reanimation to recover a deleted object.

Tombstone reanimation involves using the ldp.exe utility to modify the attributes of the deleted object so that it no longer has the deleted attribute. You should use tombstone reanimation only if no backups of the system state data exist and you haven't enabled the Active Directory Recycle Bin because it can lead to unpredictable results.

Although Active Directory snapshots do represent copies of the Active Directory database at a particular point in time, you should use mounted snapshots to determine which backup contains the items you want to authoritatively restore. It is possible to export objects from snapshots and to reimport them into Active Directory using tools such as LDIFDE, but this can lead to unpredictable results.

Lesson summary

- The Active Directory Recycle Bin is enabled on a per-forest basis and can't be disabled after it's enabled.
- The Active Directory Recycle Bin requires a minimum forest functional level of Windows Server 2008 R2.
- By default, objects stay in the Active Directory Recycle Bin for 180 days. You can modify this length of time by changing the value of the msDS-deletedObjectLifetime attribute using the Set-ADObject cmdlet or the ldp.exe utility.
- Items recovered from the Active Directory Recycle Bin retain their original attributes, such as group membership and permissions.
- You can't use the Active Directory Recycle Bin to recover an item deleted before you enabled Active Directory Recycle Bin.
- You can back up the Active Directory database by backing up the system state data of a domain controller.
- Perform an authoritative restore from DSRM to recover deleted objects if the Active Directory Recycle Bin has not been enabled.
- Where possible, you should perform authoritative restore operations on a Global Catalog server.

Lesson review

Answer the following questions to test your knowledge of the information in this lesson. You can find the answers to these questions and explanations of why each answer choice is correct or incorrect in the "Answers" section at the end of this chapter.

1. What is the minimum forest functional level required to enable Active Directory Recycle Bin?

   A. Windows Server 2003

   B. Windows Server 2008

   C. Windows Server 2008 R2

   D. Windows Server 2012

2. Which console enables you to use Active Directory Recycle Bin? (Choose all that apply.)

   A. Active Directory Users And Computers

   B. Active Directory Administrative Center

   C. Active Directory Sites And Services

   D. Active Directory Domain

3. A domain controller's AD DS database has become corrupt. You have a backup of all critical volumes, which include system state data, from earlier in the week. No important Active Directory objects have been deleted. Which of the following steps do you need to take to recover Active Directory? (Choose all that apply.)

   A. Restart in DSRM.

   B. Restore system state data.

   C. Perform an authoritative restore.

   D. Perform a non-authoritative restore.

4. Which of the following techniques can you use to recover deleted user accounts in a three-domain forest configured to run at the Windows Server 2008 forest functional level? (Choose all that apply.)

   A. Authoritative restore using DSRM.

   B. Non-authoritative restore using DSRM.

   C. Restore by using the Active Directory Recycle Bin.

   D. Restore by editing Active Directory attributes with ldp.exe.

5. You want to minimize the chance that important user and computer accounts can be deleted. Which of the following steps can you take to accomplish this goal?

   A. Enable the Active Directory Recycle Bin.

   B. Configure Deleted Item Protection.

   C. Enable DSRM.

   D. Change the value of the msDS-deletedObjectLifetime attribute.

Practice exercises

The goal of this section is to provide you with hands-on practice with the following:

- Managing operations master roles
- Deploying a read-only domain controller
- Configuring Global Catalog server placement
- Defragmenting the AD DS database
- Performing file and semantic integrity checks in the Active Directory database
- Creating and viewing snapshots of the AD DS database
- Enabling and using Active Directory Recycle Bin
- Performing Active Directory backup and restore

To perform the exercises in this section, you need access to an evaluation version of Windows Server 2012 R2. You should also have access to virtual machines SYD-DC, MEL-DC, CBR-DC, and ADL-DC, the setup instructions for which are described in the Introduction. You should ensure that you have a checkpoint of these virtual machines that you can revert to at the end of the practice exercises. You should revert the virtual machines to this initial state prior to beginning these exercises.

Exercise 1: Domain controller installation

In this exercise, you perform several domain controller management tasks, including transferring operations master roles, deploying an RODC, configuring a Global Catalog server, and using UGMC. To complete this exercise, perform the following steps:

1. Power on computers SYD-DC and MEL-DC.
2. Sign on to MEL-DC as Administrator with the password **Pa$$w0rd.**
3. Open the Windows PowerShell prompt and type the following commands.

   ```
   Add-Computer -DomainName contoso.com
   ```

4. In the Windows PowerShell Credentials dialog box type **don_funk@contoso.com** and **Pa$$w0rd**, and click OK.
5. Type the following command in the Windows PowerShell prompt to restart the computer.

   ```
   Restart-Computer
   ```

6. Sign on to computer SYD-DC as **Contoso\don_funk**.
7. In Server Manager, click All Servers.
8. On the Manage menu, click Add Servers.
9. In the Add Servers dialog box, click Find Now.

10. In the list of servers, click MEL-DC, click the arrow to add MEL-DC to the selected list, as shown in Figure 4-29, and click OK.

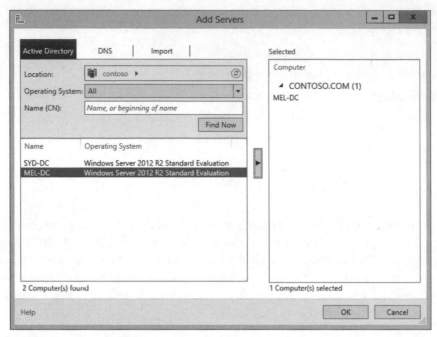

FIGURE 4-29 Adding a server

11. In Server Manager, click All Servers, and click MEL-DC.

12. In the Manage menu, click Add Roles And Features.

13. On the Before You Begin page of the Add Roles And Features Wizard, click Next.

14. On the Installation Type page, click Role-Based Or Feature-Based Installation, and click Next.

15. On the Select Destination Server page, shown in Figure 4-30, click MEL-DC.contoso.com, and click Next.

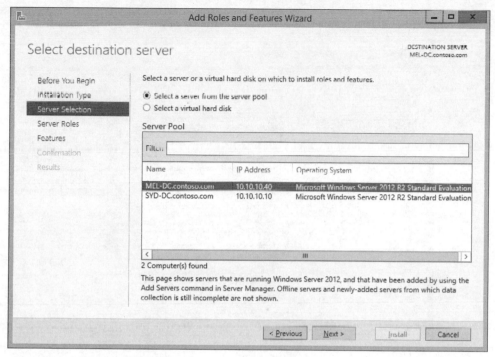

FIGURE 4-30 Selecting a destination server

16. In the Select Server Roles dialog box, click Active Directory Domain Services, as shown in Figure 4-31. The Add Roles And Features dialog box opens.

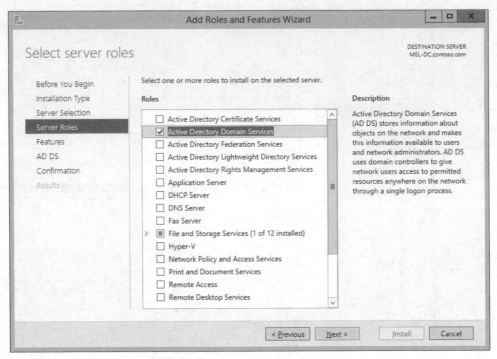

FIGURE 4-31 Adding the Active Directory Domain Services role

17. In the Add Roles And Features dialog box, click Add Features.

18. On the Select Server Roles page, click Next.

19. On the Select Features page, click Next.

20. On the Active Directory Domain Services page, click Next.

21. On the Confirmation page, select the Restart The Destination Server Automatically If Required check box, as shown in Figure 4-32, click Install, and click Close.

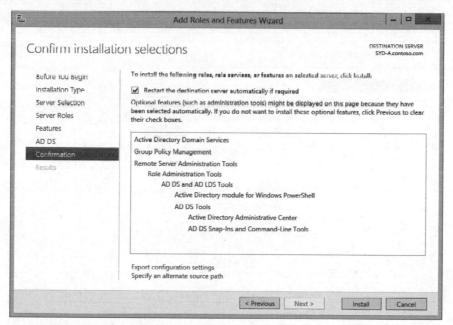

FIGURE 4-32 Restart the server if required

22. In Server Manager, click All Servers, and click MEL-DC. Click the Warning notification item. Click Promote This Server To A Domain Controller.

23. On the Deployment Configuration page of the Active Directory Domain Services Configuration Wizard, click Add A Domain Controller To An Existing Domain, and ensure that the Domain option is set to Contoso.com, as shown in Figure 4-33.

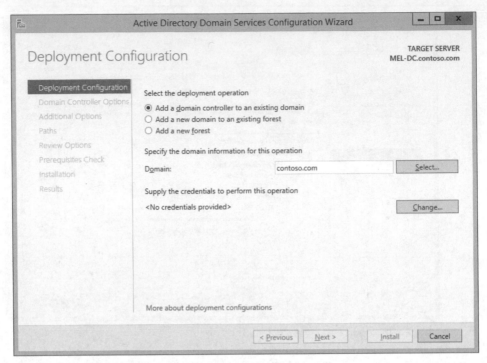

FIGURE 4-33 Adding a domain controller to an existing domain

24. Click Change. In the Windows Security dialog box, configure the following credentials and click OK:

    ■ Username: **Contoso\don_funk**

    ■ Password: **Pa$$w0rd**

25. In the Deployment Configuration dialog box, click Next.

26. On the Domain Controller Options page, configure and confirm the DSRM password **Pa$$w0rd**, as shown in Figure 4-34.

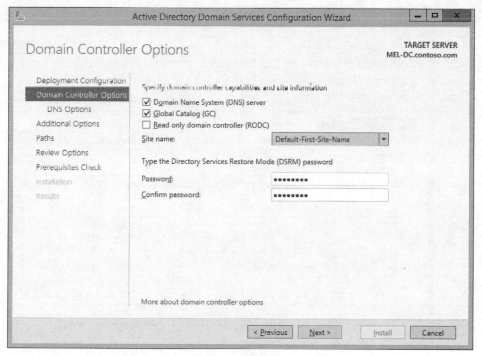

FIGURE 4-34 Configuring domain controller options

27. On the DNS Options page, click Next.

28. On the Additional Options page, click the arrow next to Replicate From, and click SYD-DC.contoso.com, as shown in Figure 4-35. Click Next.

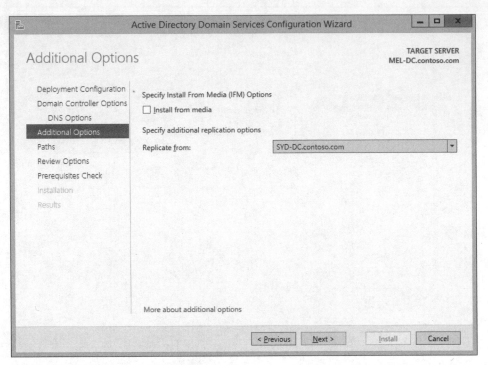

FIGURE 4-35 Configuring additional options

29. On the Paths page, click Next.

30. On the Review Options page, click Next.

31. On the Prerequisites Check page, review the results to ensure that only Warning messages are present and no Error messages are present, as shown in Figure 4-36, and then click Install.

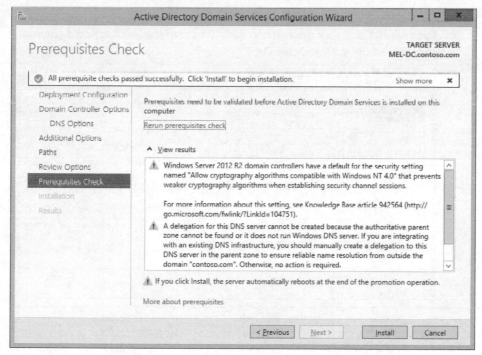

FIGURE 4-36 Prerequisite check

32. Click Close.

33. In Server Manager, click the AD DS node, and verify the presence of MEL-DC as a domain controller.

Exercise 2: RODC deployment

In this exercise, you deploy an RODC. To complete this exercise, perform the following steps:

1. Power on ADL-DC and sign on as Administrator with the password **Pa$$w0rd**.

2. Open the Windows PowerShell prompt and type the following commands.

```
Add-Computer -DomainName contoso.com
```

3. In the Windows PowerShell Credentials dialog box type **don_funk@contoso.com** and **Pa$$w0rd**, and click OK.

4. Type the following command in the Windows PowerShell prompt to restart the computer.

```
Restart-Computer
```

5. Ensure you are signed on to SYD-DC as contoso\don_funk.

6. In Server Manager on SYD-DC, click All Servers.

7. Click Manage, and click Add Servers.

8. In the Add Servers dialog box, click Find Now.

9. Click ADL-DC and click the arrow to add ADL-DC to the list of selected computers, as shown in Figure 4-37, and click OK.

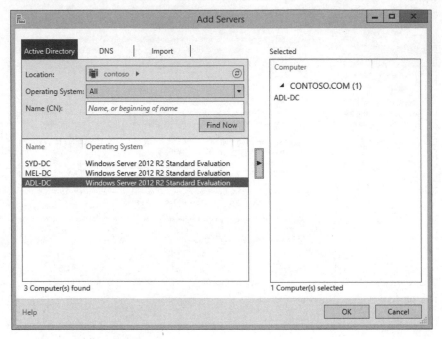

FIGURE 4-37 Adding servers

10. Click All Servers, and then click ADL-DC. On the Manage menu, click Add Roles And Features.

11. On the Before You Begin page, click Next.

12. On the Installation Type page, click Role-Based Or Feature-Based Installation, and click Next.

13. On the Select Destination Server page, click ADL-DC.contoso.com, as shown in Figure 4-38, and click Next.

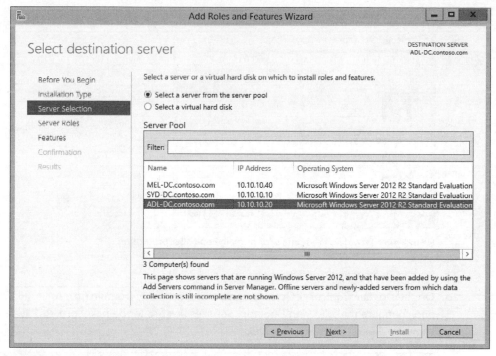

FIGURE 4-38 Selecting ADL-DC.contoso.com

14. On the Server Roles page, click Active Directory Domain Services. You will be prompted by the Add Roles And Features dialog box. Click Add Features, and click Next.

15. On the Features page, click Next.

16. On the Active Directory Domain Services page, click Next.

17. On the Confirmation page, click Restart The Destination Server Automatically If Required, click Install, and click Close.

18. In Server Manager, click All Servers, and click ADL-DC.

19. Click the Warning notification icon, and click Promote This Server To A Domain Controller.

20. On the Deployment Configuration page, click Add A Domain Controller To An Existing Domain, and click Change next to <No Credentials Provided>.

21. In the Windows Security dialog box, configure the following credentials, as shown in Figure 4-39, and click OK.

  ■ Username. **Contoso\don_funk**
  ■ Password: **Pa$$w0rd**

FIGURE 4-39 Providing credentials for domain controller promotion

22. On the Deployment Configuration page, click Next.

23. On the Domain Controller Options page, click Read Only Domain Controller (RODC), and configure the following Directory Services Restore Mode password: **Pa$$w0rd**, as shown in Figure 4-40, and click Next.

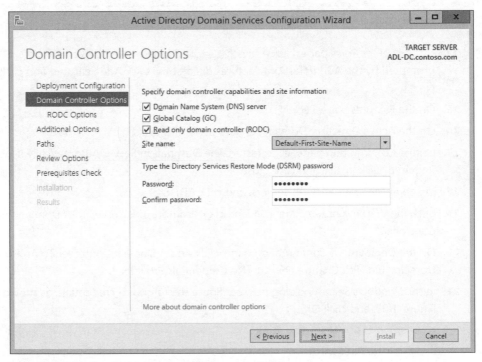

FIGURE 4-40 Configuring a domain controller as an RODC

24. On the RODC Options page, click BUILTIN\Backup Operators, and click Remove. Click BUILTIN\Account Operators, and click Remove, as shown in Figure 4-41, and click Next.

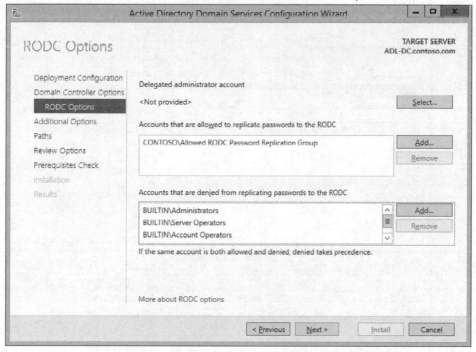

FIGURE 4-41 Configuring RODC password replication

25. On the Additional Options page, click Any Domain Controller, and then click MEL-DC. contoso.com. Click Next.

26. On the Paths page, shown in Figure 4-42, review the default paths, and then click Next.

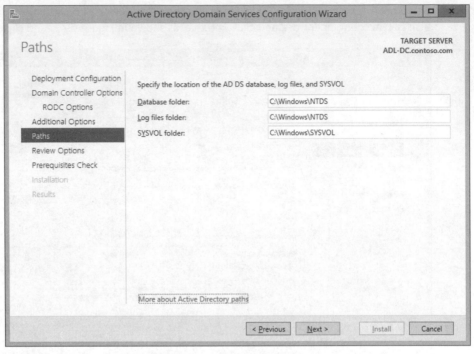

FIGURE 4-42 Configuring database, log files, and SYSVOL location

27. On the Review Options page, click Next.

28. On the Prerequisites Check page, verify that no error messages are present, and click Install. When the installation completes, click Close.

Exercise 3: Transfer operations master roles

In this exercise, you transfer several operations master roles from SYD-DC to MEL-DC. To complete this exercise, perform the following steps:

1. In Server Manager on SYD-DC, click the Tools menu, and then click Active Directory Users And Computers.

2. Click Contoso.com. On the Action menu, click Change Domain Controller.

3. In the Change Directory Server dialog box, click MEL-DC.contoso.com, as shown in Figure 4-43, and then click OK.

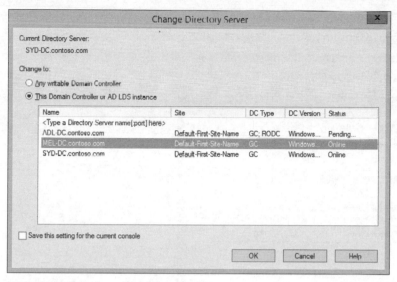

FIGURE 4-43 Selecting a domain controller

4. In Active Directory Users And Computers, click Contoso.com. On the Action menu, click Operations Masters.

5. In the PDC tab of the Operations Masters dialog box, click Change.

6. In the Active Directory Domain Services dialog box, click Yes, and then click OK.

7. Verify that the PDC tab of the Operations Master dialog box shows the PDC operations master as MEL-DC.contoso.com, as shown in Figure 4-44, and then click the Infrastructure tab.

FIGURE 4-44 Transferring the PDC emulator role

8. On the Infrastructure tab, click Change.

9. In the Active Directory Domain Services dialog box, click Yes, and then click OK.

10. Verify that the infrastructure master role is assigned to MEL-DC.contoso.com, as shown on Figure 4-45, and click Close.

FIGURE 4-45 Transferring the infrastructure master role

11. Close Active Directory Users And Computers.

12. Right-click the Windows PowerShell item on the taskbar, and click Run As Administrator.

13. Type the following command to register the Active Directory Schema snap-in.

```
Regsvr32.exe schmmgmt.dll
```

14. In the RegSvr32 dialog box, click OK.

15. Close the Windows PowerShell window.

16. Right-click the Start icon, click Run, and type **mmc.exe**.

17. In the Console1 – Console Root dialog box, click File, and click Add/Remove Snap-In.

18. In the Add Or Remove Snap-Ins dialog box, click Active Directory Schema, and click Add, as shown in Figure 4-46. Click OK.

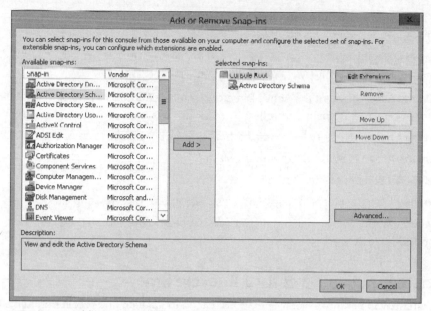

FIGURE 4-46 Adding an Active Directory Schema snap-in

19. In Console1, click Active Directory Schema.

20. On the Action menu, click Change Active Directory Domain Controller.

21. In the Change Directory Server dialog box, click MEL-DC.contoso.com, and click OK.

22. In the Active Directory Schema dialog box, click OK.

23. In Console1, click Active Directory Schema.

24. On the Action menu, click Operations Master.

25. In the Change Schema Master dialog box, shown in Figure 4-47, click Change.

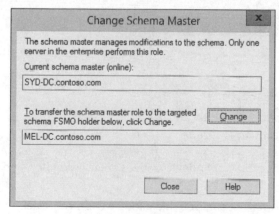

FIGURE 4-47 Changing the schema master

26. In the Active Directory Schema dialog box, click Yes, and then click OK.

27. Verify that the schema master role has been transferred to MEL-DC.contoso.com, and click Close.

28. Close Console1.

29. On the Tools menu, click Active Directory Domains And Trusts.

30. On the Action menu of the Active Directory Domains And Trusts console, click Change Active Directory Domain Controller.

31. In the Change Directory Server dialog box, click MEL-DC.contoso.com, and click OK.

32. On the Action menu, click Operations Master.

33. In the Operations Master dialog box, click Change.

34. In the Active Directory Domains And Trusts dialog box, click Yes, and click OK.

35. Verify that the domain naming master role has been moved to MEL-DC.contoso.com, and click Close.

Exercise 4: Active Directory Recycle Bin

In this exercise, you perform several operations related to deleting and recovering items from Active Directory. To complete this exercise, perform the following steps:

1. On the Tools menu of the Server Manager console, click Active Directory Administrative Center.

2. In the Active Directory Administrative Center, click Contoso (Local).

3. In the Tasks pane, click Change Domain Controller.

4. In the Change Domain Controller dialog box, click MEL-DC, and click Change.

5. In the Tasks pane of the Active Directory Administrative Center, click Enable Recycle Bin.

6. In the Enable Recycle Bin Confirmation dialog box, shown in Figure 4-48, click OK.

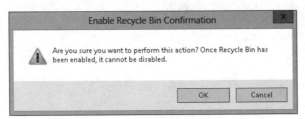

FIGURE 4-48 Enabling the Active Directory Recycle Bin

7. Review the message in the Active Directory Administrative Center dialog box, and click OK.

8. In the Active Directory Administrative Center, double-click the Users container.

9. In the Tasks pane, click New, and click User.

10. In the Create User dialog box, configure the following information and click OK:

- Full name: **Kim Akers**
- User SamAccountName: **contoso\kim_akers**

11. In the Tasks pane, click New, and click Group.

12. In the Create Group dialog box, configure the following information and click OK:

- Group Name: **Don_Funk_Reports**
- Members: **Contoso\don_funk, Contoso\kim_akers**

13. In the Active Directory Administrative Center, hold down the Ctrl key and click Kim Akers and Don_Funk_Reports.

14. In the Tasks pane, click Delete.

15. In the Delete Confirmation dialog box, click Yes.

16. In Active Directory Administrative Center, click Contoso (Local).

17. Double-click the Deleted Objects container. If this container is not present, click Refresh.

18. Verify that Kim Akers and Don_Funk_Reports are present, as shown in Figure 4-49

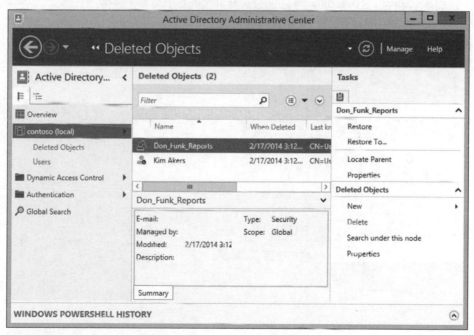

FIGURE 4-49 Recycle Bin contents

19. Select both Don_Funk_Reports and Kim Akers.

20. In the Tasks pane, click Restore.

21. Click the Users container. Verify that Kim Akers and Don_Funk_Reports have been restored.

22. Verify that Don Funk and Kim Akers are members of the restored Don_Funk_Reports security group.

Suggested practice exercises

The following additional practice exercises are designed to give you more opportunities to practice what you've learned and to help you successfully master the lessons presented in this chapter.

- **Exercise 1**   Remove the Global Catalog server role from SYD-DC.
- **Exercise 2**   Shut down MEL-DC to simulate irrecoverable failure of this server. Use Active Directory Users And Computers to clean up the Active Directory metadata. Verify that the operations master roles have been restored to SYD-DC.
- **Exercise 3**   Create a new OU and populate it with two user accounts. Configure one of the user accounts to be protected from deletion. Attempt to delete the user account. Remove the deletion protection and then delete the OU and the two user accounts. Recover only one of the user accounts.

Answers

This section contains the answers to the lesson review questions in this chapter.

Lesson 1

1. **Correct answers: A, B, and D**

   A. **Correct.** To create copies of virtualized domain controllers, the hypervisor on which the virtual machine (VM) is running must support VM GenerationID.

   B. **Correct.** To create a copy of a virtualized domain controller, the source domain controller must be a member of the Cloneable Domain Controllers security group.

   C. **Incorrect.** The schema master does not need to be online or running Windows Server 2012 or Windows Server 2012 R2 for domain controller cloning to function.

   D. **Correct.** The PDC emulator must be online and running Windows Server 2012 or Windows Server 2012 R2 for domain controller cloning to function.

2. **Correct answer: B**

   A. **Incorrect.** The infrastructure master is responsible for keeping track of changes made in other domains that influence objects in the local domain.

   B. **Correct.** The PDC emulator is responsible for managing password changes, synchronizing clocks, functioning as the master browser, and managing updates to Group Policy.

   C. **Incorrect.** The RID master generates pools of relative identifiers. They are combined with identifiers generated by domain controllers to ensure that domain SIDs are unique.

   D. **Incorrect.** The domain-naming master is responsible for managing the addition and deletion of domains and application partitions in the forest.

   E. **Incorrect.** The schema master is responsible for managing updates made to the Active Directory schema.

3. **Correct answer: E**

   A. **Incorrect.** The infrastructure master is responsible for keeping track of changes made in other domains that influence objects in the local domain.

   B. **Incorrect.** The PDC emulator is responsible for managing password changes, synchronizing clocks, functioning as the master browser, and managing updates to Group Policy.

   C. **Incorrect.** The RID master generates pools of relative identifiers. They are combined with identifiers generated by domain controllers to ensure that domain SIDs are unique.

   D. **Incorrect.** The domain-naming master is responsible for managing the addition and deletion of domains and application partitions in the forest.

E. **Correct.** The schema master is responsible for managing updates made to the Active Directory schema.

4. **Correct answer: C**

A. **Incorrect.** The infrastructure master is responsible for keeping track of changes made in other domains that influence objects in the local domain.

B. **Incorrect.** The PDC emulator is responsible for managing password changes, synchronizing clocks, functioning as the master browser, and managing updates to Group Policy.

C. **Correct.** The RID master generates pools of relative identifiers. They are combined with identifiers generated by domain controllers to ensure that domain SIDs are unique.

D. **Incorrect.** The domain-naming master is responsible for managing the addition and deletion of domains and application partitions in the forest.

E. **Incorrect.** The schema master is responsible for managing updates made to the Active Directory schema.

5. **Correct answer: D**

A. **Incorrect.** The infrastructure master is responsible for keeping track of changes made in other domains that influence objects in the local domain.

B. **Incorrect.** The PDC emulator master is responsible for managing password changes, synchronizing clocks, functioning as the master browser, and managing updates to Group Policy.

C. **Incorrect.** The RID master generates pools of relative identifiers. They are combined with identifiers generated by domain controllers to ensure that domain SIDs are unique.

D. **Correct.** The domain-naming master is responsible for managing the addition and deletion of domains, and application partitions in the forest.

E. **Incorrect.** The schema master is responsible for managing updates made to the Active Directory schema.

Lesson 2

1. **Correct answer: B**

A. **Incorrect.** You use this command to dismount a snapshot.

B. **Correct.** You use this command to mount a snapshot.

C. **Incorrect.** You use this command to create a snapshot.

D. **Incorrect.** You use this command to perform a semantic analysis of the Active Directory database.

2. **Correct answer: B**

    A. **Incorrect**. You use this command to perform an integrity check of the file that hosts the Active Directory database.

    B. **Correct.** You use this command to defragment the AD DS database.

    C. **Incorrect.** You use this command to dismount a snapshot.

    D. **Incorrect.** You use this command to mount a snapshot.

3. **Correct answers: A and D**

    A. **Correct.** You use this command to create a snapshot.

    B. **Incorrect.** You use this command to perform a check of the logical integrity of the Active Directory database.

    C. **Incorrect.** You use this command to perform an integrity check of the file that hosts the Active Directory database.

    D. **Correct.** You use this command to defragment the AD DS database.

4. **Correct answer: C**

    A. **Incorrect.** You use this command to perform a check of the logical integrity of the Active Directory database.

    B. **Incorrect.** You use this command to defragment the AD DS database.

    C. **Correct.** You use this command to perform an integrity check of the file that hosts the Active Directory database.

    D. **Incorrect.** You use this command to mount a snapshot.

5. **Correct answer: D**

    A. **Incorrect.** You use this command to create a snapshot.

    B. **Incorrect.** You use this command to perform an integrity check of the file that hosts the Active Directory database.

    C. **Incorrect.** You use this command to mount a snapshot.

    D. **Correct.** You use this command to perform a check of the logical integrity of the Active Directory database.

Lesson 3

1. **Correct answer: C**

    A. **Incorrect.** The minimum forest functional level required to enable the Active Directory Recycle Bin is Windows Server 2008 R2.

    B. **Incorrect.** The minimum forest functional level required to enable the Active Directory Recycle Bin is Windows Server 2008 R2.

    C. **Correct.** The minimum forest functional level required to enable the Active Directory Recycle Bin is Windows Server 2008 R2.

    D. **Incorrect.** The minimum forest functional level required to enable the Active Directory Recycle Bin is Windows Server 2008 R2.

2. **Correct answer: B**

   A. **Incorrect:** The Active Directory Recycle Bin is available through Active Directory Administrative Center.

   B. **Correct.** The Active Directory Recycle Bin is available through Active Directory Administrative Center.

   C. **Incorrect.** The Active Directory Recycle Bin is available through Active Directory Administrative Center.

   D. **Incorrect.** The Active Directory Recycle Bin is available through Active Directory Administrative Center.

3. **Correct answers: B and D**

   A. **Incorrect.** You only have to restart in DSRM when performing an authoritative restore.

   B. **Correct.** Restoring the system state data restores the uncorrupted Active Directory database.

   C. **Incorrect.** You only have to perform an authoritative restore when you are recovering deleted items.

   D. **Correct.** Performing a non-authoritative restore enables you to recover the AD DS database when it has become corrupted.

4. **Correct answers: A and D**

   A. **Correct.** In environments in which the Active Directory Recycle Bin is not available, you need to perform an authoritative restore to recover deleted Active Directory objects.

   B. **Incorrect.** You can't use a non-authoritative restore to recover deleted items.

   C. **Incorrect.** You can't use the Active Directory Recycle Bin with a forest configured to run at the Windows Server 2008 forest functional level.

   D. **Correct.** Although it is possible to restore items by editing active directory attributes, this method is not recommended.

5. **Correct answer: B**

   A. **Incorrect.** Enabling the Active Directory Recycle Bin does not minimize the chance that items will be deleted.

   B. **Correct.** Configuring deleted item protection minimizes the chance that a specific item will be deleted.

   C. **Incorrect.** You use DSRM to recover deleted items. You can't use this mode to minimize the chance that items will not be deleted.

   D. **Incorrect.** Changing the value of this attribute modifies how long you have to recover items using Active Directory Recycle Bin.

CHAPTER 5

Managing Group Policy application and infrastructure

There is far more to managing Group Policy than knowing the location of specific policy items. After your environment has more than a couple of Group Policy Objects (GPOs), you have to start thinking about issues such as how they apply, who can edit them, what to do if substantive changes in policy need to be rolled back, and how you can track changes in Group Policy over time. In this chapter, you'll learn how to back up, restore, import, and export GPOs. You'll learn how to delegate the process of editing and applying GPOs, and how to resolve configuration problems related to the application of Group Policy.

Lessons in this chapter:

- Lesson 1: Maintaining Group Policy Object **241**
- Lesson 2: Managing the application of Group Policy **253**

Before you begin

To complete the practice exercises in this chapter:

- You need to have deployed computers SYD-DC, MEL-DC, and ADL-DC, as described in the Introduction, using the evaluation edition of Windows Server 2012 R2.

Lesson 1: Maintaining Group Policy Object

As an experienced systems administrator pursuing certification, you have a reasonable idea of how to use Group Policy. The administration of Group Policy doesn't just occur at the level of configuring individual policies. In large organizations with many policies, it's necessary to have a maintenance strategy. Ensuring that important Group Policy Objects (GPOs) are backed up and recoverable is as important as backing up and recovering other critical services such as DNS and Dynamic Host Configuration Protocol (DHCP). In this lesson, you'll learn how to back up, restore, import, and copy GPOs. You'll also learn how to delegate the management of GPOs.

Managing Group Policy Objects

As an experienced systems administrator, you are aware that GPOs enable you to configure settings for multiple users and computers. After you get beyond editing GPOs to configure settings, you need to start thinking about issues such as GPO maintenance. For example, if an important document is lost, you need to know how to recover it from backup. Do you know what to do if someone accidentally deletes a GPO that has hundreds of settings configured over a long period of time?

The main tool you'll use for managing GPOs is the Group Policy Management Console (GPMC), shown in Figure 5-1. You can use this console to back up, restore, import, copy, and migrate. You can also use this console to delegate GPO management tasks.

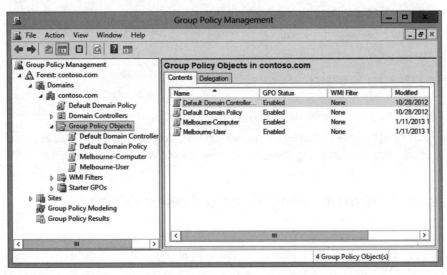

FIGURE 5-1 GPMC

There are also a substantial number of cmdlets available in the Windows PowerShell Group Policy module, including the following:

- **Get-GPO**   Enables you to view GPOs. The output of this cmdlet is shown in Figure 5-2.
- **Backup-GPO**   Enables you to back up GPOs.
- **Import-GPO**   Enables you to import a backed-up GPO into a specified GPO.

- **New-GPO** Enables you to create a new GPO.
- **Copy-GPO** Enables you to copy a GPO.
- **Rename-GPO** Enables you to change a GPO's name.
- **Restore-GPO** Enables you to restore a backed up GPO to its original location.
- **Remove-GPO** Enables you to remove a GPO.

```
UserVersion        : AD Version: 0, SysVol Version: 0
ComputerVersion    : AD Version: 0, SysVol Version: 0
WmiFilter          :

DisplayName        : Default Domain Policy
DomainName         : contoso.com
Owner              : CONTOSO\Domain Admins
Id                 : 31b2f340-016d-11d2-945f-00c04fb984f9
GpoStatus          : AllSettingsEnabled
Description        :
CreationTime       : 2/11/2014 7:10:18 PM
ModificationTime   : 2/11/2014 7:21:40 PM
UserVersion        : AD Version: 0, SysVol Version: 0
ComputerVersion    : AD Version: 3, SysVol Version: 3
WmiFilter          :

DisplayName        : Melbourne-Users
DomainName         : contoso.com
Owner              : CONTOSO\Domain Admins
Id                 : 544d784e-8fe9-4e8e-bcec-fbf0a7e5a02c
GpoStatus          : AllSettingsEnabled
Description        :
CreationTime       : 2/18/2014 4:38:55 AM
ModificationTime   : 2/18/2014 4:38:54 AM
UserVersion        : AD Version: 0, SysVol Version: 0
ComputerVersion    : AD Version: 0, SysVol Version: 0
WmiFilter          :

DisplayName        : Default Domain Controllers Policy
DomainName         : contoso.com
Owner              : CONTOSO\Domain Admins
Id                 : 6ac1786c-016f-11d2-945f-00c04fb984f9
GpoStatus          : AllSettingsEnabled
Description        :
CreationTime       : 2/11/2014 7:10:18 PM
ModificationTime   : 2/18/2014 4:38:42 AM
UserVersion        : AD Version: 0, SysVol Version: 0
ComputerVersion    : AD Version: 2, SysVol Version: 2
WmiFilter          :


PS C:\Users\Administrator> get-gpo -all_
```

FIGURE 5-2 Output of the Get-GPO cmdlet

Backing up a GPO enables you to create a copy of a GPO as it exists at a specific point in time. A user must have read permission on a GPO to back it up. When you back up a GPO, the backup version of the GPO is incremented. It is good practice to back up GPOs prior to editing them so that if something goes wrong, you can revert to the unmodified GPO.

> **REAL WORLD BACKING UP GPOS**
>
> If your organization doesn't have access to the Microsoft Desktop Optimization Pack (MDOP), you should back up GPOs before you or other people modify them. If a problem occurs, it's quicker to restore a backup than it is to reconfigure the modified GPO with the existing settings. MDOP provides the ability to use GPO versioning as well as other advanced functionality.

To back up a GPO, perform the following steps:

1. Open the GPMC.

2. Right-click the GPO that you want to back up, and click Back Up.In the Back Up Group Policy Object dialog box, shown in Figure 5-3, enter the location of the backup and a description for the backup.

FIGURE 5-3 Backing up a GPO

You can restore a GPO using the Restore-GPO cmdlet. Restoring a GPO overwrites the current version of the GPO if one exists or re-creates the GPO if the GPO has been deleted. To restore a GPO, right-click the Group Policy Objects node in the GPMC, and click Manage Backups. In the Manage Backups dialog box, shown in Figure 5-4, select the GPO that you want to restore and click Restore. If multiple backups of the same GPO exist, you can select which version of a GPO to restore.

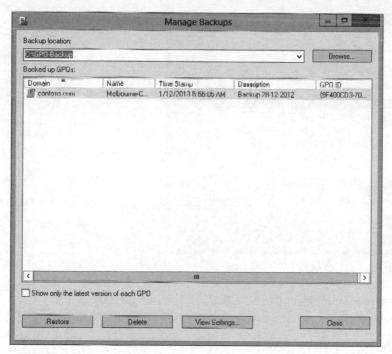

FIGURE 5-4 Restoring a GPO from backup

Import and copy GPOs

Importing a GPO enables you to take the settings in a backed up GPO and import them into an existing GPO. To import a GPO, perform the following steps:

1. Right-click an existing GPO in the GPMC and click Import Settings.

2. In the Import Settings Wizard, you are given the option of backing up the destination GPO's settings. This enables you to roll back the import.

3. Specify the folder that hosts the backed-up GPO.

4. On the Source GPO page of the Import Settings Wizard, shown in Figure 5-5, select the source GPO. You can view the settings that have been configured in the source GPO prior to importing it. Complete the wizard to finish importing the settings.

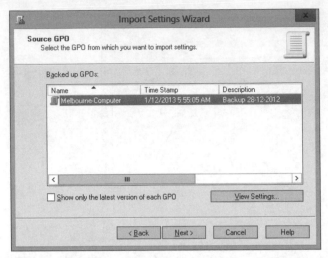

FIGURE 5-5 Importing GPO settings

Remember that when you import settings from a backed-up GPO, the settings in the backed-up GPO overwrite the settings in the destination GPO.

Copying a GPO creates a new GPO and copies all configuration settings from the original to the new. You can copy GPOs from one domain to another. You can also use a *migration table* when copying a GPO to map security principals referenced in the source domain to security principals referenced in the destination domain.

To copy a GPO, perform the following steps:

1. Right-click the GPO that you want to copy and click Copy.

2. Right-click the location that you want to copy the GPO to and click Paste.

3. In the Copy GPO dialog box, choose between using the default permissions and preserving the existing permissions assigned to the GPO (see Figure 5-6).

FIGURE 5-6 Copying a GPO

Fixing GPO problems

Windows Server 2012 and Windows Server 2012 R2 include command line utilities that allow you to repair GPO after you perform a domain rename or recreate default GPOs. If you need to recreate the default GPOs for a domain, use the DCGPOFix.exe command. If you perform a domain rename, you can use the GPFixup.exe command to repair name dependencies in GPOs and Group Policy links.

Migrate Group Policy Objects

When moving GPOs between domains or forests, you need to ensure that any domain-specific information is accounted for, so locations and security principals in the source domain aren't used in the destination domain. You can account for these locations and security principals using migration tables. You use migration tables when copying or importing GPOs.

Migration tables enable you to alter references when moving a GPO from one domain to another, or from one forest to another. An example is when you are using GPOs for software deployment and need to replace the address of a shared folder that hosts a software installation file so that it is relevant to the target domain. You can open the Migration Table Editor (MTE), shown in Figure 5-7, by right-clicking Domains in the GPMC, and clicking Open Migration Table Editor.

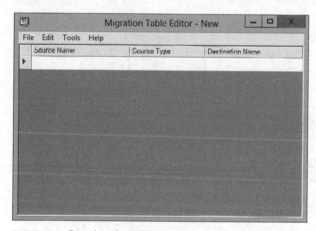

FIGURE 5-7 Opening the MTE

When you use the MTE, you can choose to populate from a GPO that is in the current domain, or choose to populate the MTE from a backed-up GPO. When you perform this action, the MTE will be populated with settings that reference local objects. If, when you perform this action, there are no results, then no local locations are referenced in the GPO that you are going to migrate.

> **MORE INFO** **WORKING WITH MIGRATION TABLES**
>
> You can learn more about working with migration tables at *http://technet.microsoft.com/ en-us/library/cc754682.aspx*.

Delegate GPO management

In larger environments, there is more than one person in the IT department. In very large organizations, one person's entire job responsibility might be creating and editing GPOs. *Delegation* enables you to grant the permission to perform specific tasks to a specific user or group of users. You can delegate some or all of the following Group Policy management tasks:

- GPO creation
- GPO modification
- GPO linking to specific sites, organizational units (OUs), or domains
- Permission to perform Group Policy Modeling analysis at the OU or domain level
- Permission to view
- Group Policy Results information at the OU, or domain level
- Windows Management Instrumentation (WMI) filter creation

Users in the Domain Admins and Enterprise Admins groups can perform all Group Policy management tasks. Users that are members of the Group Policy Creator Owners domain group can create GPOs. They also have the right to edit and delete any GPOs that they have created.

You can delegate permissions to GPOs directly using the GPMC, as shown in Figure 5-8.

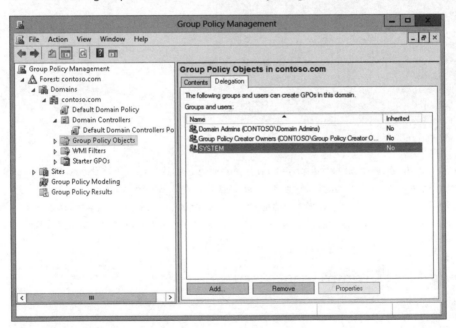

FIGURE 5-8 Group Policy permissions

Creating GPOs

If you want to delegate the ability for users to create GPOs, you can add them to the Group Policy Creator Owners group. You can also explicitly grant them permission to create GPOs using the GPMC. To do this, perform the following steps:

1. Open the GPMC from the Tools menu of Server Manager.

2. Expand the domain in which you want to delegate the ability to create GPOs, click Group Policy Objects, and click the Delegation tab.

3. Click Add and select the group or user that you want to give the ability to create GPOs in that domain.

> ✔ **Quick check**
>
> - What group should you add users to if you want to enable them to create GPOs in the domain, but not add them to the Domain Admins or Enterprise Admins groups?
>
> **Quick check answer**
>
> - Add them to the Group Policy Creator Owner group.

Editing GPOs

To edit a GPO, users must be either a member of the Domain Admins or Enterprise Admins group. They can edit a GPO if they created it. They can also edit a GPO if they have been given Read/Write permissions on the GPO through the GPMC.

To grant a user permission to edit a GPO, perform the following steps:

1. Click the GPO in the GPMC.

2. Click the Delegation tab, as shown in Figure 5-9.

3. Click Add, specify the user or group that should have permission to edit the GPO, and then specify the permissions that you want to give this user or group. You can choose from one of the following permissions:

   - Read
   - Edit Settings
   - Edit Settings, Delete, Modify Security

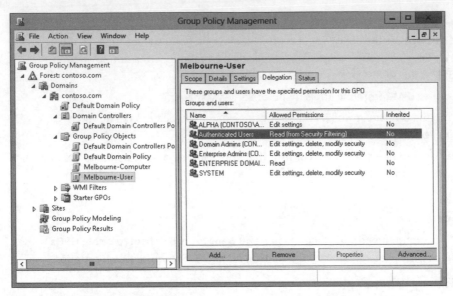

FIGURE 5-9 Delegating permissions

Linking GPOs

To enable a user to link a GPO to a specific object, you need to edit the permission on that object. You can perform this task in the GPMC, as shown in Figure 5-10. For example, to grant a user or group permission to link a GPO to an OU, select the OU in the GPMC, select the Delegation tab, click Add, and then select the user or group to which you want to grant this permission.

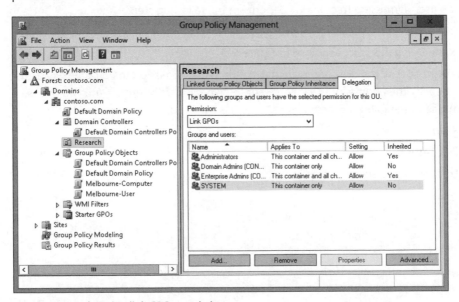

FIGURE 5-10 Delegating link GPO permission

Modeling, results, and WMI filters

Delegating permissions to perform tasks related to Group Policy Modeling and Group Policy Results is performed at the domain level, as shown in Figure 5-11. You can delegate the ability to create *WMI filters* by selecting the WMI Filters node in the GPMC and granting the permission on the Delegation tab.

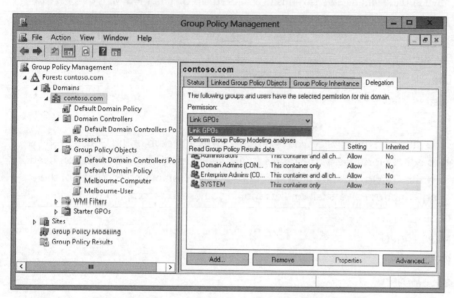

FIGURE 5-11 Delegating Group Policy Modeling and Group Policy Results permissions

Lesson summary

- Each time you back up a GPO, it creates a copy of that GPO at a particular point in time.

- Restoring a GPO overwrites the existing GPO if it still exists, or recovers it if it has been deleted.

- Importing a GPO overwrites the settings in the destination GPO with the settings from the imported GPO.

- Copying a GPO creates a duplicate of the GPO.

- You use migration tables when moving GPOs between domains and forests to account for local references in the source domain.

- You can delegate the permission to create, edit, and link using the GPMC. Non-administrative users can then perform some Group Policy tasks, such as editing policies, without giving them unnecessary privileges.

Lesson review

Answer the following questions to test your knowledge of the information in this lesson. You can find the answers to these questions and explanations of why each answer choice is correct or incorrect in the "Answers" section at the end of this chapter.

1. You have 200 individual GPO settings in a backed-up GPO named Melbourne-2012 that you want to include in an existing GPO named Sydney-2013. Which of the following Windows PowerShell cmdlets should you use to accomplish this goal?

   A. Backup-GPO

   B. Import-GPO

   C. Restore-GPO

   D. Copy-GPO

2. Prior to editing a Group Policy, your assistant makes a backup of the GPO that she is going to edit. Unfortunately, she makes a mistake in configuring the GPO. You need to revert the GPO to the state it was in prior to your assistant's edits. Which of the following Windows PowerShell cmdlets should you use to accomplish this goal?

   A. Copy-GPO

   B. Restore-GPO

   C. Import-GPO

   D. Backup-GPO

3. You want to copy a GPO from one domain to another in a forest. Which tool should you use to ensure that references to objects in the source domain updated are relevant to the destination domain? (Choose all that apply.)

   A. Active Directory Sites and Services

   B. Active Directory Users and Computers

   C. Migration Table Editor

   D. Group Policy Management Editor

4. Which of the following security groups have the right to create GPOs by default? (Choose all that apply.)

   A. Group Policy Creator Owners

   B. Enterprise Admins

   C. Domain Admins

   D. Domain Controllers

5. You are about to make substantial modifications to the default domain GPO. You want to ensure that you can return to the current state of the GPO if the modifications cause problems. Which of the following Windows PowerShell cmdlets should you use?

   A. Copy-GPO

B. Restore-GPO

C. Import-GPO

D. Backup-GPO

Lesson 2: Managing Group Policy application

For environments in which you need to apply more than one Group Policy, understanding the rules of precedence is critical. Not only do you need to understand that where you apply a Group Policy determines its overall influence but also that GPOs may or may not apply due to inheritance blocks, security filtering, or loopback processing. In this lesson, you'll learn the rules on Group Policy application and how to determine which Group Policy settings have precedence in complex environments.

After this lesson, you will be able to:

- Determine policy processing order and precedence.
- Configure policy enforcement and blocking.
- Perform Group Policy security filtering.
- Configure WMI filtering.
- Enable loopback processing.
- Configure slow-link processing.

Estimated lesson time: 45 minutes

Policy processing precedence

In organizations with large Group Policy deployments, multiple GPOs might apply to a single user account or computer account; or when a user is signed on to a specific computer, to both. Group Policy processing *precedence* is the set of rules that determines which Group Policy items apply when multiple GPOs are configured.

Group Policies are processed in the following manner:

- **Local** Settings configured at the local level apply first. If multiple local policies apply, settings in machine policies apply first, settings in admin and nonadmin local policies override them, and settings in per-user policies override any configured at the machine and admin/nonadmin level.

- **Site** Policies based on location apply next. Any settings configured at the site level override settings configured at the local level. You can link multiple GPOs at the site level. When you do this, policies with a lower numerical link order override policies with a higher numerical link order. For example in Figure 5-12, settings in the Melbourne-Computer policy override settings configured in the Melbourne-User policy.

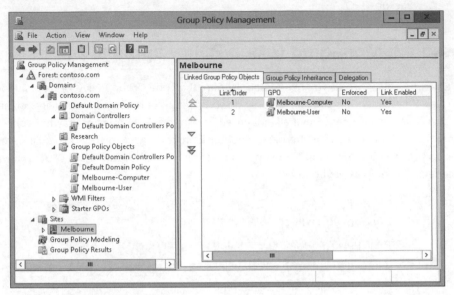

FIGURE 5-12 GPO link order

- **Domain** Settings applied at the domain level override settings applied at the site and local levels. You can link multiple GPOs at the domain level. The Default Domain Policy is linked at this level.

- **Organizational unit (OU)** Settings applied at the organizational unit level override settings applied at the domain, site, and local levels. When an account is a member of a child OU, policies applied at the child OU level override policies applied at the parent OU level. You can apply multiple GPOs at the OU level. Policies with a lower numerical link order override policies with a higher numerical link order.

Group Policy processing precedence is relevant only when there are conflicts in policies. If policy A applies at the domain level, and policy B applies at the OU level, both policy A and policy B apply.

Policy enforcement and blocking

When configuring a Group Policy, you can choose to enforce that policy. To enforce a Group Policy, right-click that policy at the location in which you link the policy and then click Enforced. When you choose to enforce a policy, that policy will apply and override settings configured at other levels. For example, normally a policy linked at the OU level would override a policy linked at the domain level. If you configure the policy at the domain level as Enforced, it instead overrides the policy linked at the OU level.

The *Block Inheritance* function enables you to block policies applied at earlier levels. For example, you can use Block Inheritance at the OU level to block policies applied at the domain and site level. Block Inheritance does not stop the application of policies configured as Enforced. For example, Figure 5-13 shows the Research OU configured with the Block Inheritance setting. The Melbourne-Computer policy, applied at the domain level as Enforced, still applies because a setting of Enforced overrides a setting of Block Inheritance.

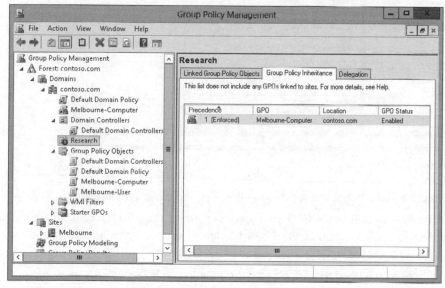

FIGURE 5-13 Override versus Enforced

Group Policy security filtering

Security filtering enables you to configure permissions on GPOs. By default, Group Policies apply to the Authenticated Users group. By changing the default permissions, you can make the Group Policy apply only to a specific group. For example, if you remove the Authenticated Users group and add another security group such as the Melbourne-Users group (shown in Figure 5-14), the Group Policy applies to only that configured security group.

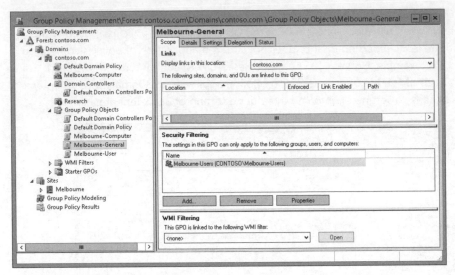

FIGURE 5-14 Security filtering

When considering whether to use security filtering, keep the following in mind:

- A security filter applies to the GPO, so it applies wherever the GPO is linked. You can't have one security filter apply to the GPO when linked at the domain level, and another security filter apply to the GPO when linked at the OU level.

- Filtered policies still need to be checked during the Group Policy processing process, which can increase the amount of time spent on Group Policy processing. Startup and logon times may increase.

It is also possible to apply a Deny permission on the basis of security account or group. Deny permissions override Allow permissions. You block a particular security group from receiving a Group Policy by setting the Apply Group Policy (Deny) advanced permission, as shown for the Sydney-Users group for the Melbourne-General GPO in Figure 5-15. You can do this on the Delegation tab of a GPO's properties instead of the Scope tab.

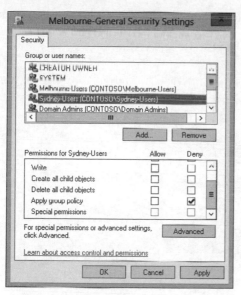

FIGURE 5-15 Security filtering

> ✔ **Quick check**
>
> ■ How would you block a GPO from applying to members of a particular security group?
>
> **Quick check answer**
>
> ■ Configure an Apply Group Policy (Deny) advanced permission on the Delegation tab of a GPO's properties.

Group Policy WMI filtering

WMI filtering enables you to filter the application of policy based on the results of a WMI query. For example, you might write a WMI query to determine whether a computer has an x86 or x64 processor, or whether there is more than a certain amount of disk space available. WMI queries are often used with policies related to software deployment to determine whether the target computer has the appropriate system resources to support the installation of the application.

The drawback of WMI queries is that they are complicated for systems administrators who are unfamiliar with programming beyond simple scripting. WMI queries also cause significant delays in Group Policy processing. In environments in which sophisticated logic needs to be applied to targeted application distribution, products such as Microsoft System Center 2012 Configuration Manager are more appropriate. System Center 2012 Configuration Manager enables administrators performing software deployment to configure ways of checking hardware configuration prior to software deployment that do not require writing queries in WMI Query Language (WQL).

You can create WMI filters by using the New WMI Filter dialog box (shown in Figure 5-16).

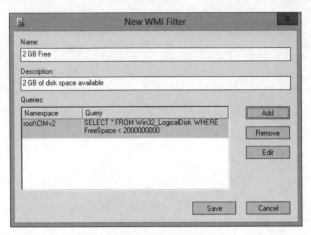

FIGURE 5-16 Creating a WMI filter

> **MORE INFO WMI QUERIES**
>
> You can learn more about WMI queries at *http://msdn.microsoft.com/en-us/library/ ms186146(VS.80).aspx*.

Loopback processing

As you are aware, each GPO has two distinct sections: Computer Configuration and User Configuration (see Figure 5-17). The resultant policies for a user are based on the cumulative user configuration settings in GPOs that apply to the user's accounts at the site, domain, and OU setting. The resultant computer policies are applied based on the cumulative computer configuration settings in GPOs that apply to the computer's account at the site, domain, and OU level.

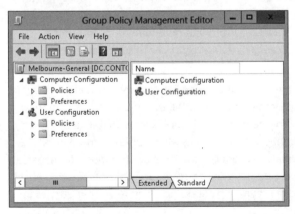

FIGURE 5-17 GPO structure

In some situations, you'll want only the GPOs that apply to the computer account to apply. You might want to do this with conference room computers, for which you want people to be able to sign on with domain accounts but to have a very controlled configuration. When you enable *loopback processing*, user settings are determined based on the settings in the User Configuration settings area of GPOs that apply to the computer account.

There are two types of loopback processing that you can configure by setting the Group Policy loopback processing mode policy, shown in Figure 5-18, and located under Computer Configuration\Administrative Templates\System\Group Policy: Replace And Merge.

- **Replace** When you configure Replace, only the GPOs that apply to the computer account will apply. Settings in the User Configuration area of the GPOs that apply to the computer account will apply.

- **Merge** The settings in the User Configuration area of GPOs that apply to the user account will still apply, but will be overridden by settings in the User Configuration area of GPOs that apply to the computer account.

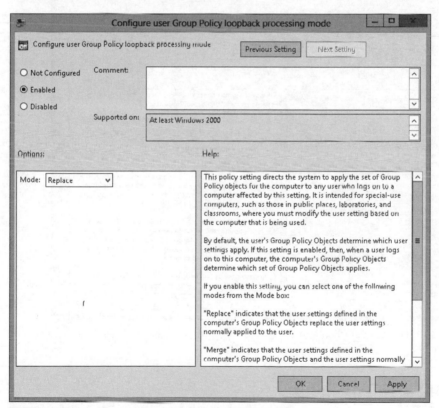

FIGURE 5-18 Loopback processing policy

Slow-link processing enables you to configure Group Policy application to be performed in a different manner, depending on the speed of the connection from the client to the domain controller. It enables you to block activities such as software deployment when the connection between Active Directory and the client is detected as falling below a particular threshold. You configure slow link detection by configuring the Group Policy slow link detection policy, as shown in Figure 5-19. This policy is located under Computer Configuration\Administrative Templates\System\Group Policy. When a slow link is detected, registry settings from administrative templates, security policies, EFS recovery policy, and IPsec policies are applied. Policies related to application deployment, scripts, folder redirection, and disk quotas will not be applied.

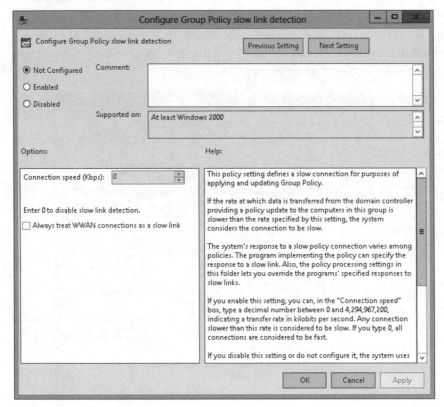

FIGURE 5-19 Slow link detection

Group Policy caching

Group Policy caching reduces the amount of time taken to process Group Policy during computer startup and user sign on. Rather than retrieve the Group Policies that apply to the computer from a domain controller when a computer starts up or a user signs on, the client will use a cached copy of the last Group Policies downloaded from the domain controller. After this initial application of the cached policies during startup and user sign on, policies will be retrieved and applied normally from a domain controller. You enable Group Policy caching by configuring the Configure Group Policy Caching policy as shown in Figure 5-20. This policy is located under Computer Configuration\Policies\Administrative Templates\System\Group Policy. Group Policy caching applies only to computers running Windows Server 2012 R2, Windows 8.1, or Windows RT 8.1.

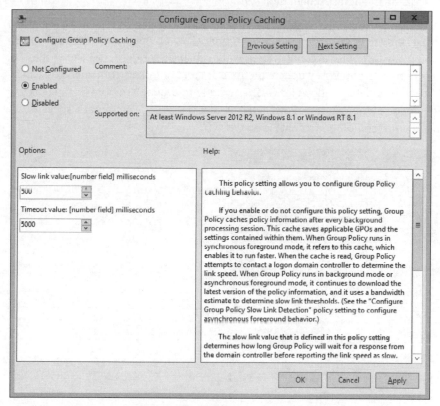

FIGURE 5-20 Configure Group Policy caching

MORE INFO   **GROUP POLICY CACHING**

You can learn more about Group Policy caching by reading this blog post by Group Policy MVP Darren Mar-Elia at *http://sdmsoftware.com/group-policy-blog/group-policy/understanding-group-policy-caching-in-windows-8-1/*.

Force Group Policy update

Windows Server 2012 and later support remote Group Policy update. Remote Group Policy update allows you to force a remote computer to perform a Group Policy update without having to sign on to the computer and run the GPUpdate.exe command. Remote Group

Policy update will work on clients running the Windows Vista and later operating system. Remote Group Policy requires the following firewall rules be enabled on clients:

- Remote Scheduled Tasks Management (RPC)
- Remote Scheduled Tasks Management (RPC-EPMAP)
- Windows Management Instrumentation (WMI-In)

You can run remote Group Policy update from the Group Policy Management Console by right-clicking on a container or OU. An update will run on all computers within the container or OU as well as on any computer accounts stored within child OUs. Figure 5-21 shows the result of running remote Group Policy update on the Domain Controllers container. You can also use the Invoke-GPUpdate Windows PowerShell cmdlet to trigger a remote Group Policy update. The advantage of the Windows PowerShell cmdlet is that you can target a specific computer rather than all computer accounts in an OU.

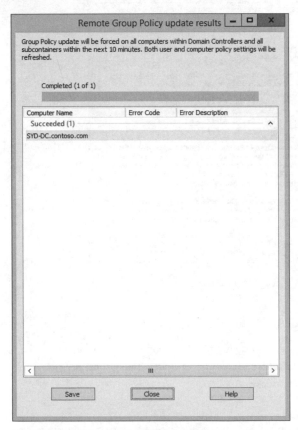

FIGURE 5-21 Remote Group Policy update

MORE INFO **USING REMOTE GPUPDATE**

You can learn more about remote Group Policy update at *https://blogs.technet.com/b/grouppolicy/archive/2012/11/27/group-policy-in-windows-server-2012-using remote gpupdate.aspx.*

Lesson summary

- Group Policies are processed in the following order: local, site, domain, and OU. Policies processed later override policies processed earlier.

- When there are parent and child OUs, and the user or computer account is a member of the child OU, the policy applied at the child OU overrides policies applied at the parent OU.

- Policy processing order is important only when policies conflict.

- A policy with the Override setting will override other policies in the processing order, including when Block Inheritance has been configured.

- Security filtering applies on a GPO, no matter where it is linked.

- Loopback processing enables GPO settings applied to the computer account to override GPO settings applied to the user account.

- Slow-link processing enables you to configure policies not to be processed when low bandwidth connections to Active Directory are detected.

- Group Policy caching allows cached copies of GPOs that apply to users and computers to be applied at startup and sign on.

- Remote Group Policy update allows you to force a Group Policy update on a remote client. Remote Group Policy update requires that 3 firewall rules be configured on clients.

Lesson review

Answer the following questions to test your knowledge of the information in this lesson. You can find the answers to these questions and explanations of why each answer choice is correct or incorrect in the "Answers" section at the end of this chapter.

1. You want to ensure that a Group Policy applies only to computers that have more than 2 gigabytes (GB) of disk space. Which of the following should you configure to accomplish this goal?

   A. Security filtering

   B. WMI filtering

   C. Loopback processing

   D. Slow-link processing

2. A Group Policy named Alpha applies at the site level. A Group Policy named Beta is assigned link order 2 at the domain level. A Group Policy named Gamma is assigned link order 1 at the domain level. A Group Policy named Delta is assigned to the Research OU. A computer account is located in the Research OU. If the same setting is configured differently in the Alpha, Beta, Gamma, and Delta GPOs, which GPO's version of this setting will apply to the computer?

   A. Alpha

   B. Beta

   C. Gamma

   D. Delta

3. A Group Policy named Alpha applies at the site level. A Group Policy named Beta is assigned link order 2 at the domain level. A Group Policy named Gamma is assigned link order 1 at the domain level. A Group Policy named Delta is assigned to the Research OU. A computer account is located in the Research OU. GPO Gamma is configured with the No Override setting. If the same setting is configured differently in the Alpha, Beta, Gamma, and Delta GPOs, which GPO's version of this setting will apply to the computer?

   A. Alpha

   B. Beta

   C. Gamma

   D. Delta

4. A Group Policy named Alpha applies at the site level. A Group Policy named Beta is assigned link order 2 at the domain level. A Group Policy named Gamma is assigned link order 1 at the domain level. A Group Policy named Delta is assigned to the Research OU. A computer account is located in the Research OU. GPO Beta is configured with the No Override setting. OU Research is configured with the Block Inheritance setting. If the same setting is configured differently in GPOs Alpha, Beta, Gamma, and Delta, which GPO's version of this setting will apply to the computer?

   A. Alpha

   B. Beta

   C. Gamma

   D. Delta

5. You have a policy applied at the domain level that you don't want applied to five computers in your organization. Which of the following should you configure to accomplish this goal?

   A. Security filtering

   B. WMI filtering

   C. Loopback processing

   D. Slow-link processing

Practice exercises

The goal of this section is to provide you with hands-on practice with the following:

- Creating, backing up, and restoring GPOs
- Delegating GPO permissions
- Enabling loopback processing
- Configuring blocking and enforcement
- Configuring GPO security filtering

To perform the exercises in this section, you need access to an evaluation version of Windows Server 2012 R2. You should also have access to virtual machines SYD-DC, MEL-DC, CBR-DC, and ADL-DC, the setup instructions for which are described in the Introduction. You should ensure that you have a checkpoint of these virtual machines that you can revert to at the end of the practice exercises. You should revert the virtual machines to this initial state prior to beginning these exercises.

Exercise 1: Prepare GPOs, security groups, and OUs

In this exercise, you prepare GPOs. To complete this exercise, perform the following steps:

1. Sign in to SYD-DC with the Contoso\Administrator account.
2. In Server Manager, click the Tools menu, and click Group Policy Management.
3. Expand the Forest: Contoso.com\Domains\Contoso.com node and click Group Policy Objects, as shown in Figure 5-22.

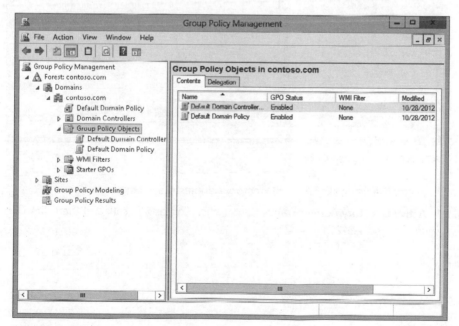

FIGURE 5-22 Clicking Group Policy Objects

4. On the Action menu, click New.

5. In the New GPO dialog box, type **Melbourne**, as shown in Figure 5-23, and click OK.

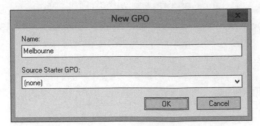

FIGURE 5-23 New GPO dialog box

6. Repeat steps 4 and 5 to create new GPOs named Sydney and Adelaide.

7. Verify that there are five GPOs listed, as shown in Figure 5-24.

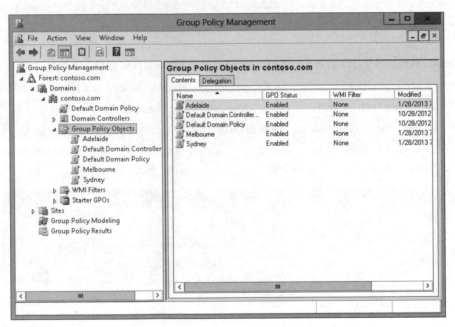

FIGURE 5-24 Three new GPOs

8. In Server Manager, click Active Directory Administrative Center.

9. In Active Directory Administrative Center, click Contoso (Local), and then click Users, as shown in Figure 5-25.

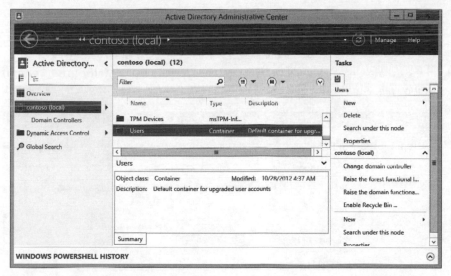

FIGURE 5-25 Users container

10. In the Tasks pane, click New, and click Group.

11. In the Create Group dialog box, type the group name **Melbourne_GPO_Editors**; click Security, Global, and Protect From Accidental Deletion, as shown in Figure 5-26; then click OK.

FIGURE 5-26 Creating a security group

12. Repeat steps 10 and 11 to create the Adelaide_Computers security group.

13. In the Active Directory Administrative Center, in the Tasks pane, under Contoso (Local), click New, and then click Organizational Unit.

14. In the Create Organizational Unit dialog box, type the name **Melbourne_Computers**, as shown in Figure 5-27, and click OK.

FIGURE 5-27 Create Organizational Unit dialog box

15. Close the Active Directory Administrative Center.

16. On the taskbar, click File Manager.

17. In File Manager, click Computer, and then double-click Local Disk (C:) .

18. On the title bar of the Local Disk (C:) window, click the New Folder icon.

19. Name the new folder **GPO_Backup**.

20. Close the Local Disk (C:) window.

Exercise 2: Manage GPOs

In this exercise, you perform several Group Policy management-related tasks. To complete this exercise, perform the following steps:

1. In the GPMC, click the Melbourne GPO.

2. When the Melbourne GPO is selected, click the Delegation tab, as shown in Figure 5-28.

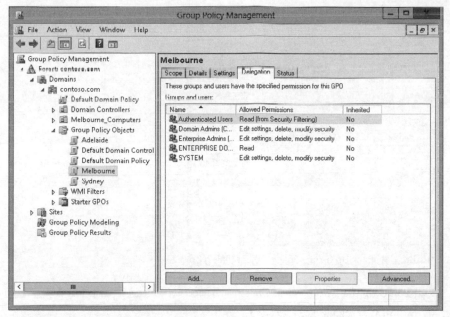

FIGURE 5-28 OU Delegation tab

3. On the Delegation tab, click Add.

4. In the Select User, Computer, Or Group dialog box, type **Melbourne_GPO_Editors**, click Check Names, and click OK.

5. In the Add Group Or User dialog box, use the drop-down menu to select Edit Settings, Delete, Modify Security, as shown in Figure 5-29, and click OK.

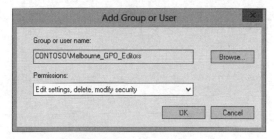

FIGURE 5-29 OU Delegation tab

6. In the GPMC, click the Sydney GPO.

7. On the Action menu, click Back Up.

8. In the Back Up Group Policy Object dialog box, type **C:\GPO_Backup** as the location, as shown in Figure 5-30, and click Back Up.

FIGURE 5-30 Back Up Group Policy Object dialog box

9. In the Backup dialog box, click OK.

10. In the GPMC, click the Sydney GPO.

11. On the Action menu, click Delete.

12. In the Group Policy Management dialog box, click Yes.

13. Verify that the Sydney GPO is no longer listed under Group Policy Objects, as shown in Figure 5-31.

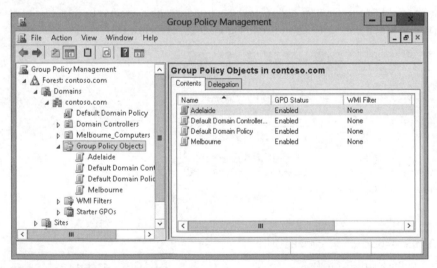

FIGURE 5-31 Verify deleted GPO

14. Click Group Policy Objects. On the Action menu, click Manage Backups.

15. In the Manage Backups dialog box, click the Sydney GPO, as shown in Figure 5-32, and click Restore.

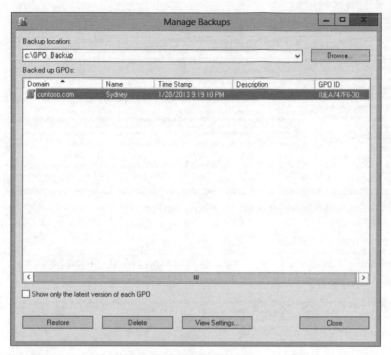

FIGURE 5-32 Manage Backups dialog box

16. In the Group Policy Management dialog box, click OK.
17. In the Restore dialog box, click OK.
18. In the Manage Backups dialog box, click Close.
19. Verify the presence of the Sydney GPO in the list of Group Policy Objects.

Exercise 3: Manage Group Policy processing

In this exercise, you perform Group Policy management tasks related to Group Policy processing. To complete this exercise, perform the following steps:

1. In the GPMC, click the Adelaide GPO.
2. On the Action menu, click Edit.
3. In the Group Policy Management Editor, expand the Computer Configuration\Administrative Templates\System\Group Policy node and select the Configure User Group Policy loopback processing mode policy, as shown in Figure 5-33.

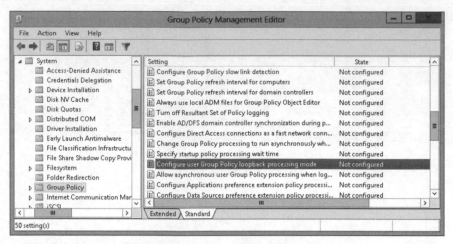

FIGURE 5-33 Select Group Policy loopback processing mode policy

4. On the Action menu, click Edit.

5. In the Configure User Group Policy Loopback Processing Mode dialog box, click Enabled. Set the mode to Replace, as shown in Figure 5-34, and click OK.

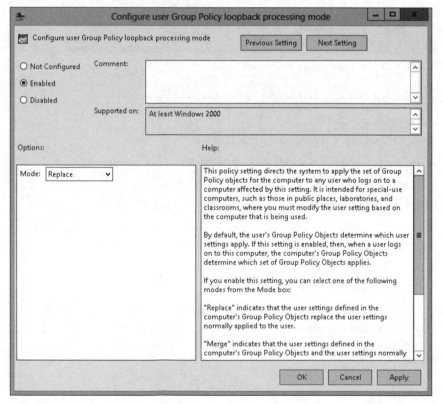

FIGURE 5-34 Configure replace mode

6. Close the Group Policy Management Editor.

7. In the GPMC, click the Adelaide GPO, and click the Scope tab.

8. On the Scope tab, click the Authenticated Users group, and click Remove.

9. In the Group Policy Management dialog box, click OK.

10. Under Security Filtering, click Add.

11. In the Select User, Computer, Or Group dialog box, type **Adelaide_Computers**, click Check Names, and click OK.

12. Verify that the security filtering properties of the Adelaide GPO match those in Figure 5-35.

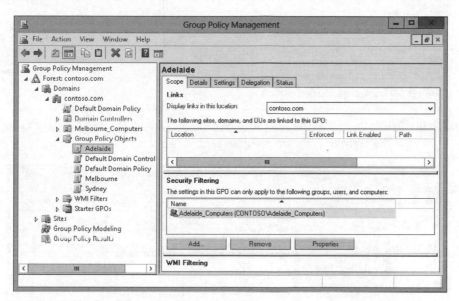

FIGURE 5-35 Configuring security filtering properties

13. In the GPMC, click Contoso.com, and click the Linked Group Policy Objects tab.

14. Click Contoso.com. On the Action menu, click Link An Existing GPO.

15. In the Select GPO dialog box, click Adelaide, as shown in Figure 5-36, and click OK.

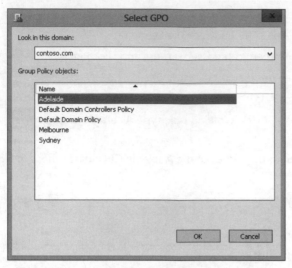

FIGURE 5-36 Selecting the GPO to link

16. In the GPMC, verify that the Adelaide GPO and the Default Domain Policy GPO are linked to the domain, as shown in Figure 5-37.

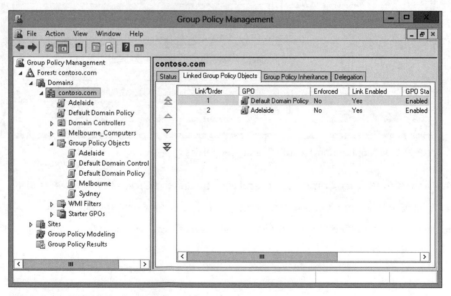

FIGURE 5-37 GPOs linked to the domain

Exercise 4: Group Policy inheritance and enforcement

In this exercise, you will perform Group Policy management tasks related to Group Policy processing. To complete this exercise, perform the following steps:

1. In the GPMC, click the Melbourne Computers OU.

2. On the Action menu, click Block Inheritance.

3. In the GPMC, click Contoso.com.

4. On the Action menu, click Link An Existing GPO.

5. In the Select GPO dialog box, click Melbourne, and then click OK.

6. Click the Melbourne GPO under Contoso.com.

7. On the Action menu, click Enforced.

8. Verify that the GPMC shows the Melbourne policy as Enforced and the Melbourne_Computers OU set to Block Inheritance, as shown in Figure 5-38.

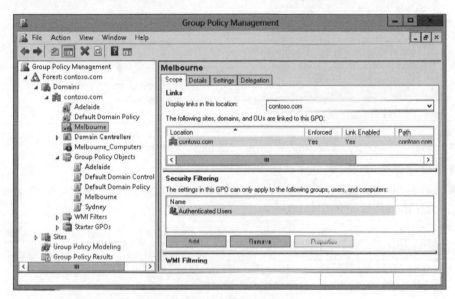

FIGURE 5-38 Block Inheritance and Enforced GPOs

9. In the GPMC, click the Group Policy Modeling node.

10. On the Action menu, click Group Policy Modeling Wizard.

11. On the Welcome page of the Group Policy Modeling Wizard, click Next.

12. On the Domain Controller Selection page, click This Domain Controller, and click SYD-DC.contoso.com. Click Next.

13. On the User And Computer Selection page, click Browse next to Container in the Computer Information section.

14. In the Choose Computer Container dialog box, click Melbourne_Computers, and click OK.

15. Verify that the User And Computer Selection page matches Figure 5-39, and click Next.

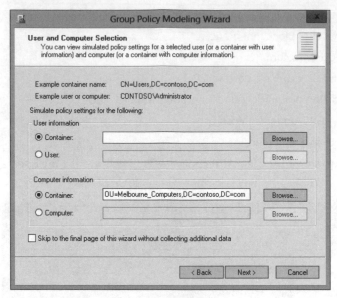

FIGURE 5-39 Group Policy Modeling Wizard

16. On the Summary Of Selections page, click Next, and then click Finish.

17. In the Warning dialog box, click OK.

18. Verify that the report for the Melbourne_Computers OU matches Figure 5-40, and that only the Melbourne GPO is listed.

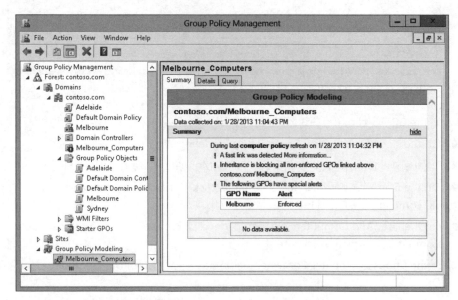

FIGURE 5-40 Group Policy Modeling results

Suggested practice exercises

The following additional practice exercises are designed to give you more opportunities to practice what you've learned and to help you successfully master the lessons presented in this chapter.

- **Exercise 1**   Configure GPO settings in the Melbourne GPO. Import these settings into the Sydney GPO.

- **Exercise 2**   Configure the Melbourne GPO so that it will not apply to members of the Adelaide_Computers group.

Answers

This section contains the answers to the lesson review questions in this chapter.

Lesson 1

1. **Correct answer: B**

   A. **Incorrect.** You use the Backup-GPO cmdlet to back up an existing GPO.

   B. **Correct.** You use the Import-GPO cmdlet to import settings from a backed-up GPO to an existing target GPO.

   C. **Incorrect.** You use the Restore-GPO cmdlet to restore a backed-up GPO to a previous state.

   D. **Incorrect.** You use the Copy-GPO cmdlet to create a copy of an existing GPO.

2. **Correct answer: B**

   A. **Incorrect.** You use the Copy-GPO cmdlet to create a copy of an existing GPO.

   B. **Correct.** You use the Restore-GPO cmdlet to restore a backed-up GPO to a previous state.

   C. **Incorrect.** You use the Import-GPO cmdlet to import settings from a backed-up GPO to an existing target GPO. Although it would import the settings from the backed-up GPO, it is possible that other settings not included in the original backed-up GPO were configured by your assistant.

   D. **Incorrect.** You use the Backup-GPO cmdlet to back up an existing GPO.

3. **Correct answer: C**

   A. **Incorrect.** You use the Active Directory Sites and Services console to manage Active Directory sites. You can't use this console to configure GPO migration settings.

   B. **Incorrect.** You use this console to manage Active Directory security principals and containers. You can't use this console to configure GPO migration settings.

   C. **Correct.** You use this tool to configure the migration table, which is necessary when migrating objects from one domain or forest to another.

   D. **Incorrect.** You use this to edit GPOs. You can't use this console to configure GPO migration settings.

4. **Correct answers: A, B, and C**

   A. **Correct.** Members of the Group Policy Creator Owners group can create GPOs by default.

   B. **Correct.** Members of the Enterprise Admins group can create GPOs by default.

   C. **Correct.** Members of the Domain Admins group can create GPOs by default.

D. Incorrect. The Domain Controllers group is a group for the accounts of domain controllers. It does not grant any permissions on GPOs.

5. **Correct answer: D**

   A. Incorrect. You use the Copy-GPO cmdlet to create a copy of an existing GPO. It does not allow you to revert the default domain GPO to its original state.

   B. Incorrect. You use the Restore-GPO cmdlet to restore a backed-up GPO to a previous state. You need to create the backup first.

   C. Incorrect. You use the Import-GPO cmdlet to import settings from a backed-up GPO to an existing target GPO.

   D. Correct. You use the Backup-GPO cmdlet to back up an existing GPO.

Lesson 2

1. **Correct answer: B**

   A. Incorrect. You use Security Filtering to filter GPO application based on security group membership.

   B. Correct. You can use a WMI query to filter GPO application based on the properties of a target computer, such as how much disk space it has available.

   C. Incorrect. You use loopback processing to enforce settings that apply to the computer account rather than the user account.

   D. Incorrect. You use slow-link processing to configure Group Policy not to apply across low-bandwidth connections.

2. **Correct answer: D**

   A. Incorrect. In this scenario, GPO Delta has precedence over the other GPOs.

   B. Incorrect. In this scenario, GPO Delta has precedence over the other GPOs.

   C. Incorrect. In this scenario, GPO Delta has precedence over the other GPOs.

   D. Correct. In this scenario, GPO Delta has precedence over the other GPOs.

3. **Correct answer: C**

   A. Incorrect. In this scenario, the No Override setting on GPO Gamma means that it has precedence.

   B. Incorrect. In this scenario, the No Override setting on GPO Gamma means that it has precedence.

   C. Correct. In this scenario, the No Override setting on GPO Gamma means that it has precedence.

   D. Incorrect. In this scenario, the No Override setting on GPO Gamma means that it has precedence.

4. **Correct answer: B**

   A. **Incorrect.** No Override settings override Block Inheritance, so the setting in GPO Beta applies to the computer.

   B. **Correct.** No Override settings override Block Inheritance, so the setting in GPO Beta applies to the computer.

   C. **Incorrect.** No Override settings override Block Inheritance, so the setting in GPO Beta applies to the computer.

   D. **Incorrect.** No Override settings override Block Inheritance, so the setting in GPO Beta applies to the computer.

5. **Correct answer: A**

   A. **Correct.** You use Security Filtering to filter GPO application based on security group membership. In this case, you configure the Apply Group Policy (Deny) advanced permission.

   B. **Incorrect.** You can use a WMI query to filter GPO application based on the properties of a target computer, such as how much disk space it has available.

   C. **Incorrect.** You use loopback processing to enforce settings that apply to the computer account rather than the user account.

   D. **Incorrect.** You use slow-link processing to configure Group Policy not to apply across low-bandwidth connections.

CHAPTER 6

Group Policy settings and preferences

Rather than having to configure settings such as mapped network drives and configured network printers on a per-computer basis, Group Policy enables you to centralize the configuration of a large number of computers. Even if you only work with server operating systems such as Exchange and SQL Server, you'll need to interact with Group Policy on a regular basis. Rather than take you through every possible Group Policy setting, this chapter includes three lessons that take you through commonly used basic Group Policy settings, discuss how to extend Group Policy through the use of administrative templates, and show how to use the Group Policy preferences feature to minimize the need for logon and startup scripts.

Lessons in this chapter:

- Lesson 1: Folder redirection, software installation, and scripts **281**
- Lesson 2: Administrative templates **296**
- Lesson 3: Group Policy preferences **303**

Before you begin

To complete the practice exercises in this chapter:

- You need to have deployed computers SYD-DC, MEL-DC, and ADL-DC, as described in the Introduction, using the evaluation edition of Windows Server 2012 R2.

Lesson 1: Folder redirection, software installation, and scripts

There are approximately 3,600 policies in a standard Group Policy Object (GPO). It is reasonable to say that few people, if anybody, knows exactly what they all do. As a server administrator, you'll tend to specialize in the areas that you find interesting and useful. If you are responsible for managing client computers running the Windows 7, Windows 8, and Windows 8.1 operating systems, you'll be interested in Group Policy items that you can use with client computers—specifically, redirecting folders; installing software; and controlling startup, shutdown, logon, and logoff scripts.

Folder Redirection

In many organizations, such as call centers and student computer labs, computer users aren't assigned a set computer. Not having a set computer provides challenges in terms of computer personalization and storage of user data. Folder Redirection enables you to redirect commonly used folders, such as the desktop and Start menu, from a local hard disk to a network location. The benefit is that by redirecting folders, users can get the same experience independently of which computer they sign on to. For example, you could redirect the desktop folder to a location on the network, and any file or folder that a user saved on the desktop would be automatically available on the desktop of any other computer that they signed on to in the domain.

You can also use Folder Redirection with offline files. When you do this, users have access to redirected folders if they are using a laptop or if the connection to the network is lost. It requires that you have Offline Files configured and that the user has made an initial connection to the network, but it provides another way to ensure that the user gets a consistent experience independent of which computer they sign on to.

You can configure Group Policy to redirect the following folders.

- AppData(Roaming)
- Desktop
- Start menu
- Documents
- Pictures
- Music
- Videos
- Contacts
- Downloads
- Links
- Searches
- Saved games

Folder Redirection policies are located in the User Configuration\Policies\Windows Settings\Folder Redirection node of a GPO, as shown in Figure 6-1.

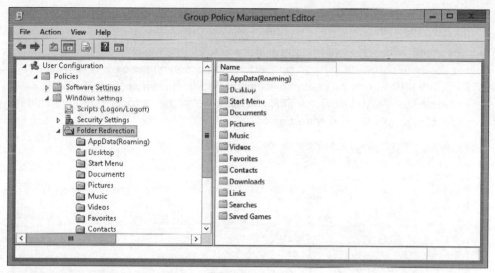

FIGURE 6-1 Folder Redirection policies

Beyond providing a consistent user experience, Folder Redirection enables you to ensure that important user data is backed up. Rather than worrying about backing up individual client computers, you configure Folder Redirection and instead ensure that the server that hosts the redirected folders is subject to stringent data protection policies.

> **REAL WORLD** **BACKING UP CLIENT DATA**
>
> In some organizations, up to 60 percent of the important data is stored on clients. People don't think about it as a big risk because if you have 60 percent of your data spread across hundreds of clients, losing one client doesn't mean losing much data. In reality, the loss of data on one client computer can cost an organization thousands, even tens of thousands, of dollars. User data stored on client machines is often worth more than the machine itself because it took someone who was getting paid a certain amount of money per hour, many hours to generate that data. Lose that data and the investment the organization made in generating that data may be lost.

You configure Folder Redirection on a per-folder basis. When you configure a Folder Redirection policy, you choose between the following options:

- **Basic** This option enables you to redirect the folders of everyone subject to the policy to the same path. When you enable this option, you can configure the following options for the target folder location:
- **Create A Folder For Each User Under The Root Path** This option is shown in Figure 6-2. The user's folder is created automatically.
- **Redirect To The Following Location** Use this when you want to redirect folders to a common shared location instead of to an individual one.

- **Redirect To The Local Userprofile Location** Use this option to redirect to the local profile path on the computer. This option disables user redirection.

- **Advanced** The Advanced option enables you to choose the same options as the Basic option, except that you can perform this action on the basis of an Active Directory security group. For example, members of the Research group might be redirected to \\FS1\FolderRedirection, and members of the Astronomy group might be redirected to \\FS2\FolderRedirection.

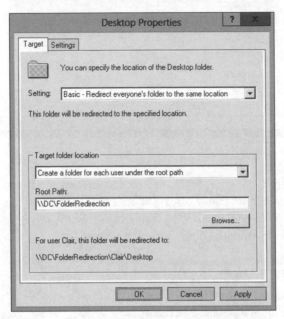

FIGURE 6-2 The Basic Folder Redirection setting

When configuring Folder Redirection for the Pictures, Music, And Videos folder, you can choose the Follow The Documents Folder option. When you do this, these folders become subfolders of the Documents folder.

REAL WORLD **SIMPLICITY BEATS COMPLEXITY**

Having the Pictures, Music, And Videos folder follow the Documents folder simplifies the management of shared folders. On the other hand, most organizations that aren't involved in producing music and video content have strict rules about the storage of that content on their servers and won't configure redirection for these specific folders.

When creating the network shares that will host redirected folders, ensure that you set the following permissions to ensure that redirected folders can be created automatically:

- Share Permissions For Root Folder
  - User's Security Group: Read and Write

- NTFS Permissions
    - User's Security Group: List Folder/Read Data, Create Folders/Append Data
    - Local System: Full Control

When configuring Folder Redirection, keep the following in mind:

- Enable Offline Files on all computers that are subject to Folder Redirection policies. Doing this ensures that redirected folders are available if network connectivity is lost. When you do this, ensure that Offline Folder functionality is also enabled at the shared folder level.
- Ensure that redirected folders are hosted on a fault tolerant storage space or volume.
- Ensure that the servers that host redirected folders are regularly backed up.
- Redirection should occur only with shared folders within the same site. Although laptop computers subject to Folder Redirection policies may occasionally be used at branch office sites (in which case Offline Files functionality applies), do not configure Folder Redirection policies that redirect local folders to locations on remote networks.

To redirect a folder, perform the following steps:

1. Configure a shared folder with the appropriate permissions.
2. Create and edit a Group Policy that applies to the users whose folders you want to redirect.
3. In the User Configuration\Policies\Windows Settings\Folder Redirection node, right-click the first folder that you want to configure redirection for and click Properties.
4. Use the Setting drop-down menu to select the Basic or Advanced option and then configure the target folder location.
5. Repeat steps 3 and 4 for each folder that you want to redirect.

> **NOTE MULTIPLE LOGONS REQUIRED**
>
> The user has to sign on several times before redirection is fully configured. This process enables folders to be created by the process and also accounts for cached credentials.

Software installation

Getting software on to a user's computers is a core task for IT professionals. In the era of Windows 95 and Windows NT 4.0, this usually meant travelling to the user's computer with a box of diskettes or CD-ROMs. Rather than having to install software locally, you can use Group Policy to deploy software to users and computers. When you do this, the software is installed over the network and it is no longer necessary to visit each computer individually to install a program. Group Policy supports software deployment for applications that use the Windows Installer (.msi) format as well as in .exe format if you use specially prepared .zap files (see the following sections).

.msi files

.msi files represent packaged applications in Microsoft Windows Installer (MSI) format. Files in this format include the information necessary to instruct an operating system on how to install the application, repair the application, and remove the application. Applications installed from .msi files are more likely to uninstall cleanly than applications deployed in other manners because the packaging process involves recording the precise system changes that occur when the application is installed on a reference computer. Applications in MSI format can be deployed using Group Policy, but you can also install them manually or deploy them using management products such as Windows Intune or System Center 2012 R2 Configuration Manager.

> **REAL WORLD** **PACKAGING APPLICATIONS**
>
> Packaging an application involves installing the application on a reference system using a traditional installer and then recording the changes the application makes to the system, including files, folders, settings, and the registry. There are third-party tools available that enable you to package applications that use installers in EXE format so that they can be deployed in MSI format. You can also use the App-V sequencer, available in the Microsoft Desktop Optimization Pack (MDOP) to create virtualized applications in MSI format, though running these requires the App-V client.

.zap files

You can use Group Policy to deploy files in EXE format through .zap files, which are files in text format that enable you to install software in EXE format using Group Policy under the following conditions:

- The installation must complete without requiring elevated privileges.
- The .zap file can only be published to users. You cannot use the Assigned deployment type for users or computers.
- When published, the user must use the Programs And Features item in the Control Panel.

Because the installation cannot require elevated privileges, most applications in EXE format cannot use .zap files to deploy many applications because many applications require elevated privileges to install on computers running Windows Vista, Windows 7, Windows 8, or Windows 8.1.

The .zap files must include the following fields:

- **FriendlyName** A simple name that enables you to identify the application.
- **SetupCommand** Provides the path to the application installer.

For example, you need to install an application named CompanyApp. The installer for this application, Setup.exe, is located on the shared folder with the UNC path \\Sydney-FS\Deployment. A .zap file created to install this application would have the following format.

```
[Application]

FriendlyName = "CompanyApp"

SetupCommand = "\\Sydney-FS\Deployment\setup.exe"
```

> **REAL WORLD** **LIMITATIONS AND UTILITY**
>
> The reason you've probably never heard of .zap files is because most .exe files require
> elevated privileges to install. As you don't want average users signing on with privileged
> accounts, it means that .zap files are pretty limited in their utility.

You have two options when deploying software using Group Policy. You can assign an
application, or you can publish the application, as shown in Figure 6-3. The Advanced option
enables you to configure advanced published or assigned settings.

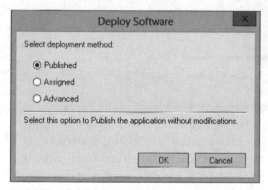

FIGURE 6-3 Publish or assign

Assign an application

Assigning an application means that the application installs automatically. How an application
installs automatically depends on whether the application is assigned to a user or to a
computer. If you assign an application to a computer, the application installs when the
computer starts up. If you assign an application to a user, the application installs after the user
signs on.

When you configure an application to be assigned, you can configure the following
deployment options, shown in Figure 6-4:

- Uninstall The Application When It Falls Out Of The Scope Of Management
- Do Not Display This Package In The Add/Remove Programs Control Panel
- Install This Application At Logon

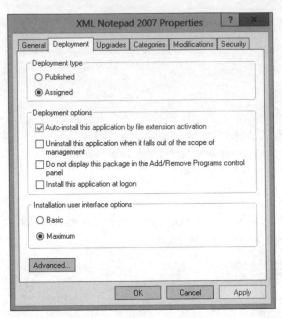

FIGURE 6-4 Assigned application options

If you enable the option to uninstall the application when it falls out of the scope of management, the application will be removed in the event that the policy that caused it to be installed no longer applies. For example, if you used a policy to assign the application to an organizational unit (OU) that contained a user account, and the application was installed because the user associated with that account signed on, the application would be removed if a user associated with a user account in a different OU signed on.

> **REAL WORLD** **OUT OF SCOPE OF MANAGEMENT**
>
> If you want to ensure that an application is removed when a user signs off from a particular computer, you're better off using App-V, which enables application streaming. This means that the application is delivered over the network automatically when a user who needs to access the application signs on. App-V is part of the MDOP.

Publishing applications

Applications can be published only to users, not computers. When you publish an application to a user, the application becomes available in the following ways:

- If the user double-clicks a file extension associated with the application, the application installs automatically.
- The user can choose to install the program through the Programs And Features item in Control Panel. The user does not require administrative privileges to perform this action.

Software deployment recommendations

There are a few things to keep in mind when deploying software using Group Policy:

- Ensure that the Everyone group has Read access at the network share level to the shared folder that hosts the installation files. In multisite organizations, consider using the Distributed File System (DFS) because it minimizes the chance that the installation will occur over a wide area network (WAN) link.

- Consider creating a GPO for each application. This reduces the amount of effort required to track which GPO is associated with each application.

- Link the GPO as close to the user or computer account as possible. For example, if you are deploying an application to users in the Astronomy OU, link the GPO to the Astronomy OU. If you then need to deploy the same application to users in another OU, link the same GPO to that OU.

- If you need to deploy to only a small number of users, configure a security filter on the GPO and then link the GPO as close as possible to the user accounts.

- Deploy commonly used applications in the installation image. Only use Group Policy to deploy applications that you have not included in the deployment image.

Performing software deployment

To assign an application, perform the following steps:

1. Place the application's .msi file on a shared folder to which the Everyone group has read access.

2. Create a new GPO and link it at the appropriate location, such as to the OU that hosts the user or to computer accounts to which you want to deploy software.

3. If deploying to a user account, expand the User Configuration\Policies\Software Settings node and right-click Software Installation. If deploying to a computer account, expand the Computer Configuration\Policies\Software Settings node and right-click Software Installation.

4. Click New and click Package.

5. Navigate to the shared folder that hosts the package, select the package, and click Open. Ensure that you don't navigate to the local address.

6. If you are performing deployment to a user, choose between Published and Assigned; otherwise, choose Published.

7. Right-click the software package and configure any advanced deployment options.

 **Quick check**
- Which one of the following options is possible: Publish or assign software to a computer through Group Policy?

Quick check answer
- You can only assign software to a computer through Group Policy. You can't publish software to a computer through Group Policy.

Upgrading packages

You can use a Group Policy software deployment to upgrade existing deployed packages. To do this, create a new software deployment using the upgraded package. When you have created the deployment, edit the properties of the new package. On the Upgrades tab, specify the package that you want to replace, as shown in Figure 6-5.

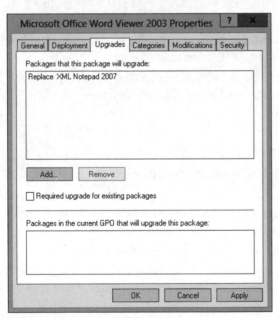

FIGURE 6-5 Upgrading an application

Scripts

As an experienced administrator, you know what a script is and how it works. You've probably even written a few of them yourself. Group Policy enables you to deploy scripts to users and computers. Most people use scripts with Group Policy to accomplish tasks that normally couldn't be accomplished with Group Policy. In the past, this primarily involved tasks such as mapping printers and shared network drives, which can now be accomplished with Group Policy preferences. Scripts can be in any format that will run on the client. It may be necessary to configure the client to support scripts that are not in .bat, .cmd, or the Windows PowerShell format.

There are four types of scripts you can configure using Group Policy:

- **Startup script**   This script executes when the computer starts up, but before a user logs on. You assign this script in a GPO that applies to the Computer account.
- **Logon script**   This script executes when the user logs on. You assign this script in a GPO that applies to the User account.
- **Logoff script**   This script executes when a user logs off. You assign this script in a GPO that applies to the User account. The Group Policy items for assigning logoff scripts are shown in Figure 6-6.
- **Shutdown script**   This script executes when a computer shuts down. You assign this script in a GPO that applies to the Computer account.

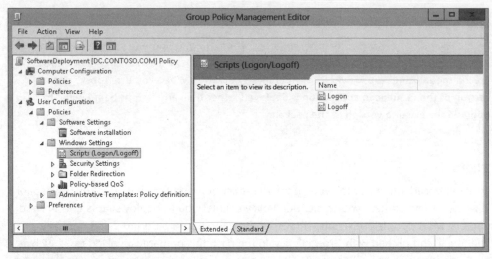

FIGURE 6-6 Assigning logon and logoff policies

Scripts assigned to the computer run using the rights and privileges assigned to the computer's Local System account. Scripts assigned to the user run using the user's rights and privileges. Scripts must be stored on shared folders on the network. You should be careful about assigning security permissions to these folders because if you enable people to modify the scripts hosted on shared folders, they can make modifications to other people's computers. Microsoft recommends using the Netlogon share for storing scripts published through Active Directory, but you can use any appropriately configured share for this purpose.

To deploy scripts, perform the following steps:

1. Create a network share to which the Everyone group has only Read access.

2. Copy the script to be deployed to this share.

3. Edit the GPO that you want to use to deploy the script.

4. If you want to configure a logon or a logoff script, navigate to the User Configuration\Policies\Windows Settings\Scripts (Logon/Logoff node).

5. If you want to configure a startup or a shutdown script, navigate to the Computer Configuration\Policies\Windows Settings\Scripts (Startup/Shutdown node).

6. Right-click the script type that you want to configure, and click Properties.

7. On the Script Properties page, shown in Figure 6-7, click Add to add a script in batch file format. If you are adding a Windows PowerShell script, select the PowerShell Scripts tab. If you want multiple scripts to run, you can use this tab to configure the order in which the scripts run.

FIGURE 6-7 Script policies

Lesson summary

- Folder redirection enables you to redirect important folders on client computers to network locations.
- You can use Folder Redirection with Offline Files to ensure that redirected folders are accessible when there is no network connectivity.
- You can use Group Policy to install software in MSI and ZAP format.
- ZAP format can only be used to install software that does not require elevated privileges to install.
- You can assign software to computers and users. When you assign software, it installs the next time the computer starts or the user logs on.
- You can publish software to users. This makes the software available to the user through Programs And Features.
- You can configure start up, shut down, logon, and logoff scripts using Group Policy. These scripts can be in any scripting format understood by the client.

Lesson review

Answer the following questions to test your knowledge of the information in this lesson. You can find the answers to these questions and explanations of why each answer choice is correct or incorrect in the "Answers" section at the end of this chapter.

1. You are planning the deployment of scripts using Group Policy. You want to have a script run each time a user logs off that copies all their local files to a backup location on the network. Which of the following Group Policy items could you configure to accomplish this goal?

   A. Startup script

   B. Logoff script

   C. Shutdown script

   D. Logon script

2. A specific user who has the sole account in a specific OU always uses the same computer. The computer account is in an OU by itself. You want a particular software package to install the next time the user's computer starts. Which of the following steps should you take to accomplish this goal?

   A. Publish the package using the Computer Configuration\Policies\Software Settings node.

   B. Assign the package using the Computer Configuration\Policies\Software Settings node.

   C. Publish the package using the User Configuration\Policies\Software Settings node.

   D. Assign the package using the User Configuration\Policies\Software Settings node.

3. You want to have three network drives automatically mapped each time a user signs on to the computer. This operation should occur using a script applied through Group Policy. Which of the following should you configure to accomplish this goal?

   A. Startup script

   B. Logoff script

   C. Shutdown script

   D. Logon script

4. You want to ensure that items such as folders and documents that a user stores on their desktop are available to them independently of which computer they sign on to in your organization's AD DS domain. Which of the following Folder Redirection policies should you configure to accomplish this goal?

   A. AppData(Roaming)

   B. Desktop

   C. Documents

   D. Favorites

5. A specific user who has the sole account in a specific OU always uses the same computer. The computer account is also in an OU by itself. You want a particular software package to install the next time the user's logs on. Which of the following steps should you take to accomplish this goal? (Choose all that apply.)

   A. Assign the package using the User Configuration\Policies\Software Settings node.

    B. Publish the package using the User Configuration\Policies\Software Settings node.

    C. Assign the package using the Computer Configuration\Policies\Software Settings node.

    D. Publish the package using the Computer Configuration\Policies\Software Settings node.

6. You want to ensure that a user's Internet Explorer bookmarks are available to the user when they sign on to any computer in your organization's Active Directory Domain Services (AD DS) domain. Which of the following Folder Redirection policies should you configure to accomplish this goal? (Choose all that apply.)

    A. Favorites

    B. Documents

    C. Desktop

    D. AppData(Roaming)

7. You want to force each computer that has an account in an Active Directory OU to perform a time synchronization against a specific time server each time the computer starts. You have created a script that performs this task. Which of the following steps must you take to ensure that the script is run in an appropriate manner? (Choose two. Each answer forms part of a complete solution.)

    A. Create a GPO and apply it to the OU that hosts the computers.

    B. Create a GPO and apply it to the domain.

    C. Configure a policy in the Computer Configuration\Policies\Windows Settings\Scripts (Startup/Shutdown) node.

    D. Configure a policy in the User Configuration\Policies\Windows Settings\Scripts (Logon/Logoff) node.

8. You want a particular package to be available to users, but they need to install it using the Programs And Features item in Control Panel. Which of the following strategies could you use to accomplish this goal?

    A. Publish the package using the User Configuration\Policies\Software Settings node.

    B. Assign the package using the User Configuration\Policies\Software Settings node.

    C. Publish the package using the Computer Configuration\Policies\Software Settings node.

    D. Assign the package using the Computer Configuration\Policies\Software Settings node.

Lesson 2: Administrative templates

Administrative templates enable you to extend Group Policies so that you can use Group Policies to manage applications as well as operating system settings. For example, you can import an administrative template into a GPO that has settings related to a specific application. You can then use that extended GPO to apply those settings to users and computers just as you would operating system settings configured in a traditional GPO. In this lesson, you learn about administrative templates, and you'll learn how to configure the Group Policy store so that you can import administrative templates and use them in GPOs. You'll also learn about the ADMX Migrator and how to filter administrative templates so only relevant templates are displayed in the Group Policy Management Editor.

> **After this lesson, you will be able to:**
> - Edit administrative template settings.
> - Import templates.
> - Use ADMX Migrator.
> - Use administrative template property filters.
>
> **Estimated lesson time: 60 minutes**

Administrative templates

Administrative templates are stored in XML format in files that use the .admx extension. .admx files are language-neutral, and the language component is stored in a region-specific .adml file. .admx files are stored in the Windows\PolicyDefinitions folder, and .adml files are stored in a subfolder of the policy definitions folder.

Prior to the release of Windows Vista, administrative templates were in a non-XML format known as ADM. ADM files are still supported for Windows Server 2012 R2 GPOs. Most applications that run on the Windows 7, Windows 8, and Windows 8.1 clients were written after the release of Windows Vista. Those that do include administrative templates are likely to include them in ADMX format.

> *MORE INFO* **MANAGING .ADMX FILES**
>
> You can learn more about managing .admx files at *http://technet.microsoft.com/en-us/library/cc709647(WS.10).aspx*.

Administrative template settings

You edit the settings in administrative templates in the same manner that you edit other Group Policy item settings. Policies located in the Administrative Templates node are processed in the same manner as other Group Policy items. There are more than 1,500 administrative template policy items available in a Windows Server 2012 R2 GPO, and some of these policy items are shown in Figure 6-8. You can add additional settings by importing administrative templates into the central store. Administrative templates are often provided with applications, or they can be downloaded from the support websites of application vendors.

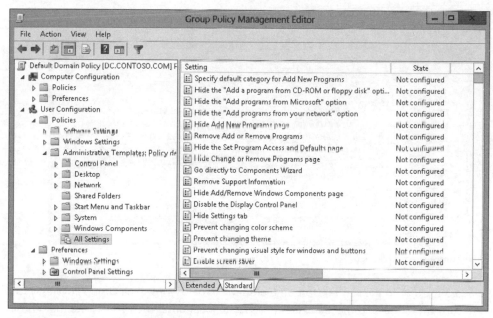

FIGURE 6-8 Administrative template settings

MORE INFO **ADMINISTRATIVE TEMPLATE SETTINGS**

You can learn more about administrative template settings at *http://technet.microsoft.com/ en-us/library/cc771104.aspx*.

Central store

To use administrative templates in ADMX format, you need to create a central store. When you create a central store, the administrative templates placed in that store will be available to all existing and new GPOs. Creating a central store is a manual process, and you need to copy new .admx and .adml files to the appropriate folders in the central store should you wish to use them with Group Policy in your organization. To create a central store, perform the following steps:

1. Log on to a domain controller in the domain with an account that has Domain Admin privileges.

2. Use File Explorer to open the following location: \\Domain.fqdn\Sysvol\Domain.fqdn\ Policies. For example, for the contoso.com domain, this would be \\Contoso.com\ Sysvol\Contoso.com\Policies.

3. Copy the C:\Windows\PolicyDefinitions folder and its contents to \\Domain.fqdn\ Sysvol\Domain.fqdn\Policies. Figure 6-9 shows the result of this process for the domain contoso.com.

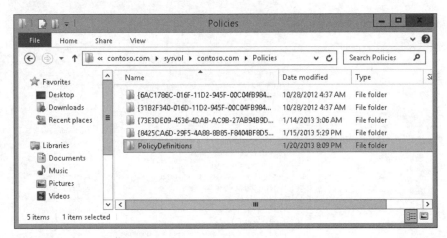

FIGURE 6-9 Group Policy store

To add templates to the central store so that they can be used with all Group Policies, you need to copy the .admx and the .adml files to separate locations. When you create the central store, a region-based subfolder is created. For computers in North America, this folder will be en-US. For computers in other regions, this subfolder uses the appropriate regional name. To import an administrative template, you need to perform the following steps:

1. Copy the .admx file to the \\Domain.fqdn\Sysvol\Domain.fqdn\Policies\ PolicyDefinitions folder.

2. Copy the .adml file to the appropriate regional folder under \\Domain.fqdn\Sysvol\ Domain.fqdn\Policies\PolicyDefinitions. For example, if contoso.com were located in North America, the location of this folder would be \\Contoso.com\Sysvol\Contoso. com\Policies\PolicyDefinitions\en-US.

If you want to import a template in ADM format and you do not want to convert it to ADMX format, you can add a template in ADM format to a single GPO using the Group Policy Management Editor, which attaches the template to the GPO. To do this, open the GPO that you want to add the template to using the Group Policy Management Editor, and on the Action menu, click Add/Remove Templates. In the Add/Remove Templates dialog box, shown in Figure 6-10, click Add to add a template. You can use this process to remove an existing template attached to the GPO.

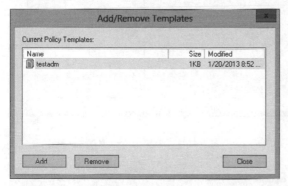

FIGURE 6-10 Importing an administrative template in ADM format

✔ Quick check

- Which folder should you copy when creating the Group Policy store?

Quick check answer

- You should copy the C:\Windows\PolicyDefinitions folder when creating the Group Policy store.

ADMX Migrator

The ADMX Migrator is a tool that you can use to convert administrative templates in ADM format to ADMX format. The ADMX Migrator is a GUI-based program. ADMX Migrator also includes a command line tool that can be used to automate the migration of administrative templates to ADMX format. The ADMX Migrator also includes an ADMX editor for creating and editing administrative templates in ADMX format. The ADMX Migrator is shown in Figure 6-11.

MORE INFO **DOWNLOAD ADMX MIGRATOR**

To download ADMX Migrator, navigate to the following website at *http://www.microsoft.com/en-in/download/details.aspx?id=15058*.

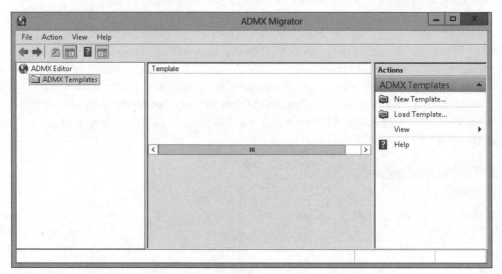

FIGURE 6-11 ADMX Migrator

REAL WORLD **CONVERTING ADM TO ADMX**

The last update of the ADMX Migrator was in 2009. Most software does not ship with administrative templates, and software that runs on the Windows 8 operating system that does ship with administrative templates almost always provides them in ADMX format.

Filter property settings

There are more than 1,800 policy settings located in the Administrative Templates section of the Computer Configuration area of a default Windows Server 2012 GPO. There are more than 1,500 policy settings in the Administrative Templates section of the User Configuration area of a default Windows Server 2012 R2 GPO. Unless you know the precise location of the policy you are looking for, this can make searching for a policy related to a specific setting or policy tedious at best.

To simplify the process of locating relevant Group Policy items, you can filter settings in administrative templates to find specific policy settings. You can use the Filter Options dialog box, shown in Figure 6-12, to filter administrative template policies based on the following:

- Managed, Configured, or Commented settings
- Group Policy keywords in the Policy Name, Help Text, or Comments
- Requirements filters to limit policies to specific products

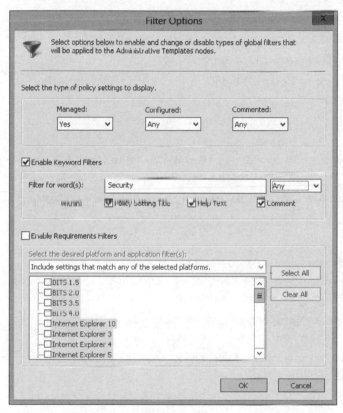

FIGURE 6-12 Filtering administrative templates

To filter policies related to administrative templates, perform the following steps:

1. Open Group Policy Management Editor. From the Action menu, click Filter Options.
2. In the Filter Options dialog box, configure filters by choosing the following options:
   - **Enable Keyword Filters**   Enter the keyword you want to search for.
   - **Enable Requirement Filters**   Specify the product that you want to view administrative template settings for.
3. Click OK. On the Action menu, click Filter On.
4. Under the Administrative Templates node of the Computer Configuration setting and the User Configuration setting, only the filtered policies will be displayed.
5. Turn the filter off by removing the Filter On selection on the Action menu.

MORE INFO **FILTERING ADMINISTRATIVE TEMPLATES**

For more information about filtering administrative templates, see *http://technet.microsoft.com/en-us/library/cc772295.aspx.*

Lesson summary

- Administrative templates enable you to extend Group Policy.
- Administrative templates in XML format use the .admx file extension.
- Older administrative templates use the ADM format.
- You need to configure a Group Policy store before you can import administrative templates in ADMX format.
- The .admx file of a template is language independent. The .adm file contains region-specific information.
- You can use the ADMX Migrator to convert templates in ADM format to ADMX and ADML format.
- You can use administrative template filters to reduce the number of policies displayed.

Lesson review

Answer the following questions to test your knowledge of the information in this lesson. You can find the answers to these questions and explanations of why each answer choice is correct or incorrect in the "Answers" section at the end of this chapter.

1. You are the administrator at contoso.com, and you want to configure the central store for Group Policy. Which of the following steps should you take to accomplish this goal?

   A. Copy the C:\Windows\PolicyDefinitions folder and its contents to \\Contoso.com\Sysvol\Contoso.com\Policies.

   B. Copy the \\Contoso.com\Sysvol\Contoso.com\Policies folder and its contents to the C:\Windows\PolicyDefinitions folder.

   C. Copy the C:\Windows\SYSVOL folder and its contents to \\Contoso.com\Sysvol\Contoso.com\Policies.

   D. Copy the \\Contoso.com\Sysvol\Contoso.com\Policies folder and its contents to C:\Windows\SYSVOL folder.

2. You are the systems administrator of contoso.com in North America, and you need to import a new administrative template into the Group Policy store. The administrative template has two files: Application.admx and Application.adml. Which of the following steps should you take to import the administrative template? (Choose two. Each answer forms part of a complete solution.)

A. Copy Application.admx to \\Contoso.com\Sysvol\Contoso.com\Policies\ PolicyDefinitions.

B. Copy Application.adml to \\Contoso.com\Sysvol\Contoso.com\Policies\ PolicyDefinitions\,

C. Copy Application.admx to \\Contoso.com\Sysvol\Contoso.com\Policies\ PolicyDefinitions\en-US.

D. Copy Application.adml to \\Contoso.com\Sysvol\Contoso.com\Policies\ PolicyDefinitions\en US.

Lesson 3: Group Policy preferences

Group Policy preferences enable you to configure settings, such as mapped drives and printers (which previously could be configured only through logon scripts) to be configured directly through Group Policy. Group Policy preferences are more reliable because they are reapplied when Group Policy applies. In this lesson, you will learn how to configure printers, network drive mappings, power plan options, and other settings using Group Policy preferences.

After this lesson, you will be able to use Group Policy preferences to configure:

- Printers
- Mapped network drives
- Power plans
- Registry settings
- Internet Explorer settings

Estimated lesson time: 60 minutes

Group Policy preference settings

Group Policy preferences enable you to configure many features that in the past had to be configured through the use of startup and logon scripts. Group Policy preferences differ from other Group Policy settings in the following ways:

- Preference settings are not enforced, whereas Group Policy settings disable the ability for the user to change a setting.
- Group Policy preferences are not removed if the policy no longer applies. A user can manually remove a configuration setting applied through Group Policy preferences.

When configuring Group Policy preferences, there is a series of options that are common to all items, shown in Figure 6-13.

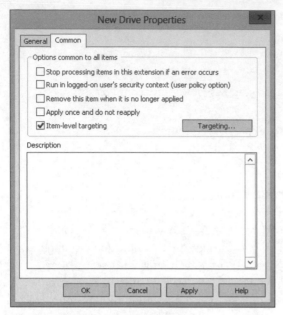

FIGURE 6-13 Common items settings

- Stop processing items in this extension if an error occurs. If a problem occurs, no preferences from this GPO will be applied to the target user or computer.

- Run in logged-on user's security context (user policy option). When the Group Policy preference is in a GPO applied to a computer account, it runs using the Local System account's privileges. Enabling this option means that a Group Policy preference applied to a computer account will run using the signed-on user's security context.

- Remove this item when it is no longer applied. When enabled, the setting will be removed if the policy that applied the setting is no longer in effect. If a policy is created without this option and applied to the computer, and then this setting is changed, it will not affect the computer. The default behavior is for these settings to persist even though they can be modified by the user.

- Apply once and do not reapply. When this option is enabled, the preference applies only at logon or startup. Otherwise, the preference is reapplied when Group Policy refreshes.

REAL WORLD **TESTING GROUP POLICY PREFERENCES**

The more complex the GPO, the more likely something is to not work as expected. Verify that each option works before you add additional options, rather than adding everything at the beginning and then trying to figure out why some of them didn't work.

Item-level targeting

Item-level targeting enables you to specify when a specific preference should apply. For example, you can use item-level targeting to ensure that a preference only applies to some, but not all, users and computers that are subject to the policy. You can configure item-level targeting based on the following categories:

- Battery Present
- Computer Name
- CPU Speed
- Date Match
- Disk Space
- Domain
- Environment Variable
- File Match
- IP Address Range
- Language
- LDAP Query
- MAC Address Range
- MSI Query
- Network Connection
- Operating System
- Organizational Unit
- PCMCIA Present
- Portable Computer
- Processing Mode
- RAM
- Registry Match
- Security Group
- Site
- Terminal Session
- Time Range
- User
- WMI Query

It is also possible to mix and match these categories. For example, you could configure item-level targeting so that a Group Policy preference applies only if the computer is running the Windows 8 operating system, has more than 4 gigabytes (GB) of RAM, has a CPU speed greater than 1 gigahertz (GHz), and there is more than 80 GB free on the system drive. This set of targeting categories is shown in Figure 6-14.

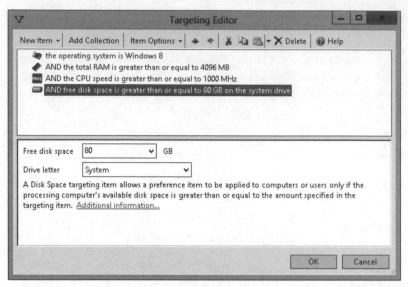

FIGURE 6-14 Targeting Editor categories

> **REAL WORLD** **ITEM-LEVEL TARGETING**
>
> Item-level targeting enables you to be specific in the way you apply Group Policy preferences. It enables you to accomplish graphically what you might have only been able to accomplish using complex Windows Management Instrumentation (WMI) queries. If you use Group Policy preferences on a regular basis, you may want to consider moving to Microsoft System Center 2012 R2 Configuration Manager. In Configuration Manager, you can create collections that enable you to define groups of computers on the basis of the properties of the system, such as operating system version, CPU speed, free disk space, and total random access memory (RAM).

Mapping network drives

One of the most common uses of logon scripts in enterprise environments is to map network drives. With Group Policy preferences, you can map network drives to occur within Group Policy without requiring the use of a net use command in a logon script.

To configure Group Policy preferences to map network drives, perform the following steps:

1. Locate the Drive Maps item under Preferences\Windows Settings in the User Configuration area of a GPO. Drive Maps is a Group Policy preference that can't be configured through the Computer Configuration area.

2. Right-click Drive Maps, click New, and then click Mapped Drive.

3. In the New Drive Properties dialog box, shown in Figure 6-15, enter the information necessary to connect the user's drive.

FIGURE 6-15 Mapping a network drive

When setting up a mapped network drive, you can configure the following options:

- **Action** The default is Update, but can also be set to Create, Replace, or Delete. This option determines what happens with the mapping. Update means that if the setting is in place, reset it with the configured settings. In most cases, the configured settings will be the same as what is already in place.

- **Location** The network share to which the drive will map.

- **Reconnect** Enable this option if you want to reconnect a mapped drive that the user has disconnected.

- **Label As** Provides the mapped network drive with a volume label.

- **Drive Letter** You can choose between assigning the first available drive letter or whether a specific drive letter is associated with the mapped drive.

- **Connect As** Use this option if you want the drive mapped with a specific set of credentials.

- **Hide/Show This Drive** Determines whether the drive is visible in File Explorer.

- **Hide/Show All Drives** Determines whether all drives are visible in File Explorer.

You can also configure the common properties for each item and item-level targeting. Because you can perform item-level targeting based on security group, you can use the Drive Maps Group Policy preferences item in a single GPO applied at the domain level to configure drive mapping based on security groups for all users in the organization.

Configuring printers

With Group Policy preferences, you can map network printers to computers. When you map a printer using Group Policy preferences, you can choose whether to set the mapped printer as the default printer or configure the mapped printer only as a default printer if a local printer is not present.

Although you can use either the Computer Configuration or the User Configuration areas of a GPO to map a printer, you can use only the User Configuration area to map a printer shared off another computer. You can use both areas to map local and TCP/IP printers. To use Group Policy preferences to map a printer, perform the following steps:

1. Navigate to the Preferences\Control Panel Settings node, right-click Printers, and click New. Then choose between Shared Printer, TCP/IP Printer, and Local Printer. Local printers must be connected to the computer and shared printers must be shared from a computer and be addressable using a Universal Naming Convention (UNC) path.

2. In the New Shared Printer Properties dialog box, shown in Figure 6-16, choose between Update/Replace, Create, and Delete. Enter the network address of the printer and whether the printer should be configured as a default printer.

FIGURE 6-16 Mapping a printer

Windows 8 clients will attempt to retrieve the printer driver either from their local driver store, from the local WSUS server or from Windows Update. In previous versions of the Windows Client operating system, the client computer attempted to obtain printer driver software from the server that hosted the shared printer.

 Quick check

- Where do client computers running the Windows 8 or Windows 8.1 operating system obtain drivers for network printers?

Quick check answer

- Client computers running the Windows 8 or Windows 8.1 operating system will check if a printer driver is locally installed. The client will then check the local WSUS server or Windows Update to find the driver.

Configuring power options

Power options enable you to configure how computers with compatible hardware use power. Power options also enable you to configure how laptop computers react when someone closes the lid or when the computer resumes operation after hibernation. When configuring a power option, you need to choose one of the following:

- Power Options (Windows XP)
- Power Schemes (Windows XP)
- Power Plans (at least Windows 7)

When configuring power options, use item-level targeting to configure the following:

- Target operating systems. For example, you can use item-level targeting to ensure that the Power Options (Windows XP) and Power Scheme (Windows XP) settings are processed by computers running Windows XP. These options don't negatively affect computers running Windows Vista, Windows 7, Windows 8, or Windows 8.1 but it's good practice to apply operating system-specific settings only to those operating systems.

- Different power options at different times of the day. You can apply settings that enable high performance during office hours and then apply power saving plans for out-of-office hours. For example, you can configure settings so that if someone doesn't interact with the computer during office hours, they have more time before the computer goes into hibernation (compared with someone who doesn't interact with the computer after business hours).

When configuring power options, it is important to understand the difference between standby and hibernation. It is also important to recognize that not all computers support these advanced power options.

- When a computer is in standby, the computer is in a low power state, but the data required to resume normal operation is stored in RAM. This has the benefit of enabling the computer to quickly return from standby to full operation. The drawback of this mode is that it requires more electricity than hibernation mode.

- When a computer is hibernating, the data required to resume normal operation is stored in a special location on the hard disk. The computer can resume without performing a full startup operation, and instead loads the contents of the special location on the hard disk straight into memory.

REAL WORLD **WINDOWS VISTA POWER PLANS**

If you have any computers in your environment running Windows Vista, they can use the Windows 7 Power Plan option.

Power Options (Windows XP)

You use this item, shown in Figure 6-17, only when you want to configure power settings for computers running Windows XP. This item enables you to configure the following items:

- Always Show Icon On The Taskbar
- Prompt For Password When The Computer Resumes From Standby
- Enable Hibernation
- Power Buttons:
    - **When I Close The Lid Of My Portable Computer** This option determines how a laptop computer with a lid reacts when the lid is closed. The options are Do Nothing, Stand By, and Hibernate.
    - **When I Press The Power Button On My Computer** This option determines how a computer reacts when the power button is pressed. The options are Do Nothing, Ask Me What To Do, Stand by, Shutdown, and Hibernate.
    - **When I Press The Sleep Button On My Computer** This option determines how a computer reacts when the sleep button is pressed. The options are Do Nothing, Ask Me What To Do, Stand By, Shutdown, and Hibernate.

FIGURE 6-17 Power Options (Windows XP)

Power Scheme (Windows XP)

Power Scheme also applies to computers running Windows XP. Power schemes differ from power options because they enable you to specify when a particular computer will have its monitor turned off, be put into standby, or put into hibernation. You can configure different settings for when the computer is plugged in to main power or is running off batteries.

You can configure the following options in Windows XP Power Scheme:

- **Power Scheme**   Enables you to choose a power scheme to configure. The options are Home/Office Desk, Portable/Laptop, Presentation, Always On, Minimal Power Management, and Max Battery (see Figure 6-18).
- **Turn Off Monitor**
- **Turn Off Hard Disks**
- **System Standby**
- **System Hibernates**   Specifies the amount of time before a supported computer enters hibernation.

FIGURE 6-18 Configuring a power scheme

Power Plans

Power Plans enable you to configure settings for computers running Windows Vista, Windows 7, and Windows 8. Rather than just being limited to determining what happens to a computer when a power button is pressed or the computer isn't used for a specific amount of time, Power Plans enable you to configure additional options including PCI Express settings and processor power management. Using a Power Plan, shown in Figure 6-19, you can configure the following settings for both on battery and plugged-in modes:

- **Additional Settings** Enables you to configure whether a password is required on wakeup.

- **Hard Disk** Enables you to specify how long before the hard disk drive is powered down.

- **Sleep** Enables you to configure the following settings: Sleep After, Enable Hybrid Sleep, and Hibernate After. Sleep functions the same way that Stand By mode does in the settings for computers with the Windows XP operating system. The computer needs to support these advanced power options for them to be enforced by this policy.

- **Power Buttons And Lid** Enables you to configure settings for lid close action, power button action, and Start menu power button. Options are Do Nothing, Sleep, Hibernate, and Shut Down.

- **PCI Express**   Enables you to configure Link State Power Management for PCI Express components that support power management. Settings include Off, Moderate Power Savings, and Maximum Power Savings.

- **Processor Power Management**   Configures settings for minimum processor state and maximum processor state as a percentage. For example, you can configure the processor to work at 50 percent of maximum capacity when the computer is on battery.

- **Display**   Configures settings for how long to wait before turning the display off when the user has not interacted with the computer.

- **Battery**   Configures critical battery action, low battery level, critical battery level, low battery notification, and low battery action. You configure the level settings as a percentage. The action setting can be set to Do Nothing, Sleep, Hibernate, or Shutdown.

FIGURE 6-19 Windows 7 Power Plan

REAL WORLD   **POWER OPTION CONFIGURATION**

System Center 2012 R2 Configuration Manager offers more advanced power options than Group Policy preferences. System Center 2012 R2 Configuration Manager also enables you to generate power utilization reports, enabling you to see the impact of power options on power consumption.

Configuring the registry

You can use Group Policy preferences to configure registry settings by adding settings, deleting settings, or modifying existing settings. You can use an existing computer's registry settings as the basis for the settings that you want to configure, or you can configure the settings manually, as shown in Figure 6-20. You can configure registry settings using the Computer Configuration or User Configuration areas of a GPO.

FIGURE 6-20 Use Group Policy preferences to configure Remote Desktop settings

> **REAL WORLD EXTRA CARE REQUIRED**
>
> Direct registry modification is a process you should undertake reluctantly and direct registry modification across a large number of computers even more so. You are most likely to use this type of Group Policy preferences when you need to respond quickly to a security threat. Vendors often suggest registry fixes as responses to security alerts while they test and develop a software-based solution. In this situation, you have the option of waiting for the software solution or using Group Policy to deploy the registry modification. Each strategy has benefits and drawbacks, and the correct choice for one organization will be the incorrect choice for another.

Internet options

You can use Group Policy preferences to configure Internet options for the following versions of Internet Explorer:

- Internet Explorer 5 and 6

- Internet Explorer 7
- Internet Explorer 8 and 9
- Internet Explorer 10 and 11

The Group Policy preferences settings for each version of Internet Explorer appear in the same manner as the Internet Explorer item in the Control Panel does. Figure 6-21 shows the Group Policy preferences settings for Internet Explorer 10. You use the Internet Explorer 10 settings to configure Group Policy preference settings for Internet Explorer 11.

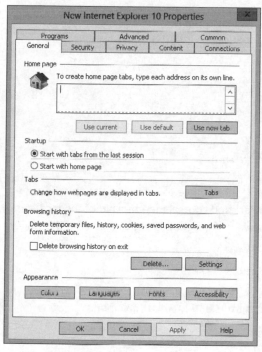

FIGURE 6-21 Use Group Policy preferences to configure Internet Explorer settings

Local Users And Groups

The Local Users And Groups option enables you to configure and create accounts for local users, as shown in Figure 6-22, and populate local groups. You can use this option to create, update, replace, and delete user accounts. When configuring local users, you should configure the password so that it is changed at next logon because this password is stored in the System Volume (SYSVOL) container in an unencrypted format. Because of this security risk, you should avoid using Group Policy preferences to populate computers with privileged local user accounts.

FIGURE 6-22 Adding a local user with Group Policy preferences

You can use the New Local Group Group Policy preference to configure the membership of local groups. You can use this policy to populate and control membership of the local Administrators group on each computer, as shown in Figure 6-23. You can also use this policy to perform the following tasks:

- Add users to a local group
- Remove users from a local group
- Delete all group members, including both users and member groups

FIGURE 6-23 Configuring a local group using Group Policy preferences

Additional settings

As you can see in Figure 6-24, there are many additional settings that you can configure using Group Policy preferences. These settings are split into Windows settings and Control Panel settings. Settings not covered earlier are covered in this section.

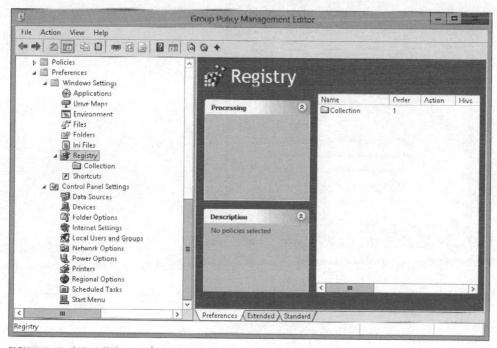

FIGURE 6-24 Group Policy preferences

Windows settings

The Group Policy preferences settings located in the Windows Settings area enable you to do the following:

- **Applications**   Enables you to configure application related settings. Applications must support Group Policy preferences before settings can be configured in this manner.

- **Environment**   Enables you to configure environment variables (for example, configuring the temporary directory variable).

- **Files**   Enables you to update files using a source and destination file. This enables you to populate computers with important files, such as ensuring that Human Resources directives on the correct utilization of the staff kitchen and coffee machine are copied to the policy documents directory on every user's desktop.

- **Folders**   Enables you to create, update, replace, or delete a folder and its contents. Figure 6-25 shows this Group Policy preference. For example, you can use Group Policy preferences to ensure that the temporary directory was automatically scrubbed each time the preference applied.

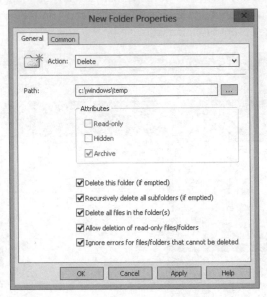

FIGURE 6-25 Deleting folder contents

- **Ini Files**   Enables you to update .ini files with specific properties and values. When using this setting, it is important to ensure that changes made to the .ini file do not stop it from being read by the computer.
- **Shortcuts**   Enables you to create shortcuts for use with desktop items, including the destination path and how the application triggered by the shortcut will be run. It is also possible for you to configure the location of a shortcut icon, as shown in Figure 6-26.

FIGURE 6-26 Shortcut settings

Control Panel settings

Additional Group Policy preferences settings can also be configured through the Control Panel settings node. This node includes settings that would normally be configured through a client computer's Control Panel.

You can configure the following settings using this Control Panel:

- **Data Sources** Enables you to configure Open Database Connectivity (ODBC) data sources. Configure this when clients need special connections configured to databases.

- **Devices** Enables you to configure whether devices are enabled or blocked. Figure 6-27 shows a Microsoft PS/2 mouse being blocked.

FIGURE 6-27 New device settings

- **Folder Options** When you configure folder options, you can configure a different set of options, for Windows XP or for computers running Windows Vista, Windows 7, Windows 8, or Windows 8.1. Folder options control how the contents of folders are displayed in File Explorer. For example, you can configure folder options to show hidden files and folders, to show encrypted and compressed NTFS files in a special color, and to hide protected operating system files. Figure 6-28 shows this Group Policy preference.

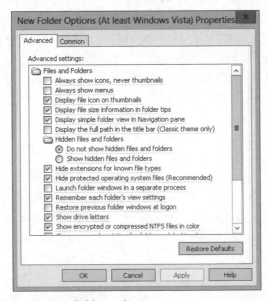

FIGURE 6-28 Folder options

- **Network Options** Use the Network Options Group Policy preference to configure VPN and dial-up connection settings for computers.
- **Regional Options** Use the Regional Options Group Policy preferences to specify the numbers, currency, time, date and other regional settings such as language.
- **Scheduled Tasks** You can use the Scheduled Tasks Group Policy preference to configure scheduled and immediate tasks. A scheduled task runs at a specific date and time configured according to the schedule. An immediate task, shown in Figure 6-29, enables you to run a specific task each time the Group Policy preference refreshes.

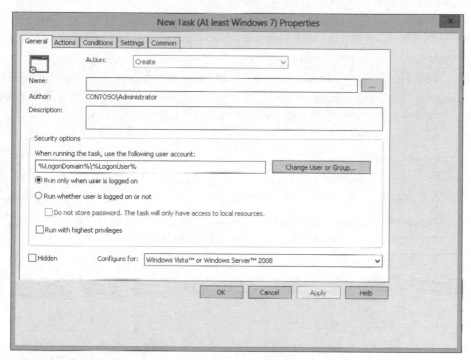

FIGURE 6-29 Running a new task

- **Start Menu** This option enables you to configure how the Start menu appears on computers running Windows client operating systems up to and including Windows 7. Using this option, you can configure whether the Computer, Control Panel, Documents, Favorites, and Games are displayed. You can also configure how many programs are displayed on the Start menu and how many recent items are displayed.

Lesson summary

- Group Policy preferences configure settings that can later be changed by users.
- Group Policy preferences are commonly used to set mapped network drives and printer settings.

- Item-level targeting enables the properties of the environment to be checked during the application of Group Policy preference items.
- You can configure Group Policy preferences so that users can't change applied settings.
- Use time-based item-level targeting to apply different power settings at different times of the day.

Lesson review

Answer the following questions to test your knowledge of the information in this lesson. You can find the answers to these questions and explanations of why each answer choice is correct or incorrect in the "Answers" section at the end of this chapter.

1. You are configuring Power Options Group Policy preferences. You want this power plan to apply only between midnight and 6 A.M. Which of the following item-level targeting options can you configure to accomplish this goal?

   A. Security Group

   B. Time Range

   C. Operating System

   D. Disk Space

2. You want to add a specific user account to all computers in an OU. Which Group Policy preferences item can you configure to accomplish this goal?

   A. Folder

   B. Devices

   C. Internet Settings

   D. Local Users And Groups

3. You want to configure a drive map, but this drive map should be configured only for computers used by executives. Which of the following item-level targeting options can you configure to accomplish this goal?

   A. Disk Space

   B. Operating System

   C. Time Range

   D. Security Group

4. You want to delete the contents of the C:\Windows\Temp folder on a number of computers in your organization each time Group Policy refreshes. Which of the following Group Policy preferences can you configure to accomplish this goal?

   A. Local Users And Groups

   B. Folder

   C. Devices

   D. Internet Settings

5. A particular set of environment variables should apply only to computers running the Windows 7 operating system, not to computers running Windows Vista or Windows 8. Which of the following item-level targeting options should you configure when setting up Group Policy preferences to apply these environment variables?

   A. Time Range

   B. Operating System

   C. Security Group

   D. Disk Space

6. You want to block users from using a specific type of USB storage drive on computers in your organization. Which of the following Group Policy preferences can you configure to accomplish this goal?

   A. Internet Settings

   B. Devices

   C. Folder

   D. Local Users And Groups

7. You are configuring a Group Policy preference immediate task to clean out the temporary directory only if the computer has less than 20 GB free space. Which of the following item-level targeting options can you configure to accomplish this goal?

   A. Security Group

   B. Time Range

   C. Operating System

   D. Disk Space

8. You want to configure VPN settings on a large number of client computers in your organization. Which of the following Group Policy preferences can you use to accomplish this goal?

   A. Local Users And Groups

   B. Folder

   C. Devices

   D. Internet Settings

Practice exercises

The goal of this section is to provide you with hands-on practice with the following:

- Configuring Folder Redirection using Group Policy
- Configuring startup, shutdown, logon, and logoff scripts using Group Policy
- Configuring the Group Policy store

- Enabling Group Policy filtering
- Creating local users using Group Policy preferences
- Mapping network drives using Group Policy preferences
- Creating power plans using Group Policy preferences

To perform the exercises in this section, you need access to an evaluation version of Windows Server 2012 R2. You should also have access to virtual machines SYD-DC, MEL-DC, CBR-DC, and ADL-DC, the setup instructions for which are described in the Introduction. You should ensure that you have a checkpoint of these virtual machines that you can revert to at the end of the practice exercises. You should revert the virtual machines to this initial state prior to beginning these exercises.

Exercise 1: Prepare Folder Redirection and scripts

In this exercise, you prepare a server to host folders for Folder Redirection and Group Policy–related scripts. To complete this exercise, perform the following steps:

1. Sign on to SYD-DC as Contoso\Administrator.
2. Click File Explorer on the taskbar and navigate to the root folder of volume C:.
3. Click the New Folder item on the title bar. Type the name of the new folder as **FolderRedirection**.
4. Right-click the FolderRedirection folder, click Share With, and then click Specific People.
5. In the File Sharing dialog box, click the down arrow next to Add and click Everyone.
6. Click Add and click the arrow next to Read. Set the Everyone group's permission to Read/Write, click Share, and click Done.
7. Right-click the FolderRedirection folder and click Properties.
8. Click the Sharing tab, click Advanced Sharing, and click Caching.
9. In the Offline Settings dialog box, shown in Figure 6-30, click All Files And Programs That Users Open From The Shared Folder Are Automatically Available Offline and click OK.

FIGURE 6-30 Offline settings

10. Click OK to close the Advanced Sharing dialog box and click Close to close the FolderRedirection Properties dialog box.

11. On the title bar of the Local Disk (C:) Window, click New Folder. Name the new folder Scripts.

12. Right-click the Scripts folder, click Share With, and click Specific People.

13. Click the down arrow next to Add, click Everyone, and then click Add.

14. Click Share and click Done.

15. Open the Scripts folder. Right-click in the empty space, click New, and click Text Document. Type the name **Logon** and press Enter.

16. Repeat step 14 and create files named Logoff, Startup, and Shutdown.

17. Click the View menu and click File Name Extensions.

18. Right-click each file and rename them as follows:

   - Logoff.txt to Logoff.bat

   - Logon.txt to Logon.bat

   - Shutdown.txt to Shutdown.bat

   - Startup.txt to Startup.bat

Exercise 2: Configure Folder Redirection

In this exercise, you configure Folder Redirection. To complete this exercise, perform the following steps:

1. In Server Manager, click the Tools menu, and then click Group Policy Management. The Group Policy Management Console (GPMC) opens.

2. In the GPMC, expand the Forest:Contoso.com node, then the Domains node, then the Contoso.com node, and then the Group Policy Objects node.

3. Right-click the Group Policy Objects node, and click New.

4. In the New GPO dialog box, shown in Figure 6-31, type the name **FolderRedirection** and click OK.

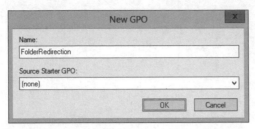

FIGURE 6-31 New GPO dialog box

5. Right-click the FolderRedirection policy and click Edit. The Group Policy Management Editor opens.

6. In the Group Policy Management Editor, expand the User Configuration\Policies\ Windows Settings\Folder Redirection node.

7. Right-click the Documents folder, and click Properties.

8. Configure the following settings, as shown in Figure 6-32, and click OK.

   - Setting: Basic - Redirect Everyone's Folder To The Same Location
   - Target Folder Location: Create A Folder For Each User Under The Root Path
   - Root Path: \\SYD-DC\FolderRedirection

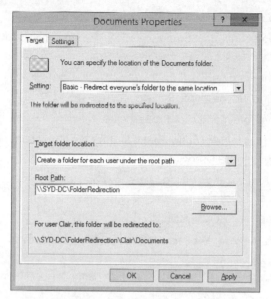

FIGURE 6-32 Redirecting the Documents folder

9. When prompted with the Warning dialog box, click Yes.

10. Right-click the Pictures folder and click Properties.

11. In the Pictures Properties dialog box, shown in Figure 6-33, configure the Setting to Follow The Documents Folder, and click OK.

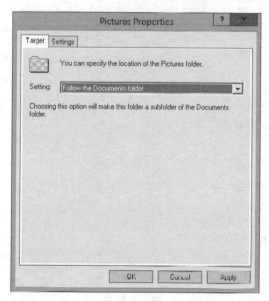

FIGURE 6-33 Redirecting the Pictures folder

12. Click Yes when presented with the warning.

13. Right-click the Music folder, and click Properties.

14. In the Music Properties dialog box, configure Setting to Follow The Documents folder, and click OK.

15. Click Yes when presented with the warning.

16. Repeat steps 13 through 15 for the Videos folder.

17. Right-click the AppData(Roaming) folder and click Properties.

18. In the AppData(Roaming) Properties folder, configure the Setting drop-down menu to Advanced – Specify Locations For Various User Groups.

19. Click Add. In the Specify Group And Location dialog box, shown in Figure 6-34, configure the following settings and click OK:

   - Security Group Membership: CONTOSO\Domain Users
   - Target Folder Location: Create A Folder For Each User Under The Root Path
   - Root Path: \\SYD-DC\FolderRedirection

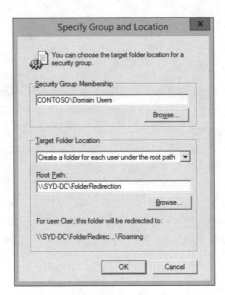

FIGURE 6-34 Advanced redirection settings

20. Click OK to close the AppData(Roaming) Properties folder.

21. Click Yes in the Warning dialog box.

Exercise 3: Configure Group Policy scripts

In this exercise, you configure Group Policy scripts. To complete this exercise, perform the following steps:

1. Click the Scripts (Logon/Logoff) node.
2. Right-click the Logon item and click Properties.
3. In the Logon Properties dialog box, click Add.
4. In the Add A Script dialog box, type **\\syd-dc\scripts\logon.bat** in the Script Name area as shown in Figure 6-35, and click OK.

FIGURE 6-35 Logon script settings

5. Click OK to close the Logon Properties dialog box. You can now right-click Logoff and click Properties; then continue.
6. In the Logoff properties dialog box, click Add.
7. In the Add A Script dialog box, type **\\syd-dc\scripts\logoff.bat** in the Script Name area and click OK.
8. Click OK to close the Logoff Properties dialog box.
9. Navigate to the Computer Configuration\Policies\Windows Settings\Scripts node.
10. Right-click Startup and click Properties.
11. In the Startup Properties dialog box, click Add.
12. In the Add A Script dialog box, type **\\syd-dc\scripts\startup.bat** in the Script Name area and click OK.

13. Click OK to close the Startup Properties dialog box.

14. Right-click Shutdown and click Properties.

15. In the Shutdown Properties dialog box, click Add.

16. In the Add A Script dialog box, type **\\syd-dc\scripts\shutdown.bat** in the Script Name area and click OK.

17. Click OK to close the Shutdown Properties dialog box.

18. Close the Group Policy Management Editor.

Exercise 4: Configure the central store and administrative template filtering

In this exercise, you configure the central store and perform administrative template filtering. To complete this exercise, perform the following steps:

1. Use File Explorer to open the following location: \\Contoso.com\Sysvol\Contoso.com\Policies.

2. Open a second File Explorer window and navigate to the C:\Windows folder.

3. Right-click the PolicyDefinitions folder and click Copy.

4. Switch to the File Explorer window that is open on \\Contoso.com\Sysvol\Contoso.com\Policies.

5. Right-click in an empty area and click Paste.

6. Open the GPMC.

7. Right-click the Forest: Contoso.com\Domains\Contoso.com\Group Policy Objects node and click New.

8. In the New GPO dialog box, type the name **Template Check** and click OK.

9. Right-click the Template Check GPO and click Edit.

10. Click the Computer Configuration\Policies\Administrative Templates node, click the Action menu, and click Filter Options.

11. Check Enable Keyword Filters. In the Filter For Word(s) text box, type **Biometrics**.

12. Check Enable Requirements Filters and then click Windows 8.1 Operating Systems, as shown in Figure 6-36. Click OK.

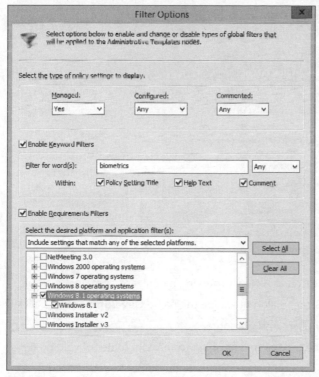

FIGURE 6-36 Logon script settings

13. Click the Computer Configuration\Policies\Administrative Templates\All Settings node and verify that only three policy items are listed.

Exercise 5: Configure Group Policy preferences

In this exercise, you configure Group Policy preferences. To complete this exercise, perform the following steps:

1. In Server Manager, click the Tools menu, and click Active Directory Users And Computers.

2. Click the Users container. In the toolbar, click the Create A New Group In The Current Container button.

3. In the New Object – Group dialog box, shown in Figure 6-37, type the name **Research** and click OK.

FIGURE 6-37 New security group

4. In the toolbar, click the Create A New Group In The Current Container button.

5. In the New Object – Group dialog box, type the name **Development** and click OK.

6. Close Active Directory Users And Computers.

7. Click File Explorer in the taskbar and navigate to the root folder of volume C:.

8. Click the New Folder icon in the title bar. Name the folder **ResearchShare**.

9. Right-click the ResearchShare folder, click Share With, and click Specific People.

10. In the File Sharing dialog box, type the name **Contoso\Research** and click Add.

11. Click the Read permission next to Research and click Read/Write, as shown in Figure 6-38.

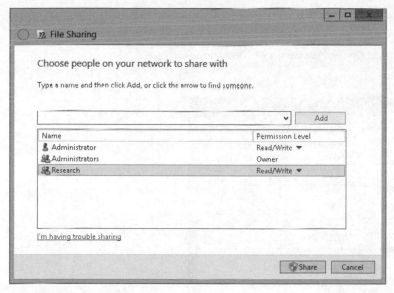

FIGURE 6-38 New security group

12. Click Share, and click Done.

13. Now it is time to deal with the title bar.

14. Click the New Folder icon in the title bar. Name the folder **DevelopmentShare**.

15. Right-click the DevelopmentShare folder, click Share With, and click Specific People.

16. In the File Sharing dialog box, type the name **Contoso\Development** and click Add.

17. Click the Read permission next to Development and click Read/Write. Click Share and click Done.

18. From the Tools menu of Server Manager, click Group Policy Management Console.

19. Right-click the Forest: Contoso.com\Domains\contoso.com\Group Policy Objects node and click New.

20. In the New GPO dialog box, type the name **GPPTest** and click OK.

21. Right-click the GPPTest GPO and click Edit.

22. In the Group Policy Management Editor, expand Computer Configuration\ Preferences\Control Panel Settings and click Local Users And Groups.

23. Right-click Local Users And Groups, click New, and click Local User.

24. In the New Local User Properties dialog box, shown in Figure 6-39, configure the following settings and click OK:

   ▪ Action: **Create**

   ▪ User name: **Generic_User**

   ▪ Full name: **Generic User**

- Password: **Pa$$w0rd**
- Confirm Password: **Pa$$w0rd**
- User Must Change Password At Next Logon
- Account Never Expires

FIGURE 6-39 New local user

25. In the Password warning dialog box, click OK.
26. Right-click Local Users And Groups, click New, and click Local Group.
27. In the New Local Group Properties dialog box, configure the following settings, as shown in Figure 6-40, and click OK:

- Action: **Create**
- Group name: **Generic_Group**
- Members: **Generic_User**

FIGURE 6-40 New security group

28. In the Group Policy Management Editor, expand the User Configuration\Preferences\ Windows Settings node.

29. Right-click Drive Maps, click New, and click Mapped Drive.

30. In the New Drive Properties dialog box, shown in Figure 6-41, configure the following settings and then click the Common tab.

- Action: **Update**
- Location: **\\SYD-DC\ResearchShare**
- Use: **R:**

FIGURE 6-41 New drive properties

31. In the Common tab, click Item-level Targeting, and then click Targeting.

32. In the Targeting Editor, click New Item and click Security Group. In the Group name, type **Contoso\Research**, as shown in Figure 6-42, and click OK.

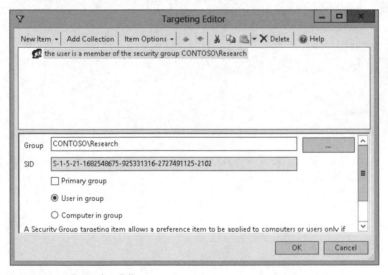

FIGURE 6-42 Targeting Editor

33. Click OK to close the New Drive Properties dialog box.

34. Right-click Drive Maps, click New, and click Mapped Drive.

35. In the New Drive Properties dialog box, configure the following settings and then click the Common tab:

- Action: **Update**
- Location: **\\SYD-DC\DevelopmentShare**
- Use: **V:**

36. On the Common tab, click Item-level targeting, and then click Targeting.

37. In the Targeting Editor, click New Item, and click Security Group. In the Group name, type **Contoso\Development** and click OK. Click OK to close the New Drive Properties dialog box.

38. Select the User Configuration\Preferences\Control Panel Settings\Power Options node.

39. Right-click the Power Options node, click New, and click Power Plan (At least Windows 7).

40. In the New Power Plan (At Least Windows 7) Properties dialog box, expand the Sleep node and configure the following settings for the Balanced power plan, as shown in Figure 6-43, and then click the Common tab.

- Sleep After: On Battery (Minutes): **10**
- Sleep after: Plugged In (Minutes): **20**
- Hibernate After: On Battery (Minutes): **20**
- Plugged In (Minutes): **30**

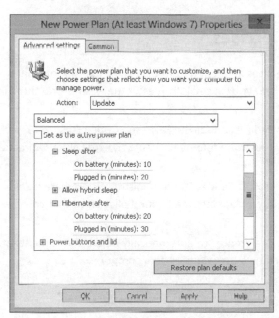

FIGURE 6-43 Power plan

41. On the Common tab, click Item-level Targeting, and click Targeting.

42. In the Targeting Editor, click New Item, and click Time Range.

43. In the Targeting Editor dialog box, set the range to between 6 P.M. and 7 A.M., as shown in Figure 6-44, and click OK.

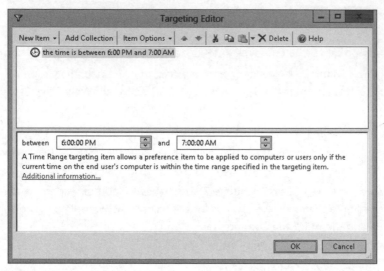

FIGURE 6-44 Power plan

44. Click OK twice and close the Group Policy Management Editor.

Suggested practice exercises

The following additional practice exercises are designed to give you more opportunities to practice what you've learned and to help you successfully master the lessons presented in this chapter.

- **Exercise 1** Configure Folder Redirection for the Favorites, Contacts, Links, Searches, and Saved Games folders. Redirect these folders to the \\SYD-DC\FolderRedirection network shared folder.

- **Exercise 2** Download the Microsoft Office 2013 administrative template from Microsoft's website. Import this template into the Group Policy store that you created in Exercise 2.

- **Exercise 3** Use Group Policy preferences to automatically delete the contents of the C:\Windows\Temp folder each time a user signs on to a computer.

Answers

This section contains the answers to the lesson review questions in this chapter.

Lesson 1

1. **Correct answer: B**

    A. **Incorrect.** Startup scripts run when the computer starts. You want to perform this action when the user logs off.

    B. **Correct.** Logoff scripts run when the user logs off. You use a logoff script to ensure that the user's files were copied to the backup location when the user logged off from the computer.

    C. **Incorrect.** Shutdown scripts run when the computer shuts down. You want to perform this action when the user logs off.

    D. **Incorrect.** Logon scripts run when the user logs on to the computer. You want to perform this action when the user logs off.

2. **Correct answer: B**

    A. **Incorrect.** You can't publish packages to computers. You can only publish packages to users.

    B. **Correct.** It installs the package the next time the computer starts.

    C. **Incorrect.** Publishing the package to the user makes the package available in Add And Remove Programs.

    D. **Incorrect.** Assigning the package means the package installs the next time the user logs on.

3. **Correct answer: D**

    A. **Incorrect.** Startup scripts run when the computer starts. You configure a logon script to accomplish the goal.

    B. **Incorrect.** Logoff scripts run when the user logs off. You configure a logon script to accomplish the goal.

    C. **Incorrect.** Shutdown scripts run when the computer shuts down. You configure a logon script to accomplish the goal.

    D. **Correct.** Logon scripts run when the user logs on to the computer. You configure a logon script to accomplish the goal.

4. **Correct answer: B**

    A. **Incorrect.** The AppData(Roaming) folder stores application-specific data.

    B. **Correct.** The Desktop folder stores all the items a user places on the desktop.

    C. **Incorrect.** The Documents folder is the default location for a user's documents.

    D. **Incorrect.** The Favorites folder stores a user's Internet Explorer favorites.

5. **Correct answer: A**

   A. **Correct.** Assigning the package means the package installs the next time the user logs on.

   B. **Incorrect.** Publishing the package to the user makes the package available in Add And Remove Programs

   C. **Incorrect.** It installs the package the next time the computer starts.

   D. **Incorrect.** You can't publish packages to computers. You can only publish packages to users.

6. **Correct answer: A**

   A. **Correct.** The Favorites folder stores a user's Internet Explorer favorites.

   B. **Incorrect.** The Documents folder is the default location for a user's documents.

   C. **Incorrect.** The Desktop folder stores all the items a user places on the desktop.

   D. **Incorrect.** The AppData(Roaming) folder stores application-specific data.

7. **Correct answers: A and C**

   A. **Correct.** You should configure a GPO and apply it to the OU that hosts the computers.

   B. **Incorrect.** You should not apply this policy at the domain level. You should configure a GPO and apply it to the OU that hosts the computers.

   C. **Correct.** You must configure a startup script.

   D. **Incorrect.** You must configure a startup script.

8. **Correct answer: A**

   A. **Correct.** Publishing the package to the user makes the package available in Add And Remove Programs.

   B. **Incorrect.** Assigning the package means the package installs the next time the user logs on.

   C. **Incorrect.** You can't publish packages to computers. You can only publish packages to users.

   D. **Incorrect.** It installs the package the next time the computer starts.

Lesson 2

1. **Correct answer: A**

   A. **Correct.** If you were the administrator at contoso.com, you would copy the C:\Windows\PolicyDefinitions folder and its contents to \\Contoso.com\Sysvol\Contoso.com\Policies to create the Group Policy store.

   B. **Incorrect.** If you were the administrator at contoso.com, you would copy the C:\Windows\PolicyDefinitions folder and its contents to \\Contoso.com\Sysvol\Contoso.com\Policies to create the Group Policy store.

C. **Incorrect.** If you were the administrator at contoso.com, you would copy the C:\Windows\PolicyDefinitions folder and its contents to \\Contoso.com\Sysvol\ Contoso.com\Policies to create the Group Policy store.

D. **Incorrect.** If you were the administrator at contoso.com, you would copy the C:\Windows\PolicyDefinitions folder and its contents to \\Contoso.com\Sysvol\ Contoso.com\Policies to create the Group Policy store.

2. **Correct answer: A and D**

A. **Correct.** The .admx file needs to go in the PolicyDefinitions folder. The .adml file needs to go in the associated regional folder, which for North America is en-US.

B. **Incorrect.** The .admx file needs to go in the PolicyDefinitions folder. The .adml file needs to go in the associated regional folder, which for North America is en-US.

C. **Incorrect.** The .admx file needs to go in the PolicyDefinitions folder. The .adml file needs to go in the associated regional folder, which for North America is en-US.

D. **Correct**. The .admx file needs to go in the PolicyDefinitions folder. The .adml file needs to go in the associated regional folder, which for North America is en-US.

Lesson 3

1. **Correct answer: B**

A. **Incorrect.** The Security Group item-level targeting option enables you to have Group Policy preferences apply only if the computer or user is found to be a member of a specific security group.

B. **Correct.** The Time Range item-level targeting option enables you to have a Group Policy preference apply only if the time is currently in the specified range.

C. **Incorrect.** The Operating System item-level targeting option enables you to have Group Policy preferences apply only if the operating system matches one of the operating systems specified.

D. **Incorrect.** The Disk Space item-level targeting option enables you to have Group Policy preferences apply only if a certain amount of free disk space exists.

2. **Correct answer: D**

A. **Incorrect.** You can use the Folder Options Group Policy preference to create or delete folders, or to delete the contents of folders.

B. **Incorrect.** You can use the Devices Group Policy preference to enable or block specific devices.

C. **Incorrect.** You can use the Internet Settings Group Policy preference to configure dial-up and VPN settings.

D. **Correct.** You can use the Local Users And Groups option to add and remove local users, or modify the membership of local groups.

3. **Correct answer: D**

   A. **Incorrect.** The Disk Space item-level targeting option enables you to have Group Policy preferences apply only if a certain amount of free disk space exists.

   B. **Incorrect.** The Operating System item-level targeting option enables you to have Group Policy preferences apply only if the operating system matches one of the operating systems specified.

   C. **Incorrect.** The Time Range item-level targeting option enables you to have a Group Policy preference apply only if the time is currently in the specified range.

   D. **Correct.** The Security Group item-level targeting option enables you to have Group Policy preferences apply only if the computer or user is found to be a member of a specific security group. In this case, you would add the computers used by executives to a security group.

4. **Correct answer: B**

   A. **Incorrect.** You can use the Local Users And Groups option to add and remove local users, or modify the membership of local groups.

   B. **Correct.** You can use the Folder Options Group Policy preference to create or delete folders, or to delete the contents of folders.

   C. **Incorrect.** You can use the Devices Group Policy preference to enable or block specific devices.

   D. **Incorrect.** You can use the Internet Settings Group Policy preference to configure dial-up and VPN settings.

5. **Correct answer: B**

   A. **Incorrect.** The Time Range item-level targeting option enables you to have a Group Policy preference apply only if the time is currently in the specified range.

   B. **Correct.** The Operating System item-level targeting option enables you to have Group Policy preferences apply only if the operating system matches one of the operating systems specified.

   C. **Incorrect.** The Security Group item-level targeting option enables you to have Group Policy preferences apply only if the computer or user is found to be a member of a specific security group.

   D. **Incorrect.** The Disk Space item-level targeting option enables you to have Group Policy preferences apply only if a certain amount of free disk space exists.

6. **Correct answer: B**

   A. **Incorrect.** You can use the Internet Settings Group Policy preference to configure dial-up and VPN settings.

   B. **Correct.** You can use the Devices Group Policy preference to enable or block specific devices.

    C. **Incorrect.** You can use the Folder Options Group Policy preference to create or delete folders, or to delete the contents of folders.

    D. **Incorrect.** You can use the Local Users And Groups option to add and remove local users, or modify the membership of local groups.

7. **Correct answer: D**

    A. **Incorrect.** The Security Group item-level targeting option enables you to have Group Policy preferences apply only if the computer or user is found to be a member of a specific security group.

    B. **Incorrect.** The Time Range item-level targeting option enables you to have a Group Policy preference apply only if the time is currently in the specified range.

    C. **Incorrect.** The Operating System item-level targeting option enables you to have Group Policy preferences apply only if the operating system matches one of the operating systems specified.

    D. **Correct.** The Disk Space item-level targeting option enables you to have Group Policy preferences apply only if a certain amount of free disk space exists.

8. **Correct answer: D**

    A. **Incorrect.** You can use the Local Users And Groups option to add and remove local users, or modify the membership of local groups.

    B. **Incorrect.** You can use the Folder Options Group Policy preference to create or delete folders, or to delete the contents of folders.

    C. **Incorrect.** You can use the Devices Group Policy preference to enable or block specific devices.

    D. **Correct.** You can use the Internet Settings Group Policy preference to configure dial-up and VPN settings.

CHAPTER 7

Administering network policies

Network policies determine the conditions under which clients can connect to a network, either locally or through remote methods such as a Remote Desktop Gateway (RD Gateway) server or a Virtual Private Network (VPN) server. On networks with Windows Server 2012 and Windows Server 2012 R2 deployed, these policies are hosted and configured on servers with the Network Policy Server (NPS) role installed. In this chapter, you'll learn how to deploy and configure an NPS, configure different networks, and understand Network Access Protection (NAP) policies, as well as learn to configure and deploy the infrastructure required to support those policies.

Lessons in this chapter:

- Lesson 1: Understanding Network Policy Server policies   **345**
- Lesson 2: Understanding Network Access Protection enforcement methods   **376**
- Lesson 3: Understanding Network Access Protection infrastructure   **392**

Before you begin

To complete the practice exercises in this chapter:

- You need to have deployed computers SYD-DC, MEL-DC, and ADL-DC, as described in the Introduction, using the evaluation edition of Windows Server 2012 R2.

Lesson 1: Understanding Network Policy Server policies

The Network Policy Server (NPS) is a central component of Windows Server 2012 and Windows Server 2012 R2-based remote access and Network Access Protection (NAP) solutions. In this lesson, you'll learn how to deploy the NPS server role, and how to configure connection request policies and client configuration. You'll learn about IP filters, encryption, IP settings, and NPS templates. You'll also learn about some of the concepts that are important in understanding the use of NPS policies in both NAP and Remote Authentication Dial-In User Service (RADIUS) scenarios.

After this lesson, you will be able to:

- Configure connection request policies.
- Configure client configuration.
- Configure IP filters.
- Configure encryption.
- Configure IP settings.
- Configure NPS templates.

Estimated lesson time: 45 minutes

NPS deployment

NPS enables you to configure network access policies. These policies can be related to remote connection requests, such as through a VPN or RD Gateway server, or they can be related to client health, which you use when deploying NAP. You can also configure a Windows Server 2012 or Windows Server 2012 R2 server with the NPS role as a *RADIUS proxy*. A RADIUS proxy forwards remote access connection requests to another RADIUS server that can authorize or deny that request.

You can configure the NPS role on Windows Server 2012 or Windows Server 2012 R2 to function in one or more of the following capacities:

- NAP policy server
- RADIUS server
- RADIUS proxy

> **NOTE RADIUS**
>
> This lesson focuses on NPS policies as they relate to NAP and RADIUS. You'll learn about using NPS as a RADIUS server and RADIUS proxy in more detail in Chapter 8, "Administering remote access."

When deploying the NPS role, you can also choose to install the Health Registration Authority (HRA) and the Host Credential Authorization Protocol (HCAP), as shown in Figure 7-1. The HRA enables you to deploy health certificates to computers in NAP scenarios. The HRA requires that web server components also be installed. The HCAP enables the integration of NAP and Cisco Network Access Control (Cisco NAC). In this configuration, the NPS server provides authorization for Cisco NAC clients.

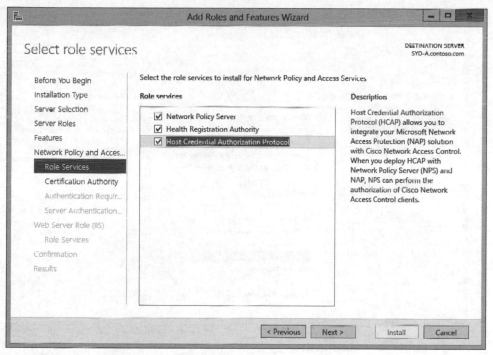

FIGURE 7-1 Selecting NPS role services

To install the NPS role on a computer running Windows Server 2012 or Windows Server 2012 R2, perform the following steps:

1. In Server Manager, click Manage, and click Add Roles and Features.

2. On the Before You Begin page of the Add Roles And Features Wizard, click Next.

3. On the Select Installation Type page, click Role-Based Or Feature-Based Installation, and click Next.

4. On the Select Destination Server page, click the server on which you want to deploy the NPS role, and click Next.

5. On the Select Server Roles page, click Network Policy And Access Services, as shown in Figure 7-2.

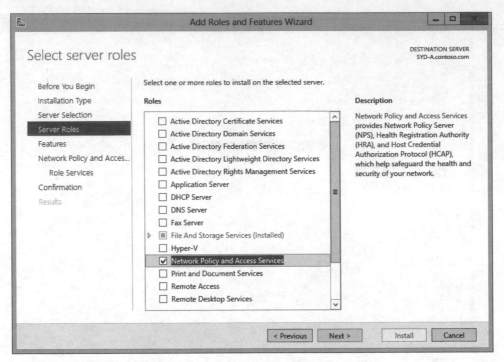

FIGURE 7-2 Installing the Network Policy And Access Services role

6. When you click Network Policy And Access Services, the Add Roles And Features Wizard dialog box prompts you to install the Remote Server Administration Tools associated with this role. Click Add Features.

7. Click Next three times until you reach the Select Role Services page.

8. On the Select Role Services page, you can choose to install the HRA and the HCAP role services. When you choose to install these role services, the Add Roles And Features Wizard automatically prompts you to install additional required components, such as Web Server components.

9. If you choose to deploy the HRA, you are prompted to choose a Certification Authority (CA), as shown in Figure 7-3. You can choose to select a CA later if one is not present, a locally installed CA, or another existing CA on the network. Click Next.

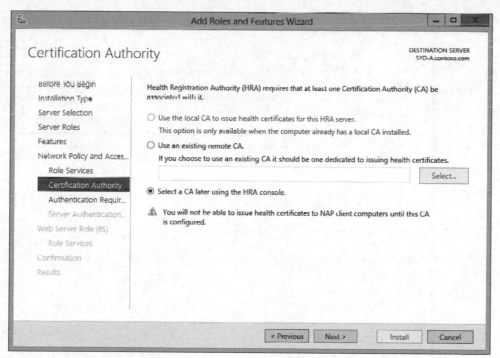

FIGURE 7-3 Selecting an HRA CA

10. When configuring the HRA, you must also determine whether you will limit the request for HRA certificates to users who are members of an Active Directory directory services domain, or enable anonymous requests for certificates. You can choose between these options on the Authentication Requirements page of the Add Roles and Features Wizard, as shown in Figure 7-4. Click Next.

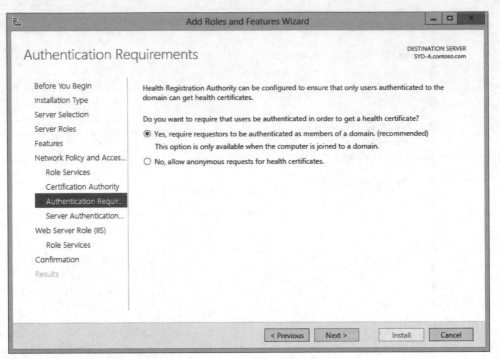

FIGURE 7-4 Configuring Authentication Requirements for the HRA

11. The HRA and HCAP role services also require that you configure an SSL certificate for communication with the server. If no existing SSL certificate is present on the server, you can enable SSL later by configuring a certificate for the default website in Internet Information Services (IIS). Click Next.

12. On the Web Server Role (IIS) And Role Services page, click Next.

13. On the Confirm Installation Selections page of the Add Roles and Features Wizard, click Install. When the installation completes, click Close.

Connection request policies

A connection request policy is a set of conditions that enable you to specify which RADIUS server performs the authorization and authentication process for specific RADIUS clients. You can configure multiple connection request policies on a server with the NPS role installed. When multiple policies are present, as shown in Figure 7-5, policies are processed according to the policy processing order. The first policy where conditions are met will be used.

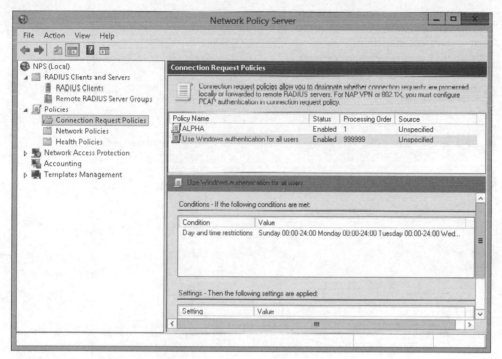

FIGURE 7-5 Policy processing order

Network access server type

One of the first steps you undertake when creating a connection request policy is to specify the type of network access server that will be sending traffic to the NPS server. You configure the type of network access server on the Specify Connection Request Policy Name And Connection Type page, as shown in Figure 7-6.

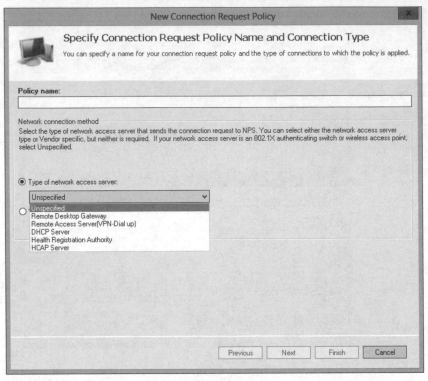

FIGURE 7-6 Default connection request policy

When configuring the policy, you can choose from the following connection types:

- **Remote Desktop Gateway** Use this option when you are configuring the NPS server to perform authentication for an RD Gateway server.

- **Remote Access Server (VPN-Dial Up)** Use this option when you are configuring the NPS server to perform authentication for remote access. You can use this method with both VPN and dial-up servers.

- **DHCP Server** Use this option when configuring NAP with the Dynamic Host Configuration Protocol (DHCP) enforcement method.

- **Health Registration Authority** Use this option when configuring NAP with the IPsec enforcement option.

- **HCAP Server** Use this option when configuring the NPS server to work with Cisco's HCAP implementation.

- **Unspecified** Use this type if you are configuring NPS to perform authentication for an 802.1x authenticating switch or wireless access point.

You can also configure a vendor-specific network access server and use the vendor-specific ID if you are configuring NPS to perform authentication from a third-party access server.

Request policy conditions

When you configure multiple policies, the policies are evaluated in numerical order, with the first policy that matches the specified conditions being used. You add conditions on the Specify Conditions page of the New Connection Request Policy dialog box. You select a condition in the Select Condition dialog box, shown in Figure 7-7.

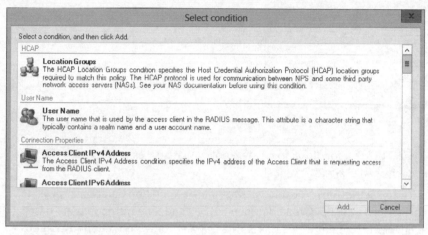

FIGURE 7-7 Adding conditions

Although at least one condition must exist, you can also use multiple conditions when you create a connection request policy. You can select from the following conditions:

- **Location Groups**   Use this condition when you are using the NPS server to authenticate clients that use Cisco's HCAP protocol.

- **User Name**   The user name as specified in the RADIUS message. This name includes both the user account name and the RADIUS realm name. You can use wildcards when configuring this condition.

- **Access Client IPv4 Address**   The IPv4 address of the client requesting access.

- **Access Client IPv6 Address**   The IPv6 address of the client requesting access.

- **Framed Protocol**   Use this condition when you want to apply the policy to clients using a specific framing protocol such as PPP.

- **Service Type**   Enables you to create a condition that depends on the type of service. The Service Type options are shown in Figure 7-8.

FIGURE 7-8 Service type options

- **Tunnel Type**   Use this condition to create a policy that applies only to a specific type of tunnel, such as an LT2P/IPsec tunnel.
- **Day And Time Restrictions**   Enables you to create a condition determining when connection attempts will be accepted or denied. Day and time restrictions are based upon the time zone set on the NPS server. The Day And Time Restrictions dialog box is shown in Figure 7-9.

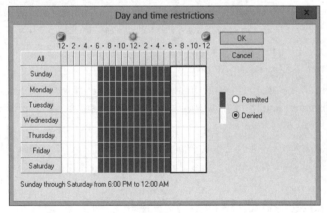

FIGURE 7-9 Day and time restrictions

- **Identity Type**   Enables the policy to be associated with a specific mechanism (for example, a NAP statement of health).
- **Calling Station ID**   This RADIUS client property enables the policy to match the telephone number of the network access server to which the client connected. For example, if the dial-up server had the phone number 555-5555, it could be used as the calling station ID.
- **Client Friendly Name**   This RADIUS client property enables the policy to match the identity of the RADIUS client that forwarded the connection request to the NPS server.

For example, if the VPN server were named VPN-ALPHA, it could be used as the client friendly name.

- **Client IPv4 Address** This RADIUS client property enables the policy to match the IPv4 address of the RADIUS client that forwarded the connection request to the NPS server. For example, you could use the IPv4 address of a VPN server as the client IPv4 address.

- **Client IPv6 Address** This RADIUS client property enables the policy to match the IPv6 address of the RADIUS client that forwarded the connection request to the NPS server. For example, you could use the IPv6 address of a VPN server as the client IPv6 address.

- **Client Vendor** Enables you to use the name of the RADIUS client vendor that is forwarding connection requests to the NPS server.

- **Called Station ID** Similar to the RADIUS client property, this property enables you to specify the telephone number of the network access server. In this and the following property items, the network access server is not using RADIUS, but is forwarding authentication traffic to the server with the NPS role installed.

- **NAS Identifier** In this scenario, NAS is the acronym of Network Access Server rather than Network Attached Storage. This property enables you to specify a character string representing the name of the network access server.

- **NAS IPv4 Address** This property enables you to specify the IPv4 address of the network access server.

- **NAS IPv6 Address** Use this property to specify the IPv6 address of the network access server.

- **NAS Port Type** Use this property to specify the types of access media, including ISDN, VPN, Ethernet, or Cable, as shown in Figure 7-10.

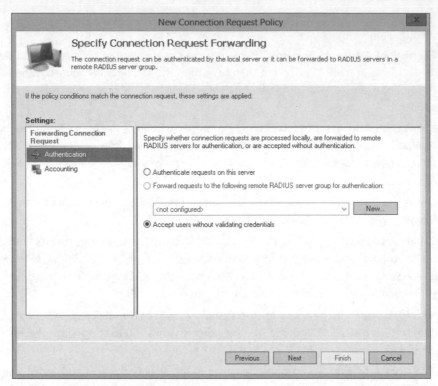

FIGURE 7-10 NAS Port Type dialog box

REAL WORLD **RADIUS CLIENTS**

RADIUS terminology can be confusing. It is important to remember that RADIUS clients are not the same as remote access clients. For example, a VPN or dial-up server that forwards authentication requests to an NPS server is a RADIUS client. The remote computer making the connection to the VPN or dial-up server is not a RADIUS client.

Connection request forwarding

By configuring a connection request forwarding setting, you can specify whether the local server performs authentication or forwards authentication traffic to a remote RADIUS server group. You can also configure connection request forwarding so that users are automatically accepted without any credential validation, as shown in Figure 7-11. You can also configure accounting on the Specify Connection Request Forwarding page. Accounting enables you to record RADIUS traffic.

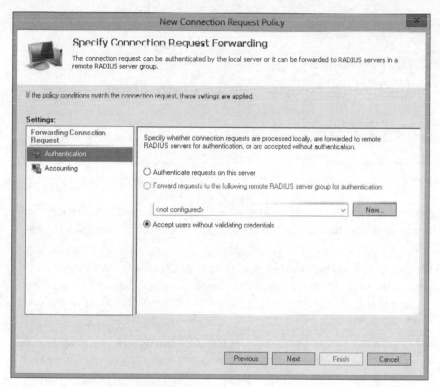

FIGURE 7-11 Connection request forwarding

Authentication methods

The Specify Authentication Methods page enables you to configure which authentication method or methods clients can use. These settings override any authentication methods specified in the network policy. When you specify multiple methods, the NPS server attempts the most-secure method, and then the next most secure method, until it reaches the least-secure specified method. The most secure authentication types are the Extensible Authentication Protocols (EAPs), which include the following (as shown in Figure 7-12):

- Microsoft: Smart Card Or Other Certificate
- Microsoft: Protected EAP (PEAP)
- Microsoft: Secured Password (EAP-MSCHAP v2)

FIGURE 7-12 Adding an EAP

You can also configure NPS to support less-secure authentication protocols, as shown in Figure 7-13. The less-secure authentication protocols, from most secure to least secure, are the following:

- **Microsoft Encrypted Authentication Version 2 (MS-CHAP-v2)**   When enabling this authentication method, you can also allow users to change passwords after that password has expired. MS-CHAP-v2 was first introduced with Windows NT 4.0 Service Pack 4.

- **Microsoft Encrypted Authentication (MS-CHAP)**   A less-secure version of MS-CHAP-v2. You can also allow users to change passwords after the password expiration date.

- **Encrypted Authentication (CHAP)**   Unless there is an excellent reason otherwise, don't use this authentication protocol. You should use this protocol only if you need to support old clients that don't support more secure authentication protocols.

- **Unencrypted Authentication (PAP, SPAP)**   You use these protocols only if you need to support old clients that don't support more-secure authentication protocols. Use these protocols with care because they pass credentials in cleartext format.

- **Allow Clients To Connect Without Negotiating An Authentication Method**   This option enables clients to connect without requiring a specific authentication method.

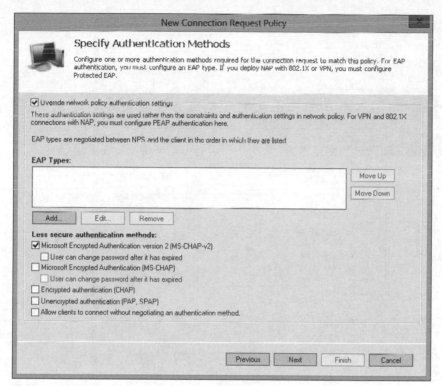

FIGURE 7-13 Authentication methods

Realm and RADIUS attributes

You can apply a realm name as well as RADIUS attributes to a connection request policy. This is often done when the computer with the NPS server role installed is functioning as a RADIUS proxy. When functioning as a proxy, the server with the NPS role installed can alter attributes that were passed to it by a RADIUS client. This process enables the RADIUS server providing authentication to use the altered attributes instead of the ones sent by the client. When functioning as a RADIUS proxy, the server with the NPS role installed can also add additional attributes to the traffic forwarded to the RADIUS server that provides authentication services. You perform these steps on the Configure Settings page shown in Figure 7-14.

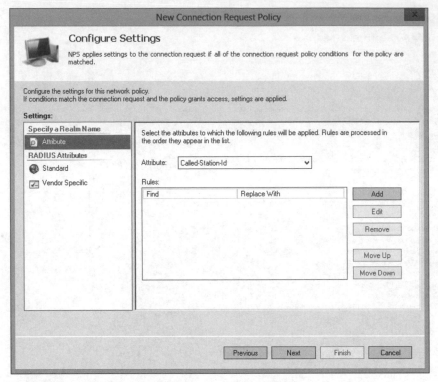

FIGURE 7-14 Configure settings page

Default connection request policy

Windows Server 2012 and Windows Server 2012 R2 create a default connection request policy when you deploy the NPS role. The name of this policy is Use Windows Authentication For All Users and it is assigned the processing order of 999999. The NPS server uses this policy as a last resort. The policy, shown in Figure 7-15, has the following properties, with all other properties not configured:

- Authentication Methods: Not Configured
- Authentication: Authenticate Requests On This Server
- Conditions: Sunday To Saturday, 00:00 To 24:00

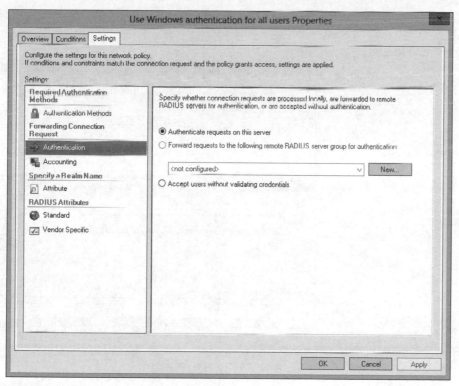

FIGURE 7-15 Default connection request policy

Creating a connection request policy

You can create a connection request policy from the NPS console. To create a connection request policy, perform the following steps:

1. Open the NPS console from the Tools menu in Server Manager.

2. Expand the Policies node, and click Connection Request Policies, as shown in Figure 7-16.

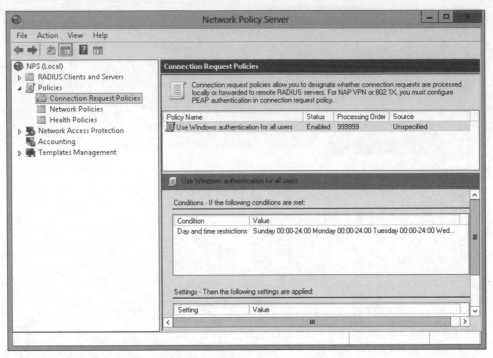

FIGURE 7-16 Connection Request Policies node of the NPS console

3. On the Action menu, click New.

4. On the Specify Connection Request Policy Name And Connection Type page, provide a policy name and specify the type of network access server to which the policy applies.

5. On the Specify Conditions page, add at least one condition that differentiates the policy from any other policies on the server with the NPS role installed.

6. On the Specify Connection Request Forwarding page, specify whether the local server will perform authentication, or whether the server with the NPS role installed will function as a RADIUS proxy and forward requests to a remote server. You can also configure accounting on this page.

> **MORE INFO**   **CONNECTION REQUEST POLICIES**
>
> For more information about connection request policies, consult the following TechNet document at *http://technet.microsoft.com/en-us/library/cc753603.aspx*.

7. On the Specify Authentication Methods page, choose whether to override network policy authentication settings. If you do, you must specify which authentication methods you will use in place of the ones specified in the network policy.

8. If the server with the NPS role installed is functioning as a RADIUS proxy, you can configure additional attributes as well as replace existing attributes forwarded by a RADIUS client on the Configure Settings page.

9. You then complete the New Connection Request Policy Wizard. The policy will be assigned the next available processing order number. You can right-click the policy and select Move Up or Move Down to change the policy processing order.

> ✔ **Quick check**
>
> - How do you ensure that one connection request policy applies to one group of users and a second connection request policy applies to a different group of users?
>
> **Quick check answer**
>
> - Configure different conditions in each connection request policy.

Client configuration

In some environments, a computer must authenticate before it can connect to a network. You can configure this authentication using 802.1X group policy items. You configure separate policies for wired networks and wireless networks.

To configure the default wired or wireless network policies, perform the following steps:

1. Open the Group Policy Management Console (GPMC) from the Tools menu of the Server Manager console.

2. Expand the Forest\Domains\Domain FQDN\Group Policy Objects (GPO) node and select the policy that you want to use to enforce 802.1X configuration. You can also create a new policy and link it to an appropriate location for this purpose, as shown in Figure 7-17.

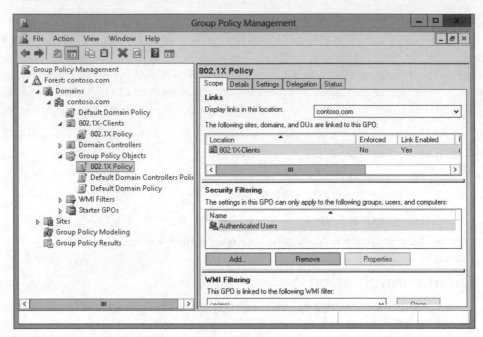

FIGURE 7-17 Custom GPO for 802.1X policies

3. On the Action menu, click Edit.

4. Expand the Computer Configuration\Policies\Windows Settings\Security Settings node.

5. Under this node there are two policy areas, as shown in Figure 7-18:

- Wired Network (IEEE 802.3) Policies
- Wireless Network (IEEE 802.11) Policies

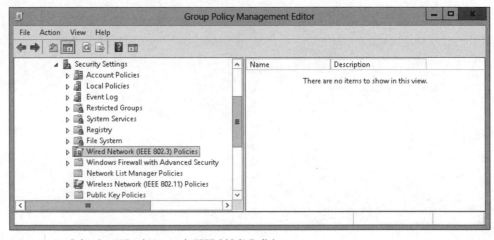

FIGURE 7-18 Selecting Wired Network (IEEE 802.3) Policies

6. You use the same technique to configure either wired network or wireless network policies. To configure these policies, click either Wired Network (IEE 802.3) Policies or Wireless Network (IEEE 802.11) Policies. On the Action menu, click Create A New Wired Network Policy For Windows Vista And Later Releases/Create A New Wireless Network Policy For Windows Vista And Later Releases.

7. On the General tab of the New Wired Network Policy Properties dialog box, shown in Figure 7-19, provide a name for the policy. The default policy setting is to use Windows Wired Auto Config. You can also configure a block on shared user credentials for computers running the Windows 7, Windows 8, or Windows 8.1 operating systems.

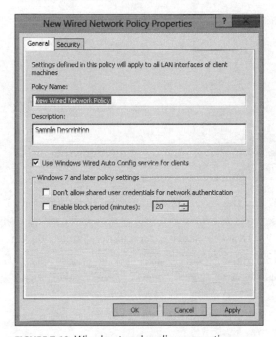

FIGURE 7-19 Wired network policy properties

8. On the Security tab, shown in Figure 7-20, you can configure a network authentication method and an authentication mode. The authentication mode determines whether a user's credentials, the computer's credentials, or both are used to authenticate to gain network access. These settings can be overridden by a connection request policy.

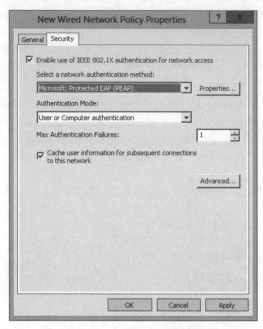

FIGURE 7-20 Wired network policy security

9. If you click the Advanced option, you can access advanced security settings for the network policy. Through these settings, shown in Figure 7-21, you can configure single sign-on settings and advanced 802.1X settings. You can configure Single Sign On to occur immediately before user logon or after user logon.

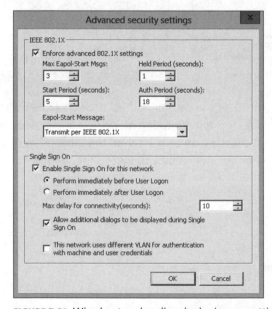

FIGURE 7-21 Wired network policy single sign-on settings

10. Click OK to commit policy changes. Close the Group Policy Management Editor.

> **MORE INFO** **CLIENT CONFIGURATION**
>
> For more information about client computer configuration, consult the following Tech-Net article at *http://technet.microsoft.com/en-us/library/cc731479.aspx*.

IP filters

IP filters enable you to control incoming and outgoing traffic based on source and destination IP address, as well as port and protocol. You use IP address filters to limit communication between clients and specific hosts and services on the network. You can configure IP filters on the Settings page of the Network Policy properties, as shown in Figure 7-22, or when creating a network policy.

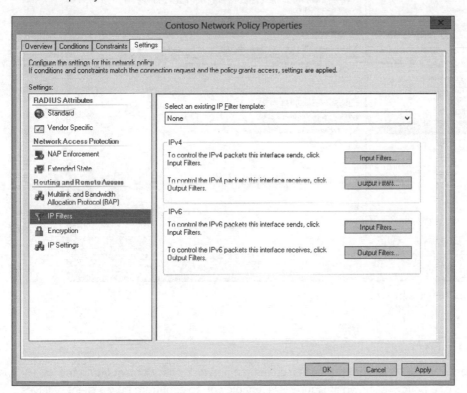

FIGURE 7-22 Network policy IP filters

Encryption

When configuring network policies, you can select which types of encryption the connection can use on the Configure Settings page of the New Network Policy Wizard or by editing the properties of an existing network policy. If you want to force network connections to use strong encryption, ensure that the No Encryption and Basic Encryption settings are not selected in the network policy, as shown in Figure 7-23. The key length determines the strength of the encryption. Although increased key length does improve security, it also comes at the cost of increased processor overhead.

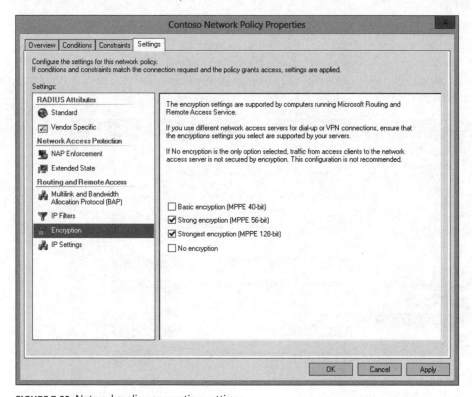

FIGURE 7-23 Network policy encryption settings

IP settings

IP settings, which you can configure when creating a network policy or by editing the properties of a policy, as shown in Figure 7-24, enable you to configure how a client receives an IP address. You can configure the following settings:

- Server Must Supply An IP Address
- Client May Request An IP Address
- Server Settings Determine IP Address Assignment
- Assign A Static IPv4 Address

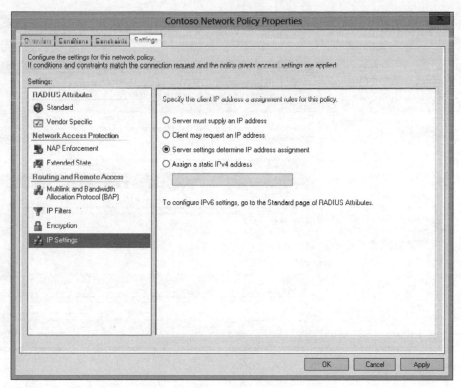

FIGURE 7-24 Network policy IP address settings

You can configure an IPv6 address on the Standard page of the RADIUS attributes section.

Creating network policies

Network policies determine which users and computers are authorized to connect to the network. Network policies are often used with NAP. The process of creating network policies is similar to creating connection request policies. Both sets of policies share many of the same elements. To create a network policy, perform the following steps:

1. In the NPS console, click Network Policies under the Policies node, as shown in Figure 7-25.

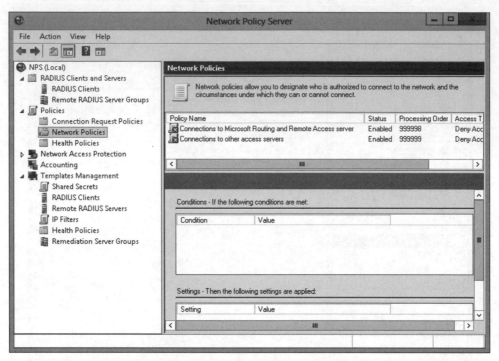

FIGURE 7-25 Network policies

2. On the Action menu, click New.

3. On the Specify Network Policy Name And Connection Type page, enter a policy name and specify the type of network access server. The options are the following:

- Remote Desktop Gateway
- Remote Access Server (VPN-Dial Up)
- DHCP Server
- Health Registration Authority
- HCAP Server

4. On the Specify Conditions page, select one or more conditions that determine whether the policy applies. The options, shown in Figure 7-26, are these:

- **Windows Groups**   The user or computer must belong to a Windows security group.
- **Machine Groups**   The computer must belong to a Windows security group.
- **User Groups**   The user must belong to a Windows security group.
- **Location Groups**   Must be part of an HCAP location group.
- **HCAP User Groups**   Must be part of an HCAP user group.
- **Day And Time Restrictions**   Policy applies only at specific dates and times.

- **Identity Type** Limits clients to those that can be identified in a specific way, such as an NAP statement of health.

- **MS-Service Class** Requires the client to have an IP address lease from a specific DHCP scope.

- **Health Policies** Client must meet the criteria of a specific health policy.

- **NAP-Capable Computers** Specifies whether the computer must or must not be participating in an NAP implementation.

- **Operating System** Enables the policy to apply to specific operating systems and processor architecture (x86, x64, ia64).

- **Policy Expiration** Determines when the policy expires.

- **Access Client IPv4 Address** The client's IPv4 address, not the RADIUS client's IP address.

- **Access Client IPv6 Address** The client's IPv6 address.

- **Authentication Type** Authentication method used, which includes CHAP, EAP, MS-CHAP v1, MS-CHAP v2, PAP, PEAP, and Unauthenticated.

- **Allowed EAP Types** Allowed EAP types, which includes Microsoft: Smart Card or other certificate, Microsoft PEAP, and Microsoft EAP-MSCHAP v2.

- **Framed Protocol** Policy applies only to clients using the specified framed protocol, such as PPP or SLIP.

- **Service Type** Applies when the client uses a particular service type.

- **Tunnel Type** Applies when the client uses a particular tunnel type.

- **Calling Station ID** RADIUS calling station ID.

- **Client Friendly Name** RADIUS client name.

- **Client IPv4 Address** RADIUS IPv4 address.

- **Client IPv6 Address** RADIUS IPv6 address.

- **Client Vendor** RADIUS client vendor.

- **MS-RAS Vendor** RADIUS vendor ID.

- **Called Station ID** Telephone number of the network access server.

- **NAS Identifier** Network access server name.

- **NAS IPv4 Address** Network access server IPv4 address.

- **NAS IPv6 Address** Network access server IPv6 address.

- **NAS Port Type** Network access server media type, including ISDN, wireless, VPN, or tunnel.

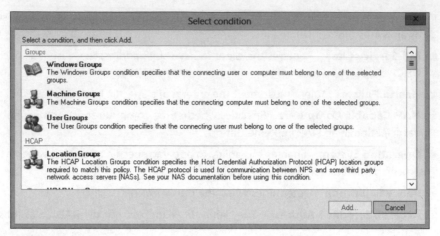

FIGURE 7-26 Selecting conditions

5. On the Specify Access Permission page, choose whether access is granted or blocked to computers or users that meet the specified conditions.

6. On the Configure Authentication Methods page, specify which authentication methods the client can use to authenticate.

7. On the Configure Constraints page, shown in Figure 7-27, you can configure the following properties:

   - Idle Timeout
   - Session Timeout
   - Called Station ID
   - Day And Time Restrictions
   - NAS Port Type

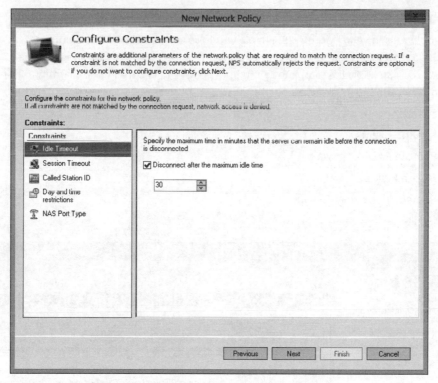

FIGURE 7-27 Configuring constraints

8. On the Configure Settings page of the New Network Policy Wizard, you can configure the following:

- RADIUS Attributes
- NAP Enforcement
- Multilink and Bandwidth Allocation Protocol
- IP Filters
- Encryption
- IP Settings

9. Clicking Next enables you to complete the wizard. You can then alter the position of the policy by moving it up and down. Clients use the first policy for which they meet the conditions.

NPS templates

NPS templates, shown in Figure 7-28, enable you to save a specific NPS component configuration so that it can be reused or exported to another server with the NPS role installed. You can apply the template to multiple policies to ensure uniform configuration. You can configure the following templates:

- Shared Secrets
- RADIUS Clients
- Remote RADIUS Servers
- Health Policies
- Remediation Server Groups
- IP Filters

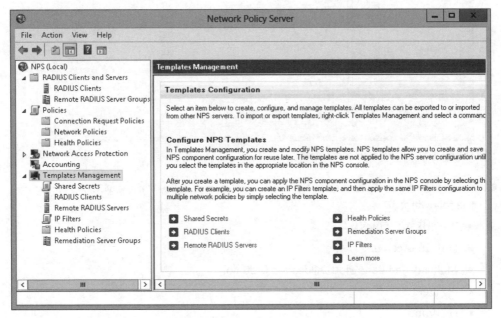

FIGURE 7-28 Network policy IP address settings

To configure a template, click the type of template that you want to configure in the NPS console. Then, from the Action menu, click New. Configure the template in the same way that you would configure the associated properties in a policy. Figure 7-29 shows the creation of an IP filters template.

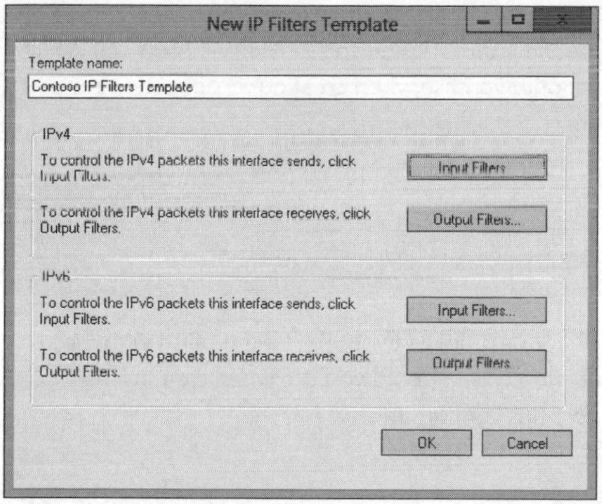

FIGURE 7-29 IP filters template

Lesson summary

- Connection request policies enable you to configure how a request for a connection is processed.
- IP filters are parts of network policy that enable you to restrict traffic on the basis of a source and destination IP address, as well as on a port and protocol.
- Encryption settings are parts of a network policy that determine the minimum level of encryption required.
- NPS templates enable you to apply settings to multiple policies.

Lesson review

Answer the following questions to test your knowledge of the information in this lesson. You can find the answers to these questions and explanations of why each answer choice is correct or incorrect in the "Answers" section at the end of this chapter.

1. You are configuring a connection request policy for clients that will be connecting to a Virtual Desktop Infrastructure (VDI) deployment on a trusted network from clients on the Internet. Clients should be able to connect using a Remote Desktop connection. Which of the following connection types should you configure when creating a connection request policy?

   A. HCAP server

   B. Remote access server

   C. DHCP server

   D. RD Gateway

2. You want to configure a connection request policy to support clients connecting to the internal network from clients on the Internet using the L2TP/IPsec protocol. Which of the following connection types should you use when creating a connection request policy to support this configuration?

   A. RD Gateway

   B. DHCP server

   C. Remote access server

   D. HCAP server

3. You want to configure a connection request policy to support integration with Cisco NAC. Which of the following connection types should you use when creating a connection request policy to support this configuration?

   A. Remote access server

   B. HCAP server

   C. DHCP server

   D. RD Gateway

4. You want to configure a network policy that applies only at certain times of the week. Which of the following conditions should you use when creating a network policy to meet this goal?

   A. Windows Groups

   B. Machine Groups

   C. User Groups

   D. Day And Time Restrictions

5. You want to configure a network policy that applies to certain computers, but not others. Which of the following conditions should you use to accomplish this goal? (Choose all that apply.)

   A. Windows Groups

   B. User Groups

   C. Day And Time Restrictions

   D. Machine Groups

Lesson 2: Understanding Network Access Protection enforcement methods

NAP enables you to limit network access to client computers that have met a specific set of health criteria. These health criteria are configurable and can include ensuring that an antimalware checker is installed and running, that Windows Firewall is enabled, and that the computer has recently checked for available software updates. There are five different methods that you can use for NAP enforcement. Some of these methods are appropriate only for specific scenarios, others require special equipment, and some can be implemented without requiring substantial changes to the existing network's configuration. In this lesson, you'll learn about the different NAP enforcement methods. In Lesson 3, you'll learn about the infrastructure required to support NAP.

After this lesson, you will be able to:

- Configure DHCP enforcement.
- Configure IPsec enforcement.
- Configure 802.1X enforcement.
- Configure VPN enforcement.
- Configure RD Gateway enforcement.

Estimated lesson time: 45 minutes

DHCP enforcement

When you configure NAP DHCP enforcement, an appropriately configured DHCP server will provide clients with an IP address for a trusted network only if they meet the NAP health policy requirements. If the client does not meet the NAP health policy requirements, the NAP can be configured to provide the client with an address on a remediation network, enabling the client to apply the updates and changes necessary to become compliant.

When you use DHCP enforcement, client health is assessed each time the client attempts to obtain or renew an IP address lease, which means that there is a direct relationship with the length of the DHCP lease and the frequency at which a NAP health check is performed. Organizations that implement long DHCP leases are more likely to have noncompliant clients with valid addresses than organizations that implement shorter DHCP lease times. DHCP enforcement works only with IPv4, and you can't use DHCP enforcement as a NAP enforcement method on IPv6-only networks.

REAL WORLD **GETTING AROUND DHCP ENFORCEMENT**

Any user who knows how to manually configure the IP address can get around DHCP enforcement. As generations of users who grew up with computers move into the workplace, basic network configuration knowledge is becoming more widespread.

Deploying NAP by using the DHCP enforcement method requires that you take the following steps:

1. Create a connection request policy and a network policy on the server with the NPS role installed. You can do it manually or by selecting Dynamic Host Configuration

Protocol (DHCP) as the Network Connection Method in the Configure NAP Wizard, as shown in Figure 7-30.

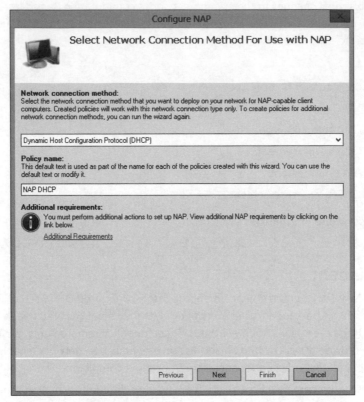

FIGURE 7-30 Configuring the DHCP enforcement method

2. Configure Group Policy to enable the NAP DHCP enforcement client, as shown in Figure 7-31, and the NAP service on computers that will be NAP clients. The DHCP Quarantine Enforcement Client is located on the Computer Configuration\Policies\Windows Settings\Security Settings\Network Access Protection\NAP Client Configuration\Enforcement Clients node.

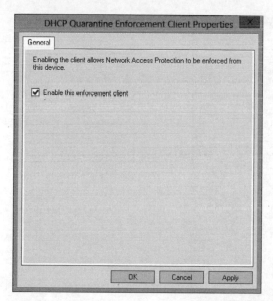

FIGURE 7-31 Enabling DHCP quarantine enforcement client policy

3. Enable NAP, either for individual DHCP scopes or for all DHCP scopes configured on the DHCP server. You can configure the properties at the DHCP server level on the Network Access Protection tab of IPv4 properties, as shown in Figure 7-32. When configuring the DHCP server for NAP, you need to specify what actions to take if the DHCP server can't reach the server with the NPS role installed. The options are to enable normal access, place clients on a restricted network, or ignore client DHCP requests.

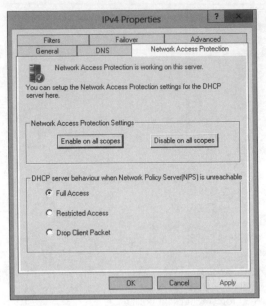

FIGURE 7-32 Enabling NAP for all DHCP scopes

4. Ensure that you configure the appropriate Windows Security Health Validator (WSHV), or System Health Agents (SHAs) and System Health Validators (SHVs). You'll learn more about these components in Lesson 3.

MORE INFO **DHCP ENFORCEMENT**

For more information about DHCP enforcement, consult the following TechNet article at *http://technet.microsoft.com/en-us/library/cc733020.aspx*.

IPsec enforcement

IPsec is a technology that enables communication to be authenticated and encrypted. When configured appropriately, any computer that uses IPsec communicates only with other hosts that it can authenticate. You can configure IPsec communication to use trusted digital certificates for authentication.

NAP using IPsec enforcement builds on this process. Instead of the client computer being directly issued a special certificate to be used for IPsec authentication from a CA, the client computer is issued a certificate used for IPsec authentication from a health certificate server. Health certificate servers issue these certificates only if a client can demonstrate that it meets the health requirements configured through NAP. After a client is issued a health certificate, that certificate is available for authentication only as long as the client remains healthy. The NAP client disallows use of the certificate when the client is noncompliant. This method enables clients to have their health status immediately remediated, unlike other NAP methods that apply only initially or on a periodic basis, such as when a DHCP lease needs to be renewed.

To configure NAP with IPsec enforcement, perform the following steps:

1. On the server with the NPS role installed, configure a connection request policy, network policy, and NAP health policy. You can do this manually, or you can select the IPsec With Health Registration Authority (HRA) network connection method in the Configure NAP Wizard, as shown in Figure 7-33.

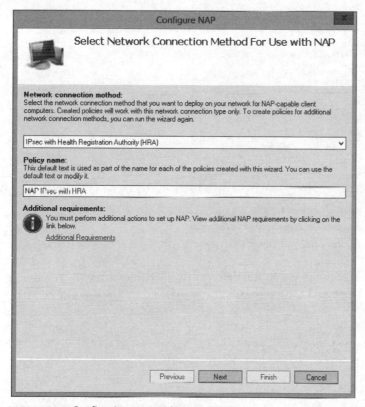

FIGURE 7-33 Configuring NAP with IPsec enforcement

2. Deploy the Health Registration Authority NPS role service. You can deploy it on the server with the NPS role installed.

3. Deploy an enterprise root or subordinate Active Directory Certificate Services (AD CS) server. This enables you to configure custom certificate templates.

> **MORE INFO** **IPSEC ENFORCEMENT**
>
> For more information about IPsec enforcement, consult the following TechNet article at *http://technet.microsoft.com/en-us/library/cc771899.aspx*.

4. Configure the IPsec Relying Party Properties policy, as shown in Figure 7-34, and enable the NAP service on clients. The IPsec Relying Party Properties policy is located in the Computer Configuration\Policies\Windows Settings\Security Settings\Network Access Protection\NAP Client Configuration\Enforcement Clients node.

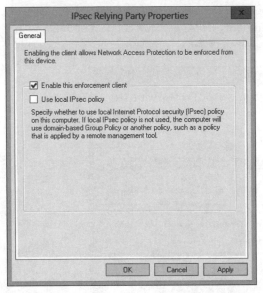

FIGURE 7-34 Configuring NAP with IPsec enforcement

5. Ensure that you configure the appropriate WSHV, or SHAs and SHVs.

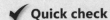**Quick check**
- Which NAP enforcement method also helps minimize the chance of intercepted network traffic being read by unauthorized third parties?

Quick check answer
- The IPsec enforcement method encrypts network traffic, meaning that any captured is enciphered and will be unintelligible to unauthorized third parties attempting to read it.

802.1X enforcement

NAP enforcement for 802.1X uses authenticating switches and wireless access points and only grants network access to computers that meet client health requirements. This enforcement method requires switches and wireless access points that can perform 802.1x network authentication. When a computer is compliant, it is placed on the trusted network. When a computer is noncompliant, it is either:

- Placed onto a separate VLAN. This VLAN is configured with access to remediation servers.

OR

- Packet filters are applied to the client that limit network access to remediation servers.

With 802.1X enforcement, changes in client health have an immediate effect, with a noncompliant client automatically placed on a restricted network until it returns to a healthy state.

REAL WORLD **MORE EXPENSIVE EQUIPMENT**

The drawback of 802.1X enforcement is its reliance on hardware that supports forwarding authentication traffic to an NPS server. Many small-sized and medium-sized organizations use consumer networking hardware that does not support this type of advanced feature.

Although you configure 802.1X enforcement for wired and wireless networks separately, both require you to enable the EAP Quarantine Enforcement Client policy shown in Figure 7-35. This policy is located in the Computer Configuration\Policies\Windows Settings\Security Settings\Network Access Protection\NAP Client Configuration\Enforcement Clients node. You also need to ensure that the NAP service is running on all NAP client computers.

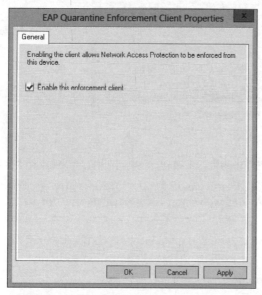

FIGURE 7-35 Enable 802.1X enforcement

To configure 802.1X enforcement for wired networks, you need to perform the following steps:

- On the server with the NPS role installed, configure a connection request policy, network policy, and NAP health policy. You can do this by configuring each policy separately, or by using the Configure NAP Wizard and selecting the IEEE 802.1X (Wired) network connection method on the Configure NAP Wizard, as shown in Figure 7-36.

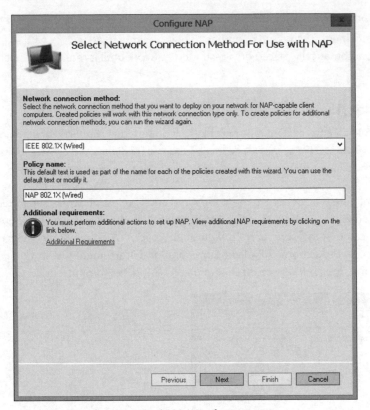

FIGURE 7-36 Configuring Wired 802.1X enforcement

- Configure 802.1X switches to forward authentication traffic to the server with the NPS role installed.
- If you want to use PEAP-TLS or EAP-TLS with smart cards or certificates for authentication, deploy AD CS.
- If you want to use PEAP-MS-CHAP v2, you can use a local AD CS deployment or purchase server certificates from a trusted third-party certification authority.
- Ensure that you configure appropriate WSHV, or SHA and SHVs.

To configure 802.1X enforcement for wireless networks, you need to perform the following steps:

- On the server with the NPS role installed, configure a connection request policy, network policy, and NAP health policy. You can do this by configuring each policy separately, or by using the Configure NAP Wizard and selecting the IEEE 802.1X (Wireless) network connection method in the Configure NAP Wizard, as shown in Figure 7-37.

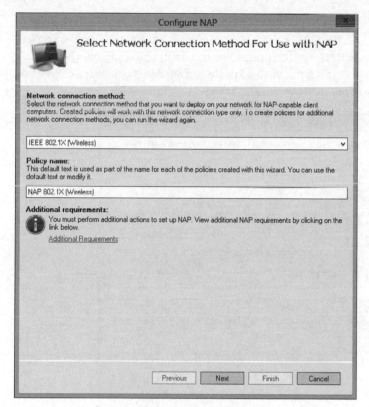

FIGURE 7-37 Configuring Wireless 802.1X enforcement

- Configure 802.1X wireless access points to forward authentication traffic to the server with the NPS role installed.
- Ensure that you configure appropriate WSHV, or SHAs and SHVs.

MORE INFO **802.1X ENFORCEMENT**

For more information about 802.1x enforcement, consult the following TechNet article at *http://technet.microsoft.com/en-us/library/cc770861.aspx.*

VPN enforcement

VPN enforcement enables you to stop clients that don't meet your organization's health requirements from successfully establishing VPN connections. When you configure VPN enforcement, you can simply block incoming connections from unhealthy clients or you can redirect unhealthy clients to a remediation network in which they can return to a healthy state. You can also allow full access for a limited time, after which the noncompliant client is disconnected.

To configure NAP VPN enforcement, perform the following steps:

1. On the server with the NPS role installed, configure a connection request policy, network policy, and NAP health policy. You can do this by configuring each policy separately or by selecting the Virtual Private Network (VPN) network connection method in the Configure NAP Wizard, as shown in Figure 7-38.

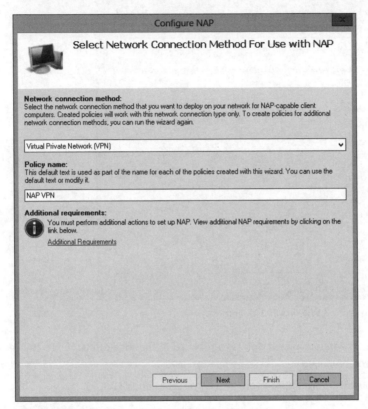

FIGURE 7-38 Configuring NAP VPN enforcement

2. Deploy the remote access role on a computer running Windows Server 2012 or Windows Server 2012 R2. Configure the remote access server as a VPN server and configure the server with the NPS role installed as the primary RADIUS server. It is also possible to use Windows Server 2008 or Windows Server 2008 R2 as a VPN server in this scenario.

3. On computers running Windows 7, Windows 8, and Windows 8.1, you enable the EAP Quarantine Enforcement Client policy when configuring NAP clients. On computers running Windows XP and Windows Vista, you enable the Remote Access Enforcement Client for Windows XP And Windows Vista policy, as shown in Figure 7-39. These policies are located in the Computer Configuration\Policies\Windows Settings\Security Settings\Network Access Protection\NAP Client Configuration\Enforcement Clients node. You also need to ensure that the NAP service is running on all NAP client computers.

FIGURE 7-39 Configuring VPN enforcement

4. If you want to use PEAP-TLS or EAP-TLS with smart cards or certificates for VPN authentication, deploy AD CS.

5. If you want to use PEAP-MS-CHAP v2 for VPN authentication, you can use a local AD CS deployment or purchase server certificates from a trusted third-party certification authority.

6. Ensure that you configure the appropriate WSHV, or SHAs and SHVs.

> **NOTE VPN ENFORCEMENT**
>
> For more information about VPN enforcement, consult the following TechNet article at
> *http://technet.microsoft.com/en-us/library/cc753622.aspx.*

RD Gateway enforcement

RD Gateway servers allow access to Remote Desktop servers on trusted networks to clients on untrusted networks, such as the Internet. Remote Desktop servers can include RD Session Host servers, RD RemoteApp applications, Remote Desktop running on Windows 7, Windows 8, and Windows 8.1 client computers, as well as connections through Remote Desktop Connection Broker to VDI.

RD Gateway servers enable you to provide access to these servers without needing to configure VPN connections or DirectAccess. The Remote Desktop connection client, built into the Windows Client operating system, supports RD Gateway servers. You can configure the Remote Desktop connection client so that it makes a direct connection to a Remote Desktop server when the client is on a protected network and attempts an indirect connection through a configured RD Gateway server when the client is connected to an untrusted network.

REAL WORLD **BYOD SCENARIOS**

RD Gateway enforcement is useful for organizations that allow Bring Your Own Device (BYOD) scenarios. Instead of allowing users to directly connect to sensitive servers and resources using their own computers, organizations can use an RD Gateway server to enable indirect connections to these resources. By combining an RD Gateway server with NAP, it is possible to ensure that the BYOD clients have met a minimum standard of computer health before successfully connecting to the RD Gateway server.

To configure NAP with RD Gateway enforcement, perform the following steps:

1. On the server with the NPS role installed, configure a connection request policy, network policy, and NAP health policy. You can do this by configuring each policy separately, or by using the Configure NAP Wizard and selecting the Remote Desktop Gateway (RD Gateway) network connection method on the Configure NAP Wizard, as shown in Figure 7-40.

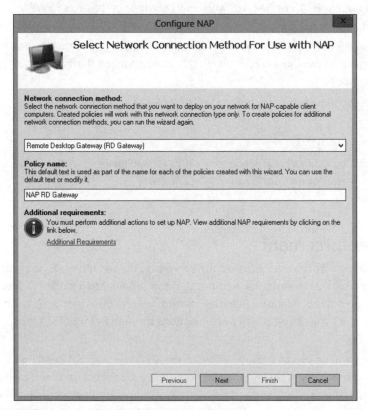

FIGURE 7-40 Configuring RD Gateway policies

2. Deploy an RD Gateway server, which must be accessible to clients on the untrusted network from which connections will be made. It also needs to be connected to the trusted network on which Remote Desktop servers are present.

3. Enable NAP health policy checks on the RD Gateway server. You can do this by adding the RD Gateway Manager snap-in to a custom Microsoft Management Console (MMC) and then configuring options on the RD CAP Store tab of the RD Gateway Server properties, as shown in Figure 7-41.

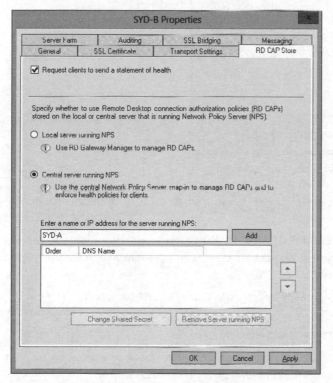

FIGURE 7-41 Configuring RD Gateway to use NAP

4. Enable the RD Gateway Quarantine Enforcement Client Properties policy shown in Figure 7-42. This policy is located in the Computer Configuration\Policies\Windows Settings\Security Settings\Network Access Protection\NAP Client Configuration\ Enforcement Clients node. You also need to ensure that the NAP service is running on all NAP client computers.

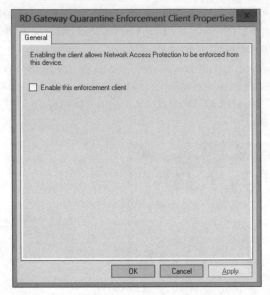

FIGURE 7-42 RD Gateway enforcement client

5. If you want to use PEAP-TLS or EAP-TLS with smart cards or certificates for RD Gateway authentication, deploy AD CS.

6. If you want to use PEAP-MS-CHAP v2 for RD Gateway authentication, you can use a local AD CS deployment or purchase server certificates from a trusted third-party certification authority.

7. Ensure that you configure the appropriate WSHV, or SHAs and SHVs.

> *MORE INFO* **RD GATEWAY ENFORCEMENT**
>
> For more information about RD Gateway enforcement, consult the following TechNet article at *http://technet.microsoft.com/en-us/library/cc771213.aspx*.

Lesson summary

- NAP enables you to limit network access to clients that are able to demonstrate that they meet configured health criteria.
- NAP DHCP enforcement restricts the leasing of IPv4 addresses to healthy clients.
- NAP IPsec enforcement issues the certificates required to communicate in an encrypted and authenticated manner with other hosts on the network, only to healthy clients.
- NAP 802.1x enforcement uses authenticating switches and wireless access points to limit network connectivity to clients that are deemed healthy.

- NAP VPN enforcement uses client health to limit VPN connections.
- NAP RD Gateway enforcement limits connections through an RD Gateway server to clients that are healthy.

Lesson review

Answer the following questions to test your knowledge of the information in this lesson. You can find the answers to these questions and explanations of why each answer choice is correct or incorrect in the "Answers" section at the end of this chapter.

1. You want to limit connections from the Internet to your organization's Remote Desktop session host servers to those clients that can demonstrate that they are healthy. Which NAP enforcement method should you implement?

   A. IPsec enforcement

   B. 802.1X enforcement

   C. VPN enforcement

   D. RD Gateway enforcement

2. You want to stop laptop computers that are not up to date with software updates and antimalware definitions from connecting to your organization's wireless access points. Which NAP enforcement method should you implement?

   A. 802.1X enforcement

   B. DHCP enforcement

   C. RD Gateway enforcement

   D. VPN enforcement

3. You want to provide IPv4 address leases only to computers that are up to date with software updates and antimalware definitions. Which NAP enforcement method should you implement?

   A. VPN enforcement

   B. 802.1X enforcement

   C. IPsec enforcement

   D. DHCP enforcement

4. You want to allow only computers that are up to date with software updates and antimalware definitions to communicate in an authenticated and encrypted manner with secure servers on a trusted internal network. Which NAP enforcement method should you implement?

   A. DHCP enforcement

   B. IPsec enforcement

   C. VPN enforcement

   D. RD Gateway enforcement

5. You want to limit remote access connections from hosts on the Internet using LT2P to client computers that are up to date with software updates and antimalware definitions. Which NAP enforcement method should you implement?

   A. RD Gateway enforcement

   B. 802.1X enforcement

   C. VPN enforcement

   D. IPsec enforcement

Lesson 3: Understanding Network Access Protection infrastructure

After you have decided on a NAP enforcement method, you need to think about what configuration settings will determine whether a client is deemed healthy or unhealthy. You do this by configuring health validators. In this lesson, you will learn how to configure SHVs and you will learn how to configure health policies and remediation server groups. You will also learn how to configure HRAs that distribute health certificates when using the NAP with the IPsec enforcement method.

> **After this lesson, you will be able to:**
> - Configure Windows Security Health Validators.
> - Configure System Health Validators.
> - Configure health policies.
> - Configure Health Registration Authorities.
> - Configure remediation server groups.
>
> **Estimated lesson time: 45 minutes**

Windows Security Health Validator

The WSHV includes a list of settings that you can configure as a benchmark for determining whether a client computer is deemed healthy or unhealthy by the NAP process. A client must meet the requirements of each setting that you enable in the WSHV, shown in Figure 7-43, to be healthy. Not meeting any enabled condition means that the client will be determined to be in an unhealthy state.

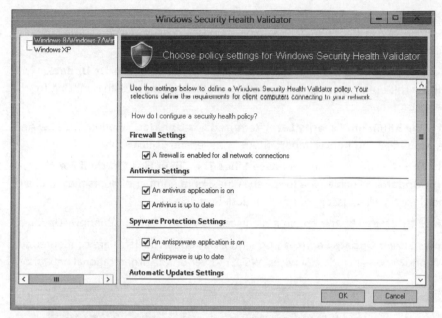

FIGURE 7-43 Configuring WSHV

You can configure the following settings in the WSHV:

- **A Firewall Is Enabled For All Network Connections** Windows Firewall or a third-party firewall recognized by the operating system component known as Action Center is enabled for all network connection types. Although it is possible that a third-party firewall may be present and functioning on the client computer, the firewall is not accounted for by NAP unless that firewall is registered with Action Center.

- **An Antivirus Application Is On** An antivirus application registered with Action Center is installed and enabled.

- **Antivirus Is Up To Date** An antivirus application registered with Action Center reports that it has recently performed a successful definition update. If the antivirus application could not update in a period specified by the application vendor, it will report to Action Center that it is not up to date.

- **An Antispyware Application Is On** An antispyware application is registered with Action Center and enabled. Some applications function as both antivirus and antispyware and register with Action Center in both these categories.

- **Antispyware Is Up To Date** The antispyware application registered with Action Center has successfully performed a definition update check recently. If the antimalware application could not update in a period specified by the application vendor, it will report to Action Center that it is not up to date.

- **Automatic Updating Is Enabled** Windows Update is enabled on the client computer.

- **Security Updates Settings** This collection of settings, shown in Figure 7-44, enables you to go beyond just ensuring that automatic updating is enabled. You can configure the following settings:

- **Restrict Access For Clients That Do Not Have All Available Security Updates Installed** This option restricts access if any available security update is missing from the client computer.

- **Specify The Minimum Severity Level Required For Updates** Options are Low And Above, Moderate And Above, Important And Above, and Critical Only.

- **Specify The Number Of Hours Allowed Since The Client Has Checked For New Security Updates** Enables you to specify a maximum number of hours that can have elapsed since the client last performed an update check.

- **Windows Update** Use this option if clients retrieve updates from Windows Update.

- **Windows Server Update Services** Configure this option if clients are configured to use a Windows Server Update Services (WSUS) server on the organizational network.

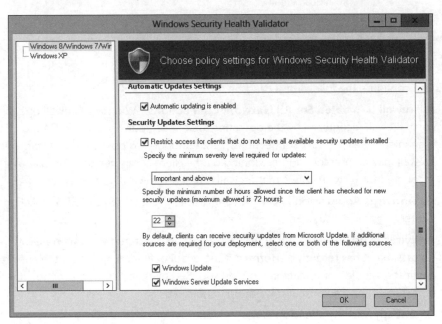

FIGURE 7-44 Windows Security Health Validator dialog box

MORE INFO **WSHVS**

For more information about WSHVs, consult the following TechNet document at *http://technet.microsoft.com/en-us/library/cc731260.aspx*.

System Health Validators and System Health Agents

SHVs and SHAs are client and server components that you can configure to validate the health of a client computer. The *SHA* resides on the client, and the *SHV* is located on the server with the NPS role installed. The WSHV is an SHV created by Microsoft.

> **MORE INFO** **SHVS**
>
> For more information about SHVs, consult the following TechNet document at *http://technet.microsoft.com/en-us/library/cc771201.aspx*.

SHVs and corresponding SHAs are also available from third parties that might deal with specific settings in the products made by those third parties. For example, it is possible to get SHVs and SHAs for third-party operating systems so that clients with those operating systems installed can participate in a NAP implementation.

> **REAL WORLD** **WSHV**
>
> For most NAP deployments, the built-in WSHV will meet organizational needs. You will need to look at third-party SHVs if there are non-Windows Client operating systems used regularly on your network.

Health policies

Health policies must include one or more SHVs. When a properly configured client attempts to connect to a network where NAP is enabled, the client computer will forward a statement of health of the server with the NPS role installed. The server with the NPS role installed compares the statement of health against the health policy and determines whether the client is compliant. You configure health policies on the server with the NPS role installed. Figure 7-45 shows a health policy. You can use any installed SHVs in a health policy.

> **MORE INFO** **HEALTH POLICIES**
>
> For more information about health policies, consult the following TechNet article at *http://technet.microsoft.com/en-us/library/cc771934.aspx*.

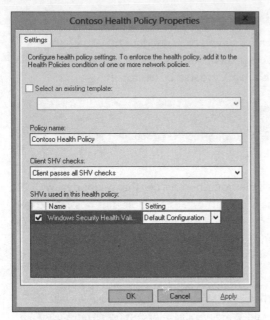

FIGURE 7-45 A health policy in the WSHV

When configuring a health policy with multiple SHVs, you can choose whether a client will be deemed healthy if only some, but not all, of the SHV checks are passed. You can configure the following options in a health policy:

- Client Passes All SHV Checks
- Client Fails All SHV Checks
- Client Passes One Or More SHV Checks
- Client Fails One Or More SHV Checks
- Client Reported As Transitional By One Or More SHVs
- Client Reported As Infected By One Or More SHVs
- Client Reported As Unknown By One Or More SHVs

A client must pass all conditions in an SHV to pass an SHV check. A failure of any condition in an SHV means that the check for that SHV has failed.

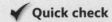 **Quick check**

- What is the minimum number of SHVs in a health policy?

Quick check answer

- A health policy requires a minimum of one SHV.

Health Registration Authorities

The HRA is an NPS role service that obtains and distributes health certificates from a CA when you deploy NAP with IPsec enforcement. You must configure the HRA to interact with a CA. You can do that when setting up the HRA or by using the Add Certification Authority task in the Actions pane, as shown in Figure 7-46.

FIGURE 7-46 CA to be used with an HRA

HRA cryptographic policies, shown in Figure 7-47, involve specifying which asymmetric keys algorithms, hash keys algorithms, and cryptographic service providers are accepted by the HRA. By default, an HRA will accept all supported asymmetric key and hash algorithms, and cryptographic service providers supported on Windows Client operating systems, but you can limit support to specific algorithms and cryptographic service providers by editing the properties of the cryptographic policy.

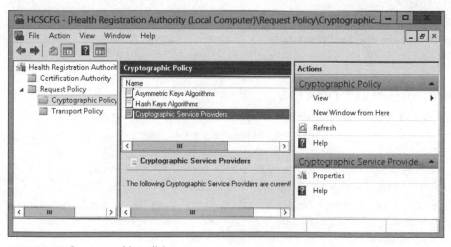

FIGURE 7-47 Cryptographic policies

Configuring a transport policy involves specifying which HTTP user agents can be used with the HRA. As Figure 7-48 shows, by default, any agent can be used with the HRA. You can limit the agent based on the agent string.

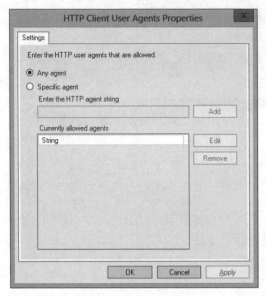

FIGURE 7-48 Transport agent policies.

It is necessary to modify the HRA cryptographic policy or transport policy only in organizations that have stringent security requirements. It is unlikely that you'll need to perform this action if your organization does not require the strictest level of security.

> **MORE INFO   HRAS**
>
> For more information about HRAs, consult the following TechNet article at *http://technet
> .microsoft.com/en-us/library/cc732365.aspx*.

Remediation server groups

A *remediation server group* is a collection of servers located on a restricted network that host the resources that allow noncompliant clients to reach a state of compliance. For example, a remediation server group may host a WSUS deployment, antivirus and antispyware definitions, and any other software necessary to bring a computer to a compliant state. You configure remediation server groups in the NPS console by clicking the Remediation Server Groups node under Network Access Protection, and clicking New in the Action menu. You then add all servers that will participate in the remediation server group in the New Remediation Server Group dialog box, shown in Figure 7-49.

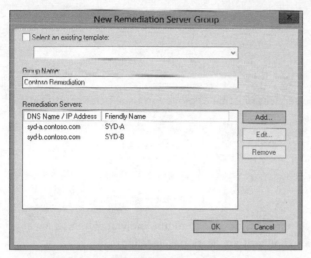

FIGURE 7-49 Remediation server group

> **MORE INFO   REMEDIATION SERVER GROUPS**
>
> For more information about remediation server groups, consult the following TechNet article at *http://technet.microsoft.com/en-us/library/cc770646.aspx.*

Lesson summary

- The WSHV is the built-in SHV available with Windows Server 2012 and Windows Server 2012 R2.
- SHVs are collections of conditions used to determine client health, such as whether a firewall is enabled.
- SHAs assess a client to determine compliance with the conditions in the SHV.
- Health policies determine which SHVs are used to calculate client health in NAP scenarios.
- HRAs are used to issue health certificates in a NAP IPsec implementation.
- Remediation server groups are collections of servers that host services that enable unhealthy clients to return to a healthy state.

Lesson review

Answer the following questions to test your knowledge of the information in this lesson. You can find the answers to these questions and explanations of why each answer choice is correct or incorrect in the "Answers" section at the end of this chapter.

1. Which of the following should you configure if you want clients to be able to return to a healthy state after being found noncompliant by the NAP process?

A. SHV

B. Health policy

C. Remediation server group

D. HRA

2. Which of the following NPS role services must be deployed to issue health certificates when you deploy NAP with IPsec?

A. Health policy

B. Remediation server group

C. SHV

D. HRA

3. In which of the following NAP components do you configure individual items such as whether a firewall is enabled or an antivirus application is installed?

A. SHV

B. HRA

C. Health policy

D. Remediation server group

4. Which of the following do you select as a benchmark for health when configuring a NAP policy?

A. Remediation server group

B. Health policy

C. SHV

D. HRA

Practice exercises

The goal of this section is to provide you with hands-on practice with the following:

- Installing the NPS role
- Configuring WSHV
- Configuring a remediation server group
- Configuring client policy for DHCP enforcement
- Configuring NAP DHCP enforcement

To perform the exercises in this section, you need access to an evaluation version of Windows Server 2012 R2. You should also have access to virtual machines SYD-DC, MEL-DC, CBR-DC, and ADL-DC, the setup instructions for which are described in the Introduction. You should ensure that you have a checkpoint of these virtual machines that you can revert to at the end of the practice exercises. You should revert the virtual machines to this initial state prior to beginning these exercises.

Exercise 1: Installing the DHCP role

In this exercise, you install the DHCP role, which is necessary to support the later implementation of NAP. To complete this exercise, perform the following steps:

1. Ensure that SYD-DC is powered on.

2. Start MEL-DC and sign in using the Administrator account with the password **Pa$$w0rd**.

3. Open the Windows PowerShell prompt and type the following commands.

   ```
   Add-Computer -DomainName contoso.com
   ```

4. In the Windows PowerShell Credentials dialog box type **don_funk@contoso.com** and **Pa$$w0rd**, and click OK.

5. Type the following command in the Windows PowerShell prompt to restart the computer.

   ```
   Restart-Computer
   ```

6. Start ADL-DC and sign in using the Administrator account with the password **Pa$$w0rd**.

7. Open the Windows PowerShell prompt and type the following commands

   ```
   Add-Computer -DomainName contoso.com
   ```

8. In the Windows PowerShell Credentials dialog box type **don_funk@contoso.com** and **Pa$$w0rd**, and click OK.

9. Type the following command in the Windows PowerShell prompt to restart the computer.

   ```
   Restart-Computer
   ```

10. Sign on to MEL-DC with the contoso\don_funk account.

11. On the Manage menu of the Server Manager console, click Add Roles And Features.

12. On the Before You Begin page of the Add Roles and Features Wizard, click Next.

13. On the Installation Type page, click Role-Based Or Feature-Based Installation, and click Next.

14. On the Select Destination Server page, click MEL-DC.contoso.com, and click Next.

15. On the Select Server Roles page, click DHCP Server.

16. In the Add Roles And Features Wizard dialog box that pops up, click Add Features, and click Next.

17. On the Features page, click Next.

18. On the DHCP Server page, click Next.

19. On the Confirmation page, click Install, and then click Close.

20. On the Tools menu, click DHCP.

21. Click MEL-DC.contoso.com, as shown in Figure 7-50.

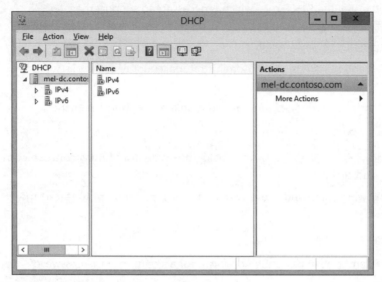

FIGURE 7-50 DHCP console

22. On the Action menu, click Authorize.

23. Close the DHCP console.

24. Click the notification icon next to the Manage menu, and click Complete DHCP configuration.

25. On the DHCP Post-Install Configuration Wizard dialog box, click Next.

26. On the Authorization page, click Commit.

27. On the Summary page, click Close.

Exercise 2: Deploying the NPS role

In this exercise, you deploy the NPS role on MEL-DC. To complete this exercise, perform the following steps:

1. On MEL-DC, click Add Roles And Features from the Manage menu.

2. On the Before You Begin page of the Add Roles and Features Wizard, click Next.

3. On the Select Installation Type page, click Role-Based Or Feature-Based Installation, and click Next.

4. On the Select Destination Server page, click MEL-DC.contoso.com, and click Next.

5. On the Select Server Roles page, click Network Policy And Access Services.

6. In the Add Roles And Features Wizard dialog box that pops up, click Add Features, and then click Next.

7. On the Select Features page, click Next.

8. On the Network Policy And Access Services page, click Next.

9. On the Role Services page, ensure that Network Policy Server is selected, as shown in Figure 7-51, and click Next.

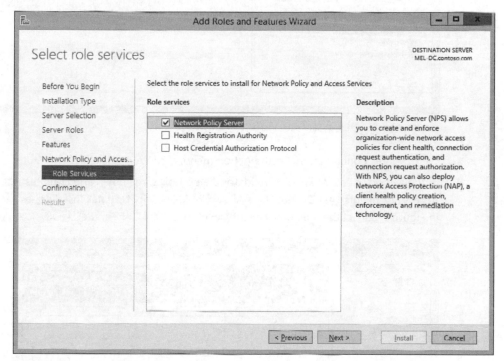

FIGURE 7-51 Selecting NPS role service

10. On the Confirmation page, click Install, and then click Close.

Exercise 3: Configuring Windows Security Health Validator

In this exercise, you configure the WSHV on the server with the NPS role installed. To complete this exercise, perform the following steps:

1. On MEL-DC, on the Tools menu, click Network Policy Server.

2. Expand Network Access Protection\System Health Validators\Windows Security Health Validator and click Settings, as shown in Figure 7-52.

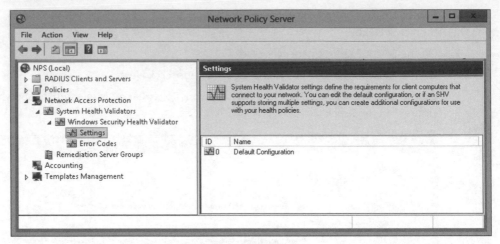

FIGURE 7-52 Selecting WSHV settings

3. Click Default Configuration. On the Action menu, click Properties.

4. In the Windows Security Health Validator dialog box, scroll down and click Restrict Access For Clients That Do Not Have All Available Security Updates Installed, as shown in Figure 7-53. Set the minimum severity level to Critical Only, and click OK.

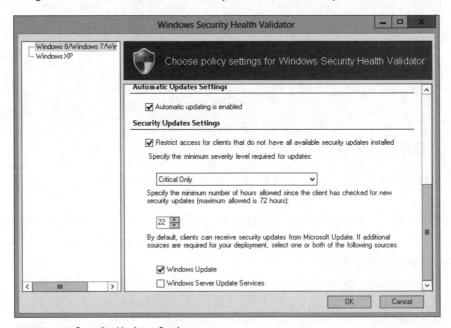

FIGURE 7-53 Security Updates Settings

Exercise 4: Configuring a remediation server group

In this exercise, you configure remediation server groups. To complete this exercise, perform the following steps:

1. On MEL-DC, in the NPS console, click Remediation Server Groups, as shown in Figure 7-54.

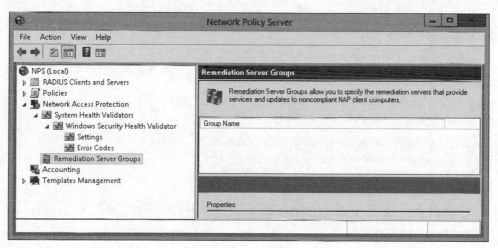

FIGURE 7-54 Remediation server groups

2. On the Action menu, click New.

3. In the New Remediation Server Group dialog box, type **Contoso Remediation Group** in the Group Name, and click Add.

4. In the Add New Server dialog box, type the friendly name **ADL-DC** and the DNS name **ADL-DC.contoso.com,** and then click Resolve. Click OK.

5. Verify that the New Remediation Server Group dialog box matches Figure 7-55, and click OK.

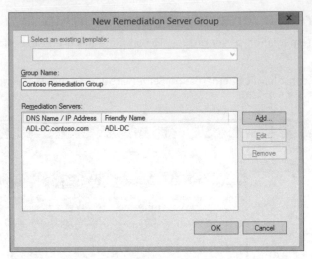

FIGURE 7-55 Remediation server groups

Exercise 5: Configuring client policies for DHCP enforcement

In this exercise, you use the GPMC and the DHCP console, and then configure client policies to support DHCP enforcement. To complete this exercise, perform the following steps:

1. On MEL-DC, right-click the Windows PowerShell icon on the taskbar, right-click Windows PowerShell, and click Run As Administrator. At the User Account Control prompt, click Yes.

2. Execute the following commands.

   ```
   Install-WindowsFeature GPMC,RSAT-ADDS
   ```

3. Close Windows PowerShell.

4. On the Tools menu of Server Manager, click Group Policy Management.

5. In the Group Policy Management Console, expand Forest: Contoso.com\Domains\ contoso.com\ and select Group Policy Objects.

6. On the Action menu, click New.

7. On the New GPO dialog box, type **DHCP-Enforcement** and click OK.

8. In the Group Policy Management Console, right-click the DHCP-Enforcement policy and click Edit.

9. Expand the Computer Configuration\Policies\Windows Settings\Security Settings\ Network Access Protection node, and click NAP Client Configuration, as shown in Figure 7-56.

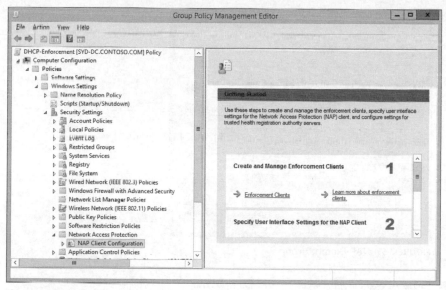

FIGURE 7-56 NAP client configuration

10. Click Enforcement Clients, and then click DHCP Quarantine Enforcement Client.

11. On the Action menu, click Enable.

12. Close the Group Policy Management Editor.

13. Close the GPMC.

14. On the Tools menu of the Server Manager console, click Active Directory Users And Computers.

15. Expand Contoso.com, and click Computers. On the Action menu, click New, and click Group.

16. In the New Object - Group dialog box, type the name **NAP-Exempt**, as shown in Figure 7-57, and click OK.

FIGURE 7-57 NAP-Exempt group

17. Close Active Directory Users And Computers.

Exercise 6: Configuring NAP DHCP enforcement

In this exercise, you configure NAP DHCP enforcement. To complete this exercise, perform the following steps:

1. In the NPS console on MEL-DC, click NPS (Local), and then click Configure NAP.

2. On the Select Network Connection Method For Use With NAP page, use the drop-down list to select Dynamic Host Configuration Protocol (DHCP), as shown in Figure 7-58, and click Next.

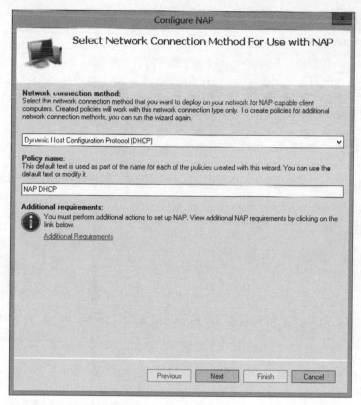

FIGURE 7-58 DHCP NAP policy

3. On the RADIUS Clients page, click Next.

4. On the Specify DHCP Scopes page, click Next.

5. On the Machine Groups page, click Add.

6. In the Select Group dialog box, type **NAP-Exempt**, click Check Names, and click OK.

7. Verify that the Configure Machine Groups page matches Figure 7-59, and click Next.

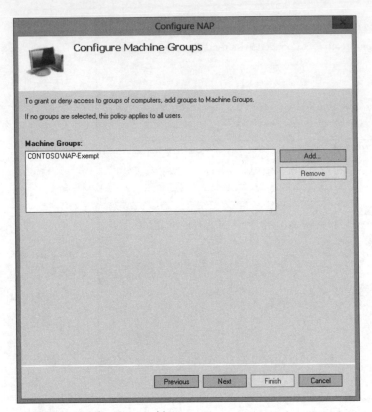

FIGURE 7-59 Configuring machine groups

8. On the Remediation Server Group page, use the drop-down list to select Contoso Remediation Group, as shown in Figure 7-60, and click Next.

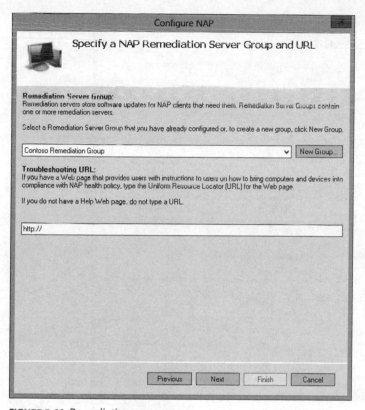

FIGURE 7-60 Remediation server groups

9. On the Define NAP Health Policy page, verify that Windows Security Health Validator is selected, that Auto-Remediation is enabled, and that Deny Full Network Access To NAP-Ineligible Client Computers is selected, as shown in Figure 7-61, and click Next.

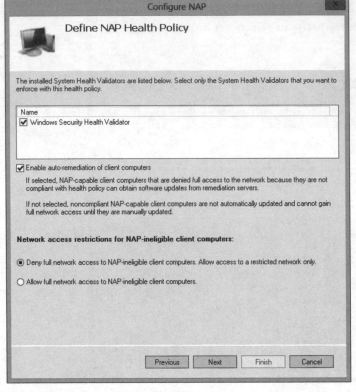

FIGURE 7-61 Defining NAP health policy

10. On the Completing NAP Enforcement Policy And RADIUS Client Configuration page, click Finish.

Suggested practice exercises

The following additional practice exercises are designed to give you more opportunities to practice what you've learned and to help you successfully master the lessons presented in this chapter.

- **Exercise 1**   Install an enterprise root CA and a Health Registration Authority
- **Exercise 2**   Configure NAP with IPsec enforcement
- **Exercise 3**   Configure a remediation server group

Answers

This section contains the answers to the lesson review questions in this chapter.

Lesson 1

1. **Correct answer: D**

   A. **Incorrect.** You use the HCAP server connection request type when configuring integration with Cisco NAC.

   B. **Incorrect.** You use the remote access server when configuring connection request policies related to dial-up and VPN services.

   C. **Incorrect.** You use DHCP server when configuring policies to support NAP with DHCP enforcement.

   D. **Correct.** You use the RD Gateway connection type for a connection request policy when you want to allow Remote Desktop Connection connections from untrusted networks.

2. **Correct answer: C**

   A. **Incorrect.** You use the RD Gateway connection type for a connection request policy when you want to allow Remote Desktop Connection connections from untrusted networks.

   B. **Incorrect.** You use DHCP server when configuring policies to support NAP with DHCP enforcement.

   C. **Correct.** You use the remote access server connection request type when configuring connection request policies related to dial-up and VPN services.

   D. **Incorrect.** You use the HCAP server connection request type when configuring integration with Cisco NAC.

3. **Correct answer: B**

   A. **Incorrect.** You use the remote access server connection request type when configuring connection request policies related to dial-up and VPN services.

   B. **Correct.** You use the HCAP server connection request type when configuring integration with Cisco NAC.

   C. **Incorrect.** You use DHCP server when configuring policies to support NAP with DHCP enforcement.

   D. **Incorrect.** You use the RD Gateway connection type for a connection request policy when you want to allow Remote Desktop Connection connections from untrusted networks.

4. **Correct answer: D**

   A. **Incorrect.** Use the Windows Groups condition if you want to configure a network policy that applies to either user or computer accounts that are members of a security group.

   B. **Incorrect.** Use the Machine Groups condition if you want to configure a network policy that applies to computer accounts in a specific group.

   C. **Incorrect.** Use the User Groups condition if you want to configure a network policy that applies to user accounts in a specific group.

   D. **Correct.** Use the Day And Time Restrictions to configure a policy that applies only at certain times of the week.

5. **Correct answer: A and D**

   A. **Correct.** Use the Windows Groups condition if you want to configure a network policy that applies to either user or computer accounts that are members of a security group.

   B. **Incorrect.** Use the User Groups condition if you want to configure a network policy that applies to user accounts in a specific group.

   C. **Incorrect.** Use the Day And Time Restrictions to configure a policy that applies only at certain times of the week.

   D. **Correct.** Use the Machine Groups condition if you want to configure a network policy that applies to computer accounts in a specific group.

Lesson 2

1. **Correct answer: D**

   A. **Incorrect.** IPsec enforcement enables healthy clients to communicate with other hosts on the network in an encrypted and authenticated manner.

   B. **Incorrect.** 802.1x enforcement enables the use of authenticating switches and wireless access points to limit network connectivity to clients that are deemed healthy.

   C. **Incorrect.** VPN enforcement limits VPN connections to clients that are healthy.

   D. **Correct.** RD Gateway enforcement limits connections through an RD Gateway server to clients that are healthy.

2. **Correct answer: A**

   A. **Correct.** 802.1x enforcement allows the use of authenticating switches and wireless access points to limit network connectivity to clients that are deemed healthy.

   B. **Incorrect.** The DHCP enforcement method enables you to restrict the leasing of IPv4 addresses to healthy clients.

C.   **Incorrect.** RD Gateway enforcement limits connections through an RD Gateway server to clients that are healthy.

D.   **Incorrect.** VPN enforcement limits VPN connections to clients that are healthy.

3.   **Correct answer: D**

A.   **Incorrect.** VPN enforcement limits VPN connections to clients that are healthy.

B.   **Incorrect.** 802.1x enforcement allows the use of authenticating switches and wireless access points to limit network connectivity to clients that are deemed healthy.

C.   **Incorrect.** IPsec enforcement enables healthy clients to communicate with other hosts on the network in an encrypted and authenticated manner.

D.   **Correct.** The DHCP enforcement method enables you to restrict the leasing of IPv4 addresses to healthy clients.

4.   **Correct answer: B**

A.   **Incorrect.** The DHCP enforcement method enables you to restrict the leasing of IPv4 addresses to healthy clients.

B.   **Correct.** IPsec enforcement enables healthy clients to communicate with other hosts on the network in an encrypted and authenticated manner.

C.   **Incorrect.** VPN enforcement limits VPN connections to clients that are healthy.

D.   **Incorrect.** RD Gateway enforcement limits connections through an RD Gateway server to clients that are healthy.

5.   **Correct answer: C**

A.   **Incorrect.** RD Gateway enforcement limits connections through an RD Gateway server to clients that are healthy.

B.   **Incorrect.** 802.1x enforcement allows the use of authenticating switches and wireless access points to limit network connectivity to clients that are deemed healthy.

C.   **Correct.** VPN enforcement limits VPN connections to clients that are healthy.

D.   **Incorrect.** IPsec enforcement enables healthy clients to communicate with other hosts on the network in an encrypted and authenticated manner.

Lesson 3

1.   **Correct answer: C**

A.   **Incorrect.** An SHV is a set of specific health conditions, such as whether a firewall is enabled and antimalware software is installed, all of which must be met to pass an SHV check in a health policy.

B.   **Incorrect.** A health policy is a collection of one or more SHVs. Health policy settings determine whether a client is compliant.

C. **Correct.** A collection of servers that hosts software updates and antimalware definitions that enable noncompliant clients to return to health.

D. **Incorrect.** An HRA is used in an NAP IPsec enforcement to issue health certificates.

2. **Correct answer: B and D**

A. **Incorrect.** A health policy is a collection of one or more SHVs. Health policy settings determine whether a client is compliant.

B. **Incorrect.** A collection of servers that host software updates and antimalware definitions that enable noncompliant clients to return to health.

C. **Incorrect.** An SHV is a set of specific health conditions, such as whether a firewall is enabled and antimalware software is installed, all of which must be met to pass an SHV check in a health policy.

D. **Correct**. An HRA is used in a NAP IPsec enforcement to issue health certificates.

3. **Correct answer: A**

A. **Correct.** An SHV is a set of specific health conditions, such as whether a firewall is enabled and antimalware software is installed, all of which must be met to pass an SHV check in a health policy.

B. **Incorrect.** An HRA is used in a NAP IPsec enforcement to issue health certificates.

C. **Incorrect.** A health policy is a collection of one or more SHVs. Health policy settings determine whether a client is compliant.

D. **Incorrect.** A collection of servers that host software updates and antimalware definitions that enable noncompliant clients to return to health.

4. **Correct answer: B**

A. **Incorrect.** A collection of servers that host software updates and antimalware definitions that enable noncompliant clients to return to health.

B. **Correct.** A health policy is a collection of one or more SHVs. Health policy settings determine whether a client is compliant.

C. **Incorrect.** An SHV is a set of specific health conditions, such as whether a firewall is enabled and antimalware software is installed, all of which must be met to pass an SHV check in a health policy.

D. **Incorrect.** An HRA is used in a NAP IPsec enforcement to issue health certificates.

CHAPTER 8

Administering remote access

In the modern workplace, work rarely stops at the door of the building. Approximately 60 percent of computers used on the networks of modern organizations are laptop and tablet computers instead of traditional desktop computers. People are just as likely to be working from home or a coffee shop as they are from a desk in the office environment. Remote access enables you to grant users on untrusted networks, such as the Internet, access to trusted networks, such as the ones that host your organization's critical servers. In this chapter, you learn how to configure RADIUS servers, clients, and proxies. You learn how to configure Windows Server 2012 and Windows Server 2012 R2 as a Routing and Remote Access server. You also learn how to configure DirectAccess.

Lessons in this chapter:

- Lesson 1: Configuring RADIUS **417**
- Lesson 2: Configuring VPN and routing **434**
- Lesson 3: Configuring DirectAccess **454**

Before you begin

To complete the practice exercises in this chapter:

- You need to have deployed computers SYD-DC, MEL-DC, and ADL-DC, as described in the Introduction, using the evaluation edition of Windows Server 2012 R2.

Lesson 1: Configuring RADIUS

Remote Authentication Dial-In User Service (RADIUS) is a standard protocol supported by almost all advanced networking devices. It enables you to configure authentication and authorization for network connections, from connections from remote access clients on the Internet, to connections made through authenticating switches and wireless access points. Deploying a RADIUS server on a trusted network enables you to keep remote access servers, such as Virtual Private Network (VPN) servers deployed on the perimeter network, more secure. If you use RADIUS for authentication, the VPN server on the perimeter network doesn't have to maintain an account database. It simply handles connections, forwarding authentication and authorization traffic to a RADIUS server. If attackers can compromise the VPN server on the perimeter network, they can't gain access to the account database because it is hosted on a RADIUS server on the protected network. In this lesson, you learn about RADIUS servers, RADIUS proxies, RADIUS clients, and RADIUS accounting.

> **After this lesson, you will be able to:**
>
> ■ Deploy RADIUS servers.
>
> ■ Manage RADIUS proxies.
>
> ■ Configure RADIUS clients.
>
> ■ Configure RADIUS accounting.
>
> **Estimated lesson time: 45 minutes**

RADIUS servers

A RADIUS server performs authentication, authorization, and accounting for VPN, 802.1x wireless access point and authenticating switches, and dial-up connections. The Network Policy Server (NPS) role is Microsoft's implementation of a RADIUS server.

You can install the NPS role by performing the following steps:

1. In Server Manager, click Add Roles And Features from the Manage menu.

2. On the Before You Begin page, click Next.

3. On the Select Installation Type page, click Role-Based Or Feature-Based Installation, and click Next.

4. On the Select Destination Server page, select the server on which you want to install the NPS role, and click Next.

5. On the Select Server Roles page, click Network Policy And Access Services, as shown in Figure 8-1.

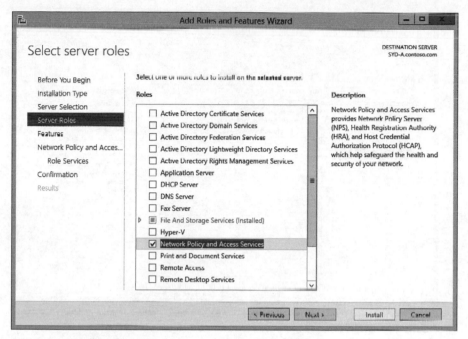

FIGURE 8-1 Installing the NPS role

6. In the Add Roles And Features Wizard dialog box, click Add Features.

7. On the Select Server Roles page, click Next.

8. On the Select Features page, click Next.

9. On the Network Policy And Access Service pace, click Next.

10. On the Select Role Services page, ensure that Network Policy Server is selected, as shown in Figure 8-2, and click Next.

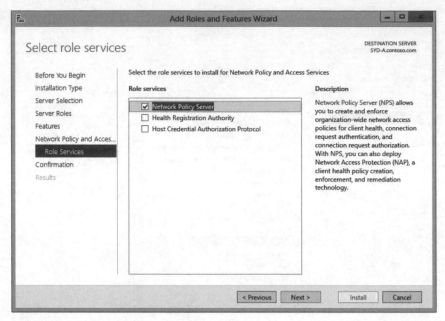

FIGURE 8-2 Installing the NPS role service

11. On the Confirm Installation Selections page, click Install, and then click Close.

Given that NPS is an implementation of the RADIUS protocol, you can use NPS with other third-party products that support the RADIUS protocol, as well as other versions of Microsoft products that support RADIUS. The NPS role's support for the RADIUS protocol means that you can integrate it with most third-party remote and network access products. Active Directory functions as the user account database when a server with the NPS role installed is a member of an Active Directory Domain Services (AD DS) domain. You configure whether the local server performs RADIUS authentication when creating a connection request policy, or by editing the properties of a connection request policy, as shown in Figure 8-3.

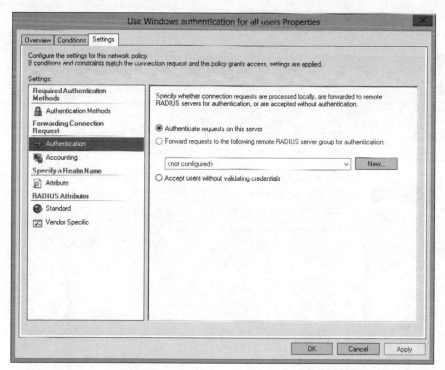

FIGURE 8-3 Configuring authentication

MORE INFO **RADIUS SERVERS**

For more information about RADIUS servers, consult the following TechNet article at *http://technet.microsoft.com/en-us/library/cc755248.aspx.*

RADIUS proxies

A *RADIUS proxy* forwards traffic from RADIUS clients to other RADIUS servers based upon the properties of the connection request. When you configure a server with the NPS role installed as a RADIUS proxy, information about messages passed on to RADIUS servers from RADIUS clients is recorded in the accounting log. A server configured as a RADIUS proxy functions as a RADIUS client from the perspective of the RADIUS server performing authentication.

You deploy a RADIUS proxy when you need to provide authentication and authorization for users that have accounts in other Active Directory forests. For example, if there are three forests in your organization in which no forest trusts have been configured, but only one VPN server, you can use a RADIUS proxy to forward authentication traffic to RADIUS servers in the other forests. If a forest trust has been configured, you don't need to use a RADIUS proxy. You can also use a RADIUS proxy when you need authentication to occur against an account database running on a third-party operating system. Figure 8-4 shows a configuration in which requests are forwarded to the CONTOSO RADIUS server group.

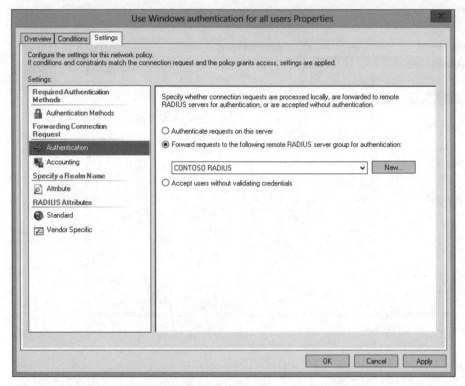

FIGURE 8-4 Configuring NPS to forward RADIUS requests

To configure a server with the NPS role installed to function as a RADIUS proxy, you need to have configured a remote RADIUS server group. You perform this task in the New Remote RADIUS Server Group dialog box, shown in Figure 8-5. A remote RADIUS server group is a collection of RADIUS servers to which a RADIUS proxy can forward authentication traffic. You configure the priority and weight of each server in the group to determine the balance of traffic forwarded from the proxy. Weight is for load balancing allocation and priority is used in high availability situations.

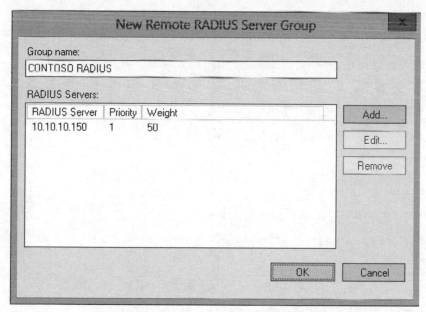

FIGURE 8-5 Remote RADIUS server group

You can add additional servers to the group if the current RADIUS servers can't cope with the current traffic load. To add a server to the group, perform the following steps:

1. In the New Remote RADIUS Server Group dialog box, click Add.

2. In the Add RADIUS Server dialog box, enter the fully qualified domain name (FQDN) or IP address of the RADIUS server that you want to add to the group, as shown in Figure 8-6, and click Verify.

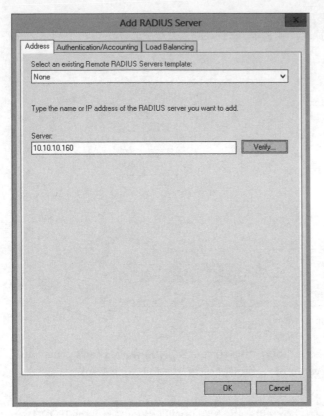

FIGURE 8-6 Adding a server to a remote RADIUS server group

MORE INFO   **RADIUS PROXIES**

For more information about RADIUS proxies, consult the following TechNet article at
http://technet.microsoft.com/en-us/library/cc731320.aspx.

---

3. On the Authentication/Accounting tab, you can configure the shared secret between
   the RADIUS proxy server and the RADIUS server. You can also configure the accounting
   port and determine whether the same shared secret is used for authentication and
   accounting, as shown in Figure 8-7.

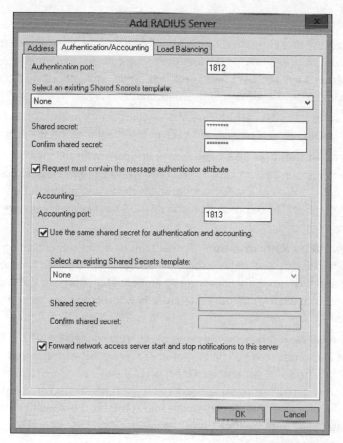

FIGURE 8-7 Configuring RADIUS server authentication and accounting

4. The Load Balancing tab enables you to configure timeout settings for a server. They determine how long the proxy will wait before sending authentication traffic to another RADIUS server in the remote RADIUS server group.

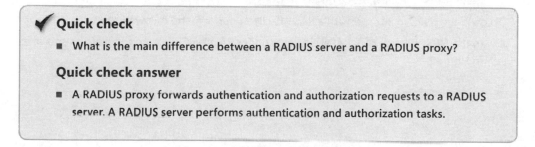

✔ Quick check

■ What is the main difference between a RADIUS server and a RADIUS proxy?

Quick check answer

■ A RADIUS proxy forwards authentication and authorization requests to a RADIUS server. A RADIUS server performs authentication and authorization tasks.

RADIUS clients

When many IT professionals are first introduced to the term *RADIUS client*, they assume that it is something similar to a laptop computer on the Internet trying to make a remote access connection. A RADIUS client is a device that forwards authentication and authorization traffic to a RADIUS server. A RADIUS client can be one of the following:

- **Another RADIUS server** In this case, the RADIUS server is acting as a proxy. The response from the RADIUS server is forwarded back to the client through the proxy.

- **A wireless access point that uses 802.1x authentication** Rather than have the wireless access point perform authentication and authorization, the wireless access point functions as a RADIUS client and forwards authentication and authorization traffic to the RADIUS server. The response from the RADIUS server determines whether the connection is allowed or denied.

- **A switch that uses 802.1x authentication** Rather than have the authenticating switch perform authentication and authorization, the authenticating switch functions as a RADIUS client and forwards authentication and authorization traffic to the RADIUS server. The response from the RADIUS server determines whether the connection is allowed or denied.

- **A VPN server** The VPN server handles the setup of the VPN connection. The authentication and authorization is handled by another server. The response from the RADIUS server determines whether the connection is allowed or denied. This configuration is more secure because the account database is not hosted on the VPN server. If the VPN server is on a perimeter network, you configure a firewall to allow RADIUS authentication and authorization traffic between the VPN server and the RADIUS server on the protected network.

- **A dial-up server** Although dial-up is less likely to be used today, especially because few recent models of laptops ship with modems that use a phone line to make a connection, dial-up servers can function as RADIUS clients. In this configuration, they forward authentication and authorization traffic to a RADIUS server and then allow or deny the connection based on the response.

To configure NPS to interact with a RADIUS client, perform the following steps:

1. In the NPS console, click RADIUS Clients under RADIUS Clients And Servers, as shown in Figure 8-8.

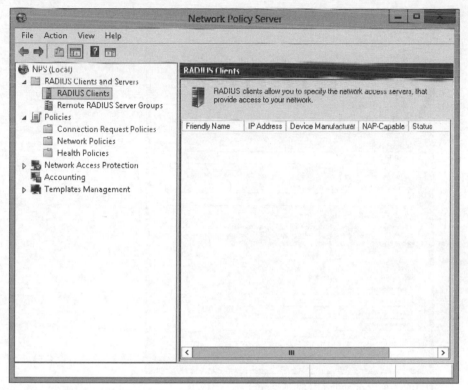

FIGURE 8-8 RADIUS clients node

2. On the Action menu, click New.

3. In the New RADIUS Client dialog box, shown in Figure 8-9, provide the following details:

- **Friendly Name** This option enables you to enter a name that reminds you of the client's function.

- **Address (IP Or DNS)** Provides the IP address or FQDN of the RADIUS client.

- **Shared Secret** You can choose a preconfigured shared secret template or configure a shared secret manually. A shared secret enables the RADIUS client and the RADIUS server to verify each other's identity.

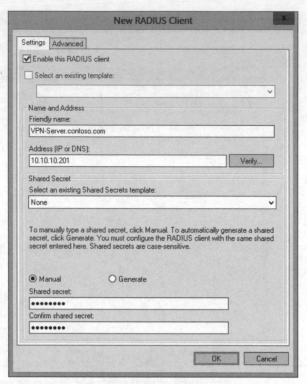

FIGURE 8-9 Configuring RADIUS client basic settings

4. On the Advanced tab of the New RADIUS Client dialog box, shown in Figure 8-10, you can configure a RADIUS client vendor from a list of 23. You can also specify whether the RADIUS client is NAP-capable and configure RADIUS attribute requirements.

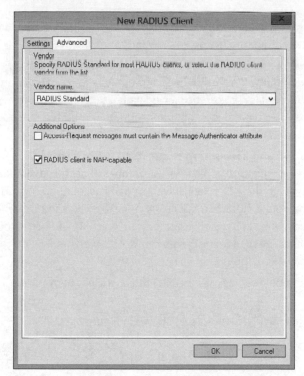

FIGURE 8-10 RADIUS client advanced settings

NOTE **RADIUS CLIENTS**

For more information about RADIUS clients, consult the following TechNet article at *http://technet.microsoft.com/en-us/library/cc754033.aspx*.

RADIUS accounting

RADIUS accounting is a function that you can configure on a server that hosts the NPS role that enables you to record successful and failed connection attempts through devices that participate in your organization's RADIUS infrastructure. You can use the RADIUS accounting function available in NPS to record the following information:

- User authentication requests
- Access-Accept messages
- Access-Reject messages
- Accounting requests and responses
- Periodic status updates

You can configure RADIUS accounting on a server with the NPS role installed in one of the following three ways:

- **Event logging** This method is the least sophisticated. You use this method to audit and troubleshoot connection attempts. The events are written to the event log.

- **Logging user authentication and accounting requests to a local file** Enables logs to be written in Internet Authentication Service (IAS) and database-compatible format. This method writes data to a flat file that can be viewed with a text file editor or a tool such as Microsoft LogParser. This type of logging is appropriate when there are only a small number of remote access clients.

- **Logging user authentication and accounting requests to a Microsoft SQL Server XML-compliant database** Logging to an SQL Server database has the advantage of enabling multiple servers with the NPS role installed to write accounting data to a single location. Because the data is stored on a SQL Server instance, it can be queried using Microsoft SQL Server syntax. In large environments in which RADIUS accounting data needs to be regularly examined, administrators can write a web application to query and extract data from this database.

To configure RADIUS accounting on a server with the NPS role installed, perform the following steps:

1. Select the Accounting node in the NPS console, as shown in Figure 8-11.

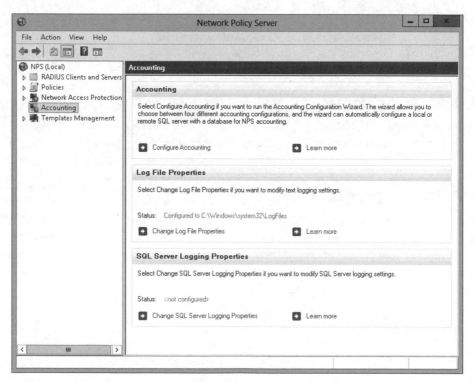

FIGURE 8-11 Accounting node of the NPS console

2. Click Configure Accounting. On the Introduction page of the Accounting Configuration Wizard, click Next.

3. On the Select Accounting Options page, shown in Figure 8-12, select one of the following options, and click Next.

   - **Log To A SQL Server Database** Choose this option if you only want to use SQL Server for logging.

   - **Log To A Text File On The Local Computer** Choose this option if you want to use only a local text file to store RADIUS accounting logs.

   - **Simultaneously Log To A SQL Server Database And A Local Text File** Choose this option if you want to use both the local text file and a SQL Server instance to record RADIUS accounting data.

   - **Log To A SQL Server Database Using Text File Logging For Failover** Use this option if you want a SQL Server database to be used for logging and a text file to be used only when logs can't be written to the SQL Server instance.

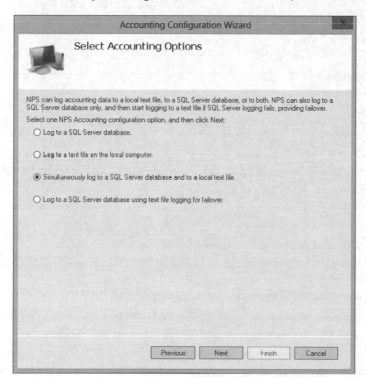

FIGURE 8-12 Accounting options

4. When configuring SQL logging, specify the information that you want logged, as shown in Figure 8-13. You can configure NPS to log the following RADIUS accounting data:

   - Accounting Requests

- Authentication Requests
- Periodic Accounting Status
- Periodic Authentication Status
- Logging Failure Action

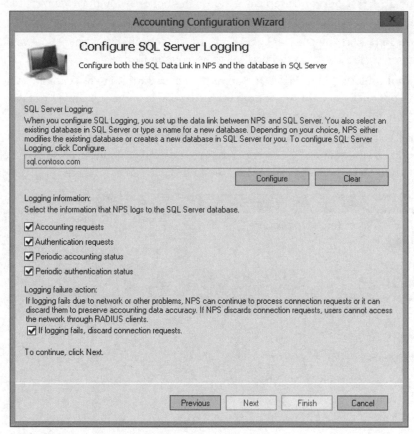

FIGURE 8-13 SQL Server logging options

5. Click Finish to complete the Accounting Configuration Wizard.

When configuring logging, you can enable an option that will block connection requests if logging fails. When considering whether to implement this option, you should balance the inconvenience of disallowing network access, which could be substantial if you have deployed NAP, against the security impact of having connections that would otherwise be authenticated and authorized being denied because a log entry cannot be written.

> *NOTE* **RADIUS ACCOUNTING**
>
> For more information about RADIUS accounting, consult the following TechNet article at
> *http://technet.microsoft.com/en-us/library/cc725566.aspx.*

Lesson summary

- NPS is the role that enables Windows Server 2012 and Windows Server 2012 R2 to function as a RADIUS server.
- A RADIUS server performs authentication and authorization for traffic forwarded to it from a RADIUS client.
- A RADIUS proxy forwards traffic from RADIUS clients to RADIUS servers. A RADIUS proxy can forward traffic to different RADIUS servers based on the properties of the traffic.
- A RADIUS client is a device that sends authentication and authorization traffic to a RADIUS server. A VPN server can be a RADIUS client.
- RADIUS accounting records authorization request data. RADIUS accounting data can be written to the event log, to a local log file, or to an SQL Server database.

Lesson review

Answer the following questions to test your knowledge of the information in this lesson. You can find the answers to these questions and explanations of why each answer choice is correct or incorrect in the "Answers" section at the end of this chapter.

1. Your organization has three Active Directory forests that don't have a trust relationship. You have a single VPN server that handles all incoming VPN connections. This VPN server is a dedicated hardware device deployed on the perimeter network. You want to configure the deployment so that authentication and authorization traffic is forwarded to existing RADIUS servers in each forest based on the connecting user's account properties. Which of the following must you deploy to accomplish this goal?

   A. RADIUS server

   B. RADIUS proxy

   C. RADIUS client

   D. RADIUS accounting

2. You want to deploy a server on your organization's internal network that will respond to authentication and authorization requests from a dedicated hardware device that functions as a VPN server that is deployed on your organization's perimeter network. Which of the following must you deploy to accomplish this goal?

   A. RADIUS accounting

   B. RADIUS server

   C. RADIUS proxy

   D. RADIUS client

3. Your organization has purchased a dedicated hardware device that functions as a VPN server, and you have deployed this device on your organization's perimeter network. You want to allow your organization's existing RADIUS server, deployed as a Windows

Server 2012 R2 server with the NPS enrolled to accept and respond to authentication and authorization traffic from this device. Which of the following should you configure on the server with the NPS role installed to accomplish this goal?

A. RADIUS client

B. RADIUS accounting

C. RADIUS server

D. RADIUS proxy

4. You want to ensure that data about authentication and authorization traffic forwarded to your server with the NPS role installed on the internal network is written to an SQL Server database rather than to a local file. Which of the following should you configure to accomplish this goal?

A. RADIUS proxy

B. RADIUS client

C. RADIUS accounting

D. RADIUS server

5. Which of the following information must you provide when configuring a RADIUS client on a RADIUS server? (Choose three. Each answer forms part of a complete solution.)

A. Friendly name

B. Authentication protocol

C. IP address or FQDN

D. Shared secret

Lesson 2: Configuring VPN and routing

You can configure Windows Server 2012 and Windows Server 2012 R2 to function as a VPN server, a local area network (LAN) router, and an NAT device. An advantage of deploying Windows Server 2012 and Windows Server 2012 R2 as a VPN server over a dedicated hardware device is that you can then use VPN protocols such as IKEv2 and advanced authentication methods, which aren't always possible with dedicated hardware devices. In this lesson, you will learn how to deploy the Routing and Remote Access role, deploy Windows Server 2012 and Windows Server 2012 R2 as a VPN server, and configure LAN routing and NAT.

Deploy Routing and Remote Access

The *Remote Access* role service enables you to provide network access and routing functionality using a computer running Windows Server 2012 and Windows Server 2012 R2 that you might otherwise provision using a dedicated hardware device. The Remote Access role enables you to provide the following services to computers:

- Access to trusted networks (such as an organization's internal network) for clients on untrusted networks (such as the Internet) through VPNs or DirectAccess.
- Network routing using the Routing Information Protocol (RIP) and static routes, enabling you to connect separate IPv4 and IPv6 networks. It also enables you to configure encrypted site-to-site tunnels that can be used as wide area network (WAN) links between branch offices across the Internet.

To deploy Routing and Remote Access on a computer running Windows Server 2012 and Windows Server 2012 R2, perform the following steps:

1. In Server Manager, click Manage, and click Add Roles And Features.
2. On the Before You Begin page of the Add Roles And Features Wizard, click Next.
3. On the Select Installation Type page, click Role-Based Or Feature-Based Installation, and click Next.
4. On the Server Selection page, select the server on which you want to deploy the Routing and Remote Access role. Any servers that are part of the management server's All Servers server pool are present in this dialog box, and Windows Server 2012 and Windows Server 2012 R2 enable you to use this wizard to install roles both locally and remotely. Click Next.
5. On the Select Server Roles page, select Remote Access, as shown in Figure 8-14.

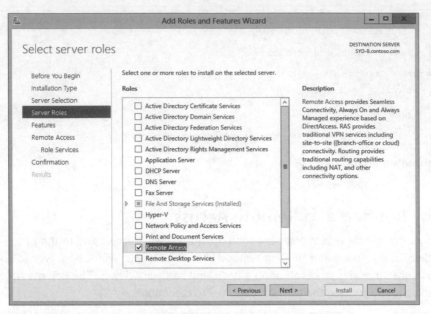

FIGURE 8-14 Adding the Remote Access role

6. On the Add Roles And Features Wizard dialog box that pops up, click Add Features, and then click Next.

7. On the Select Features page, click Next.

8. On the Remote Access page, click Next.

9. On the Select Role Services page, shown in Figure 8-15, you can choose one or both of the following role services:

   - **DirectAccess And VPN (RAS)** Choose this option if you want to configure Windows Server 2012 or Windows Server 2012 R2 as a DirectAccess or VPN server, or to allow the server to perform both those functions.

   - **Routing** Choose this option if you want to configure Windows Server 2012 or Windows Server 2012 R2 as a router between subnets or to provide NAT services.

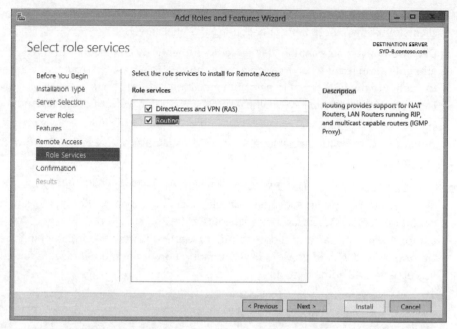

FIGURE 8-15 Adding VPN, DirectAccess, and Routing role services

10. Click Next. On the Confirmation page, click Install, and then click Close.

> **NOTE DIRECTACCESS**
>
> Configuring and deploying DirectAccess is covered in Lesson 3, "Configuring DirectAccess."

Configure VPN settings

After you install the Remote Access role on a computer running Windows Server 2012 or Windows Server 2012 R2, you can configure the server as a *VPN server*. Before you deploy Windows Server 2012 or Windows Server 2012 R2 as a VPN server, ensure that you have met the following requirements:

- The computer that will function as the VPN server needs to have two network adapters. Prior to configuring the VPN server, you need to determine which interface will accept incoming traffic from untrusted networks. You specify this network interface during VPN setup.

- Determine how clients from untrusted networks will receive IP addresses on the trusted network. You can configure the VPN server to interact with an existing Dynamic Host Configuration Protocol (DHCP) server on the trusted network. When you do this, the VPN server leases blocks of 10 IP addresses and assigns them to remote clients. You also have the option of manually configuring an address pool from which the VPN server can lease IP addresses. When you do this, you must ensure that the manually selected IP addresses are not already in use and are not used in future by clients other than those that connect using the VPN server.

■ Decide whether you want the VPN server to authenticate connections or pass authentication requests on to a server with the NPS role installed. You might choose to configure the VPN server to pass authentication requests on to a server with the NPS role installed if you have multiple servers or if you have configured a stand-alone server as a VPN server as a way of enhancing security.

To configure a server with the Remote Access role installed as a VPN server, perform the following steps:

1. On the Tools menu in Server Manager, click Remote Access Management.

2. In the Remote Access Management console, select the server on which you want to configure Remote Access, as shown in Figure 8-16, and click Run The Remote Access Setup Wizard. You can also choose to run the Getting Started Wizard. Running the Getting Started Wizard provides fewer configuration options, but it may be suitable for less experienced administrators.

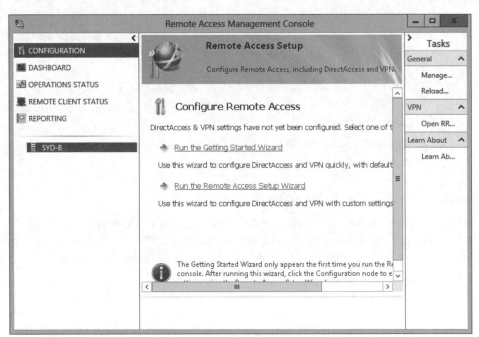

FIGURE 8-16 Remote Access Management console

3. In the Configure Remote Access dialog box, shown in Figure 8-17, click Deploy VPN Only. You'll learn about configuring DirectAccess in Lesson 3, "Configuring DirectAccess."

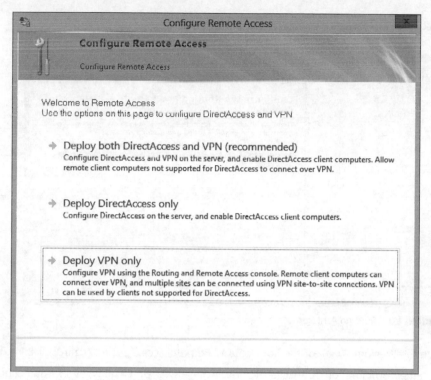

FIGURE 8-17 Selecting Deploy VPN Only

4. When you choose this option, the Routing And Remote Access console opens.
5. Click the server that will function as the remote access server, as shown in Figure 8-18, and click Configure And Enable Routing And Remote Access on the Action menu.

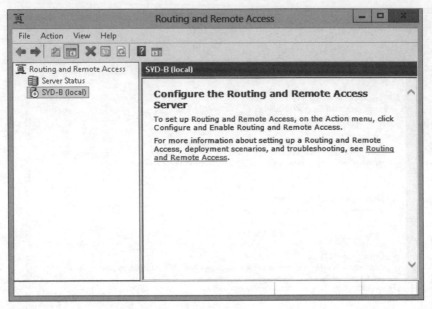

FIGURE 8-18 Routing And Remote Access console

6. On the Welcome page of the Routing And Remote Access Setup Wizard, click Next.

7. On the Configuration page, click Remote Access (Dial-Up Or VPN) as shown in Figure 8-19, and click Next.

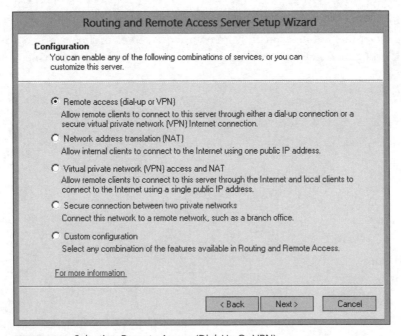

FIGURE 8-19 Selecting Remote Access (Dial-Up Or VPN)

8. On the Remote Access page, you have the option of selecting both dial-up and VPN connections. Select VPN and click Next.

9. On the VPN Connection page, select the adapter that is connected to the Internet, as shown in Figure 8-20, and click Next. Note that the simulated Internet connection in the figure is a private IP address, whereas in a production deployment it would be a public IP address.

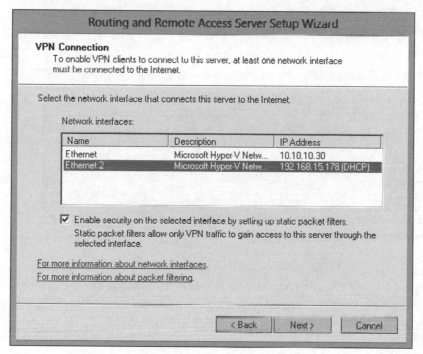

FIGURE 8-20 Selecting network interface

10. On the IP Address Assignment page, choose whether you want to assign IP addresses automatically, such as having the VPN server lease them from a DHCP server, or configure them manually. Click Next.

11. If you choose to configure IP addresses manually, you can add an IP address range on the Address Range Assignment page of the wizard, shown in Figure 8-21, and then click Next.

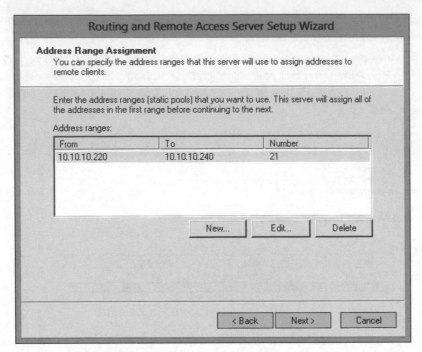

Routing and Remote Access Server Setup Wizard

Address Range Assignment
You can specify the address ranges that this server will use to assign addresses to remote clients.

Enter the address ranges (static pools) that you want to use. This server will assign all of the addresses in the first range before continuing to the next.

Address ranges:

From	To	Number
10.10.10.220	10.10.10.240	21

New...   Edit...   Delete

< Back   Next >   Cancel

FIGURE 8-21 Selecting a network interface

12. On the Managing Multiple Remote Access Servers page, shown in Figure 8-22, choose whether you want Routing And Remote Access to authenticate connections or whether you want to forward authentication requests to a RADIUS server. This example uses Routing And Remote Access.

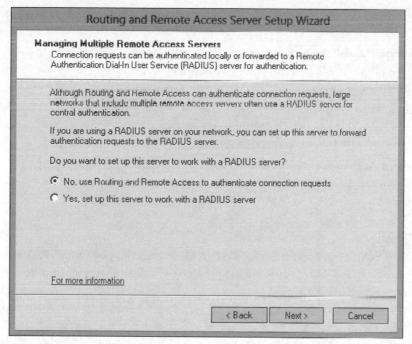

FIGURE 8-22 Configuring authentication

13. If you configure Routing And Remote Access, the next page finishes the wizard. When you complete the wizard, VPN connections will be enabled from the server.

VPN authentication

When planning to allow clients to remotely connect to trusted networks, consider the authentication protocols that can be used to establish those connections. Although Windows Server 2012 and Windows Server 2012 R2 support many protocols that have been in use for some time, these protocols are often less secure than more recently developed protocols. Windows Server 2012 and Windows Server 2012 R2 support the following protocols, listed from most secure to least secure:

- **Extensible Authentication Protocol-Transport Level Security (EAP-TLS)** You use this protocol with smart cards or digital certificates. You can use this protocol only if you are using RADIUS authentication or if the remote access server performing authentication is domain-joined.

- **Microsoft Challenge Handshake Authentication Protocol version 2 (MS-CHAPv2)** Provides mutual authentication. This means that not only is the user authenticated but the service that the user is connecting to is also authenticated. Allows for the encryption of the authentication process and the session.

- **Extensible Authentication Protocol-Message Digest 5 Challenge Handshake Authentication (EAP-MD5 CHAP)** Supports encryption of authentication data through MD5 hashing and also uses the EAP framework. Used to support third-party clients.

- **Challenge Handshake Authentication Protocol (CHAP)**   Authentication data is encrypted through MD5 hashing. The data is not encrypted.
- **Shiva Password Authentication Protocol (SPAP)**   This 1990s protocol is supported by Windows Server 2012 and Windows Server 2012 R2. It provides basic encrypted authentication that can be deciphered using automated techniques if the appropriate traffic is captured. Not recommended for use.
- **Password Authentication Protocol (PAP)**   This protocol does not encrypt authentication data, meaning that if the authentication is captured, user name and password data can be read directly without having to be decrypted.

VPN protocols

A Windows Server 2012 or Windows Server 2012 R2 VPN server supports four VPN tunneling protocols. In most organizations, you leave the protocols enabled. Clients attempt to negotiate a connection using the most secure protocol available to them. The protocols that are available depend on the operating system, with protocols available to computers running Windows 7, Windows 8, and Windows 8.1, and not available to computers running Windows XP. VPN servers on computers running Windows Server 2012 and Windows Server 2012 R2 support the following protocols:

- IKEv2
- SSTP
- L2TP/IPSec
- PPTP

IKEv2

IKEv2 is the most recent VPN protocol supported by Microsoft. The drawback of IKEv2 is that you can use it only with VPN clients running the Windows 7, Windows 8, and Windows 8.1 operating systems. IKEv2 has the following features:

- Supports IPv6
- Enables VPN reconnect
- Supports EAP and Computer certificates for client authentication
- Does not support PAP or CHAP
- Only supports MS-CHAPv2 with EAP
- Supports data origin authentication, data integrity, replay protection, and data confidentiality
- Uses UDP port 500

VPN reconnect enables the automatic reconnection of VPN connections without requiring users to perform manual authentication. VPN reconnect works across different connections, so a VPN connection can remain active when a user switches between hotspots or a wired and wireless connection. VPN reconnect allows for automatic reconnection without authentication for periods of disruption for up to 8 hours.

SSTP

SSTP became available with the release of Windows Vista and Windows Server 2008. It is supported on clients running Windows Vista, Windows 7, Windows 8, and Windows 8.1, but not supported on clients running the Windows XP operating system. SSTP functions by encapsulating PPTP traffic over the Secure Sockets Layer (SSL) channel of the Secure Hypertext Transfer Protocol (HTTPS). The advantage of SSTP is that it uses TCP port 443, which means that it is likely to work in locations in which other protocols, such as IKEv2, L2TP/IPsec, and PPTP, do not work because of intervening firewalls.

SSTP has the following requirements:

- Supported only on clients running Windows Vista, Windows 7, Windows 8, and Windows 8.1.
- Requires that the client trusts the Certification Authority (CA) that issued the VPN server's SSL certificate.
- The SSL certificate must be configured with a name that matches the FQDN of the IP address of the external interface of the VPN server.
- Can't be used to create VPN connections if there is a web proxy that requires authentication.

L2TP/IPsec

L2TP/IPsec is supported by clients running the Windows XP, Windows Vista, Windows 7, Windows 8, and Windows 8.1 operating systems. It is the most secure VPN protocol that you can deploy with a Windows Server 2012 or Windows Server 2012 R2 VPN server if you need to support clients running the Windows XP operating system. Although L2TP/IPsec usually requires the deployment of digital certificates, it is possible, with special configuration, to get L2TP/IPsec to work with preshared keys. When used with digital certificates, L2TP/IPsec VPN clients must trust the CA that issued the certificate to the VPN server, and the VPN server must trust the CA that issued the certificates to the clients. The simplest way to implement L2TP/IPsec is by also deploying an Enterprise CA on the trusted network. L2TP/IPsec supports all authentication protocols that are supported with Windows Server 2012 and Windows Server 2012 R2, which means you can use the protocol with advanced authentication methods such as smart cards.

PPTP

PPTP is the oldest VPN protocol supported by Windows Server 2012 and Windows Server 2012 R2. It is also the least secure. It is most often used when organizations that need to support clients running Windows XP haven't deployed the certificate infrastructure required to implement L2TP/IPsec. PPTP connections provide data confidentiality, but do not provide data integrity or data origin protection. That means that captured data can't be read, but you can't be sure that the transmitted data was the same data sent by the client.

 Quick check

- Which protocols can you use if you need to support VPN clients running the Windows XP operating system?

Quick check answer

- You can use the PPTP or L2TP/IPSec protocols if you need to support VPN clients running the Windows XP operating system. SSTP is supported only on clients running the Windows Vista, Windows 7, Windows 8, and Windows 8.1 client operating systems. IKEv2 is supported only on clients running the Windows 7, Windows 8, and Windows 8.1 client operating systems.

Configure routing

 You can configure Windows Server 2012 and Windows Server 2012 R2 to function as a network router in the same way that you configure a traditional hardware device to perform this role. To perform this function, the computer must have two or more network adapters. Windows Server 2012 and Windows Server 2012 R2 support using *Routing Information Protocol v2* (RIP) for route discovery. You can also use the Routing And Remote Access console to configure static routes.

To configure Windows Server 2012 or Windows Server 2012 R2 to function as a router, perform the following steps:

1. From the Tools menu of Server Manager, click Routing And Remote Access.

2. In the Routing And Remote Access console, click the server that you want to configure. On the Action menu, click Configure And Enable Routing And Remote Access.

3. On the Welcome page of the Routing And Remote Access Server Setup Wizard, click Next.

4. On the Configuration page, select Custom Configuration, and click Next.

5. On the Custom Configuration page, select LAN Routing, as shown in Figure 8-23, and click Next.

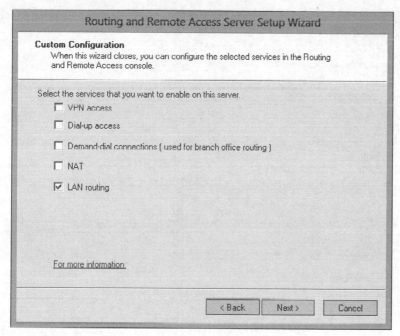

FIGURE 8-23 LAN routing

6. Click Finish. In the Routing And Remote Access dialog box, click Start Service.

7. In the Routing And Remote Access console, right-click the server, and click Properties.

8. On the General tab of the server properties dialog box, select IPv6 Router, as shown in Figure 8-24, to enable the server to also route IPv6 traffic.

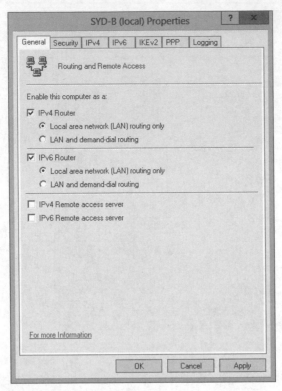

FIGURE 8-24 Enabling IPv6 routing

Network address translation (NAT)

Network address translation (NAT) enables you to share an Internet connection with computers on an internal network. In a typical NAT configuration, the NAT server has two network interfaces. One network interface is connected to the Internet. The second network interface connects to a network with a private IP address range. Computers on the private IP address range can then establish communication with computers on the Internet. It is also possible to configure port forwarding so that all traffic sent to a particular port on the NAT server's public interface is directed to a specific IP address/port combination on a host on the private IP address range.

To configure a computer running the Windows Server 2012 or Windows Server 2012 R2 operating system with two network adapters to function as a NAT device, one of which is connected to the Internet, perform the following steps:

1. Open the Routing And Remote Access console from the Tools menu in Server Manager.

2. Select the server that you want to configure. On the Action menu, click Configure and Enable Routing And Remote Access.

3. On the Welcome To The Routing And Remote Access Server Setup Wizard, click Next.

4. On the Configuration page, select Network Address Translation (NAT), as shown in Figure 8-25, and click Next.

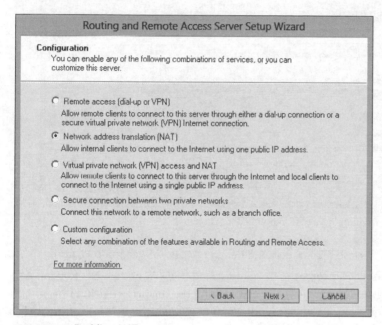

FIGURE 8-25 Enabling NAT

5. On the NAT Internet Connection page, select the network interface that connects to the Internet, as shown in Figure 8-26, and click Next. In this figure, the interface connected to the Internet uses a private IP address.

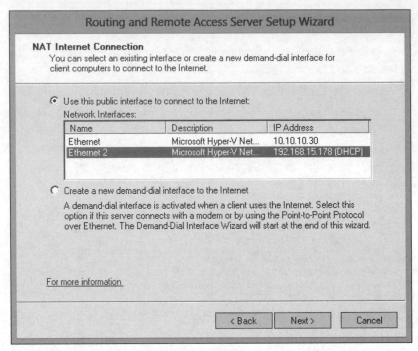

FIGURE 8-26 Configuring a NAT Internet connection

6. Click Finish to close the Routing And Remote Access Server Setup Wizard.

You can configure NAT properties by right-clicking the NAT node in the Routing And Remote Access console and clicking Properties. Using this properties dialog box, you can configure the assignment of addresses for hosts on the private network, as shown in Figure 8-27. You can use the Name Resolution tab to determine how name resolution works on the private network. It enables clients to communicate using single names or FQDNs rather than IP addresses.

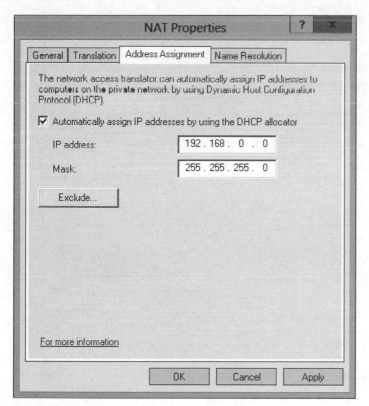

FIGURE 8-27 NAT address allocation

Web Application Proxy in pass-through mode

Web Application Proxy is a remote access role that allows you to configure a reverse proxy to publish applications and services hosted on protected networks to hosts on untrusted networks, such as the Internet. When you publish an application through Web Application Proxy, you can choose to use AD FS to perform pre-authentication, and configure pass-through mode. When you configure pass-through mode, as shown in Figure 8-28, the Web Application Proxy passes all authentication traffic through to the server hosting the published application.

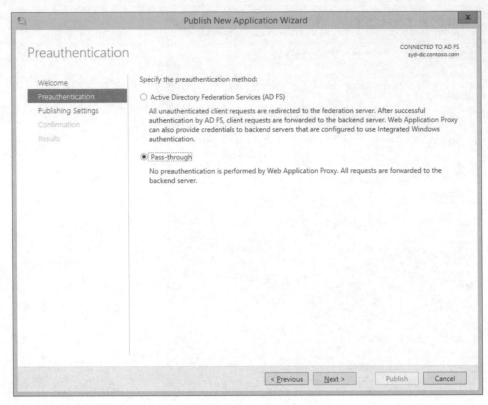

FIGURE 8-28 Publishing an application in pass-through mode

To deploy Web Application Proxy, you need to already have deployed AD FS on a server in the domain. When you deploy the Web Application Proxy, you specify the address of the AD FS server. You also need to import a copy of the web server certificate used with AD FS, including the private key, onto the server that will host the Web Application Proxy. As the server that hosts the Web Application Proxy will be responsible for proxying traffic from hosts on untrusted networks to applications hosted on protected networks, it should be configured as a stand alone server rather than be domain joined.

> **MORE INFO** **WEB APPLICATION PROXY WITH PASS-THROUGH PREAUTHENTICATION**
>
> For more information about configuring Web Application Proxy with Pass-through preauthentication, consult the following TechNet article at *http://technet.microsoft.com/ en-us/library/dn383655.aspx.*

Lesson summary

- The Routing And Remote Access role enables you to configure a computer running Windows Server 2012 or Windows Server 2012 R2 to provide dial-up, VPN, NAT, and LAN routing services.
- NAT enables a single Internet connection to be shared by multiple computers.
- LAN routing enables the routing of network traffic between subnets. LAN routing supports routing of both IPv4 and IPv6 traffic.
- The SSTP VPN protocol uses HTTPS to carry VPN traffic. It can be used in firewalled environments that block other VPN protocols.
- IKEv2 supports VPN reconnect. VPN reconnect enables disrupted VPN connections to be reestablished up to 8 hours later without requiring user reauthentication.
- Web Application Proxy in pass-through mode allows you to publish web applications that perform their own authentication to clients on untrusted networks using a reverse proxy.

Lesson review

Answer the following questions to test your knowledge of the information in this lesson. You can find the answers to these questions and explanations of why each answer choice is correct or incorrect in the "Answers" section at the end of this chapter.

1. You have a number of VPN clients that are running the Windows XP operating system. You have deployed a computer running Windows Server 2012 R2 as a VPN server. Which of the following VPN protocols can be used with Windows XP clients? (Choose all that apply.)

    A. SSTP

    B. IKEv2

    C. L2TP/IPSec

    D. PPTP

2. Which of the following VPN protocols can be used only with clients running the Windows 7, Windows 8, or Windows 8.1 client operating system?

    A. PPTP

    B. L2TP/IPSec

    C. IKEv2

    D. SSTP

3. Several users in your organization regularly stay at hotels that have firewalls that allow only outbound traffic on TCP port 80 and 443. Which of the following VPN protocols should you enable to allow these users to connect to your organization's Windows Server 2012 R2 VPN server?

  A. IKEv2

  B. L2TP/IPSec

  C. SSTP

  D. PPTP

4. Which of the following VPN protocols support automatic reconnection of VPN connections for up to 8 hours without requiring manual user reauthentication?

  A. SSTP

  B. IKEv2

  C. PPTP

  D. L2TP/IPSec

5. You are in the process of running the Routing And Remote Access Setup Wizard. Which of the following options should you select if you want to allow a group of computers on your organization's network that don't need to be able to accept direct inbound communication from hosts on the Internet to share an Internet connection?

  A. VPN access

  B. Dial-up access

  C. NAT

  D. LAN router

Lesson 3: Configuring DirectAccess

DirectAccess provides an always-on, computer-authenticated VPN solution that enables client computers to maintain connections to an organization's internal network without requiring that a user perform manual authentication. In this lesson, you learn how to deploy and configure DirectAccess as well as learn DirectAccess' infrastructure requirements.

After this lesson, you will be able to:

- Understand DirectAccess.
- Understand DirectAccess infrastructure.
- Configure DNS to support DirectAccess.
- Configure certificates for DirectAccess.
- Configure DirectAccess clients.

Estimated lesson time: 45 minutes

Understanding DirectAccess

DirectAccess is an always-on, computer-authenticated IPv6 VPN connection that becomes active any time a client computer can establish an Internet connection when on an untrusted network. Any IPv6 capable application on the DirectAccess client has full access to resources on the trusted network. DirectAccess has the following benefits:

- Automatic connection to a trusted network when a client connects to the Internet. Does not require user authentication as is the case with a traditional VPN connection.

- Uses a variety of protocols including HTTPs to enable IPv6 connectivity. This enables DirectAccess to establish connections in almost all circumstances in which an Internet connection is present.

- Supports remote management of clients, including manage-out support. Manage-out support is a Windows Server 2012 and Windows Server 2012 R2 feature that enables remote management functionality of DirectAccess clients, enabling incoming access to the client for the purposes of maintenance and administration.

- DirectAccess integrates with server and domain isolation as well as NAP. This enables organizations to maintain the health state of clients as long as the client has an active Internet connection.

DirectAccess in Windows Server 2012 and Windows Server 2012 R2 have the following changes from the implementation available in Windows Server 2008 R2:

- DirectAccess no longer requires that two consecutive public IPv4 addresses be assigned to the network adapter connected to the Internet.

- It isn't necessary to deploy Active Directory Certificate Services (AD CS) on the trusted network.

REAL WORLD   **SIMPLIFYING REMOTE ACCESS**

The real reason to go to the trouble of configuring DirectAccess is that it vastly simplifies providing remote access. Users simply have a connection to the trusted internal network without having to mess with configuring their VPN connection. In some organizations, establishing a VPN connection involves complex authentication routines such as using a special identification device in which users have to type the number currently displayed on the device within a short period of time before they can connect.

DirectAccess infrastructure

The biggest change between DirectAccess in Windows Server 2008 R2 and DirectAccess in Windows Server 2012 and Windows Server 2012 R2 is how much simpler the process of configuring DirectAccess is. DirectAccess is also included with the Essentials version of Windows Server 2012. The Essentials versions of Windows Server 2012 and Windows Server 2012 R2 are aimed at small businesses and simplifies many complex systems administration tasks in the way that the Small Business Server line of products once did. The main thing to remember about deploying DirectAccess is that unlike other remote access technologies, the computer making the DirectAccess connection must be a member of the same Active Directory forest as the DirectAccess server. DirectAccess uses computer authentication, whereas most other remote access solutions authenticate based on the user's credentials.

> *MORE INFO* **DIRECTACCESS INFRASTRUCTURE**
>
> For more information about DirectAccess infrastructure, consult the following TechNet article at *http://technet.microsoft.com/en-us/library/jj574174.aspx*.

DirectAccess topology

DirectAccess supports multiple deployment topologies. You don't have to deploy the DirectAccess server with a network adapter directly connected to the Internet. You can integrate the DirectAccess server with your organization's existing edge topology. During deployment of the DirectAccess server, the Remote Access Server Wizard asks you which of the topologies reflects your server configuration, as shown in Figure 8-29.

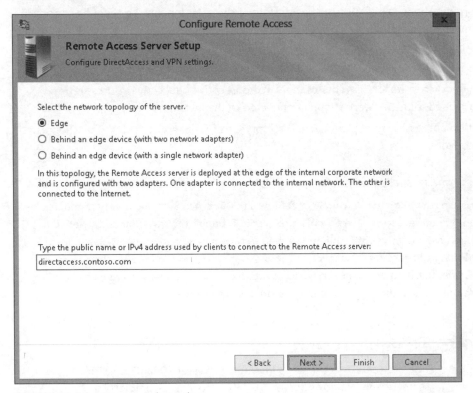

FIGURE 8-29 Selecting network topology

The difference between them is as follows:

- **Edge**   This is the traditional DirectAccess deployment. The computer hosting the server has two network adapters. The first network adapter is connected directly to the Internet and has been assigned one or more public IPv4 addresses. The second network adapter connects directly to the internal trusted network.

- **Behind An Edge Device (With Two Network Adapters)**   In this deployment, the DirectAccess server is located behind a dedicated edge firewall. This can be a computer running Forefront Threat Management Gateway 2010, Unified Access Gateway 2010, or a third-party hardware firewall device. In this configuration, one of the network adapters on the DirectAccess server is connected to the perimeter network behind the edge firewall. The second network adapter connects directly to the internal trusted network. Figure 8-30 shows the process of configuring this topology.

- **Behind An Edge Device (With A Single Network Adapter)**   The DirectAccess server has a single network adapter connected to the internal network. The edge firewall passes traffic to the DirectAccess server.

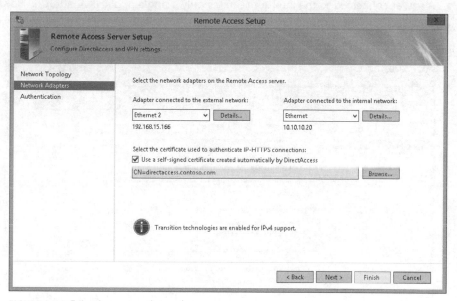

FIGURE 8-30 Selecting network topology

DirectAccess server

The DirectAccess server is a domain-joined computer running Windows Server 2012 or Windows Server 2012 R2 that accepts connections from DirectAccess clients on untrusted networks, such as the Internet, and provides access to resources on trusted networks. The DirectAccess server performs the following roles:

- Authenticates DirectAccess clients connecting from untrusted networks
- Functions as an IPsec tunnel mode endpoint for DirectAccess traffic from untrusted networks

Before you can configure a computer running Windows Server 2012 or Windows Server 2012 R2 to function as a DirectAccess server, you must ensure that it meets the following requirements:

- The server must be a member of an Active Directory Directory Services domain.
- If the server is connected directly to the Internet, it must have two network adapters: one that has a public IP address and one that is connected to the trusted internal network.
- The server does not need to be directly connected to the Internet if it is published through Microsoft Forefront Threat Management Gateway (TMS) 2010 or Microsoft Forefront Unified Access Gateway (UAG) 2010. In this scenario, the DirectAccess server can have only one network adapter that is connected to the trusted network.
- The DirectAccess server can be deployed behind a NAT device, which limits DirectAccess to use IP over HTTPS (IP-HTTPS).
- A server connected to the Internet requires only a single public IPv4 address. However, Two-Factor Authentication (Smart Card Or One-Time Password [OTP]), shown in Figure 8-31, requires two consecutive public IPv4 addresses.

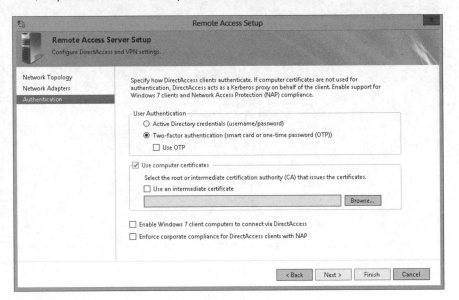

FIGURE 8-31 Configuring two-factor authentication

- The DirectAccess server can also host a VPN server. This functionality was not present in the Windows Server 2008 R2 version of DirectAccess.
- You can configure DirectAccess in a network load-balanced configuration of up to eight nodes.
- The SSL certificate installed on the DirectAccess server must contain an FQDN that resolves through DNS servers on the Internet to the public IP address assigned to

the DirectAccess server or to the gateway through which the DirectAccess server is published.

- The SSL certificate installed on the DirectAccess server must have a Certificate Revocation List (CRL) distribution point that is accessible to clients on the Internet.

REAL WORLD **CERTIFICATE REQUIREMENTS**

You should strongly consider obtaining the SSL certificate for your organization's DirectAccess server from a public CA. If you do this, you don't have to worry about publishing the CRL from your internal certificate services deployment out to a location that is accessible to the Internet. Using a trusted third-party CA ensures that the CRL will be available to clients on the Internet. Although purchasing a certificate costs money, the financial cost is likely to be less than the cost to the organization of having you install and configure a CRL distribution point on a location accessible to clients on the Internet.

A DirectAccess implementation also relies on the following infrastructure being present:

- **Active Directory domain controller**   DirectAccess clients and servers must be members of an Active Directory domain. By necessity, when you deploy a domain controller, you also deploy a DNS server. By its nature, Active Directory also makes Group Policy available.
- **Group Policy**   When you configure DirectAccess, the setup wizard creates a set of Group Policy Objects (GPOs) that are configured with settings that you choose in the wizard. They apply to DirectAccess clients, DirectAccess servers, and servers that you use to manage DirectAccess.

Prepare DNS servers by removing the ISATAP name from the global query block list. You must take this step on all DNS servers hosted on computers running the Windows Server 2008, Windows Server 2008 R2, Windows Server 2012, and Windows Server 2012 R2 operating systems. You can do this by removing ISATAP from the GlobalQueryBlockList value on the Computer\HKEY_LOCAL_MACHINE\SYSTEM\CurrentControlSet\Services\DNS\ Parameters hive of the registry so that it contains only the wpad entry, as shown in Figure 8-32. You'll have to restart the DNS server after making this configuration change.

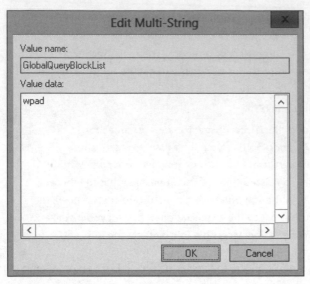

FIGURE 8-32 The wpad entry

You can also remove ISATAP from the DNS global query block list by issuing the following command on each DNS server.

```
Dnscmd /config /globalqueryblocklist wpad
```

> **MORE INFO** **DIRECTACCESS INFRASTRUCTURE**
>
> For more information about configuring a DirectAccess server, consult the following TechNet article at *http://technet.microsoft.com/en-us/library/jj574180.aspx*.

Network Location Server

The *Network Location Server* (NLS) is a specially configured server that enables clients to determine whether they are on a trusted or an untrusted network. The NLS server's only function is to respond to specially crafted HTTPS requests. When the client determines that it has a connection to any network, it sends this specially crafted HTTPS request. If there is a response to this request, the client determines that it is on a trusted network and disables the DirectAccess components. If there is no response to this request, the client assumes that it is connected to an untrusted network and initiates a DirectAccess connection.

DirectAccess clients are informed of the location of the NLS through Group Policy. You don't have to configure these policies manually because they are created automatically when you use the DirectAccess Setup Wizard. Any server that hosts a website and has an SSL certificate installed can function as the NLS. You should ensure that the NLS is highly available because a failure of this server will cause all clients configured for DirectAccess on the trusted network to assume that they are on an untrusted network.

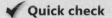

Quick check

- What is the name of the server that the DirectAccess client contacts to determine whether it is on the trusted network?

Quick check answer

- The DirectAccess client contacts the NLS to determine whether it is on the trusted network.

DirectAccess clients

DirectAccess clients have the following requirements:

- The computer either must already be a member of an Active Directory domain or be configured for offline domain join. The computer must be a member of the domain prior to actually using DirectAccess to connect to internal network resources.
- The computer must be running one of the following operating systems:
  - Windows 8.1 Enterprise edition (x86 and x64)
  - Windows 8 Enterprise edition (x86 and x64)
  - Windows 7 Enterprise and Ultimate editions

DirectAccess clients are configured through GPOs. The configuration GPO is automatically created through the DirectAccess setup process. This GPO is filtered so that it applies only to the security group that you've designated as hosting the DirectAccess clients. These GPOs are shown in Figure 8-33.

Although you can use all editions of Windows Server 2008 R2, Windows Server 2012, and Windows Server 2012 R2 as DirectAccess clients, this configuration is not recommended because these operating systems are rarely used as desktop operating systems (except for a few IT professionals). A server at a branch office site should use a statically configured WAN link instead of a DirectAccess connection to connect back to resources in the head office.

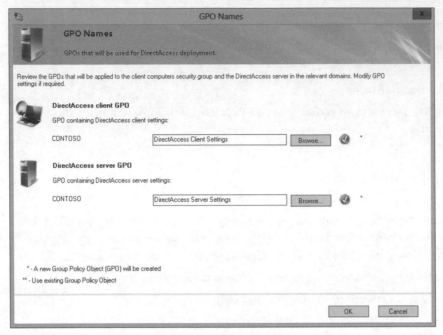

FIGURE 8-33 DirectAccess GPOs

Configure DirectAccess

After you understand the infrastructure requirements, configuring DirectAccess is straight-forward. To configure DirectAccess, perform the following steps:

1. Create a security group in Active Directory. Add the computer accounts of all computers that will be DirectAccess clients. This security group can have any name, but a name such as DirectAccess_Clients makes it easy to remember why you created it. Figure 8-34 shows the selection of the custom created DirectAccess_Clients group when running the Remote Access Setup Wizard.

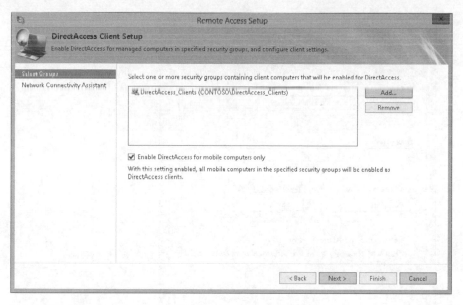

FIGURE 8-34 Creating a security group for DirectAccess clients

2. Ensure that you configure DNS with the following information:

   - The externally resolvable DNS zone needs to have a record mapping the FQDN of the external interface of the DirectAccess server to the public IPv4 address of the DirectAccess server.

   - If you use a certificate issued by your organization's CA, ensure that a DNS record exists for the CRL location.

   - The internal DNS zone needs a record mapping the name of the NLS to an IP address.

   - Remove ISATAP from the global query block list on all DNS servers in the organization.

3. If you use your organization's CA, you have to configure an appropriate certificate template as well as deploy a CRL distribution point in a location that can be accessed by clients on the Internet. This certificate template can be a duplicate of the Web Server Certificate Template, as shown in Figure 8-35. You can use this certificate for both the SSL certificate for the NLS and the IP-HTTPS certificate for the DirectAccess server. If you don't use your organization's CA to issue certificates, you can use certificates from a public CA for the NLS and the DirectAccess server.

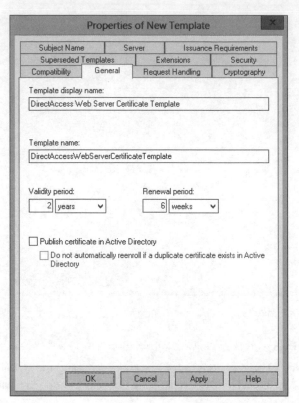

FIGURE 8-35 Certificate and Web Server Certificate templates

4. Configure firewall rules for all hosts on the trusted network that should be accessible to DirectAccess clients so they enable inbound and outbound ICMPv6 echo requests. You can configure these rules in a GPO that applies to hosts that should be accessible to DirectAccess clients. The rules should have the following properties:

- Rule Type: Custom
- Protocol Type: ICMPv6
- Specific ICMP Types: Echo Request (see Figure 8-36).

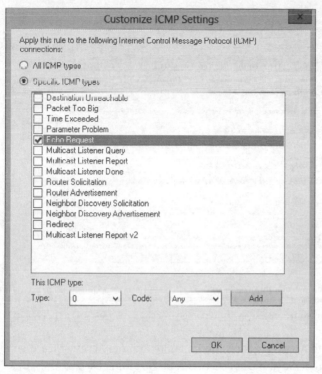

FIGURE 8-36 IPv6 ICMP echo request

5. Install the Remote Access role on the computer that will function as the DirectAccess server.

6. Open the Remote Access console. As Figure 8-37 shows, you can choose between running the Getting Started Wizard and the Remote Access Setup Wizard. The Getting Started Wizard enables administrators to quickly deploy DirectAccess by requiring a minimal amount of information. The Remote Access Setup Wizard requires a detailed response, but enables administrators to customize their deployment. The rest of this procedure deals with the Remote Access Setup Wizard.

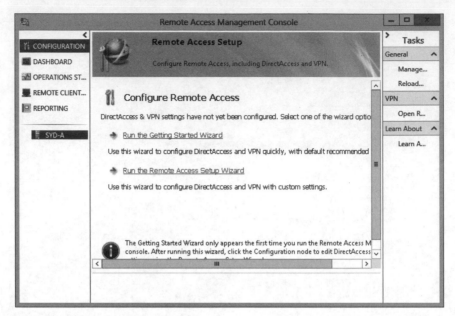

FIGURE 8-37 Choosing a wizard option

7. The Configure Remote Access page of the Configure Remote Access Wizard enables you to choose among deploying DirectAccess And VPN, DirectAccess Only, or VPN Only.

8. When you select Deploy DirectAccess Only, you are provided with the Remote Access Setup diagram shown in Figure 8-38. This diagram involves a series of steps that enable you to configure the DirectAccess server, clients, and infrastructure. There are four steps:

- Step 1: Remote Clients
- Step 2: Remote Access Server
- Step 3: Infrastructure Servers
- Step 4: Application Servers

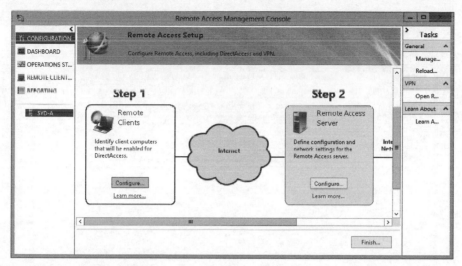

FIGURE 8-38 Remote Access Setup

Step 1: Remote Clients

The Step 1: Remote Clients section of Remote Access Setup enables you configure which computers will function as DirectAccess clients. When you click the Configure button in the Step 1 area, a three-page wizard appears that enables you to configure the following settings:

1. Choose Deploy Full DirectAccess For Client Access And Remote Management or Deploy DirectAccess For Remote Management Only, as shown in Figure 8-39. If you choose the first option, the people using DirectAccess clients can access internal network resources when they have an active Internet connection. If you choose the second option, you can perform management tasks on the computer when it's connected on the Internet, but the user can't access internal resources.

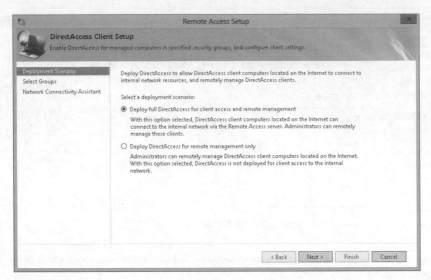

FIGURE 8-39 Select client access and remote management, or remote management only

2. Select which security groups that contain computer accounts will be enabled for DirectAccess, as shown in Figure 8-40. On this page, you can choose Enable DirectAccess For Mobile Computers Only and Use Force Tunneling. When you enable force tunneling, computers designated as DirectAccess clients connect through the remote access server when they connect to both the Internet and the internal trusted network.

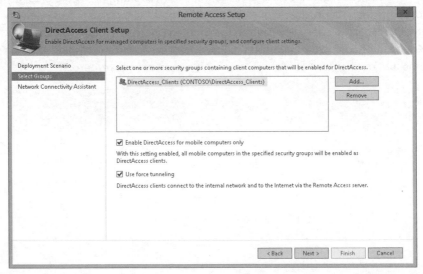

FIGURE 8-40 Selecting which security groups that contain computer accounts are enabled for DirectAccess

3. On the Network Connectivity Assistant (NCA) page shown in Figure 8-41, you can configure connectivity information for clients, such as providing the DirectAccess connection name, the email address of the helpdesk, and whether DirectAccess clients use local name resolution.

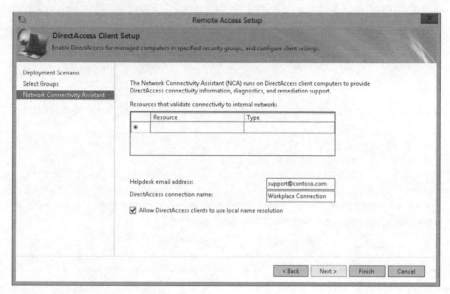

FIGURE 8-41 NCA configuration

Step 2: Remote Access Server

The Step 2: Remote Access Server section of the Remote Access Setup diagram has a three-page wizard that enables you to do the following:

1. Configure the network topology and specify the public name or IPv4 address that clients use to connect to DirectAccess. The topology options are Edge, Behind Edge (Two Network Adapters), and Behind Edge (Single Network Adapter). These topologies were described earlier in the chapter in the DirectAccess topology section.

2. On the Network Adapters page, verify the network adapter configuration. You can also choose the certificate used to authenticate IP-HTTPS connections. It should be a typical SSL certificate that uses an FQDN that clients use for connections. You can also choose to have a self-signed certificate used, although this is not recommended except on test deployments.

3. On the authentication page, choose whether you want to use Active Directory or Two-Factor Authentication. You can also configure authentication to use computer certificates. When you do this, you must specify the CA from which the computer certificates must be issued. As Figure 8-42 shows, you can also determine whether you will allow computers running the Windows 7 operating system to connect and whether you will enforce NAP policies on clients that have made DirectAccess connections.

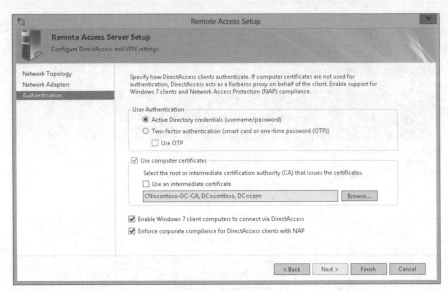

FIGURE 8-42 Configuring remote access authentication

Step 3: Infrastructure Servers

After you have configured the remote access clients and the remote access server, the next step is to configure infrastructure servers. The Infrastructure Server Setup Wizard takes you through the following steps:

1. On the first page, specify the location of the NLS by using the URL of the server. If specifying a separate server, remember to use https rather than http in the address. You also have the option of configuring the DirectAccess server as the remote access server and using a self-signed certificate, as shown in Figure 8-43. Self-signed certificates are more appropriate for tests rather than production deployments.

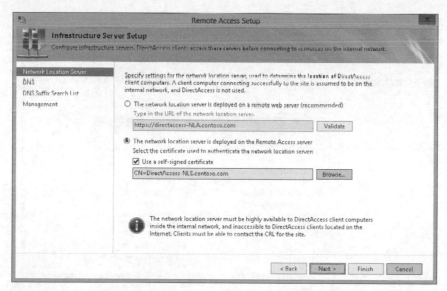

FIGURE 8-43 NLS address configuration

2. The DNS page enables you to specify the DNS suffixes that should be used with the name resolution and the address of the internal DNS server. On this page, shown in Figure 8-44, you can also configure how clients should use the DNS server of their local Internet connection. These are the options:

- Use the DNS server of the local connection if the name isn't resolvable using the DNS server on the trusted network.

- Use the DNS server of the local connection if the name isn't resolvable using the DNS server on the trusted network, or if the DNS server on the trusted network cannot be contacted.

- Use the DNS server of the local connection if any DNS error occurs.

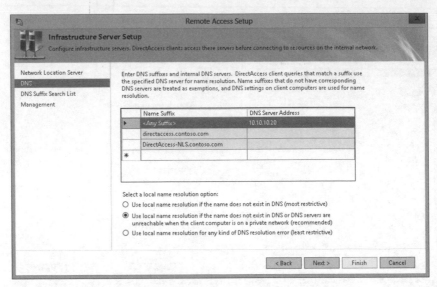

FIGURE 8-44 DirectAccess DNS configuration

3. The DNS Suffix Search List enables you to configure any DNS suffixes that should be used by the client for any unqualified names. The default settings add the domain name suffix.

4. The Management Servers page, shown in Figure 8-45, enables you to configure the servers used for DirectAccess client management. You can also configure NAP remediation servers if you are using NAP with DirectAccess.

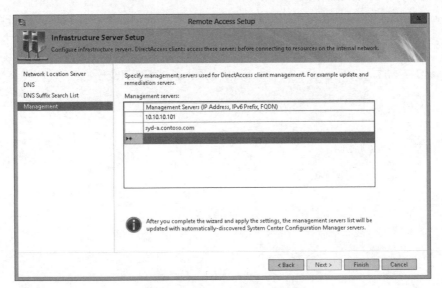

FIGURE 8-45 DirectAccess Management Server configuration

Step 4: Application Servers

Step 4 of the Remote Access Management Console setup enables you to configure the addresses of application servers that require end-to-end authentication when interacting with DirectAccess clients. Unlike the other steps, this step involves configuring only one dialog box, in which you specify the security group that contains the computer accounts for which you want to require end-to-end authentication and encryption. This dialog box is shown in Figure 8-46. You can also use this dialog box to limit DirectAccess clients so they can connect only to servers in the listed groups and can't connect to other servers on the trusted network. You use this option in environments with stringent security requirements.

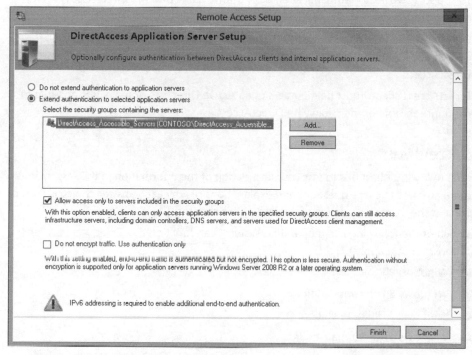

FIGURE 8-46 Configuring authentication between DirectAccess clients and servers

Lesson summary

- DirectAccess clients send traffic to the NLS server to determine whether they are located on the trusted network or on the Internet.
- You need to install an SSL/web server certificate from a trusted CA on the NLS server and the DirectAccess server.
- You must remove ISATAP from the DNS global query block list on all DNS servers in order to use DirectAccess.

- A DirectAccess Edge deployment requires two network adapters. One adapter is connected to the Internet. The other adapter is connected to an internal trusted network.
- A DirectAccess server can be deployed behind an edge device, such as a firewall, with one or two network adapters.
- The DirectAccess server must be a member of an Active Directory domain.
- If deployed behind a NAT device, DirectAccess can use only IP over HTTPS.
- DirectAccess can be deployed with a single public IPv4 address.
- To support two-factor authentication or one-time password, the DirectAccess server requires two consecutive public IPv4 addresses.
- Only computers running Windows 8.1 Enterprise Edition, Windows 8 Enterprise edition and Windows 7 Enterprise and Ultimate editions can be configured to use DirectAccess.
- DirectAccess clients must be members of an Active Directory domain. It is possible to configure remote domain join with DirectAccess.

Lesson review

Answer the following questions to test your knowledge of the information in this lesson. You can find the answers to these questions and explanations of why each answer choice is correct or incorrect in the "Answers" section at the end of this chapter.

1. Which of the following client operating systems can function as a DirectAccess client? (Choose all that apply.)

   A. Windows RT

   B. Windows 8 Enterprise edition

   C. Windows 7 Ultimate edition

   D. Windows Vista Ultimate edition

2. You want to use two-factor authentication with DirectAccess clients. Which of the following conditions must be met to implement this configuration?

   A. The DirectAccess server's Internet interface must be assigned a single public IPv4 address.

   B. The DirectAccess server's Internet interface must be assigned two consecutive public IPv4 addresses.

   C. The DirectAccess server must be configured to use RADIUS authentication.

   D. ISATAP must be added to the DNS global query block list on all DNS servers.

3. On which of the following servers must you deploy a web server/SSL certificate when deploying DirectAccess? (Choose all that apply.)

   A. Active Directory domain controller

   B. DNS server

C. DirectAccess server

   D. NSL server

4. Which server does a client attempt to contact to determine whether it is on an internal trusted network before initiating a DirectAccess connection?

   A. DirectAccess server

   B. DNS server

   C. NLS server

   D. DHCP server

5. In which of the following situations can a DirectAccess client use only IP over HTTPS?

   A. The DirectAccess server has a network interface connected directly to the Internet.

   B. The DirectAccess server has a network interface with a public IP address and is located on a perimeter network.

   C. The DirectAccess server is behind a NAT device.

   D. The DirectAccess server's public interface is assigned two nonconsecutive public IPv4 addresses.

Practice exercises

The goal of this section is to provide you with hands-on practice with the following:

- Configure a RADIUS server
- Configure a RADIUS server group
- Configure a RADIUS client
- Set up RADIUS accounting
- Deploy a VPN server

To perform the exercises in this section, you need access to an evaluation version of Windows Server 2012 R2. You should also have access to virtual machines SYD-DC, MEL-DC, CBR-DC, and ADL-DC, the setup instructions for which are described in the Introduction. You should ensure that you have a checkpoint of these virtual machines that you can revert to at the end of the practice exercises. You should revert the virtual machines to this initial state prior to beginning these exercises.

Exercise 1: Configure a RADIUS server

In this exercise, you configure SYD-DC as a RADIUS server. To complete this exercise, perform the following steps:

1. Start SYD-DC.

2. Start MEL-DC and sign on as Administrator.

3. Open the Windows PowerShell prompt and type the following commands.

```
Add-Computer -DomainName contoso.com
```

4. In the Windows PowerShell Credentials dialog box type **don_funk@contoso.com** and **Pa$$w0rd**, and click OK.

5. Type the following command in the Windows PowerShell prompt to restart the computer.

```
Restart-Computer
```

6. Sign on to SYD-DC as Contoso\don_funk.

7. In the Server Manager console, click Manage, and click Add Roles And Features.

8. On the Before You Begin page of the Add Roles And Features Wizard, click Next.

9. On the Select Installation Type page, click Role-Based Or Feature-Based Installation, and click Next.

10. On the Select Destination Server page, click SYD-DC.contoso.com, and click Next.

11. On the Server Roles page, click Network Policy And Access Services.

12. In the Add Roles And Features Wizard dialog box, click Add Features. Click Next.

13. On the Select Features page, click Next.

14. On the Network Policy And Access Services page, click Next.

15. On the Select Role Services page, verify that Network Policy Server is selected, as shown in Figure 8-47, and click Next.

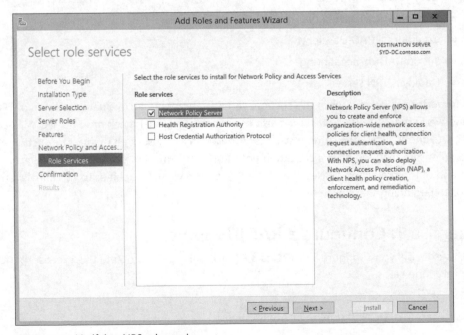

FIGURE 8-47 Verifying NPS role service

16. On the Confirmation page, click Install, and then click Close.

Exercise 2: Configure a remote RADIUS server group

In this exercise, you configure a RADIUS server group. To complete this exercise, perform the following steps:

1. In the Server Manager console on SYD-DC, click Tools, and then click Network Policy Server.

2. In the NPS console, expand RADIUS Clients And Servers and click Remote RADIUS Server Groups, as shown in Figure 8-48.

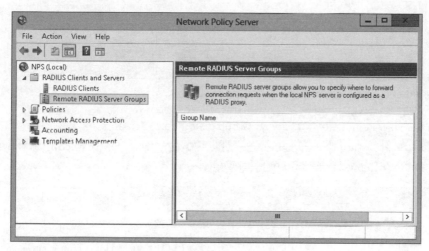

FIGURE 8-48 Remote RADIUS Server Groups node

3. On the Action menu, click New.

4. In the New Remote RADIUS Server Group dialog box, type the name **CONTOSO REMOTE GROUP**, as shown in Figure 8-49.

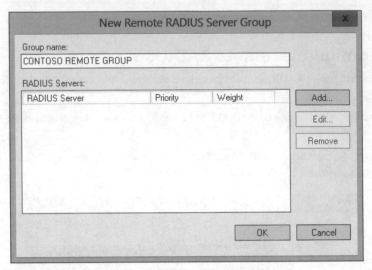

FIGURE 8-49 Contoso remote RADIUS server group

5. In the New Remote RADIUS Server Group dialog box, click Add.

6. In the Add RADIUS Server dialog box, type **SYD-RADIUS-1.contoso.com**, as shown in Figure 8-50, and click OK. Do not click Verify.

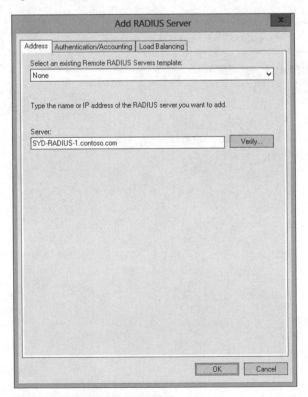

FIGURE 8-50 New remote RADIUS server

7. Click OK to close the New Remote RADIUS Server Group dialog box.

Exercise 3: Configure a RADIUS client

In this exercise, you configure a RADIUS client. To complete this exercise, perform the following steps:

1. On SYD-DC, in the NPS console, click RADIUS Clients under RADIUS Clients And Servers.

2. On the Action menu, click New.

3. In the New RADIUS client dialog box, configure the following information and click OK (see Figure 8-51).

   - Friendly Name: **MEL-DC**
   - Address: **MEL-DC.contoso.com**
   - Shared Secret: **Pa$$w0rd**
   - Confirm Shared Secret: **Pa$$w0rd**

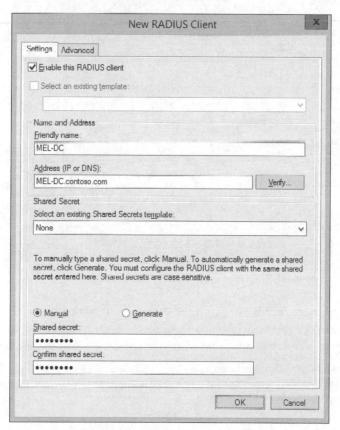

FIGURE 8-51 New RADIUS client

Exercise 4: Set up RADIUS accounting

In this exercise, you configure RADIUS accounting. To complete this exercise, perform the following steps:

1. In the NPS console on SYD-DC, click Accounting, and then click Configure Accounting.

2. On the Introduction page of the Accounting Configuration Wizard, click Next.

3. On the Select Accounting Options page, click Log To A Text File On The Local Computer, as shown in Figure 8-52, and click Next.

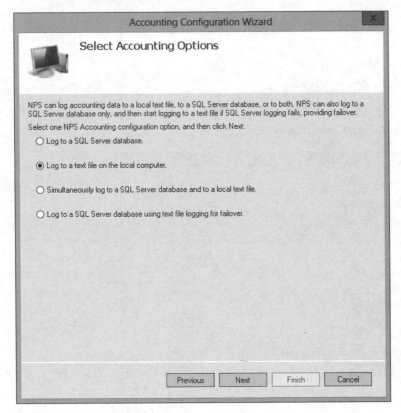

FIGURE 8-52 Accounting options

4. On the Configure Local File Logging page, ensure that Accounting Requests, Authentication Requests, Periodic Accounting Status, and Periodic Authentication Status are selected. Also ensure that logs are written to the C:\Windows\System32\ LogFiles folder.

5. Remove the option If Logging Fails, Discard Connection Requests, as shown in Figure 8-53, and click Next.

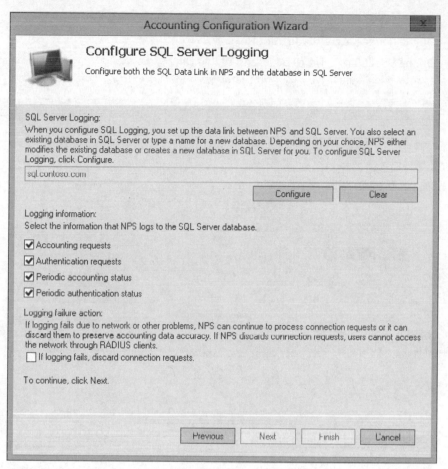

FIGURE 8-53 Local file logging options

6. On the Summary page, click Next, and then click Close.

Exercise 5: Install a VPN server

In this exercise, you configure MEL-DC as a VPN server. To complete this exercise, perform the following steps:

1. Sign on to MEL-DC as Contoso\don_funk.

2. On the Manage menu of the Server Manager console, click Add Roles And Features.

3. On the Before You Begin page, click Next.

4. On the Select Installation Type page, click Role-Based Or Feature-Based Installation, and click Next.

5. On the Select Destination Server page, click MEL-DC.contoso.com, and click Next.

6. On the Select Server Roles page, click Remote Access.

7. On the Select Features page, click Next.

8. On the Remote Access page, click Next.

9. On the Select Role Services page, ensure that DirectAccess And VPN (RAS) is selected, as shown in Figure 8-54, click Add Features, and click Next.

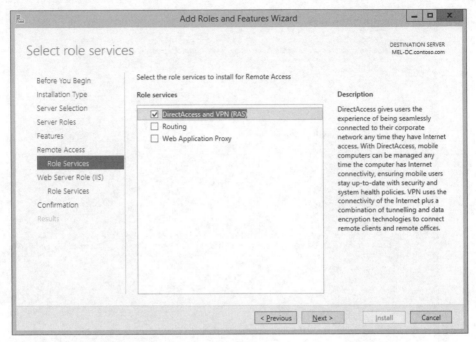

FIGURE 8-54 Local file logging options

10. On the Web Server Role (IIS) page, click Next.

11. On the Select Role Services page, click Next.

12. On the Confirmation page, click Install, and then click Close.

Exercise 6: Configure a VPN server

In this exercise, you configure MEL-DC as a VPN server. To complete this exercise, perform the following steps:

1. On the Tools menu of the Server Manager console on MEL-DC, click Routing And Remote Access.

2. In the Routing And Remote Access console, click MEL-DC.

3. On the Action menu, click Configure and Enable Routing And Remote Access.

4. On the Welcome To The Routing And Remote Access Server Setup Wizard page of the Routing And Remote Access Server Setup Wizard, click Next.

5. On the Configuration page, click Custom Configuration, and click Next.

6. On the Custom Configuration page, click VPN Access, as shown in Figure 8-55, and click Next.

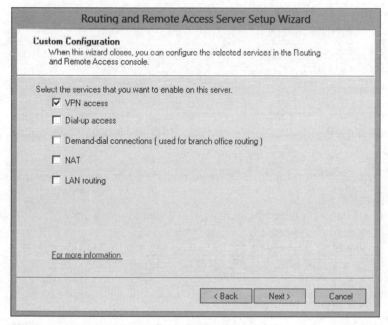

FIGURE 8-55 Choosing VPN Access

7. Click Finish to complete the setup wizard.
8. In the Routing And Remote Access dialog box, click Start Service.

Exercise 7: Prepare for Web Application Proxy

In this exercise, you configure the necessary certificate services infrastructure so that you can deploy ADL-DC as a Web Application Proxy server. To complete this exercise, perform the following steps:

1. While signed on to SYD-DC as contoso\don_funk, right-click the Windows PowerShell icon on the taskbar, right-click Windows PowerShell, and click Run As Administrator.
2. In the Windows PowerShell window, type the following command and press Enter.

    ```
    Install-WindowsFeature ADCS-Cert-Authority,ADFS-Federation -IncludeManagementTools
    ```

3. In the Windows PowerShell window, type the following command and press Enter.

    ```
    Add-KdsRootKey -EffectiveTime (Get-Date).AddHours(-10)
    ```

4. Close the Windows PowerShell window.
5. On the Server Manager console, click the Refresh icon, and then click the Notification icon.

6. Click Configure Active Directory Certificate Services On The Destination Server.

7. On the Credentials page of the AD CS Configuration Wizard, continue to click Next, accepting the default settings until you reach the Confirmation page.

8. On the Confirmation page, click Configure, and then click Close.

9. On the Server Manager console, click Tools, and then click Certification Authority.

10. In the Certification Authority console, expand Contoso-SYD-DC-CA, and click Certificate Templates.

11. On the Action menu, click Manage.

12. In the Certificate Templates Console, click on the Web Server certificate template.

13. On the Action menu, click Duplicate Template.

14. On the General tab of the Properties Of New Template dialog box, set the name to Web Server 2.

15. On the Request Handling tab of the Properties Of New Template dialog box, select Allow Private Key To Be Exported, as shown in Figure 8-56.

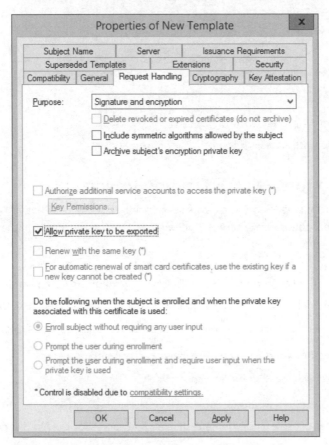

FIGURE 8-56 Allow private key export

16. On the Security tab of the Properties Of New Template dialog box, click Authenticated Users and assign the Read(Allow), Write(Allow), and Enroll(Allow) permissions as shown in Figure 8-57. Click OK to close the Properties Of New Template dialog box.

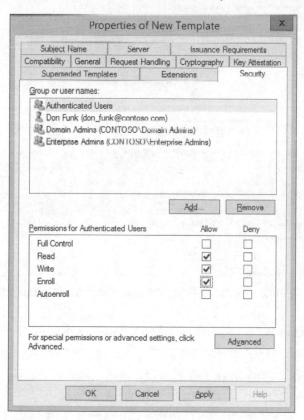

FIGURE 8-57 Configure template permissions

17. Close the Certificate Templates console.
18. In the Certification Authority console, click the Certificate Templates node. On the Action menu click New, and click Certificate Template To Issue.
19. On the Enable Certificate Templates dialog box, click Web Server 2, as shown in Figure 8-58, and click OK.

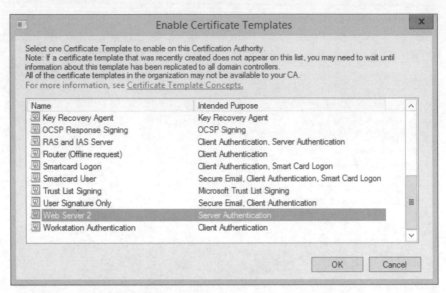

FIGURE 8-58 Select certificate template

20. Right-click the Start button, and click Run.

21. In the Run dialog box, type **mmc.exe**. On the User Account Control dialog box, click Yes.

22. On the File menu of the Console1 dialog box, click Add/Remove Snap-In.

23. In the Add Or Remove Snap-Ins dialog box, click Certificates, and click Add.

24. On the Certificates Snap-In dialog box, click Computer account, click Next, and then click Finish. Click OK to close the Add Or Remove Snap-Ins dialog box.

25. In the Console1 dialog box, expand Certificates, expand Personal, and click Certificates.

26. From the Action menu, click All Tasks, and click Request New Certificate.

27. On the Before You Begin page of the Certificate Enrollment dialog box, click Next twice.

28. On the Request Certificates page, shown in Figure 8-59, click More Information Is Required To Enroll For This Certificate.

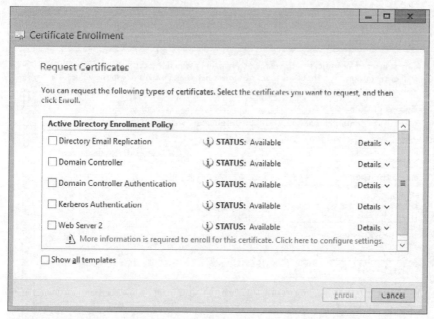

FIGURE 8-59 Configure more information

29. On the Certificate Properties dialog box, click Full DN, and click Common Name.

30. In the value box, type **syd-dc.contoso.com** and click Add, as shown in Figure 8-60, and then click OK.

FIGURE 8-60 Specify common name

31. Click Web Server 2, click Enroll, and click Finish.

32. In console 1, click on the Syd-dc.contoso.com certificate.

33. On the Action menu, click All Tasks, and click Export.

34. On the Welcome To The Certificate Export Wizard, click Next.

35. On the Export Private Key page, click Yes, Export The Private Key, as shown in Figure 8-61, and click Next twice.

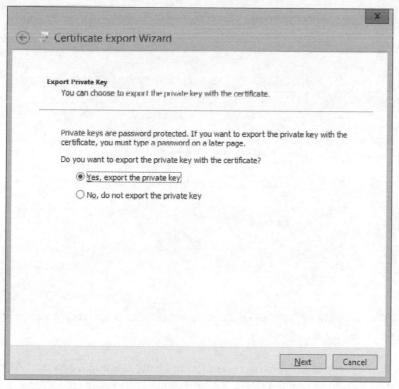

FIGURE 8-61 Allow private key export

36. On the Security page of the Certificate Export Wizard, set the password as **Pa$$wurd** and click Next.

37. On the File To Export dialog box, type **c:\SYD-DC-CERT**, click Next, click Finish, and click OK.

Exercise 8: Configure AD FS to support Web Application Proxy

In this exercise, you configure AD FS on SYD-DC, as this role is needed to support the deployment of ADL-DC as a Web Application Proxy server. To complete this exercise, perform the following steps:

1. On the Server Manager console, click the Notification icon, and then click Configure The Federation Service On This Server.

2. On the Welcome page of the Active Directory Federation Services Configuration Wizard, click Next twice.

3. On the Specify Service Properties page, click the drop down menu next to SSL Certificate and click Syd-dc.contoso.com. Set the Federation Service Display Name to Syd-dc.contoso.com, as shown in Figure 8-62, and click Next.

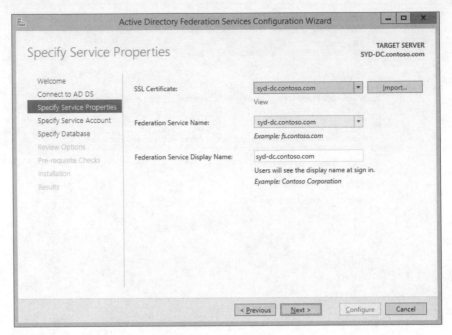

FIGURE 8-62 Allow private key export

4. On the Specify Service Account name page, click Create A Group Managed Service Account, and set the name to CONTOSO\ADFSGMSA as shown in Figure 8-63, and click Next.

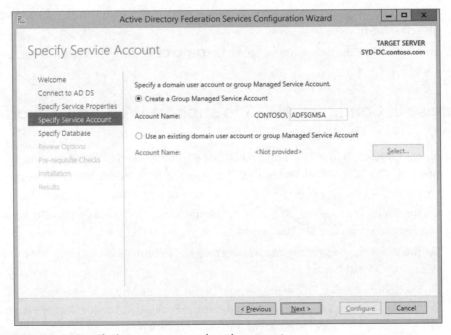

FIGURE 8-63 Specify the group managed service account

5. On the Specify Database page, click Create A Database On This Server Using Windows Internal Database, and click Next twice.

6. On the Pre-requisite Checks page, click Configure.

7. Ignore the warnings on the results page and click Close.

Exercise 9: Deploy Web Application Proxy with pass-through preauthentication

In this exercise, you deploy ADL-DC as a Web Application Proxy server and configure the publication of an application using pass-through preauthentication. To complete this exercise, perform the following steps:

1. Start and sign in to ADL-DC as Administrator with the password **Pa$$w0rd**.

2. Right-click the Start button, and click Run.

3. In the Run dialog box, type **\\SYD-DC\C$\SYD-DC-CERT.pfx** and click OK.

4. On the Welcome To The Certificate Import Wizard, click Local Machine, as shown in Figure 8-64, and click Next.

FIGURE 8-64 Import certificate

5. On the File To Import page, click Next.

6. On the Private Key Protection page, type the password **Pa$$w0rd** and click Next.

7. On the Certificate Store page, select Automatically Select The Certificate Store Based On The Type Of Certificate, click Next, click Finish, and click OK.

8. On the Manage menu of the Server Manager console, click Add Roles And Features.

9. On the Before You Begin page of the Add Roles And Features Wizard, click Next three times.

10. On the Select Server Roles page, click Remote Access, and click Next three times.

11. On the Select Role Services page, click Web Application Proxy, as shown in Figure 8-65, and then click Add Features. Click Next, click Install, and click Close.

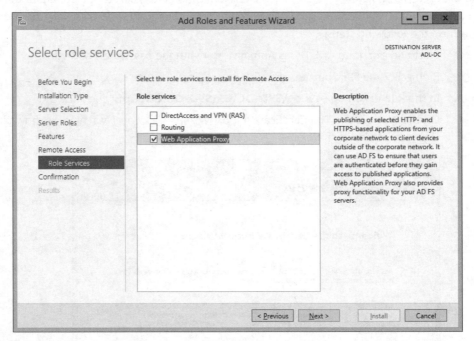

FIGURE 8-65 Import certificate

12. Click the Notification icon on the Server Manager console and click Open The Web Application Proxy Wizard.

13. On the Welcome page of the Web Application Proxy Configuration Wizard, click Next.

14. On the Federation Server page, type the federation service as **syd-dc.contoso.com**, the user name as **contoso\don_funk** and the password as **Pa$$w0rd** as shown in Figure 8-66, and click Next.

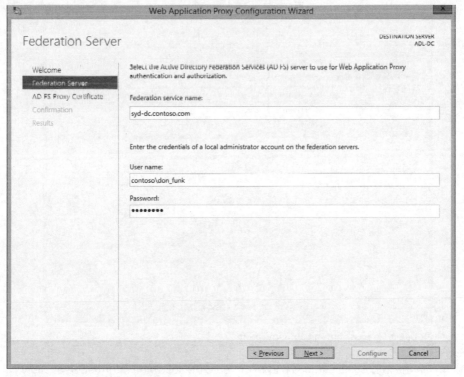

FIGURE 8-66 Federation Service name

15. On the AD FS Proxy Certificate page, click the down arrow, click SYD-DC.contoso.com, and click Next.

16. On the Confirmation page, click Configure, and then click Close.

17. In the Tasks pane of the Remote Access Management Console, click Publish.

18. On the Welcome page of the Publish New Application Wizard, click Next.

19. On the Preauthentication page, click Pass-Through as shown in Figure 8-67, and click Next.

FIGURE 8-67 pass-through authentication

20. On the Publishing Settings page, configure the following information as shown in Figure 8-68 and click Next, click Publish, and click Close.

- Name: **syd-dc.contoso.com**
- External URL: **https://syd-dc.contoso.com**
- External Certificate: **syd-dc.contoso.com**
- Backend Server URL: **https://syd-dc.contoso.com**

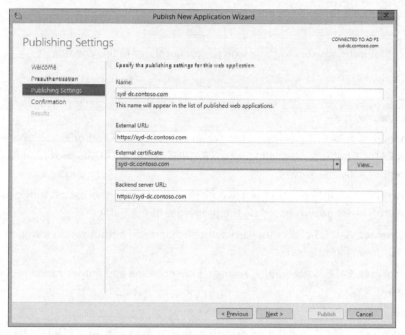

FIGURE 8-68 Publishing settings

Suggested practice exercises

The following additional practice exercises are designed to give you more opportunities to practice what you've learned and to help you successfully master the lessons presented in this chapter.

- **Exercise 1** Deploy the NPS role on ADL-DC. Configure ADL-DC as a RADIUS client of MEL-DC.
- **Exercise 2** Configure ADL-DC as a NAT router.
- **Exercise 3** Configure CBR-DC as a DirectAccess server.

Answers

This section contains the answers to the lesson review questions in this chapter.

Lesson 1

1. **Correct answer: B**

    A. **Incorrect**. A RADIUS server performs authentication and authorization operations on RADIUS traffic forwarded to it by a RADIUS client. A RADIUS proxy is a RADIUS client of a RADIUS server.

    B. **Correct**. A RADIUS proxy forwards authentication and authorization traffic to RADIUS server groups based on the properties of the traffic.

    C. **Incorrect**. RADIUS clients forward authentication and authorization traffic to RADIUS servers or proxies.

    D. **Incorrect**. RADIUS accounting records authentication and authorization request data.

2. **Correct answer: B**

    A. **Incorrect**. RADIUS accounting records authentication and authorization request data.

    B. **Correct**. A RADIUS server performs authentication and authorization operations on RADIUS traffic forwarded to it by a RADIUS client. A RADIUS proxy is a RADIUS client of a RADIUS server.

    C. **Incorrect**. A RADIUS proxy forwards authentication and authorization traffic to RADIUS server groups based on the properties of the traffic.

    D. **Incorrect**. RADIUS clients forward authentication and authorization traffic to RADIUS servers or proxies.

3. **Correct answer: A**

    A. **Correct**. RADIUS clients forward authentication and authorization traffic to RADIUS servers or proxies.

    B. **Incorrect**. RADIUS accounting records authentication and authorization request data.

    C. **Incorrect**. A RADIUS server performs authentication and authorization operations on RADIUS traffic forwarded to it by a RADIUS client. A RADIUS proxy is a RADIUS client of a RADIUS server.

    D. **Incorrect**. A RADIUS proxy forwards authentication and authorization traffic to RADIUS server groups based on the properties of the traffic.

4. **Correct answer: C**

    A. **Incorrect**. A RADIUS proxy forwards authentication and authorization traffic to RADIUS server groups based on the properties of the traffic.

    B. **Incorrect**. RADIUS clients forward authentication and authorization traffic to RADIUS servers or proxies.

    C. **Correct**. RADIUS accounting records authentication and authorization request data.

    D. **Incorrect**. A RADIUS server performs authentication and authorization operations on RADIUS traffic forwarded to it by a RADIUS client. A RADIUS proxy is a RADIUS client of a RADIUS server.

5. **Correct answers: A, C, and D**

    A. **Correct**. You specify a friendly name when configuring a RADIUS client on a RADIUS server.

    B. **Incorrect**. You don't specify an authentication protocol when configuring a RADIUS client on a RADIUS server.

    C. **Correct**. You specify an IP address or FQDN when configuring a RADIUS client on a RADIUS server.

    D. **Correct**. You specify a shared secret when configuring a RADIUS client on a RADIUS server.

Lesson 2

1. **Correct answers: C and D**

    A. **Incorrect**. The SSTP protocol VPN protocol can be used by computers running the Windows Vista, Windows 7, Windows 8, and Windows 8.1 client operating systems.

    B. **Incorrect**. The IKEv2 protocol can be used by computers running the Windows 7, Windows 8, and Windows 8.1 client operating systems.

    C. **Correct**. The L2TP/IPsec protocol can be used by computers running the Windows XP, Windows Vista, Windows 7, Windows 8, and Windows 8.1 client operating systems.

    D. **Correct**. The L2TP/IPsec protocol can be used by computers running the Windows XP, Windows Vista, Windows 7, Windows 8, and Windows 8.1 client operating systems.

2. **Correct answer: C**

    A. **Incorrect**. The L2TP/IPsec protocol can be used by computers running the Windows XP, Windows Vista, Windows 7, Windows 8, and Windows 8.1 client operating systems.

    B. **Incorrect**. The L2TP/IPsec protocol can be used by computers running the Windows XP, Windows Vista, Windows 7, Windows 8, and Windows 8.1 client operating systems.

    C. **Correct**. The IKEv2 protocol can be used by computers running Windows 7 and Windows 8 client operating systems.

D. Incorrect. The SSTP protocol VPN protocol can be used by computers running the Windows Vista, Windows 7, and Windows 8, and Windows 8.1 client operating systems.

3. **Correct answer: C**

   A. Incorrect. You can't use IKEv2 through firewalls in hotels that allow both secure and insecure web traffic only.

   B. Incorrect. You can't use L2TP/IPSec through firewalls in hotels that allow both secure and insecure web traffic only.

   C. Correct. SSTP uses port 443, making it possible to use this VPN protocol through firewalls in hotels that allow secure web traffic.

   D. Incorrect. You can't use PPTP through firewalls in hotels that allow both secure and insecure web traffic only.

4. **Correct answer: B**

   A. Incorrect. SSTP doesn't support VPN reconnect.

   B. Correct. This VPN protocol supports VPN reconnect. VPN reconnect enables reestablishment of disrupted VPN connections for up to 8 hours after the disruption occurred without requiring manual user reauthentication.

   C. Incorrect. PPTP doesn't support VPN reconnect.

   D. Incorrect. L2TP/IPsec doesn't support VPN reconnect.

5. **Correct answer: C**

   A. Incorrect. You configure VPN access to provide protected network access to clients on the Internet. You can't use VPN access to enable protected network clients to share an Internet connection.

   B. Incorrect. You configure dial-up access if you want to enable access to your organization's internal network for clients that have modems. You can't use dial-up access to allow protected network clients to share an Internet connection.

   C. Correct. You can use NAT to enable a group of computers on a private network to share an Internet connection.

   D. Incorrect. You choose LAN router if you need to make a group of computers on your organization's network that has public IP addresses accessible to hosts on the Internet.

Lesson 3

1. **Correct answers: B and C**

   A. Incorrect. Windows RT can't be joined to a domain and can't function as a DirectAccess client.

   B. Correct. Windows 8 Enterprise edition can be configured as a DirectAccess client. This is the only edition of Windows 8 that can be used with DirectAccess.

C. **Correct**. Windows 7 Ultimate edition can be configured as a DirectAccess client. You can also configure computers running Windows 7 Enterprise edition as DirectAccess clients.

D. **Incorrect**. Windows Vista can't be configured as a DirectAccess client.

2. **Correct answer: D**

A. **Incorrect**. The DirectAccess server's Internet interface must be assigned two consecutive public IPv4 addresses.

B. **Correct**. The DirectAccess server's Internet interface must be assigned two consecutive public IPv4 addresses.

C. **Incorrect**. DirectAccess does not use RADIUS authentication.

D. **Correct**. You must remove ISATAP from the DNS global query block list on all DNS servers to use DirectAccess.

3. **Correct answer: D**

A. **Incorrect**. You don't need to deploy a web server/SSL certificate on a domain controller when deploying DirectAccess.

B. **Incorrect**. You don't need to deploy a web server/SSL certificate on a DNS server when deploying DirectAccess.

C. **Incorrect**. You must deploy a web server/SSL certificate on the NLS server when deploying DirectAccess.

D. **Correct**. You must deploy a web server/SSL certificate on the NLS server when deploying DirectAccess.

4. **Correct answer: C**

A. **Incorrect**. DirectAccess clients attempt to contact the NLS server to determine their network location before attempting to initiate a DirectAccess connection.

B. **Incorrect**. DirectAccess clients attempt to contact the NLS server to determine their network location before attempting to initiate a DirectAccess connection.

C. **Correct**. DirectAccess clients attempt to contact the NLS server to determine their network location before attempting to initiate a DirectAccess connection.

D. **Incorrect**. DirectAccess clients attempt to contact the NLS server to determine their network location before attempting to initiate a DirectAccess connection.

5. **Correct answer: C**

A. **Incorrect**. IP over HTTPS is the option only when a DirectAccess server is deployed behind a NAT device.

B. **Incorrect**. IP over HTTPS is the option only when a DirectAccess server is deployed behind a NAT device.

C. **Correct**. IP over HTTPS is the option only when a DirectAccess server is deployed behind a NAT device.

D. **Incorrect**. IP over HTTPS is the option only when a DirectAccess server is deployed behind a NAT device.

CHAPTER 9

Managing file services

The management of file servers is an important, if somewhat less than invigorating, task that Windows Server administrators need to perform on a regular basis because file servers are the most commonly deployed workload for computers running a Windows Server operating system. The main thing that administrators need to ensure is that file servers remain available. To ensure that a file server remains available, you need to be able to control what files are stored there, not only by type and size, but also by age and content. In this chapter, you'll learn how to use File Server Resource Manager (FSRM) to control the type of files that are stored on file servers. You'll learn how to simplify the location of specific shared folders in an organization that has a large number of file servers. You'll also learn how to protect volumes and individual files with encryption.

Lessons in this chapter:

- Lesson 1: Configuring File Server Resource Manager **501**
- Lesson 2: Configuring a Distributed File System **511**
- Lesson 3: Configuring file and disk encryption **522**

Before you begin

To complete the practice exercises in this chapter:

- You need to have deployed computers SYD-DC, MEL-DC, and ADL-DC, as described in the Introduction, using the evaluation edition of Windows Server 2012 R2.

Lesson 1: Configuring File Server Resource Manager

File Server Resource Manager (FSRM) enables you to simplify the management of file servers by the following:

- Enabling you to apply storage quotas
- Using file screens
- Performing file classification
- Generating reports on the properties of volumes, folder trees, and folders

In this lesson, you'll learn how to stop users from consuming more than a specified amount of storage space in a folder, how to block them from writing specific file types to a folder, and also learn how to generate reports listing the biggest files stored on a volume, and files that have not been accessed recently.

> **After this lesson, you will be able to:**
> - Configure quotas.
> - Configure file screens.
> - Enable file classification.
> - Configure file management tasks
> - Generate storage reports.
>
> **Estimated lesson time: 45 minutes**

Configuring quotas

Quotas enable you to control the amount of storage space consumed by a user on a volume, folder tree, or individual folder. In previous versions of the Windows server operating system, NTFS quotas enabled you to apply quotas on a per-volume basis. FSRM quotas are more sophisticated, enabling you to apply different quotas to different folder trees on the same volume.

You apply quotas to different locations using a quota template. As Figure 9-1 shows, a quota template enables you to specify a space limit, determine whether the quota is hard or soft, and provide notification thresholds.

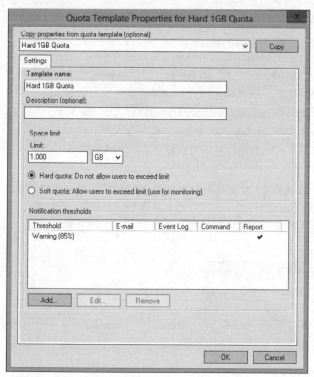

FIGURE 9-1 Quota template

The difference between a hard quota and a soft quota is as follows:

- A hard quota blocks users from exceeding the specified limit. They can't write additional data to the folder tree to which the quota template applies.

- A soft quota doesn't block users from exceeding the specified limit.

You can configure notification thresholds at any percentage of the quota, including values above the quota value, such as 150 percent. Each notification threshold can be configured separately. You can configure the following options at a notification threshold:

- **Threshold** Value at which the threshold action is triggered.

- **E-mail** Sends an email message when storage utilization exceeds the threshold value.

- **Event Log** Writes an item to the event log when storage utilization exceeds the threshold value.

- **Command** Runs a command when storage utilization exceeds the threshold value.

- **Report** Generates a report when storage utilization exceeds the threshold value.

Configuring file screens

File screens enable you to block specific file types, on the basis of the file name extension, from being written to volumes, folder trees, or individual folders. You configure file screens by selecting a specific file group to the screen or by selecting a file screen template and applying it to a specific location.

A file group is a collection of file types associated with a particular kind of file. For example, the Image Files file group includes the file extensions associated with common image file formats such as .bmp, .jpg, .gif, and .png. You can edit which file extensions are associated with existing file groups or create custom file groups.

A file screen template, shown in Figure 9-2, includes file groups, email settings, event log settings, command prompt settings, and report settings related to the file screen. You use these additional settings to configure a response when a user attempts to write a file to a location that is screened.

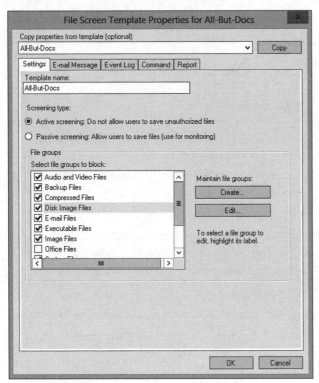

FIGURE 9-2 File screen template

REAL WORLD GETTING AROUND FILE SCREENS

Clever users can get around file screens by changing the file name extension. If you find a clever user who perpetrates this type of shenanigan, draft her into the IT department.

A file screen exception enables you to create an exemption to an existing file screen. For example, you might have a file screen that blocks a number of file types being written to a specific volume, but you might need to allow one of those blocked file types to be written to a specific folder on that volume. To deal with this scenario, you configure a file screen exception. You specify the exception path, as shown in Figure 9-3, and the file groups to be excluded from screening. The exception applies only to the specified path.

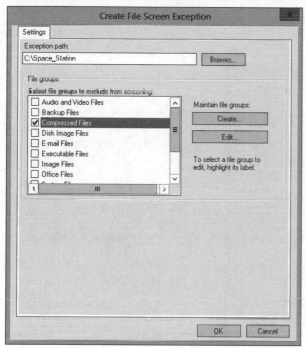

FIGURE 9-3 File screen exception

✔ **Quick check**

■ You want to allow file types to be written to a subfolder that are blocked by a file screen applied to the folder. How can you accomplish this goal?

Quick check answer

■ Configure a file screen exception.

Enabling file classification

File classification enables you to apply metadata to files based on file properties. File classification properties can use one of the following property types:

■ **Yes/No** A Boolean value of either YES or NO. When multiple values apply, NO overrides YES.

■ **Date-Time** A date and time property.

- **Number**   A numeric property.

- **Multiple Choice List**   A list of values that can be assigned to a property. Multiple values are allowed.

- **Ordered List**   A fixed list of values. If multiple values apply, the one closest to the top of the list is used.

- **String**   A text string that can be assigned to the property.

- **Multi-string**   A list of strings that can be assigned to a property.

Figure 9-4 shows a file classification property.

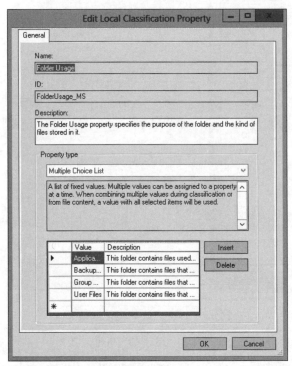

FIGURE 9-4 File classification property

A file classification rule applies a property to a file. When configuring a classification rule, you specify a scope, a classification mechanism, the property to be assigned to the file, and additional classification parameters.

Configuring file management tasks

File management tasks enable you to perform operations, from simply moving files to running a program (as shown in Figure 9-5) on files that have a specific classification property applied. For example, you can configure a file management task to automatically move files over a certain age to a shared folder on another server. When configuring a file management task, specify the following:

- The scope of files to be checked for a condition
- The condition checked for
- The action taken
- The task schedule
- Notification and report settings

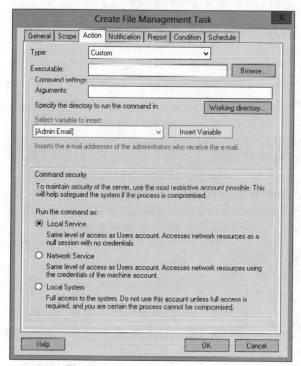

FIGURE 9-5 File management task

Generating reports

A *storage report* enables you to generate information about the type and nature of files stored on a storage server. Storage reports give you the information that you need to configure effective file screens and quotas. FSRM in Windows Server 2012 and Windows Server 2012 R2 support the following storage reports:

- **Duplicate Files** Enables you to locate duplicate files.
- **File Screening Audit** Enables you to generate a list of files blocked by a file screen on a per-user basis.
- **Files By File Group** Lists files by file group. For example, all files on a file share that match the properties of the Office Files file group. You configure file groups when configuring file screens.

- **Files By Owner**   Enables you to view files by owner. You can use this report to determine which users are consuming a disproportionate amount of disk space.
- **Files By Property**   Enables you to view files on the basis of file classification property.
- **Folders By Property**   Enables you to view folders on the basis of classification property.
- **Large Files**   A report of files that are larger than a specified size.
- **Least Recently Accessed Files**   A report of files that have not been accessed in a specified number of days.
- **Most Recently Accessed Files**   A report of files that have been accessed in a specified number of days.
- **Quota Usage**   A report of information on quotas where the quota usage exceeds a benchmark value.

When you want to generate reports, you create a report task. You use the Storage Reports Task Properties dialog box, shown in Figure 9-6, to configure which reports to include in a report task. You can also configure the parameters and scope of the reports. The parameters and scope of the reports determine which folders will be checked, whether the reports are emailed, and how often the reports are generated. Reports can be output in HTML, DHTML, XML, CSV, and Text format. Reports can also be run on an on-demand basis if necessary.

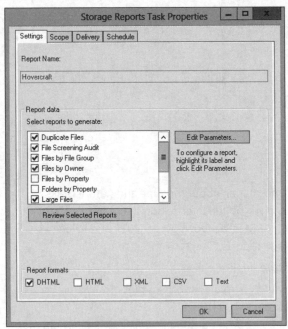

FIGURE 9-6 Configure storage reports

NOTE FILE SERVER RESOURCE MANAGER

For more information about FSRM, consult the following TechNet article at *http://technet .microsoft.com/en-us/library/hh831701.aspx.*

Lesson summary

- Quotas enable you to apply limits on the amount of data that a user can store in a particular folder or folder tree.
- File screens enable you to block users from writing specific types of files to folders.
- File classification enables you to assign metadata to files based on file properties.
- File management tasks enable you to perform tasks on files based on the file metadata.
- Storage reports enable you to generate reports about files stored in particular locations, including largest files, least recently accessed files, and duplicate files.

Lesson review

Answer the following questions to test your knowledge of the information in this lesson. You can find the answers to these questions and explanations of why each answer choice is correct or incorrect in the "Answers" section at the end of this chapter.

1. You want to stop users from saving audio and video files to shared folders hosted on your organization's Windows Server 2012 R2 file servers. You have installed FSRM on each file server. Which of the following must you configure to accomplish this goal?

    A. File Classification Rule

    B. File Screen

    C. File Screen Template

    D. File Groups

2. You have configured a file screen for the Research shared folder. This file screen currently blocks all files except Office document files. You want to keep this file screen in place, but allow compressed files, which can't be written to the Research folder, to be able to be stored in the Old_Projects folder, a subfolder of the Research folder. It should not be possible for users to store compressed files in the Research folder or in other subfolders of the Research folder. Which of the following should you configure to accomplish this goal?

    A. File Screen Template

    B. File Screen Exception

    C. Classification Rule

    D. File Groups

3. You want to apply the same file screen to 20 different shares hosted on a Windows Server 2012 R2 file server. This file screen includes six different file groups. Which of the following should you configure to minimize the amount of work you need to do to accomplish this goal?

   A. Configure a file group

   B. Configure a file screen exception

   C. Configure a file screen template

   D. Configure a quota template

4. You are in the process of configuring a file server that hosts 40 separate shared folders and you want to ensure that all users of these shared folders are subject to the same storage limit. Which of the following should you create and apply to accomplish this goal?

   A. File screen

   B. Quota

   C. File screen template

   D. Quota template

5. You want to have alerts automatically sent to users who consume more than 500 MB in a specific shared folder. Users should not be able to put more than 1 GB on the file share. Which of the following properties should you configure when creating a quota?

   A. 500 MB hard quota

   B. 1 GB hard quota

   C. 500 MB soft quota

   D. 1 GB soft quota

6. You want to have alerts automatically sent to users who consume more than 500 MB in a shared folder. Users should not be blocked from storing more data, but should be sent a storage report in the event that they exceed 750 MB. Which of the following properties should you configure when creating a quota?

   A. 500 MB hard quota

   B. 750 MB hard quota

   C. 500 MB soft quota

   D. 1 GB hard quota

7. You have applied a quota to a file share. You are configuring a notification for the 90 percent threshold. This notification should forward reports to users detailing files that they have stored that they haven't used recently, as well as the name and location of any large files. Which of the following reports should you include when configuring this threshold notification? (Choose all that apply.)

   A. Least Recently Accessed Files

   B. Quota Usage

C. Large Files

D. Duplicate Files

Lesson 2: Configuring a Distributed File System

A Distributed File System (DFS) enables you to create a unified namespace that users can browse when attempting to locate a specific network folder. You can also use a DFS to create replicas of important shared folders. In this lesson, you will learn how to configure a DFS in both domain-based and stand-alone configuration. You will also learn about the different types of replication topologies and technologies that you can use to support a DFS.

> **After this lesson, you will be able to understand:**
>
> - DFS namespaces.
> - Replication topology.
> - Replication targets.
> - Replication schedules.
> - Cloning the DFS Replication database
> - DFSR and database recovery
>
> **Estimated lesson time: 45 minutes**

Understanding Distributed File System namespaces

A *Distributed File System* (DFS) enables you to simplify the process of locating shared folders. If you don't implement a DFS, users who don't have network drives mapped need to remember not only the shared folder name but also the name of the server that hosts that shared folder. With a DFS, all shared folders can be located off the same namespace, meaning that a user needs to remember only the shared folder name. A DFS also enables shared folders to be replicated, providing fault tolerance and a mechanism to enable the same shared folder content to be distributed to multiple locations in a way that's transparent to the user. Users simply navigate to the folder they want, and a DFS redirects them to the closest available replica of that folder. DFS on Windows Server 2012 R2 supports up to 70 million files per volume, with a maximum of 120 million files per DFS server.

DFS namespaces enable you to group shared folders hosted on different servers into one or more logical namespaces. For example, instead of having these folders:

- \\FS-1\Accounting
- \\FS-2\Research
- \\FS-3\Management

You could have the following:

- \\Contoso.com\Accounting
- \\Contoso.com\Research
- \\Contoso.com\Management

In this scenario, the folders are still hosted on machines named FS-1, FS-2, and FS-3. By implementing DFS namespaces, the folders are much easier to locate because it is no longer necessary for users to remember which server is hosting them.

There are two types of DFS namespaces that you can create on computers running Windows Server 2012 and Windows Server 2012 R2 (as shown in Figure 9-7):

- Domain-based namespace
- Stand-alone namespace

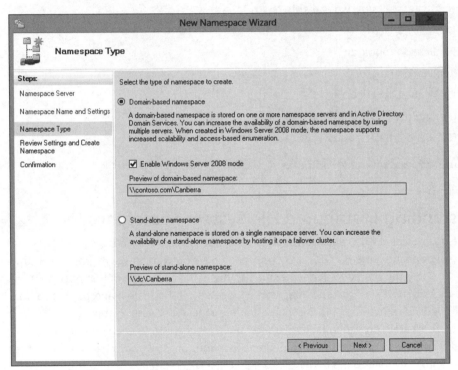

FIGURE 9-7 Configuring a new namespace

Domain-based namespaces

Domain-based DFS namespaces are stored in Active Directory, and you deploy them when you need to ensure that the namespace remains available, even if one of the servers hosting the namespace is offline. With domain-based namespaces, multiple servers can host the same namespace as long as they have the DFS role installed.

You can deploy two types of *domain-based namespace*: Windows 2008 mode or Windows 2000 mode. Windows 2008 mode provides better features, increasing the number of folder targets from 5,000 to 50,000 and providing support for accessed-based enumeration. The 50,000 folder targets supported by domain-based namespaces can all be located on the same server or spread across up to 50,000 file servers, although this would limit each server to a single folder.

> **NOTE** **ACCESS-BASED ENUMERATION**
>
> Access-based enumeration enables users to see only files and folders they have permissions set up on. When you configure access-based enumeration, users can't see files and folders they can't open.

Windows 2008 mode has the following requirements:

- The domain that hosts the DFS namespace must be at the Windows Server 2008 domain functional level or higher.
- The Active Directory forest functional level must be Windows Server 2003 or higher.
- Namespace servers need to be running Windows Server 2008, Windows Server 2008 R2, Windows Server 2012 or Windows Server 2012 R2.

Stand-alone namespaces

Stand-alone namespaces enable you to deploy a DFS on file servers that are not members of an Active Directory domain. You can also deploy a stand-alone namespace on a server that is a member of an Active Directory domain. Stand-alone DFS namespaces support up to 50,000 folders spread across up to 50,000 separate servers. You might consider deploying a stand-alone DFS namespace when you need to support more than 5,000 DFS folders, but you can't deploy a domain-based DFS because the domain isn't at the Windows Server 2008 or higher functional level.

> **MORE INFO** **DFS NAMESPACES**
>
> For more information about DFS namespaces, consult the following article at *http://technet .microsoft.com/en-us/library/ee404780.aspx*.

You can have only one namespace server with a stand-alone namespace. This means if the server hosting the stand-alone namespace fails, the whole namespace is unavailable, even if servers hosting folder targets remain online. You can make a stand-alone namespace highly available by deploying it on a failover cluster.

Understanding DFS replication

DFS replication enables you to configure folder replication so that folder replicas remain synchronized. When deployed on computers running Windows Server 2008, Windows Server 2008 R2, Windows Server 2012 or Windows Server 2012 R2, DFS replication uses a process known as remote differential compression, which improves replication by using block-level replication. This means that instead of replicating a file in its entirety when there is a small change, only the data blocks that have been changed are replicated. Block-level replication, instead of file-level replication, dramatically reduces the amount of network traffic generated by DFS replication.

When the same file is edited on different replicas, DFS replication uses a "last writer wins" to resolve conflicts related to file modification and "earliest creator wins" for name conflicts. For example, if a user in Melbourne and a user in Sydney are editing the same file, the user that performs the most recent save operation has the changes saved. Similarly, if a user in Melbourne and a user in Sydney create a file with the same name before replication occurs, the user that created the file first, even if it is by a microsecond, will win the conflict.

When conflicts occur, the files and folders that lose the conflict resolution are automatically moved to the Conflict and Deleted folder, which is located under the local path of the replicated folder in the DfsrPrivate\ConflictandDeleted directory. By default, deleted files are also automatically moved to this directory, as shown in Figure 9-8.

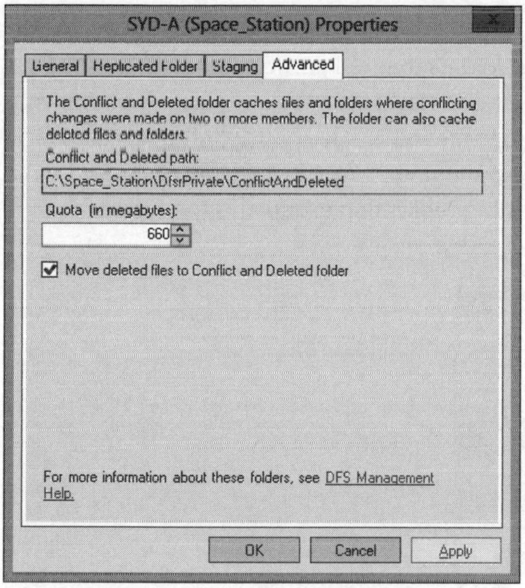

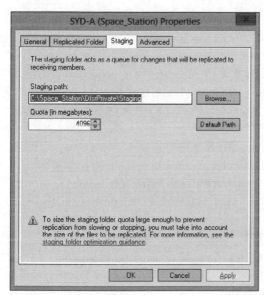

FIGURE 9-8 Conflict and deleted path

DFS uses a special folder, named the staging folder, to store a file before sending or receiving it. When remote differential compression is enabled, calculations are performed on files in the staging folder to determine which blocks need to be replicated. The receiving folder uses its own staging folder to build the modified file. The staging folder is located under the local path of the replicated folder and has a default quota of 4096 MB, as shown in Figure 9-9.

FIGURE 9-9 Staging folder

Understanding replication targets

Replication targets enable you to specify shared folders that will participate in a DFS. You can add a target to an existing replicated folder in the New Folder Target dialog box, shown in Figure 9-10. When adding a replication target, you need to specify the Universal Naming Convention (UNC) path of the folder that will host the target. You also need to specify whether you will add this folder target to an existing replication group and the type of connection that the folder will use.

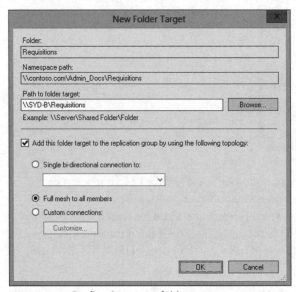

FIGURE 9-10 Configuring a new folder target

Understanding replication topology

Replication topology determines how DFS servers that are members of a replication group communicate with each other. When you create a replication group, you need to decide which topology you will use. As Figure 9-11 shows, you can choose between two topologies in the New Topology Wizard:

- **Hub And Spoke** In this topology, you designate central servers as hub servers. Other servers in the topology replicate with hub servers and don't replicate directly with non-hub servers. Choose this topology if you have a large number of servers in the replication group. This topology works best when you have a central server in which most updates occur and few updates occurring on spoke servers. You can choose this topology only when there are three or more servers in the replication group.

- **Full Mesh** This topology is appropriate if you have 10 or fewer servers in the replication group. In this topology, any server in the replication group will replicate with any other server in the replication group.

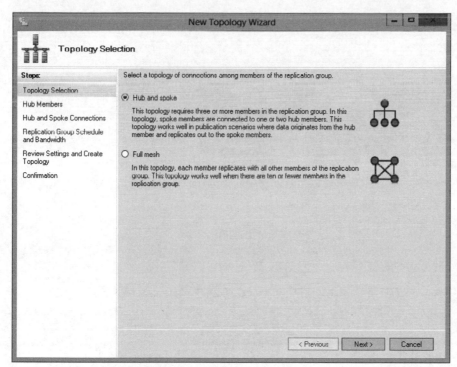

FIGURE 9-11 Configuring replication topology

Understanding replication schedules

Replication schedules, shown in Figure 9-12, enable you to specify when replication occurs and how bandwidth is utilized. The default is for replication to occur 24 hours per day and to use all available bandwidth. This is appropriate for organizations with high bandwidth, wide area network (WAN) connections, in which replica synchronization must happen as quickly as possible.

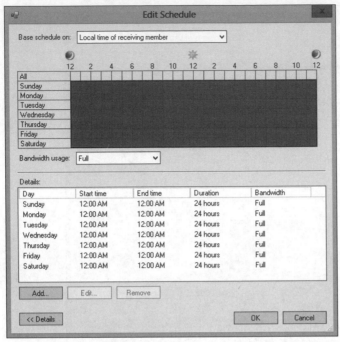

FIGURE 9-12 Replication schedule

MORE INFO **DFS REPLICATION**

For more information about DFS replication, consult the following TechNet article at
http://technet.microsoft.com/en-us/library/cc773238.aspx.

You can also configure a custom schedule, as shown in Figure 9-13. Using a custom
schedule, you might configure limited bandwidth utilization during office hours and full
bandwidth utilization during off-peak periods.

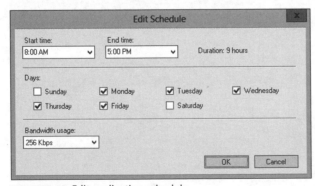

FIGURE 9-13 Edit replication schedule

The trick to understanding a DFS is that you use it when you want to distribute the same content to multiple sites in your organization. A DFS isn't a backup solution because an error introduced in one document will replicate out to all other locations. When configuring a DFS to host files, remember to ask yourself whether the files really need to be replicated to more than one location. If the answer is yes, a DFS is appropriate.

Cloning the DFS Replication database

Windows Server 2012 R2 supports being able to export a clone of the DFS Replication database. This allows you to pre-seed a replicated folder with content when deploying a new replication partner or when replacing a failed server. Using a clone of the DFS replication database and pre-seeding content reduces initial synchronization time.

The following prerequisites must be met before you can create a clone of the DFS replication database:

- The DFS Replication service must be running.

- The account used to perform the operation must be a member of the Domain Admins or Enterprise Admins groups, or have been delegated the appropriate permissions to create DFS replication groups.

- The DFS Replication database must be on a volume that has at least one Read-Write replicated folder.

- All replicated folders on the volume must be in a normal state, and cannot be in the initial sync, initial building, or recovery state.

- Cloning takes the DFS Replication volume manager offline, preventing replication of content from that volume during the cloning process.

The volume on the destination server on which you will import the cloned database cannot host a replicated folder. You can import single-cloned databases on multiple servers. You perform the export operation using the Export-DfsrClone Windows PowerShell cmdlet. You can monitor the process of creating the cloned database using the Get-DfsrCloneState cmdlet. Running the Export-DfsrClone cmdlet will generate sample Robocopy commands that you can use to move the copy of the data to the destination server. Once the content is copied, you use the Import-DfsrClone cmdlet on the destination server to import the cloned content.

For more information about cloning DFS Replication databases, consult the following TechNet article at *http://technet.microsoft.com/en-us/library/dn482443.aspx*.

Understanding DFSR and database recovery

The DFSR database can become corrupted when hardware fails or when there is an unexpected loss of power. Windows Server 2012 R2 improves the recovery process for a corrupted DFS database so that recovery is likely to occur more successfully in the case where multiple servers experience corruption at the same time. When multiple servers suffered corruption at the same time in previous versions of DFS, it was possible that replication would stop entirely because each server was waiting for the others to return to a normal state before attempting self-repair. The implementation of DFSR on Windows Server 2012 R2 minimizes the chance that corruption will cause replication to pause, requiring administrator intervention to get it restarted.

> *MORE INFO*   DFS DATABASE RECOVERY
>
> To learn more about DFS database recovery, consult this TechNet blog post at *https://blogs.technet.com/b/filecab/archive/2013/07/31/dfs-replication-in-windows-server-2012-r2-revenge-of-the-sync.aspx.*

Lesson summary

- DFS enables you to simplify the location of shared folders by enabling their placement under a single tree.
- A domain-based DFS enables you to deploy multiple namespace servers for redundancy.
- If a domain is at the Windows Server 2008 or higher functional level, and the forest is at the Windows Server 2003 functional level, you can implement Windows 2008 mode.
- A Windows 2008 domain-based DFS enables up to 50,000 folder targets, access-based enumeration, and remote differential compression.
- Stand-alone mode enables you to support up to 50,000 folder targets, but does not provide redundancy for namespace servers.
- Hub and spoke mode is appropriate for replication groups in which updates occur on few servers and replication topology must be managed.
- Full mesh topology is appropriate for replication groups that have fewer than 10 members.
- Replication schedules enable you to configure replication times and how much bandwidth is allocated to replication.

Lesson review

Answer the following questions to test your knowledge of the information in this lesson. You can find the answers to these questions and explanations of why each answer choice is correct or incorrect in the "Answers" section at the end of this chapter.

1. You have 30 Windows Server 2012 R2 member servers that are members of an Active Directory domain that is running at the Windows Server 2003 functional level. You want to implement a DFS to simplify accessing of shared folders and to enable replication to different sites. You estimate that you will need to support approximately 6,000 folder targets. Which of the following solutions should you implement? (Choose all that apply.)

   A. Create a replication group. Configure the replication group to use the hub and spoke topology.

   B. Create a replication group. Configure the replication group to use a full mesh topology.

   C. Configure a domain-based DFS namespace.

   D. Configure a stand-alone DFS namespace.

2. You have nine Windows Server 2012 R2 member servers that are members of an Active Directory domain that is running at the Windows Server 2012 R2 functional level. The forest is also running at the Windows Server 2012 R2 functional level. You want to deploy DFS so the namespace is still available if one namespace server is offline. You want to enable replication between any two servers hosting content. Which of the following solutions should you implement? (Choose all that apply.)

   A. Configure a stand-alone DFS namespace.

   B. Configure a domain-based DFS namespace.

   C. Create a replication group. Configure the replication group to use a full mesh topology.

   D. Create a replication group. Configure the replication group to use the hub and spoke topology.

3. You have five servers running Windows Server 2012 R2 that you want to use with a DFS, each located in a different building on the same university campus. Each building on the campus is connected to each other with a high-speed link. The domain that hosts the servers is running at the Windows Server 2003 functional level. You need to support 12,000 folder targets. Which of the following solutions should you implement? (Choose all that apply.)

   A. Create a replication group. Configure the replication group to use the hub and spoke topology.

   B. Create a replication group. Configure the replication group to use a full mesh topology.

   C. Configure a domain-based DFS namespace.

   D. Configure a stand-alone DFS namespace.

4. Your organization's head office is located in Melbourne, Australia, with branch offices in Sydney, Brisbane, Adelaide, Perth, Darwin, and Hobart. Your organization has a single Active Directory domain running at the Windows Server 2008 functional

level. The forest is also configured to run at this functional level. You have deployed Windows Server 2012 R2 file servers at the head office and branch office locations. Each branch office location has a WAN link to the Melbourne office. There are no WAN links between branch offices. Which of the following steps should you take when configuring a DFS in your environment? (Choose all that apply.)

A. Configure a stand-alone DFS namespace.

B. Configure a domain-based DFS namespace.

C. Create a replication group. Configure the replication group to use a full mesh topology.

D. Create a replication group. Configure the replication group to use the hub and spoke topology.

Lesson 3: Configuring file and disk encryption

Encryption enables you to protect data from being accessed by unauthorized people. Unlike file and folder permissions, which are often incorrectly applied, decryption of encrypted data can occur only if a user or computer has access to the correct private key. In this lesson, you will learn about the Encrypting File System (EFS), which enables you to encrypt file and folder data. You'll also learn about BitLocker encryption, which enables you to encrypt entire volumes and protect the boot environment.

> **After this lesson, you will be able to:**
> - Configure BitLocker encryption.
> - Configure Network Unlock.
> - Configure Encrypting File System.
> - Configure EFS recovery agent.
> - Manage BitLocker and EFS certificates.
>
> **Estimated lesson time: 45 minutes**

Configuring BitLocker

BitLocker is a full-volume encryption and boot environment protection technology. By deploying BitLocker, you can ensure that a nefarious third party can't use a USB boot device to boot a computer in your organization and extract data from the hard disk, or simply remove the hard disk for later data extraction. The boot environment protection technology protects against modifications to the boot environment. When a change to the boot environment is detected, the BitLocker recovery key must be entered to authorize the changes.

BitLocker is often deployed with client computers, but it can also be deployed on servers to protect stored data. BitLocker protects data from being extracted from the hard drive only while the operating system is functioning. Users who can sign on to a computer are usually unaware that the data they are accessing is stored in an encrypted manner on the hard disk. It is only when the hard disk is connected to another computer that it is inaccessible unless the appropriate recovery keys are available. When using BitLocker with Virtual Machines (VMs), enable BitLocker on the volumes that store the VM files on the Hyper-V host. It is possible to use BitLocker with VMs, but you need to disable the Trusted Platform Module (TPM) requirement using Group Policy and configure a startup password.

In Windows Server 2012, Windows Server 2012 R2, Windows 8, and Windows 8.1, BitLocker has the following new options:

- **BitLocker Provisioning**   You can now deploy Windows 8, and Windows 8.1, Windows Server 2012 and Windows Server 2012 R2 in an encrypted state instead of deploying the operating system, enabling BitLocker, and waiting for volumes to be encrypted. Deploying the operating system in an encrypted state substantially improves operating system deployment times in secure environments.

- **Used Disk Space Only Encryption**   Previous versions of BitLocker encrypted the entire volume. The full-volume encryption option remains available, but it is also possible to configure BitLocker so that only used space on the volume is encrypted. Deploying BitLocker in this way speeds up the BitLocker deployment process.

- **Standard User PIN And Password Change**   This option enables users to alter their BitLocker PIN or password. A user-selected password is more likely to be remembered than a randomly assigned one.

- **Network Unlock**   Enables computers on wired networks to bypass the requirement for BitLocker PIN/passwords when booting.

BitLocker requirements

BitLocker can be used with or without a *TPM chip*. A TPM chip provides the highest level of security, and if you go to the trouble of deploying BitLocker, you should strongly consider having computers that have these chips. With a TPM chip, you can configure boot environment protection. When boot environment protection is enabled, the integrity of the boot environment is checked each time the computer boots. If a modification to the boot environment has been made, the computer will be forced into BitLocker Recovery mode.

You configure the BitLocker mode using Group Policy (see Figure 9-14). You can configure the following modes:

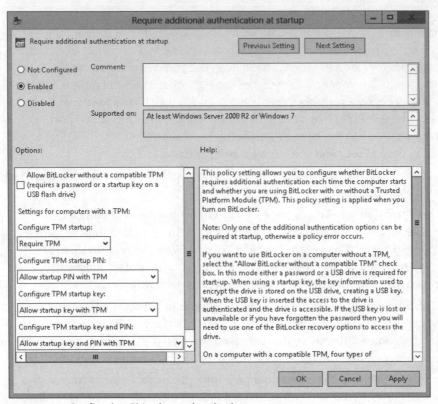

FIGURE 9-14 Configuring BitLocker authentication

- **TPM-Only Mode** When you configure this mode, the user is not prompted for a password or a PIN. This mode offers boot integrity protection. You can use this mode on servers when you have a TPM; don't have Unified Extensible Firmware Interface (UEFI) that supports Dynamic Host Configuration Protocol (DHCP) and therefore doesn't support Network Unlock; and want to protect the volume and have environment protection, but don't want to enter a password or PIN each time a reboot is required.

- **TPM Allow Startup Key** When you configure this mode, the computer can boot only when a specially prepared USB device is connected. This mode provides boot environment protection and can be used with Network Unlock on computers that meet the Network Unlock requirements.

- **TPM With PIN/Password** This is the most commonly used secure method of using BitLocker. It requires someone to perform authentication to boot without all the hassle of ensuring you never lose the startup key USB device. To boot, a password or PIN must be entered manually. In environments with Network Unlock, the PIN or password is not necessary.

- **TPM With PIN/Password And Startup Key** This option is the most secure because it requires a TPM, a boot PIN/password, and that a USB device with a startup key be connected. This level of security might be appropriate if you have an offline root Certification Authority (CA).

- **Startup Key** This option enables a computer to boot if the startup key is present. This option encrypts the hard drive, but does not provide boot integrity protection.
- **PIN/Password** This option enables a computer to boot if a password/PIN is entered. This option encrypts the hard drive, but does not provide boot integrity protection. This option can be used with VMs so that the virtual hard disk file is encrypted and can't be mounted and read.

BitLocker To Go is a version of BitLocker that can be used with removable storage devices. When connecting the BitLocker-protected device, a user needs to enter a password. After the password is entered for the device, it can be used with a compatible operating system. You can use BitLocker To Go with Windows 7 Enterprise and Ultimate editions, Windows 8, and Windows 8.1 Enterprise edition, Windows Server 2008 R2, Windows Server 2012, and Windows Server 2012 R2. BitLocker To Go does not require a TPM chip.

BitLocker Group Policy

You configure BitLocker using the policies located in the \Computer Configuration\Policies\ Administrative Templates\Windows Components\BitLocker Drive Encryption node of a Group Policy Object (GPO). These policies enable you to perform the following tasks:

- Configure BitLocker to store recovery information in Active Directory
- Choose a default network folder location of recovery passwords
- Configure encryption method and strength
- Configure startup authentication
- Configure organizational identifiers
- Block access to removable volumes not encrypted and configured with the organizational identifier

You can configure separate policies for operating system drives, fixed data drives, and removable data drives. If you configure a computer to use BitLocker, you should ensure that all drives are protected because it minimizes the chance that an unauthorized third party can recover data.

BitLocker recovery

BitLocker enables you to use a recovery key if you need to boot a computer with a TPM chip when the boot environment has changed or if you need to recover data from a BitLocker-protected volume if something has happened to the computer that originally hosted the volume. When you use BitLocker to encrypt a drive, you have the option of saving the BitLocker key in a location on a volume that is not encrypted. This file is saved as a text file that includes an identifier and a recovery key, as shown in Figure 9-15. The drawback of this method is that managing the text files quickly becomes difficult after you have more than a few computers using BitLocker.

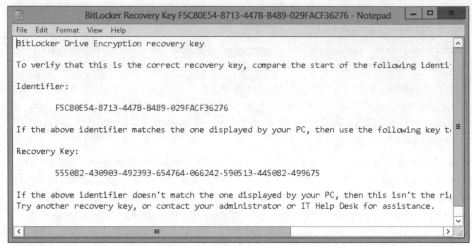

FIGURE 9-15 BitLocker recovery key

There are two better methods that you can use to manage BitLocker recovery keys:

- Active Directory backup
- Data recovery agent (DRA)

When enabled, the Store BitLocker Recovery Information In The Active Directory Domain Services (AD DS) policy, shown in Figure 9-16, backs up BitLocker recovery information to Active Directory. It's necessary to run several scripts to prepare Active Directory to support this functionality, but when enabled, administrators can view BitLocker recovery information, as in Active Directory Users And Computers, through a computer account's properties. You can configure this policy so that BitLocker is enabled only when successful backup occurs. When there are changes, these changes are automatically backed up. You can back up passwords/PINs, recovery keys, or both.

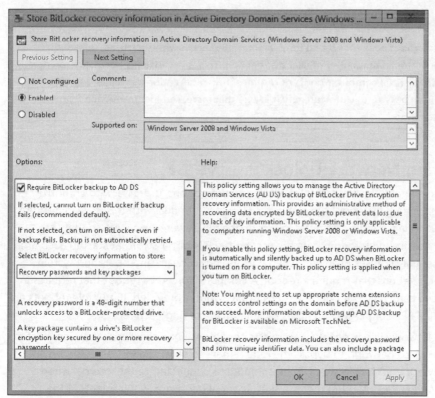

FIGURE 9-16 Configuring Active Directory BitLocker recovery

> **MORE INFO   BITLOCKER BACKUP TO ACTIVE DIRECTORY**
>
> **For more information about backing up BitLocker to Active Directory,** *see http://technet .microsoft.com/en-us/library/dd875529(v=ws.10).aspx.*

Recovering data from a BitLocker-protected volume if the host computer fails requires that you have access to the recovery key, which you use with a special utility that can then mount and read the volume, or have configured a DRA. You configure the BitLocker DRA by adding a DRA certificate to the Computer Configuration\Policies\Windows Settings\Security Settings\ Public Key Policies\BitLocker Drive Encryption node. If a volume has been encrypted prior to the configuration of this policy, you need to remove and then reapply BitLocker to ensure that the DRA certificate can decrypt encrypted volumes. When BitLocker is configured with a DRA, any computer with the appropriate certificate installed can mount and access BitLocker-encrypted volumes.

Configuring Network Unlock

When you implement BitLocker using the PIN/password options, users need to enter their PIN or password each time they boot the computer. Users tend to deal with this issue in a variety of ways, including leaving the computer in a permanently powered-on state so that they don't have to go through the rigmarole of entering the PIN or password at startup each time. This requirement also causes problems when performing software and operating system maintenance operations that require a reboot. A computer forced to reboot that requires a PIN or password can't fully boot until that PIN or password is provided. If multiple reboots are required, multiple PIN or password entries must be made during each reboot.

BitLocker Network Unlock enables computers configured for BitLocker that are connected to the internal wired network, to bypass the requirement to enter the PIN or password. BitLocker Network Unlock works only if the computer is connected to the internal wired network and only if the computer meets a specific set of hardware requirements. If the computer, such as a laptop computer, reboots when disconnected from the internal wired network, then the BitLocker PIN or password must be entered as normal.

BitLocker Network Unlock has the following requirements:

- Computers must be running Windows 8, Windows 8.1, Windows Server 2012 or Windows Server 2012 R2.

- Computer hardware must have UEFI DHCP drivers. Because Hyper-V doesn't emulate UEFI with DHCP functionality, you can't use Network Unlock with BitLocker-protected VMs. You can use Network Unlock with Hyper-V hosts protected by BitLocker.

- The BitLocker Network Unlock feature, shown in Figure 9-17, must be installed.

- Windows Deployment Services (WDS) must be installed and configured on a domain-joined computer.

- The DHCP server role must be installed and configured on a domain-joined computer.

- A network key must be installed on each computer configured with BitLocker's system volume. This key must be encrypted using a 2048-bit RSA public key stored on the server hosting the BitLocker Network Unlock feature. The Network Unlock key requires you to configure a custom certificate template based off the user template. This certificate requires a minimum key size of 2048 bits, and must use the RSA algorithm and an object identifier (OID) of 1.3.6.1.4.1.311.67.1.1

- BitLocker Network Unlock Group Policy settings must be configured. You configure this policy by adding the BitLocker Network Unlock certificate to the \Computer Configuration\Policies\Windows Settings\Security Settings\Public Key Policies\BitLocker Drive Encryption Network Unlock Certificate node.

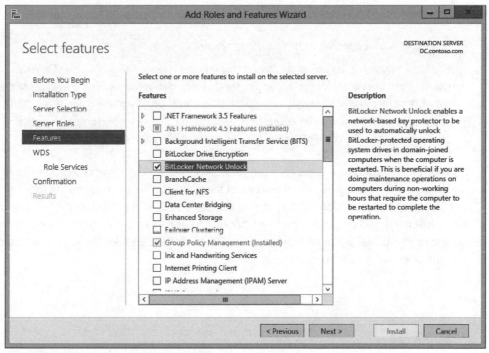

FIGURE 9-17 BitLocker Network Unlock feature

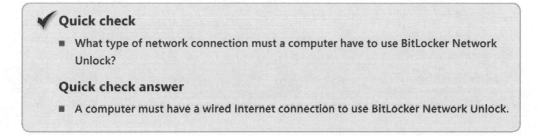

✔ **Quick check**

- What type of network connection must a computer have to use BitLocker Network Unlock?

Quick check answer

- A computer must have a wired Internet connection to use BitLocker Network Unlock.

Configuring Encrypting File System

The Encrypting File System (EFS) enables per-user encryption of files and folders. EFS has been available in Windows operating systems since the release of Windows 2000 and has supported encrypting files for multiple users since the release of Windows XP. When a user encrypts a file using EFS, only that user and a user who holds a DRA certificate (if one is configured) can read the contents of that file.

EFS is supported only on NTFS file system (NTFS) volumes; you can't use EFS on ReFS volumes. You also can't use EFS on FAT and FAT32-formatted volumes. When you copy or move an EFS encrypted file that you can decrypt to a volume that doesn't support EFS, the file is automatically decrypted. If you don't have the necessary certificate to perform decryption, the file is copied in an encrypted state.

> **REAL WORLD** **COPYING ACROSS THE NETWORK**
>
> You have to use EFS in conjunction with IPsec if EFS-encrypted files are copied across the network because the copy process copies a decrypted version of the file across the network before re-encrypting it at the destination location. If you are using IPsec, the entire process is protected by encryption. If you aren't, someone performing a packet capture can read the contents of the file as it passes from source to destination.

You can add additional users on a per-user basis through the advanced properties of a file, as shown in Figure 9-18. The drawback of this process is that it involves the user editing the file's properties, clicking Advanced, and clicking Details in the Advanced Attributes dialog box. Most users find this process too complicated to bother with on a regular basis. Active Directory Rights Management Services, a newer technology, enables the same goals to be accomplished without as many complicated steps.

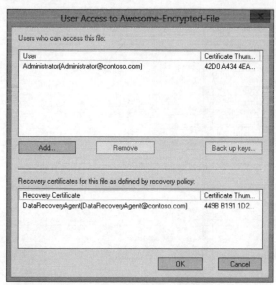

FIGURE 9-18 Sharing an EFS-encrypted file

Using EFS with an enterprise CA

When a user attempts to encrypt a file using EFS, the operating system performs a check to determine whether there is an existing EFS certificate. If there is, the operating system uses it to encrypt the file. If there isn't, the computer generates a self-signed EFS certificate. The drawback of self-signed EFS certificates is that problems can occur when a user encrypts a file on a network folder and then attempts to access that file using another computer. The problem occurs because unless credential roaming is enabled, the private key for the self-signed EFS certificate won't be available on the other computer.

If you plan to use EFS in Active Directory domain environments, you should configure EFS certificates to automatically be deployed to users by configuring autoenrollment. You should also enable credential roaming, configure the certificate to be published to Active Directory, and configure the archiving of the private key, as shown in Figure 9-19. To accomplish this, you need to make a duplicate of the basic EFS template and enable these advanced features.

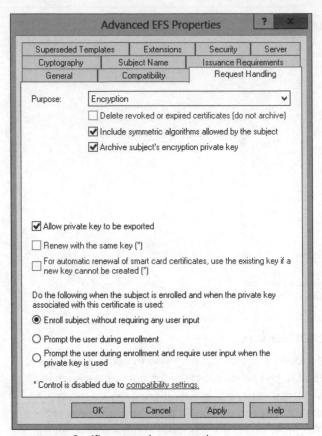

FIGURE 9-19 Certificate template properties

Taking these steps accomplishes the following goals:

- **Enabling autoenrollment**   Enables automatic deployment of an EFS certificate.

- **Enabling credential roaming**   Ensures that user credentials, including certificates, are available, independent of which computer a user logs on to.

- **Publishing certificates to Active Directory**   To encrypt a file so that it can be opened by another user, the user encrypting the file must have access to the other user's public EFS certificate. Publishing certificates to Active Directory simplifies this, providing a central repository of all users' public EFS certificates.

- **Archiving the private key**   Enables the private key to be recovered by a key recovery agent from the certificate services database.

Key and data recovery

A problematic issue with respect to enabling users to encrypt their own data is this: "How do you recover the data if the user loses the private key?" There are two general methods that you can implement to recover data encrypted by EFS:

- **Data recovery agent** A user who holds the private key for the public key configured as the DRA can read any EFS encrypted files in the organization. By default, the first Administrator account in a domain is the DRA for that domain. This presents a security risk because it means that anyone logged in with this account can read the contents of any EFS-encrypted files. You can instead issue a different user account with a data recovery certificate and configure this account as the DRA for the domain, locking out this account unless data recovery must occur. The DRA certificate uses the EFS recovery agent template. You configure this account using the \Computer Configuration\ Policies\Windows Settings\Security Settings\Public Key Policies\Encrypting File System node.

- **Key recovery agent** You can use a key recovery agent (KRA) only if key archiving is enabled on the certificate template used to issue EFS certificates. Unlike a DRA, which can be used to read any EFS-encrypted file in the domain, when you implement a KRA, the specific private key of the user who encrypted the file is recovered. That means that only that user's encrypted files can be read. This is more cumbersome to implement, but improves security because it enables the person performing data recovery to access only one user's files.

REAL WORLD **USING EFS**

There are a couple of problems with EFS. It's difficult to use when documents need to be accessed by more than one user because the only way you can configure it to work with more than one user is to edit the properties of the file, and each user needs to have the certificate published in Active Directory. The file also doesn't stay encrypted when sent as an email attachment or moved to a USB storage device formatted with a non-NTFS file system. Active Directory Rights Management Services (AD RMS) enables you to accomplish the same tasks as EFS, while making it easier to share encrypted content with other users and protect that content when transferred to other devices or sent as an email attachment.

Lesson summary

- BitLocker provides a full volume encryption solution that is transparent to users of the operating system.
- BitLocker Network Unlock enables computers connected to a wired network to bypass the requirement for entering a password or PIN at startup.
- BitLocker Network Unlock requires computers that support UEFI DHCP. It also requires the deployment of the BitLocker Network Unlock role, DHCP, WDS, and specially prepared certificates.
- BitLocker recovery passwords and keys can be backed up to Active Directory.
- You can configure a DRA for BitLocker, which enables data recovery on BitLocker-protected drives without needing to enter a specific recovery key.

- EFS enables file-level and folder-level encryption.
- You can configure a DRA for EFS. The DRA can access all EFS encrypted data.
- If you configure a custom certificate template for EFS, you can configure a KRA. This enables individual EFS private keys to be recovered from the certificate services database, enabling the decryption on a per-user basis.

Lesson review

Answer the following questions to test your knowledge of the information in this lesson. You can find the answers to these questions and explanations of why each answer choice is correct or incorrect in the "Answers" section at the end of this chapter.

1. Which of the following technologies enable a user to access an encrypted file on a file share without encrypting all files stored on the file share?

   A. EFS

   B. BitLocker

   C. IPsec

   D. SSL

2. You are planning to deploy EFS certificates through certificate services to users in your organization. You have created a new certificate services template. What should you configure to ensure that individual EFS certificates could be recovered without configuring the deployment so that a single certificate can decrypt any EFS-encrypted file?

   A. DRA

   B. KRA

   C. Credential roaming

   D. Autoenrollment

3. You want to configure a computer so that the contents of any BitLocker-encrypted volume from one of your organization's domain-joined computers are accessible, without having to extract a recovery key from Active Directory. Which of the following could you configure to accomplish this goal?

   A. Autoenrollment

   B. Credential roaming

   C. KRA

   D. DRA

4. Your organization does not have an Active Directory Certificate Services deployment. You want to ensure that BitLocker recovery keys for encrypted volumes on domain-joined computers are easy to locate on a per-computer basis, even if the computer's name is changed. Which of the following Group Policy items should you configure to accomplish this goal?

A. Provide the unique identifiers for your organization.

B. Choose drive encryption method and cipher strength.

C. Store BitLocker recovery information in AD DS.

D. Choose the default folder for the recovery password.

5. You have deployed BitLocker for all computers running Windows 8.1 in your organization. Each of these computers has a DHCP drive implemented in UEFI firmware. During software update deployment, when these computers need to reboot, it is necessary for a technician or the computer's user to enter a PIN to enable the computer to restart. You want to enable automatic restarts to occur when computers are connected to the wired network without requiring a PIN to be entered. A PIN should be required if the computer is restarting and is not connected to the wired network. Which of the following solutions should you deploy to resolve this problem? (Choose all that apply.)

A. BitLocker To Go

B. BitLocker Network Unlock

C. Domain isolation policy

D. Wake on LAN

6. Which of the following components, besides the BitLocker Network Unlock feature, are required to enable Network Unlock for BitLocker? (Choose all that apply.)

A. WDS server role

B. DHCP server role

C. WINS server role

D. Online certificate status protocol (OCSP) array

Practice exercises

The goal of this section is to provide you with hands-on practice with the following:

- Deploying FSRM
- Configuring file quotas
- Setting up a file screen
- Managing file expiration
- Configuring storage reports
- Deploying DFS
- Configuring a DFS namespace and replication
- Configuring EFS
- Enabling a DRA

To perform the exercises in this section, you need access to an evaluation version of Windows Server 2012 R2. You should also have access to virtual machines SYD-DC, MEL-DC, CBR-DC, and ADL-DC, the setup instructions for which are described in the Introduction. You should ensure that you have a checkpoint of these virtual machines that you can revert to at the end of the practice exercises. You should revert the Virtual Machines (VMs) to this initial state prior to beginning these exercises.

Exercise 1: Install the File Server Resource Manager role service and create a shared folder

In this exercise, you deploy FSRM roles. To complete this exercise, perform the following steps:

1. Start SYD-DC.

2. Start MEL-DC and sign on as Administrator.

3. Open the Windows PowerShell prompt and type the following commands.

   ```
   Add-Computer -DomainName contoso.com
   ```

4. In the Windows PowerShell Credentials dialog box, type **don_funk@contoso.com** and **Pa$$w0rd**, and click OK.

5. Type the following command in the Windows PowerShell prompt to restart the computer.`Restart-Computer`

6. Sign on to SYD-DC as Contoso\don_funk.

7. On the Manage menu, click Add Roles And Features.

8. On the Before You Begin page of the Add Roles and Features Wizard, click Next.

9. On the Select Installation Type page, click Role-Based Or Feature-Based Installation and click Next.

10. On the Select Destination Server page, click SYD-DC.contoso.com, and click Next.

11. On the Select Server Roles page, expand File And Storage Services (Installed).

12. Expand File And iSCSI Services (Installed) and click File Server Resource Manager, as shown in Figure 9-20.

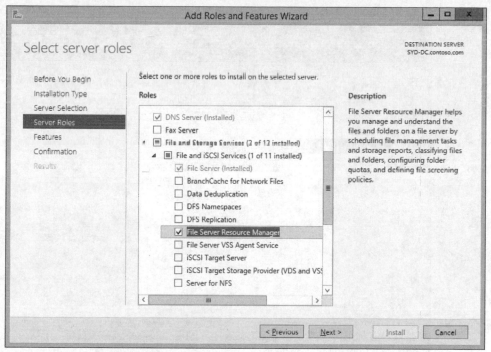

FIGURE 9-20 Adding File Server Resource Manager

13. When prompted to add features that are required for FSRM, click Add Features.

14. On the Select Server Roles page, click Next twice, and click Install.

15. Click Close to close the Add Roles and Features Wizard.

16. In Server Manager, click File And Storage Services, and then click Shares, as shown in Figure 9-21.

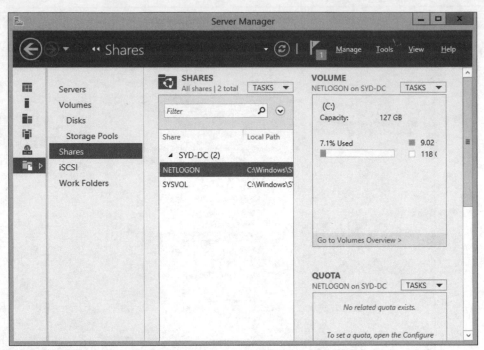

FIGURE 9-21 Configuring file shares

17. In the Central pane, click Tasks, and click New Share.

18. On the Select The Profile For This Share page, click SMB Share – Quick, as shown in Figure 9-22, and click Next.

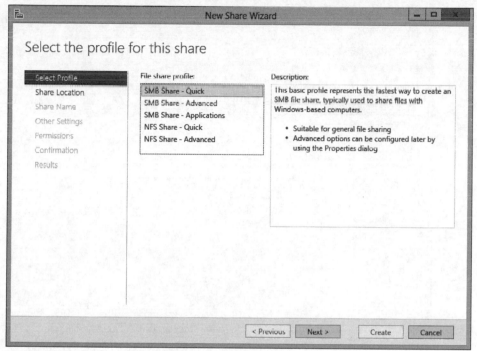

FIGURE 9-22 Creating a new SMB share

19. On the Share Location page, ensure that volume C: is selected, and click Next.

20. On the Share Name page, type the name **Hovercraft**, as shown in Figure 9-23, and click Next.

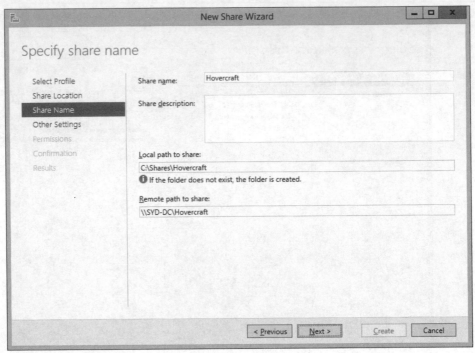

FIGURE 9-23 Share settings

21. On the Other Settings page, click Next twice.

22. On the Confirm Selections page, shown in Figure 9-24, click Create, and then click Close.

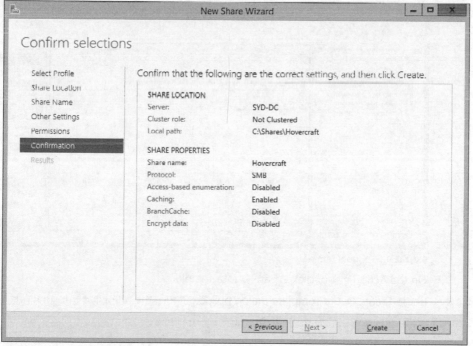

FIGURE 9-24 Confirm share settings

Exercise 2: Configure file quotas

In this exercise, you use FSRM to configure file quota templates and a file quota. To complete this exercise, perform the following steps:

1. On the Tools menu of the Server Manager console, click File Server Resource Manager.

2. In the File Server Resource Manager console, expand Quota Management and click Quota Templates, as shown in Figure 9-25.

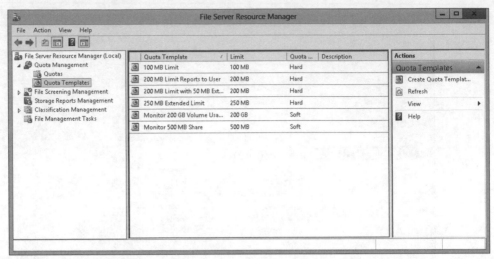

FIGURE 9-25 Quota templates

3. On the Action menu, click Create Quota Template.

4. In the Create Quota Template dialog box, configure the following information:

   - Template Name: Hard 1GB Quota

   - Limit: 1GB

5. Click Add. In the Add Threshold dialog box, click the Report tab.

6. On the Report tab, select Generate Reports and select Duplicate Files, Large Files, Least Recently Accessed Files, and Send Reports To The User Who Exceeded The Threshold, as shown in Figure 9-26. Click OK.

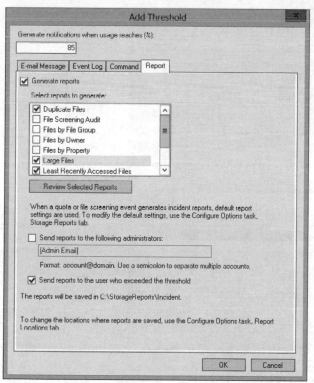

FIGURE 9-26 Configuring reports

7. Verify that the Create Quota Template dialog box matches Figure 9-27, and click OK.

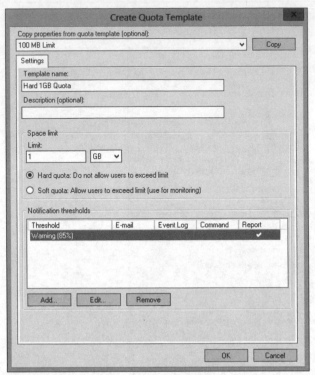

FIGURE 9-27 Creating a quota template

8. In the File Server Resource Manager node, click the Quotas node.

9. On the Action menu, click Create Quota.

10. In the Create Quota dialog box, click Browse.

11. In the Browse For Folder dialog box, expand Local Disk (C:), expand Shares, and select Hovercraft, as shown in Figure 9-28. Click OK.

FIGURE 9-28 Selecting a folder

12. In the Create Quota dialog box, click the Derive Properties From This Quota Template (Recommended) drop-down menu and click Hard 1GB Quota, as shown in Figure 9-29. Click Create.

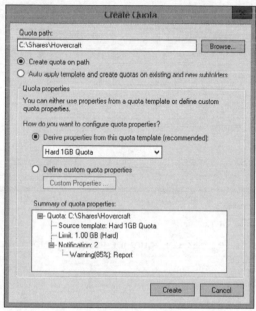

FIGURE 9-29 Creating a quota

Exercise 3: Configure file screen

In this exercise, you configure file groups, file screen templates, and a file screen. To complete this exercise, perform the following steps:

1. In the FSRM console, expand the File Screening Management node and click File Groups, as shown in Figure 9-30.

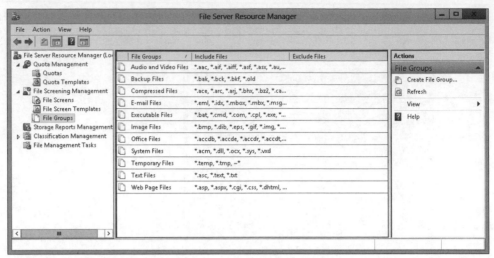

FIGURE 9-30 File groups

2. On the Actions pane, click Create File Group.

3. In the Create File Group Properties dialog box, configure the following information and click Add, as shown in Figure 9-31:

   - File Group Name: Disk Image Files

   - Files To Include: *.iso, *.wim, *.vhd, *.vhdx

FIGURE 9-31 Creating a file group

4. Click OK to close the Create File Group Properties dialog box.

5. In the FSRM console, click File Screen Templates.

6. In the Actions pane, click Create File Screen Template.

7. In the Create File Screen Template dialog box, configure the following information, as shown in Figure 9-32:

- Template Name: **Block Disk Images And Compressed Files**
- Screening Type: **Active Screening**
- Select File Groups To Block: **Compressed Files, Disk Image Files**

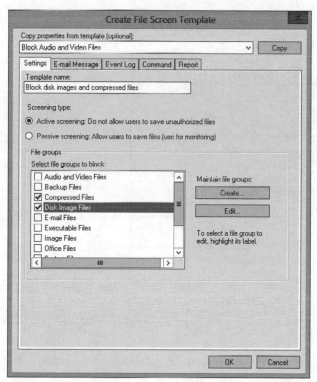

FIGURE 9-32 Creating a file screen template

8. On the Report tab, select Generate Reports, File Screening Audit, and Send Reports To The User Who Attempted To Save An Unauthorized File; then click OK, as shown in Figure 9-33.

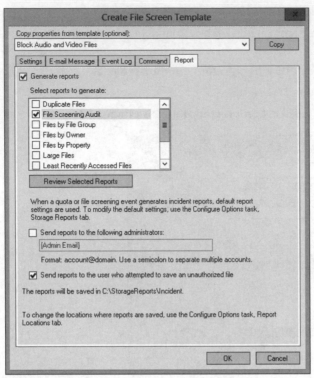

FIGURE 9-33 Selecting reports on the Report tab

9. Click the File Screens node.

10. On the Action menu, click Create File Screen.

11. In the Create File Screen dialog box, click Browse, navigate to Local Disk (C:)\Shares\Hovercraft, and click OK.

12. On the Derive Properties From This File Screen Template (Recommended) drop-down menu, click Block Disk Images And Compressed Files, as shown in Figure 9-34, and click Create.

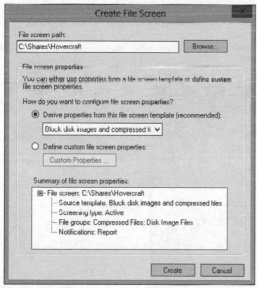

FIGURE 9-34 Configuring a file screen

Exercise 4: Configure file expiration

In this exercise, you configure a file expiration task for files stored on the Hovercraft share. To complete this exercise, perform the following steps:

1. On SYD-DC, click File Explorer on the taskbar.

2. Double-click Local Disk (C:)

3. Click the New Folder item on the title bar.

4. Name the new folder **Expired_Files**.

5. Close File Explorer.

6. In the FSRM, click File Management Tasks.

7. In the Actions pane, click Create File Management Task.

8. On the General tab of the Create File Management Task dialog box, type the task name **Move Old Files**.

9. On the Scope tab of the Create File Management Tasks dialog box, configure the following:

   - Application Files
   - Backup And Archival Files
   - Group Files
   - User Files

10. Next to the Set Folder Management Properties link, click Add.

11. In the Browse For Folder dialog box, expand Local Disk (C:), expand Shares, click Hovercraft, and click OK.

12. Verify that the Scope tab of the Create File Management Task dialog box looks the same as Figure 9-35.

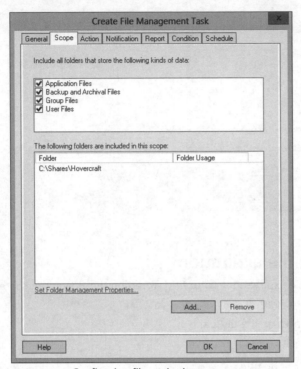

FIGURE 9-35 Configuring file expiration scope

13. On the Action tab, click Browse.

14. On the Browse For Folder directory, expand Local Disk (C:), click Expired_Files, and click OK.

15. Verify that File Expiration is selected next to Type.

16. On the Condition tab, select Days Since File Was Last Accessed, and set the value to 365, as shown in Figure 9-36.

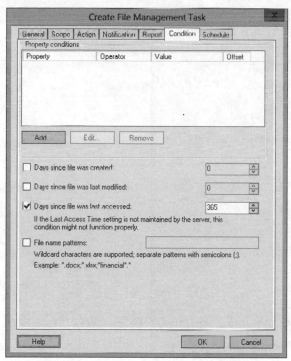

FIGURE 9-36 Configuring file expiration task conditions

17. On the Schedule tab, set the task to run at 1:00 P.M. every Monday, as shown in Figure 9-37. Click OK.

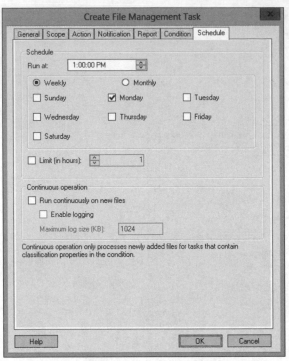

FIGURE 9-37 Configuring the file expiration task schedule

Exercise 5: Configure storage reports

In this exercise, you use FSRM to configure storage reports. To complete this exercise, perform the following steps:

1. In FSRM, click the Storage Reports Management node.
2. In the Actions pane, click Schedule A New Report Task.
3. In the Storage Reports Task Properties dialog box, type the name **Hovercraft**, as shown in Figure 9-38.

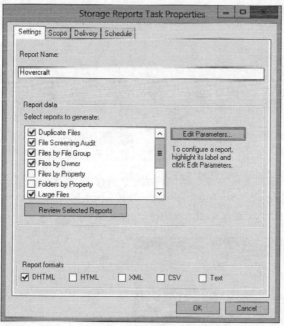

FIGURE 9-38 Selecting storage reports

4. Click Large Files, and then click Edit Parameters.

5. In the Report Parameters dialog box, set the minimum file size to 25 MB, as shown in Figure 9-39, and click OK.

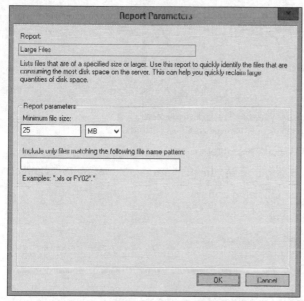

FIGURE 9-39 Configuring large file report settings

6. Click Files By File Group, and click Edit Parameters.

7. In the Report Parameters dialog box, click Selected File Groups, select the following file groups and click OK:

   ■ Audio And Video Files

   ■ Backup Files

   ■ Compressed Files

   ■ Disk Image Files

   ■ Image Files

   ■ Office Files

8. Click Least Recently Accessed Files, and click Edit Parameters.

9. In the Report Parameters dialog box, in the Minimum Days Since The Last File Was Accessed text box, type a value of **300**, as shown in Figure 9-40, and click OK.

FIGURE 9-40 Configuring the least recently accessed files settings

10. Click Quota Usage and click Edit Parameters.

11. In the Report Parameters dialog box, set the minimum quota usage to 76 and click OK.

12. On the Scope tab, select the following options:

    ■ Application Files

    ■ Backup And Archival Files

    ■ Group Files

    ■ User Files

13. On the Scope tab, next to the Set Folder Management Properties link, click Add.

14. In the Browse For Folder dialog box, expand Local Disk (C:), expand Shares, select Hovercraft, and click OK.

15. On the Schedule tab, click Weekly, and configure the report to run on Friday at 3:00 P.M., as shown in Figure 9-41, and click OK.

FIGURE 9-41 Configuring task schedules

Exercise 6: Install DFS

In this exercise, you install DFS on SYD-DC and MEL-DC. To complete this exercise, perform the following steps:

1. Ensure that SYD-DC and MEL-DC are powered on.

2. On SYD-DC, in the Server Manager console, click Dashboard, and click Add Other Servers To Manage.

3. In the Add Servers dialog box, click Find Now, click MEL-DC, and then click the arrow button to add MEL-DC to the list of selected computers (see Figure 9-42). Click OK.

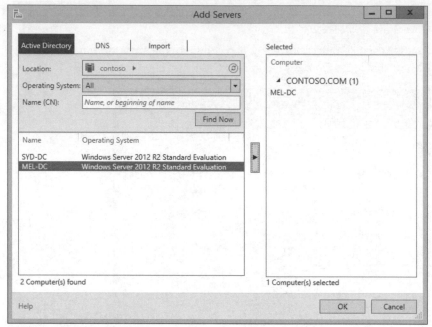

FIGURE 9-42 Adding servers

4. Click All Servers. On the Manage menu, click Add Roles And Features.

5. On the Before You Begin page of the Add Roles and Features, click Next.

6. On the Select Installation Type page, click Role-Based Or Feature-Based Installation and click Next.

7. On the Select Destination Server page, click MEL-DC.contoso.com, and click Next.

8. On the Select Server Roles page, expand File And Storage Services (Installed), expand File And iSCSI Services, and select DFS Namespaces and DFS Replication, as shown in Figure 9-43.

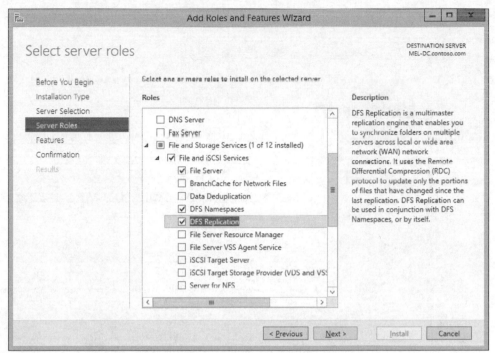

FIGURE 9-43 Adding DFS namespaces and replication

9. When prompted to add features, click Add Features, click Next twice, click Install, and click Close.

10. Repeat steps 4 through 9, except select SYD-DC.contoso.com instead of MEL-DC in step 7 (see Figure 9-44).

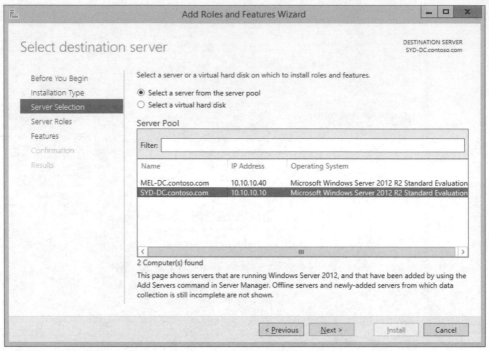

FIGURE 9-44 Selecting a destination server

Exercise 7: Create a DFS namespace and add a namespace server

In this exercise, you create a DFS namespace and add a namespace server. To complete this exercise, perform the following steps:

1. In Server Manager on SYD-DC, click Tools and click DFS Management.

2. Click the Namespaces node. In the Actions pane, click New Namespace.

3. On the Namespace Server page of the New Namespace Wizard, click Browse.

4. In the Select Computer dialog box, type **SYD-DC**, click Check Names, and click OK.

5. On the Namespace Server page, click Next.

6. On the Namespace Name And Settings page, type **Admin_Docs** and click Next.

7. On the Namespace Type page, click Domain-Based Namespace and ensure that Enable Windows Server 2008 Mode is enabled, as shown in Figure 9-45. Click Next.

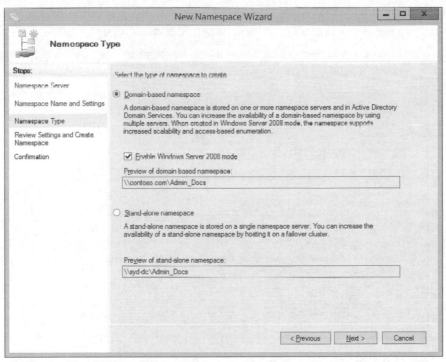

FIGURE 9-45 Choosing the namespace type

8. On the Review Settings and Create Namespace page, click Create. When the namespace is created, click Close.

9. In the DFS Management console, click the \\Contoso.com\Admin_Docs node, as shown in Figure 9-46, and click Add Namespace Server.

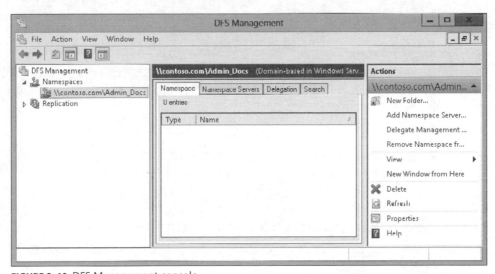

FIGURE 9-46 DFS Management console

10. In the Add Namespace Server dialog box, click Browse.

11. In the Select Computer dialog box, type **MEL-DC**, click Check Names, and click OK.

12. Verify that the Add Namespace Server dialog box appears the same as the one shown in Figure 9-47, and click OK.

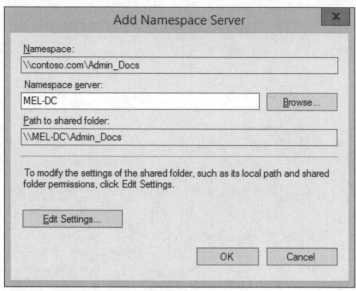

FIGURE 9-47 Adding a namespace server

13. Click the Namespace Servers tab and verify that the entries for both SYD-DC and MEL-DC are present, as shown on Figure 9-48.

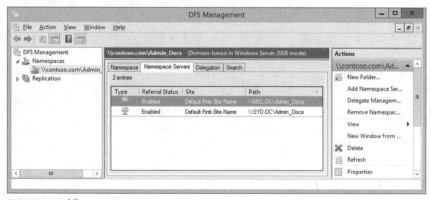

FIGURE 9-48 View namespace servers

Exercise 8: Configure DFS replication

In this exercise, you configure DFS replication. To complete this exercise, perform the following steps:

1. Sign on to MEL-DC as contoso\don_funk.

2. On the taskbar, click File Manager.

3. Click Computer, and double-click Local Disk (C:).

4. Click the New Folder icon on the title bar. Name the new folder **Space_Station**.

5. Sign off from MEL-DC and switch to SYD-DC.

6. On SYD-DC, in the DFS Management console, click Replication.

7. In the Actions pane, click New Replication Group.

8. On the Replication Group Type page of the New Replication Group Wizard, click Multipurpose Replication Group, as shown in Figure 9-49, and click Next.

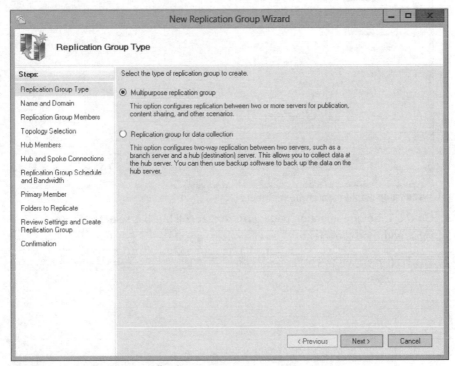

FIGURE 9-49 Configuring a replication group

9. On the Name And Domain page, type the name **Admin_Docs_Repl_Group** in the Name Of Replication Group box, and click Next.

10. On the Replication Group Members page, click Add.

11. In the Select Computers dialog box, type **SYD-DC; MEL-DC**, click Check Names, and click OK.

12. Verify that the Replication Group Members page matches Figure 9-50, and click Next.

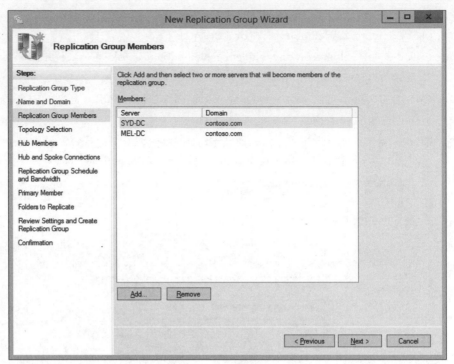

FIGURE 9-50 Replication group members

13. On the Topology Selection page, ensure that Full Mesh is selected, as shown in Figure 9-51, and then click Next.

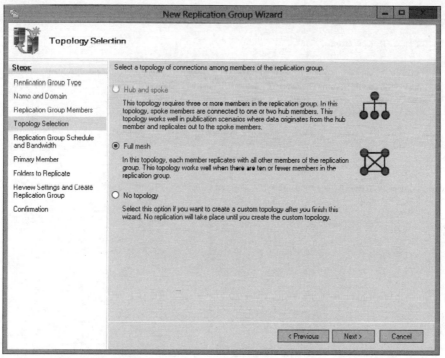

FIGURE 9-51 Replication topology

14. On the Replication Group Schedule And Bandwidth page, click Replicate Continuously Using The Specified Bandwidth, and click Next.

15. On the Primary Member page, use the drop-down menu to select MEL-DC, as shown in Figure 9-52, and click Next.

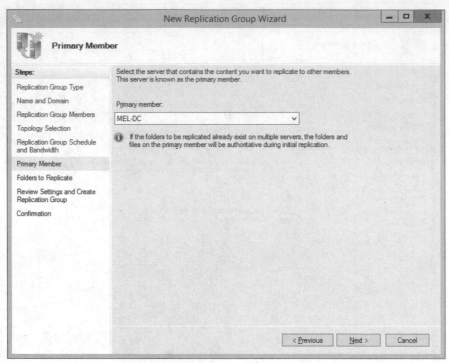

FIGURE 9-52 Configuring the primary member

16. On the Folders To Replicate page, click Add.

17. In the Add Folder To Replicate dialog box, click Browse.

18. In the Browse For Folder dialog box, click Space_Station, and click OK twice.

19. Verify that the Folders To Replicate dialog box looks the same as Figure 9-53, and click Next.

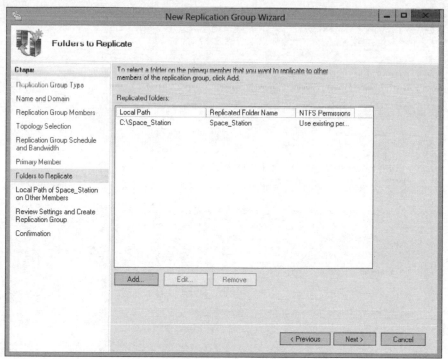

FIGURE 9-53 Choosing folders to replicate

20. On the Local Path of Space_Station On Other Members, click SYD-DC, and click Edit.

21. In the Edit dialog box, click Enabled, and click Browse.

22. In the Browse For Folder dialog box, click C:\ and then click Make New Folder.

23. Name the new folder **Space_Station** and click OK.

24. Verify that the Edit dialog box matches Figure 9-54, and click OK.

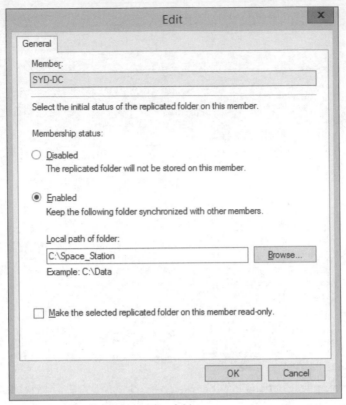

FIGURE 9-54 Configuring a replica folder

25. On the Local Path of Space_Station On Other Members page, click Next.

26. On the Review Settings And Create Replication Group page, click Create, and then click Close.

27. In the Replication Delay dialog box, click OK.

Exercise 9: Install Enterprise CA

In this exercise, you install an enterprise root CA to support BitLocker and EFS. To complete this exercise, perform the following steps:

1. On the Manage menu of the Server Manager console on SYD-DC, click Add Roles And Features.

2. On the Before You Begin page of the Add Roles and Features, click Next.

3. On the Select Installation Type page, click Role-Based Or Feature-Based Installation, and click Next.

4. On the Select Destination Server page, click SYD-DC.contoso.com, and click Next.

5. On the Select Server Roles page, click Active Directory Certificate Services, as shown in Figure 9-55.

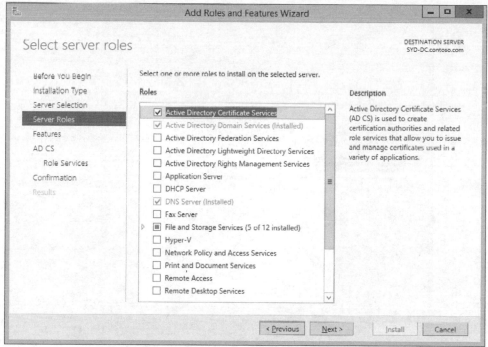

FIGURE 9-55 Adding an AD CS role

6. In the Add Roles And Features Wizard, click Add Features, and then click Next.

7. On the Select Features page, click Next.

8. On the AD CS page, click Next.

9. On the Select Role Services page, ensure that Certification Authority is selected, as shown in Figure 9-56, and click Next.

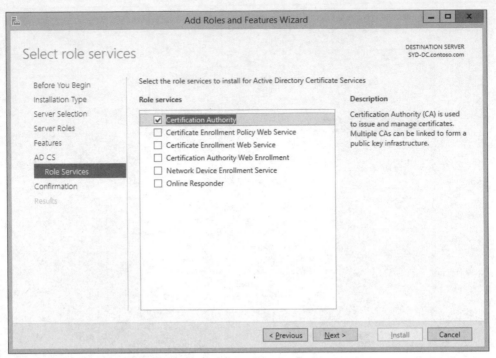

FIGURE 9-56 Adding Certification Authority

10. On the Confirmation page, click Install, and then click Close.

11. In Server Manager, click Refresh.

12. Click the Warning icon, and then click Configure Active Directory Certificate Services.

13. On the Credentials page of the AD CS Configuration Wizard, verify that the Credentials setting is configured as CONTOSO\don_funk, and click Next.

14. On the Role Services page, click Certification Authority, and click Next.

15. On the Setup Type page, click Enterprise CA, as shown in Figure 9-57, and click Next.

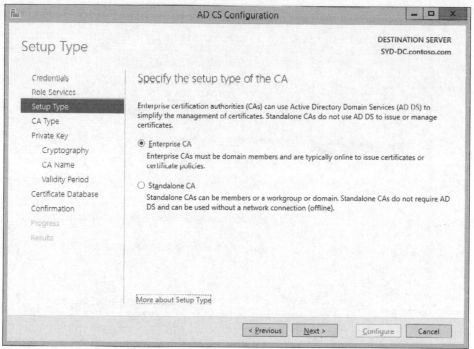

FIGURE 9-57 Configuring an Enterprise CA

16. On the CA Type page, click Root CA, and click Next.

17. On the Private Key page, click Create A New Private Key, and click Next.

18. On the Cryptography page, select SHA256 and specify a key length of 4096, as shown in Figure 9-58, and click Next.

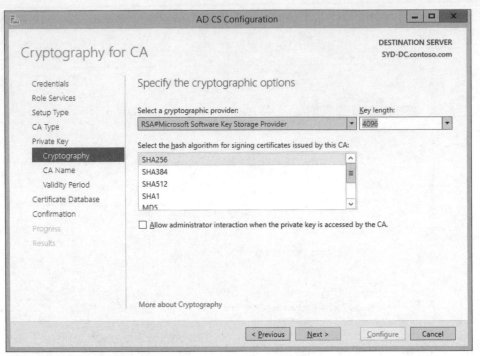

FIGURE 9-58 Selecting CA cryptography

19. On the CA Name page, click Next.

20. On the Validity Period page, set a period of 10 years, as shown in Figure 9-59, and then click Next.

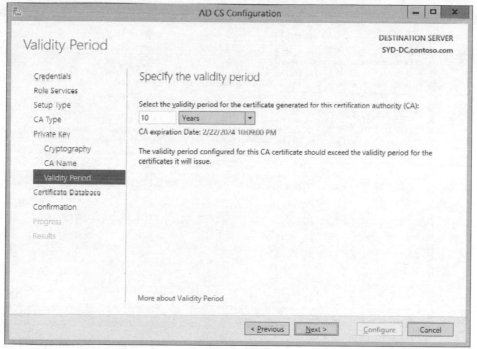

FIGURE 9-59 Configuring the CA certificate validity period

21. On the Certificate Database page, click Next.

22. On the Confirmation page, click Configure, and then click Close.

Exercise 10: Configure certificate templates

In this exercise, you configure certificate templates to be used to support data recovery and EFS. To complete this exercise, perform the following steps:

1. In Server Manager on SYD-DC, click the Tools menu, and then click Certification Authority.

2. In the Certification Authority console, expand Contoso-SYD-DC-CA, and click Certificate Templates, as shown in Figure 9-60.

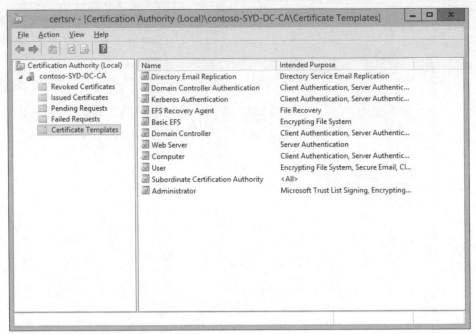

FIGURE 9-60 Certificate templates

3. On the Action menu, click Manage.

4. In the Certificate Templates console, click Basic EFS.

5. On the Action menu, click Duplicate Template.

6. On the Compatibility tab, set the Compatibility Settings For Certification Authority to Windows Server 2012 R2. In the Resulting Changes dialog box, click OK.

7. Under Certificate Recipient, click Windows 7 / Windows 2008 R2. In the Resulting Changes dialog box, click OK.

8. On the General tab, set the template display name to Advanced EFS.

9. On the Superseded Templates tab, click Add.

10. In the Add Superseded Template dialog box, click Basic EFS, as shown in Figure 9-61, and click OK.

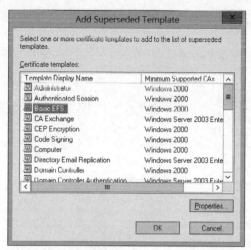

FIGURE 9-61 Configuring superseded templates

11. On the Security tab, click Authenticated Users and select the Read (Allow), Enroll
(Allow), and Autoenroll (Allow) permissions (see Figure 9-62), and click OK.

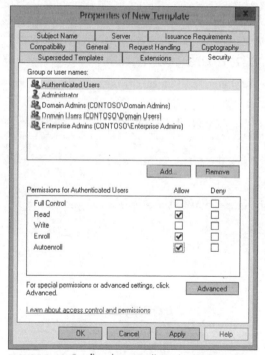

FIGURE 9-62 Configuring enrollment permissions

12. Right-click the EFS Recovery Agent template, and click Properties.

13. On the Security tab, click Authenticated Users, click Enroll, and then click OK.

14. Close the Certificates Templates console.

15. In the Certification Authority console, right-click the Certificate Templates node, and click New Certificate Template To Issue.

16. In the Enable Certificate Templates dialog box, click Advanced EFS, as shown in Figure 9-63, and click OK.

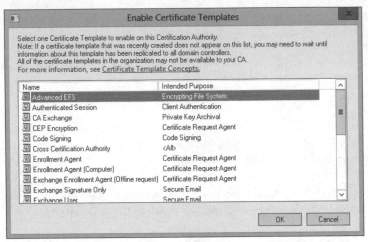

FIGURE 9-63 Selecting a template

Exercise 11: Configure certificate enrollment

In this exercise, you configure certificate enrollment and enroll certificates. To complete this exercise, perform the following steps:

1. In Server Manager on SYD-DC, click Tools, and click Active Directory Users And Computers.

2. Click the Users container, and then click the Administrator account.

3. On the Action menu, click Copy.

4. Set the Full Name and User Logon Name fields to **DataRecoveryAgent**, as shown in Figure 9-64, and click Next.

FIGURE 9-64 Creating an account

5. On the Copy Object – User page, set the Password and Confirm Password text boxes to **Pa$$w0rd**, click Next, and click Finish.

6. Sign off from SYD-DC and sign on as DataRecoveryAgent with the password **Pa$$w0rd**.

7. Click the Windows PowerShell icon on the taskbar.

8. In the Windows PowerShell window, type **mmc.exe** and press Enter.

9. In the User Account Control dialog box, click Yes.

10. In the Console1 (Console Root) dialog box, click File, and click Add/Remove Snap-In.

11. In the Add Or Remove Snap-Ins dialog box, click Certificates, as shown in Figure 9-65, and then click Add.

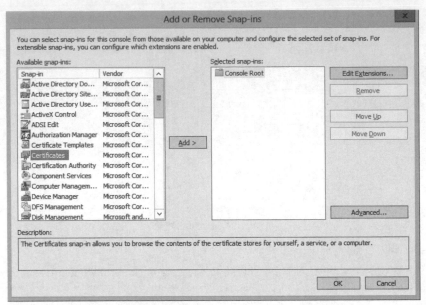

FIGURE 9-65 Adding the Certificates snap-in

12. In the Certificates Snap-In Dialog Box, click My User Account, and click Finish. Click OK to close the Add Or Remove Snap-Ins dialog box.

13. Expand the Certificates – Current User node, and click the Personal node.

14. On the Action menu, click All Tasks, and click Request New Certificate.

15. On the Before You Begin page, click Next.

16. On the Select Certificate Enrollment Policy page, click Active Directory Enrollment Policy, and click Next.

17. On the Request Certificates page, click EFS Recovery Agent, as shown in Figure 9-66, click Enroll, and then click Finish.

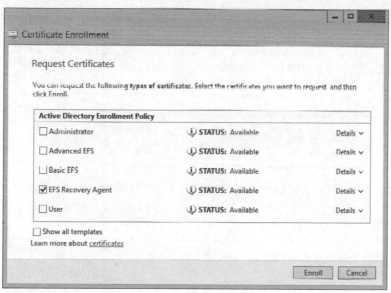

FIGURE 9-66 Selecting the certificate template

18. In Console1, expand Personal, and click Certificates.

19. Right-click DataRecoveryAgent, click All Tasks, and click Export.

20. On the Welcome To The Certificate Export Wizard page of the Certificate Export Wizard, click Next.

21. On the Export Private Key page, click No, Do Not Export The Private Key, as shown in Figure 9-67, and click Next.

FIGURE 9-67 Exporting the private key

22. On the Export File Format page, click Next.

23. On the File To Export page, click Browse.

24. In the Save As dialog box, click Local Disk (C:), and click New Folder. Name the folder **DRA**. Set the file name to C:\DRA\DRA-CERT.cer, click Save, click Next, click Finish, and click OK.

25. Close the Certificates console (Console 1) without saving changes.

26. Sign off SYD-DC and then sign back on as Contoso\Administrator.

Exercise 12: Configure EFS-related Group Policies

In this exercise, you configure EFS-related Group Policy items. To complete this exercise, perform the following steps:

1. In Server Manager, click Tools, and then click Group Policy Management.

2. In the Group Policy Management Console (GPMC), expand Forest: Contoso.com, Domains, and Contoso.com; then click Group Policy Objects (see Figure 9-68).

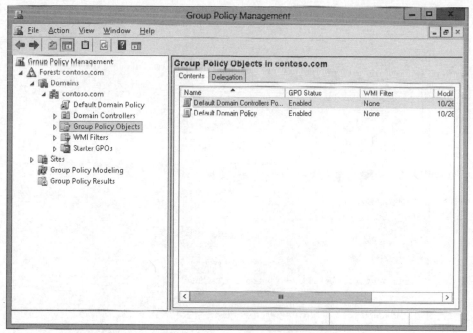

FIGURE 9-68 Configuring GPOs

3. Right-click the Default Domain Policy, and click Edit.

4. In the Group Policy Management Editor, expand the User Configuration\Policies\ Windows Settings\Security Settings\Public Key Policies node.

5. Double-click Certificate Services Client – Certificate Enrollment Policy. Set the Configuration Model setting to Enabled, as shown in Figure 9-69, and click OK.

FIGURE 9-69 Configuring client enrollment policy

6. Double-click the Certificate Services Client – Credential Roaming policy.

7. In the Certificate Services Client – Credential Roaming properties dialog box, click Enabled, and click OK twice.

8. Double-click the Certificate Services Client – Auto-Enrollment policy.

9. In the Certificate Services Client – Auto-Enrollment policy, set the Configuration Model to Enabled, and select Update Certificates That Use Certificate Templates, as shown in Figure 9-70. Click OK.

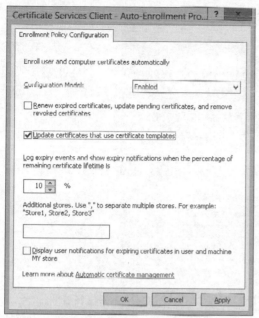

FIGURE 9-70 Configuring client autoenrollment

10. In the Group Policy Management Editor, expand the Computer Configuration\Policies\ Windows Settings\Security Settings\Public Key Policies node.

11. Click the Encryption File System node, and then click the Administrator certificate.

12. Click Action, and then click Delete. In the Certificates dialog box, click Yes.

13. Right-click the Encrypting File System node, and click Add Data Recovery Agent.

14. On the Welcome To The Add Recovery Agent Wizard page of the Recovery Agent Wizard, click Next.

15. On the Select Recovery Agents page, click Browse Folders.

16. In the Open dialog box, navigate to C:\DRA, click Dra-cert, and click Open.

17. Verify that the Select Recovery Agents page matches the one in Figure 9-71, click Next, and click Finished.

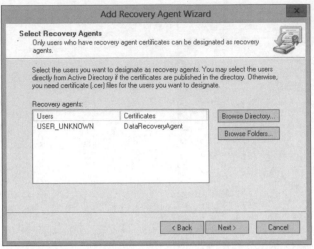

FIGURE 9-71 Configuring the recovery agent

Exercise 13: Configure BitLocker-related policies

In this exercise, you configure BitLocker-related Group Policy items. To complete this exercise, perform the following steps:

1. Ensure that the Group Policy Management Editor is open from the previous exercise and that you are editing the Default Domain Policy.

2. Navigate to the Computer Configuration\Policies\Windows Settings\Security Settings\ Public Key Policies node.

3. Right-click the BitLocker Drive Encryption node, and click Add Data Recovery Agent.

4. In the Welcome To The Add Recovery Agent Wizard dialog box, click Next.

5. On the Select Recovery Agents page, click Browse Folders.

6. In the Open dialog box, navigate to C:\DRA, click Dra-cert, and click Open.

7. Click Next, and click Finish.

8. Verify that the certificate issued to DataRecoveryAgent is listed when the BitLocker Drive Encryption node is selected, as shown in Figure 9-72.

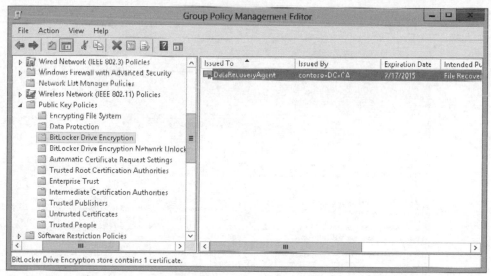

FIGURE 9-72 Configuring the BitLocker DRA

9. Expand the Computer Configuration\Policies\Administrative Templates\Windows Components node, and select BitLocker Drive Encryption.

10. Double-click the Store BitLocker Recovery Information In Active Directory Domain Services policy.

11. Set the Store BitLocker Recovery Information In Active Directory Domain Services policy to Enabled. Ensure that the policy is configured so that Require BitLocker Backup To AD DS is selected and that Recovery Passwords And Key Packages are stored, as shown in Figure 9-73, and click OK.

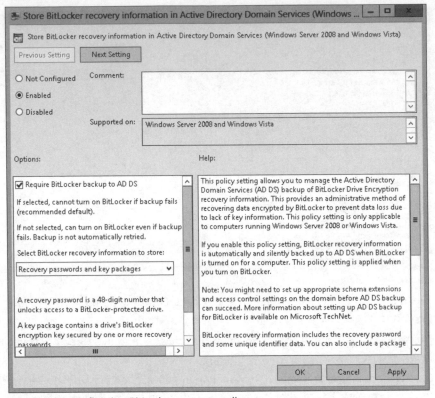

FIGURE 9-73 Configuring BitLocker recovery policy

12. Close the GPME.

Suggested practice exercises

The following additional practice exercises are designed to give you more opportunities to practice what you've learned and to help you successfully master the lessons presented in this chapter.

- **Exercise 1**   Configure a new file screen on the Hovercraft share that blocks text files. Create a text file on MEL-DC and attempt to copy this file to the Hovercraft share.
- **Exercise 2**   Verify that DFS works by copying a file to the Space_Station folder on volume C of MEL-DC, and checking that it automatically replicates to the Space_Station folder on Volume C of SYD-DC.
- **Exercise 3**   Create an additional domain-based user account that can sign on to ADL-DC. Sign on and verify that this account is automatically issued a certificate for EFS. Create a file and use EFS to encrypt it. Verify that the file cannot be opened when logged in as Contoso\Administrator, but that the file can be opened when using the DataRecoveryAgent account.
- **Exercise 4**   Add a DFS replica of the Space_Station folder on CBR-DC.

Answers

This section contains the answers to the lesson review questions in this chapter.

Lesson 1

1. **Correct answer: B**
   - **A.** **Incorrect.** A file classification rule enables a classification to be assigned to a file based on the file's properties.
   - **B.** **Correct.** A file screen enables you to block files from being written to shared folders. In this case, you can create a file screen using the existing Audio And Video Files file group.
   - **C.** **Incorrect.** It is not necessary to create a file screen template to screen files. You use a file screen template when you want to apply the same file screen settings to multiple file shares.
   - **D.** **Incorrect.** File groups are collections of files, such as audio files or office documents. Because there is an existing file group for audio and video files, it is not necessary to create a new one.

2. **Correct answer. B**
   - **A.** **Incorrect.** A file screen already applies to the shared folder. You should use a file screen template only when you want to apply the same file screen to multiple shared folders on the same server.
   - **B.** **Correct.** You use a file screen exception to create an exception, enabling certain file types to be stored that a file screen on an existing shared folder currently blocks. You can apply file screen exceptions to subfolders.
   - **C.** **Incorrect.** A file classification rule enables a classification to be assigned to a file based on the file's properties.
   - **D.** **Incorrect.** File groups are collections of files, such as audio files or office documents. You don't configure a file group to accomplish this goal; you configure a file screen exception.

3. **Correct answer: C**
   - **A.** **Incorrect.** A file group is a collection of files. Although it is possible to create a file group that incorporates the contents of the six different file groups, it is less effort to configure a file screen template.
   - **B.** **Incorrect.** You use a file screen exception to allow files blocked by a file screen to be written to the target folder.
   - **C.** **Correct.** File screen templates enable you to apply the same file screen settings to multiple folders.
   - **D.** **Incorrect.** Quota templates enable you to apply the same quotas to multiple folders.

4. **Correct answer: D**

A. **Incorrect.** You use a file screen to block specific file types from being written to a location. You can't use a file screen to apply storage limits.

B. **Incorrect.** A quota is an applied quota template. In this instance, you are creating 40 quotas by applying a single quota template.

C. **Incorrect.** File screen templates enable you to apply the same file screen to multiple locations. You can't use a file screen template to apply storage limits.

D. **Correct.** Quota templates are quota settings that you can apply to multiple file shares.

5. **Correct answer: B**

A. **Incorrect.** A 500 MB hard quota would block users from storing more than 500 MB on the file share.

B. **Correct.** You configure a 1 GB hard quota and a 50 percent notification threshold.

C. **Incorrect.** You don't configure a soft quota because it enables users to exceed the 1 GB limit.

D. **Incorrect.** You don't configure a soft quota because this enables users to exceed the 1 GB limit.

6. **Correct answer: C**

A. **Incorrect.** Hard quotas block users from storing data.

B. **Incorrect.** Hard quotas block users from storing data.

C. **Correct.** You can configure a 500 MB soft quota to send one type of notification at the 100 percent threshold and a different type of notification at the 150 percent threshold.

D. **Incorrect.** Hard quotas block users from storing data.

7. **Correct answers: A and C**

A. **Correct.** Selecting this report enables users to see which files they haven't used recently.

B. **Incorrect.** This report enables users that are subject to the quota to see how much of the assigned quota they are consuming.

C. **Correct.** Selecting this report enables users to see large files that they have stored.

D. **Incorrect.** Selecting this report enables users to see which files stored in the folder subject to the quota are duplicates.

Lesson 2

1. **Correct answers: A and D**

A. **Correct.** Hub and spoke topology enables you to configure replication with hub servers, on which content updates occur; and spoke servers, on which content updates rarely occur. Hub servers replicate with each other as well as with spoke servers. Spoke servers replicate only with hub servers.

B. **Incorrect.** Full mesh topology enables replication between all members of the replication group. It is unsuitable if there are more than 10 servers in the replication group.

C. **Incorrect.** A domain-based DFS namespace can support more than 5,000 folder targets and remote differential compression only if the hosting domain is running at the Windows Server 2008 level or higher, and the forest is at the Windows Server 2003 level or higher.

D. **Correct.** A stand-alone DFS namespace is suitable when you don't require fault tolerance namespace servers or you're willing to place the namespace server on a failover cluster, but when you do need to support between 5,000 and 50,000 folder targets in a domain that isn't running at the Windows Server 2008 functional level or higher.

2. **Correct answers: B and C**

A. **Incorrect.** A stand-alone DFS namespace is suitable when you don't require fault tolerance namespace servers or are willing to place the namespace server on a failover cluster, but when you do need to support between 5,000 and 50,000 folder targets in a domain that isn't running at the Windows Server 2008 functional level or higher.

B. **Correct.** A domain-based DFS namespace can support more than 5,000 folder targets and remote differential compression only if the hosting domain is running at the Windows Server 2008 level or higher, and the forest is at the Windows Server 2003 level or higher.

C. **Correct.** Full mesh topology enables replication between all members of the replication group. It is unsuitable if there are more than 10 servers in the replication group.

D. **Incorrect.** Hub and spoke topology enables you to configure replication with hub servers, on which content updates occur; and spoke servers, on which content updates rarely occur. Hub servers replicate with each other as well as with spoke servers. Spoke servers replicate only with hub servers.

3. **Correct answers: B and D**

A. **Incorrect.** Hub and spoke topology enables you to configure replication with hub servers, on which content updates occur, and spoke servers, on which content updates rarely occur. Hub servers replicate with each other as well as with spoke servers. Spoke servers replicate only with hub servers.

B.   Correct. Full mesh topology enables replication between all members of the replication group. It is unsuitable if there are more than 10 servers in the replication group.

C.   Incorrect. A domain-based DFS namespace can support more than 5,000 folder targets and remote differential compression only if the hosting domain is running at the Windows Server 2008 level or higher, and the forest is at the Windows Server 2003 level or higher.

D.   Correct. A stand-alone DFS namespace is suitable when you don't require fault tolerance namespace servers or are willing to place the namespace server on a failover cluster, but when you do need to support between 5,000 and 50,000 folder targets in a domain that isn't running at the Windows Server 2008 functional level or higher.

4.   **Correct answers: B and D**

A.   Incorrect. A stand-alone DFS namespace is suitable when you don't require fault tolerance namespace servers or are willing to place the namespace server on a failover cluster, but when you do need to support between 5,000 and 50,000 folder targets in a domain that isn't running at the Windows Server 2008 functional level or higher.

B.   Correct. A domain-based DFS namespace can support more than 5,000 folder targets and remote differential compression only if the hosting domain is running at the Windows Server 2008 level or higher, and the forest is at the Windows Server 2003 level or higher.

C.   Incorrect. Full mesh topology enables replication between all members of the replication group. It is unsuitable if there are more than 10 servers in the replication group.

D.   Correct. Hub and spoke topology enables you to configure replication with hub servers, on which content updates occur; and spoke servers, on which content updates rarely occur. Hub servers replicate with each other as well as with spoke servers. Spoke servers replicate only with hub servers.

Lesson 3

1.   **Correct answer: A**

A.   Correct. EFS enables you to encrypt individual files and folders.

B.   Incorrect. BitLocker enables you to fully encrypt a volume. You can't use BitLocker to encrypt specific files.

C.   Incorrect. IPsec enables encrypted and authenticated communication between hosts on a network. You can't use this technology.

D.   Incorrect. Secure Sockets Layer (SSL) certificates enable secure communication, usually with web servers, but also with other servers such as FTP servers.

2. **Correct answer: B**

   A. **Incorrect.** When you specify a DRA, the specified certificate can decrypt encrypted data. You can configure a DRA for both EFS and BitLocker.

   B. **Correct.** You can use a KRA to recover a specific EFS certificate. You can't use a KRA to decrypt any encrypted file, but you can just use it to recover the certificate that was used to encrypt the file.

   C. **Incorrect.** Although it is advisable to configure credential roaming for EFS certificates, it isn't necessary if you want to perform certificate recovery.

   D. **Incorrect.** Although it is advisable to configure autoenrollment for EFS certificates, it's not necessary if you want to perform certificate recovery.

3. **Correct answer: D**

   A. **Incorrect.** Autoenrollment enables you to deploy certificates automatically. You can't use autoenrollment to configure a computer to be able to recover data from an organization's BitLocker-protected volumes.

   B. **Incorrect.** You can't use credential roaming to configure a computer to be able to recover data from an organization's BitLocker-protected volumes.

   C. **Incorrect.** You can use a KRA to recover a specific certificate. You can't use a KRA to decrypt data on a BitLocker-encrypted volume.

   D. **Correct.** When you specify a DRA, the specified certificate can decrypt encrypted data. You can configure a DRA for both EFS and BitLocker.

4. **Correct answer: C**

   A. **Incorrect.** This policy enables you to provide BitLocker identifiers related to your organization. You can use BitLocker identifiers to block BitLocker-encrypted volumes from third parties.

   B. **Incorrect.** This policy determines the method of encryption and the strength of the cipher. You can't use this policy to configure centralized BitLocker recovery.

   C. **Correct.** Configure the Store BitLocker Recovery Information In Active Directory Domain Services policy to ensure that BitLocker recovery information can be centrally determined.

   D. **Incorrect.** Although this policy does enable BitLocker recovery passwords to be stored on a central network folder, this solution doesn't work well in large organizations in which computers might be relocated and have their names changed. Storing BitLocker recovery information in Active Directory enables recovery information to be extracted, even if the computer name is changed.

5. **Correct answers: A and B**

   A. **Correct.** BitLocker To Go enables the use of BitLocker on removable hard disk drives. It doesn't enable the entry of BitLocker PINs to be bypassed if the computer is connected to the wired corporate network.

B. **Correct.** BitLocker Network Unlock enables the requirement for the entry of BitLocker PINs to be bypassed if the computer is connected to the wired corporate network.

C. **Incorrect.** It doesn't allow the entry of BitLocker PINs to be bypassed if the computer is connected to the wired corporate network.

D. **Incorrect.** Wake On LAN is a technology that enables computers to be woken to perform maintenance operations such as software update deployment. It doesn't enable the entry of BitLocker PINs to be bypassed if the computer is connected to the wired corporate network.

6. **Correct answers: A and B**

A. **Correct.** The WDS server role must be deployed to support Network Unlock for BitLocker.

B. **Correct.** The DHCP server role must be deployed to support Network Unlock for BitLocker.

C. **Incorrect.** You don't need to deploy a WINS server to deploy Network Unlock for BitLocker.

D. **Incorrect.** Although a public and private key are necessary for Network Unlock for BitLocker, it is not necessary to deploy an Online Certificate Status Protocol array. This array enables CRL information to be published through websites.

CHAPTER 10

Monitoring and auditing

Properly monitoring servers is a critical component in administering them. If you monitor servers correctly, you'll know well in advance if the server is under resource pressure from lack of disk space, RAM, or processor resources. You'll be able to deal with those issues before they start to affect the people that use the servers on a day-to-day basis. Auditing servers enables you to track object access and configuration changes, from modifications to security settings, to users who are accessing a particularly sensitive spreadsheet.

In this chapter, you will learn how to monitor and configure auditing for computers running the Windows Server 2012 and Windows Server 2012 R2 operating system.

Lessons in this chapter:

- Lesson 1: Monitoring servers **591**
- Lesson 2: Configuring advanced audit policies **614**

Before you begin

To complete the practice exercises in this chapter:

- You need to have deployed computers SYD-DC, MEL-DC, and ADL-DC, as described in the Introduction, using the evaluation edition of Windows Server 2012 R2.

Lesson 1: Monitoring servers

Unwatched servers, like unwatched children, invariably end up in a chaotic state. Monitoring a server using data collector sets, alerts, and events enables you to keep an eye on the server's performance and configuration. Although effective monitoring is unlikely to stop a server from ever experiencing problems, it often provides warning signs about developing problems, giving you a chance to resolve them before they cause a service disruption. In this lesson, you learn how to configure data collector sets, manage alerts, monitor events, and perform network monitoring.

> **After this lesson, you will be able to:**
> - Configure data collector sets.
> - Manage alerts.
> - Monitor events.
> - Configure event subscriptions.
> - Attach event-driven tasks
> - Perform network monitoring.
>
> **Estimated lesson time: 45 minutes**

Configuring data collector sets

Data collector sets enable you to collect performance data, system configuration information, and statistics into a single file. You can use Performance Monitor or other third-party tools to analyze this information to make a determination about how well a server is functioning against an assigned workload.

You can configure data collector sets to include the following:

- **Performance counter data**   The data collector set not only includes specific performance counters but also the data generated by those counters.
- **Event trace data**   Enables you to track events and system activities. Event trace data can be useful when troubleshooting misbehaving applications or services.
- **System configuration information**   Enables you to track the state of registry keys and record any modifications made to those keys.

Windows Server 2012 and Windows Server 2012 R2 include the following built-in data collector sets, as shown in Figure 10-1.

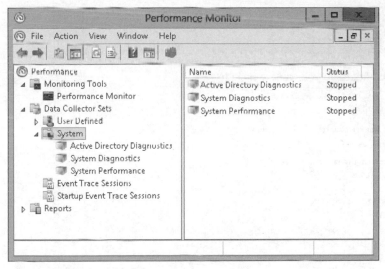

FIGURE 10-1 Built-in data collector sets

- **Active Directory diagnostics** Available if you have installed the computer as a domain controller; it provides data on Active Directory health and reliability.

- **System diagnostics** Enables you to troubleshoot problems with hardware, drivers, and STOP errors.

- **System performance** Enables you to diagnose problems with sluggish system performance. You can determine which processes, services, or hardware may be causing performance bottlenecks.

To create a data collector set, perform the following steps:

1. Open Performance Monitor from the Tools menu of the Server Manager console.

2. Expand Data Collector Sets.

3. Click User Defined. On the Action menu, click New, and click Data Collector Set.

4. You are given the option of creating the data collector set from a template, which enables you to select from an existing data collector set, or to create a data collector set manually. If you choose to create a data collector set manually, you have the option of creating a data log, which can include a performance counter, event trace data, and system configuration information; or a performance counter alert. This choice is shown in Figure 10-2.

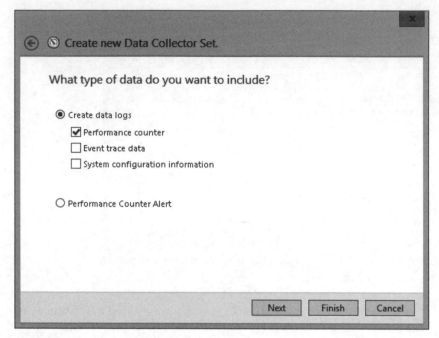

FIGURE 10-2 Creating a new data collector set

5. If you select Performance Counter, you then choose which performance counters to add to the data collector set. You also specify how often Windows should collect data from the performance counters. Figure 10-3 shows data being collected once every 15 seconds.

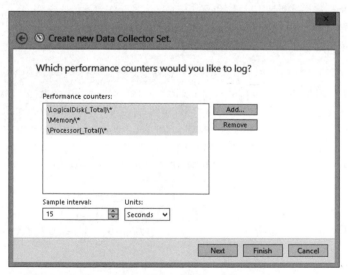

FIGURE 10-3 Setting an interval for the data collector set

6. If you choose to include event trace data, you need to enable event trace providers. As Figure 10-4 shows, a large number of event trace providers are available with Windows Server 2012 R2. You use event trace providers when troubleshooting a specific problem. For example, the Microsoft Windows-AppLocker event trace provider helps you diagnose and troubleshoot issues related to AppLocker.

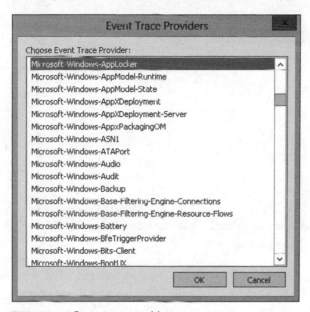

FIGURE 10-4 Event trace providers

7. If you choose to monitor system configuration information, you can select registry keys to monitor, as shown in Figure 10-5. Selecting a parent key enables you to monitor all registry changes that occur under that key while the data collector set is running.

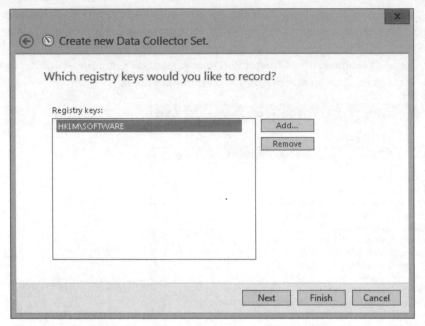

FIGURE 10-5 Setting registry keys to record

8. You then specify where you want data collected by the data collector set to be stored. The default location is the %systemdrive%\PerfLogs\Admin folder. If you intend to run the data collector set for an extended period of time, you should store the data on a volume separate from the one that hosts the operating system.

9. The final step in setting up a data collector set is to specify the account under which the data collector set runs. The default is Local System, but you can configure the data collector set to use any account for which you have the credentials.

You can schedule when a data collector set runs by configuring the Schedule tab of a data collector set's properties as shown in Figure 10-6.

FIGURE 10-6 Configure data collector set schedule

> **MORE INFO   DATA COLLECTOR SETS**
>
> For more information about data collector sets, consult the following TechNet article at
> *http://technet.microsoft.com/en-us/library/cc749337.aspx.*

Managing alerts

Performance counter *alerts* enable you to configure a task to run when a performance
counter, such as available disk space or memory, falls under or exceeds a specific value. To
configure a performance counter alert, you create a new data collector set, choose the Create
Manually option, and select the Performance Counter Alert option, as shown in Figure 10-7.

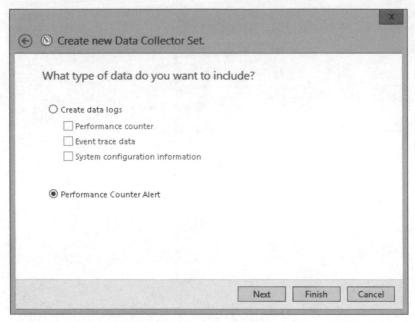

FIGURE 10-7 Configuring the performance counter alert

You add the performance counter, threshold value, and whether the alert should be triggered if the value exceeds or falls below this value. Figure 10-8 shows an alert that is triggered when the amount of available memory falls below 512 megabytes.

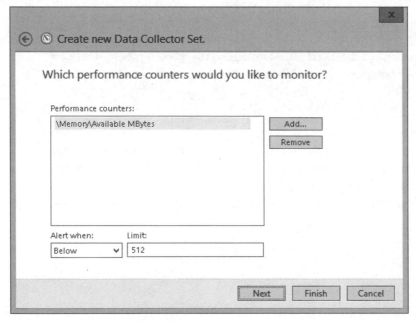

FIGURE 10-8 Setting an alert threshold

When you create an alert, all it does when triggered is to add an event to the event log. You can also configure an alert to run a scheduled task when triggered. You do this by editing the properties of the alert and specifying the name of the scheduled task on the Task tab, as shown in Figure 10-9.

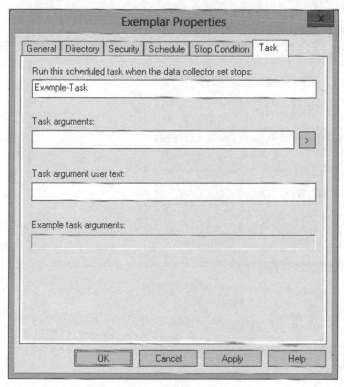

FIGURE 10-9 Running a scheduled task

Monitoring events with viewer

Event Viewer, shown in Figure 10-10, enables you to access recorded event information. The Windows Server 2012 and Windows Server 2012 R2 Event Viewer differs from the Event Viewer in earlier versions of the Windows Server operating system, such as Windows Server 2003, in that it not only offers the application, security, setup, and system logs, but it also contains separate application and service Logs. These logs are designed to provide information on a per-role or per-application basis, rather than having all application and role service-related events funneled into the application log. When searching for events related to a specific role service, feature, or application, check to see whether that role service, feature, or application has its own application log.

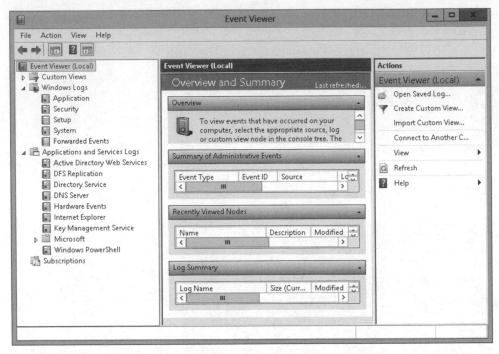

FIGURE 10-10 Event Viewer

> **MORE INFO** **EVENT VIEWER**
>
> For more information about Event Viewer, consult the following TechNet article at *http://technet.microsoft.com/en-us/library/cc766042.aspx*.

Event log filters

Filters and event logs enable you to view only those events that have specific characteristics. Filters apply only to the current Event Viewer session. If you constantly use a specific filter or set of filters to manage event logs, you should instead create a custom view. Filters apply only to a single event log. You can create filters on a log based on the following properties:

- **Logged**   Enables you to specify the time range for the filter.
- **Event Level**   Enables you to specify event levels. You can choose the following options: Critical, Warning, Verbose, Error, and Information.
- **Event Sources**   Enables you to choose the source of the event.
- **Event IDs**   Enables you to filter based on event ID. You can also exclude specific event IDs.
- **Keywords**   Enables you to specify keywords based on the contents of events.
- **User**   Enables you to limit events based on user.
- **Computer**   Enables you to limit events based on the computer.

To create a filter, perform the following steps:

1. Open Event Viewer and select the log that you want to filter.

2. Determine the properties of the event that you want to filter.

3. On the Actions pane, click Filter Current Log.

4. In the Filter Current Log dialog box, shown in Figure 10-11, specify the filter properties.

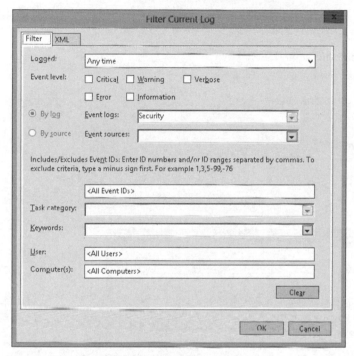

FIGURE 10-11 Specifying filter properties

Event log views

Event log views enable you to create customized views of events across any event log stored on a server, including events in the forwarded event log. Rather than looking through each event log for specific items of interest, you can create event log views that target only those specific items. Event Viewer includes a custom view named Administrative Events. This view displays critical, warning, and error events from a variety of important event logs such as the application, security, and system logs.

Views differ from filters in the following ways:

■ **Persistent** You can use a view across multiple Event Viewer sessions. If you configure a filter on a log, it is not available the next time you open the Event Viewer.

■ **Include multiple logs** A custom view can display events from separate logs. Filters are limited to displaying events from one log.

■ **Exportable** You can import and export event log views between computers.

Creating an event log view is a similar process to creating a filter. The primary difference is that you can select events from multiple logs, and you give the event log view a name and choose a place to save it. To create an event log view, perform the following steps:

1. Open Event Viewer.

2. Click the Custom Views node, and then click Create Custom View from the Actions menu.

3. In the Create Custom View dialog box, shown in Figure 10-12, select the properties of the view, including:

   - When the events are logged
   - The event level
   - Which event log to draw events from
   - Event source
   - Task category
   - Keywords
   - User
   - Computer

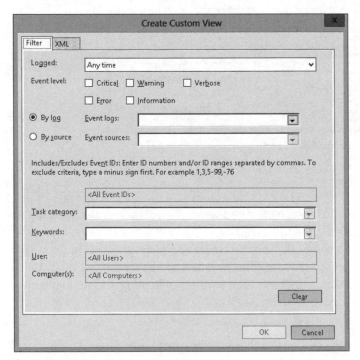

FIGURE 10-12 Creating a custom view

4. In the Save Filter To Custom View dialog box, enter a name for the custom view and a location in which to save the view (see Figure 10-13). Click OK.

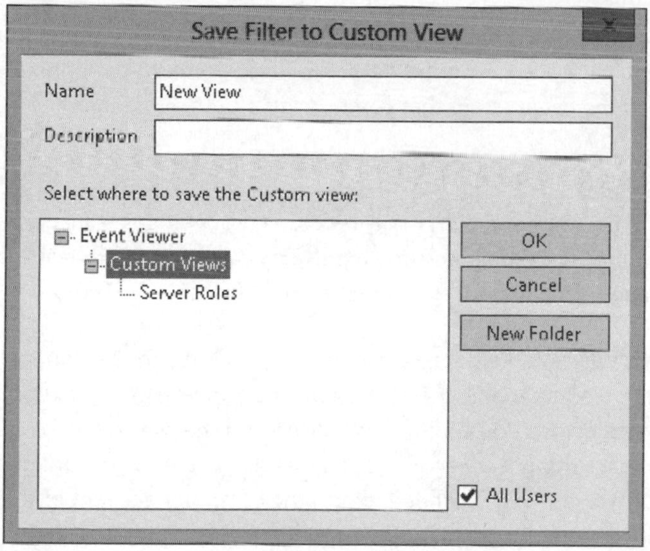

FIGURE 10-13 Entering the custom view name

5. Verify that the new view is listed as its own separate node in the Event Viewer.

You can export a custom event log view by selecting the event log view and clicking Export Custom View. Exported views can be imported on other computers running Windows Server 2012 and Windows Server 2012 R2.

> **MORE INFO** **EVENT LOG VIEWS**
>
> For more information about event log views, consult the following TechNet article at *http://technet.microsoft.com/en-us/library/cc766522.aspx*.

Configuring event subscriptions

Event log forwarding enables you to centralize the collection and management of events from multiple computers. Rather than having to examine the event log of each computer by making a remote connection to that computer, event log forwarding enables you to do one of the following:

- Configure a central computer to collect specific events from source computers. Use this option in environments in which you need to consolidate events from only a small number of computers.
- Configure source computers to forward specific events to a collector computer. Use this option when you have a large number of computers from which you want to consolidate events. You configure this method using Group Policy.

Event log forwarding enables you to configure the specific events that are forwarded to the central computer. This enables the computer to forward important events. It isn't necessary to forward all events from the source computer. If you discover something that warrants further investigation from the forwarded traffic, you can log on to the original source computer and view all the events from that computer in a normal manner.

Event log forwarding uses Windows Remote Management (WinRM) and the Windows Event Collector (wecsvc). You need to enable these services on computers that function as event forwarders and event collectors. You configure WinRM using the winrm quickconfig command. You configure wecsvc using the wecutil qc command. If you want to configure subscriptions from the security event log, you need to add the computer account of the collector computer to the local Administrators group on the source computer.

To configure a collector-initiated event subscription, configure WinRM and Windows Event Collector on the source and collector computers. In the Event Viewer, configure the Subscription Properties dialog box, shown in Figure 10-14, with the following information:

- **Subscription Name** The name of the subscription.
- **Destination Log** The log where collected events will be stored.
- **Subscription Type And Source Computers: Collector Initiated** Use the Select Computers dialog box to add the computers that the collector will retrieve events from. The collector must be a member of the local Administrators group or the Event Log Readers group on each source computer, depending on whether access to the security log is required.
- **Events To Collect** Create a custom view to specify which events are retrieved from each of the source computers.

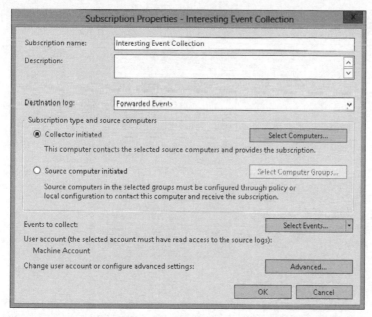

FIGURE 10-14 Configuring a collector-initiated event subscription

If you want to instead configure a source computer-initiated subscription, you need to configure the following group policies on the computers that will act as the event forwarders:

- **Configure Forwarder Resource Usage**   This policy determines the maximum event forwarding rate in events per second. If this policy is not configured, events will be transmitted as soon as they are recorded.

- **Configure Target Subscription Manager**   This policy enables you to set the location of the collector computer.

> **MORE INFO**   **EVENT SUBSCRIPTIONS**
>
> For more information about event subscriptions, see *http://technet.microsoft.com/en-us/library/cc749183.aspx*.

Both of these policies are located in the Computer Configuration\Policies\Administrative Templates\Windows Components\Event Forwarding node. When configuring the subscription, you must also specify the computer groups that hold the computer accounts of the computers that will be forwarding events to the collector. You do this in the Computer Groups dialog box, as shown in Figure 10-15.

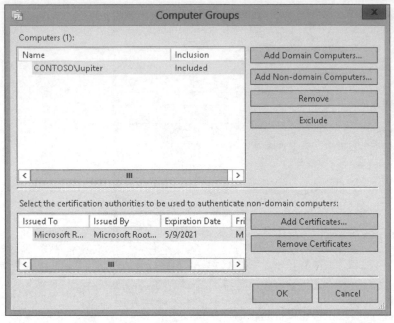

FIGURE 10-15 Configuring subscription computer groups for the subscription

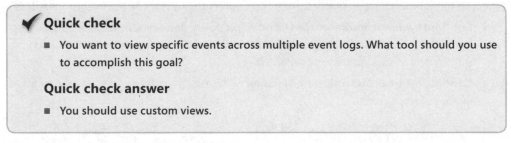

✔ **Quick check**

- You want to view specific events across multiple event logs. What tool should you use to accomplish this goal?

Quick check answer

- You should use custom views.

Attaching event-driven tasks

Event Viewer enables you to attach tasks to specific events. A drawback to the process of creating event-driven tasks is that you need to have an example of the event that triggers the task already present in the event log. Events are triggered based on an event having the same log, source, and event ID.

To attach a task to a specific event, perform the following steps:

1. Open Event Viewer. Locate and select the event upon which you want to base the new task.

2. On the Event Viewer Actions pane, click Attach Task To This Event. The Create Basic Task Wizard displays.

3. On the Create A Basic Task page, review the name of the task that you want to create. By default, the task is named after the event. Click Next.

4. On the When An Event is Logged page, review the information about the event. This will list the log from which the event originates, the source of the event, and the event ID. Click Next.

5. On the Action page, shown in Figure 10-16, you can choose the task to perform. The Send An E-Mail and Display A Message tasks are deprecated, and you get an error if you try to create a task using these actions. Click Next.

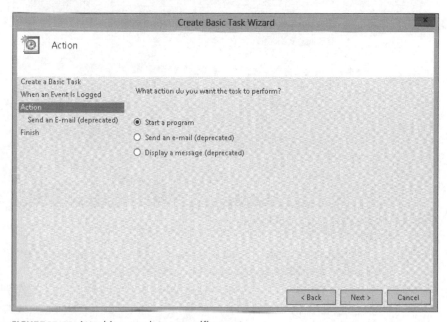

FIGURE 10-16 Attaching a task to a specific event

6. On the Start A Program page, shown in Figure 10-17, specify the program or script that should be automatically triggered as well as additional arguments.

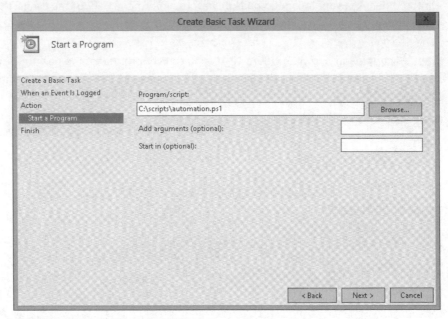

FIGURE 10-17 Specifying a triggered script

7. After you complete task creation, you can modify the task to specify the security context under which the task executes. By default, event tasks run only when the user is signed on. You can configure the task to run whether the user is signed on or not, as shown in Figure 10-18.

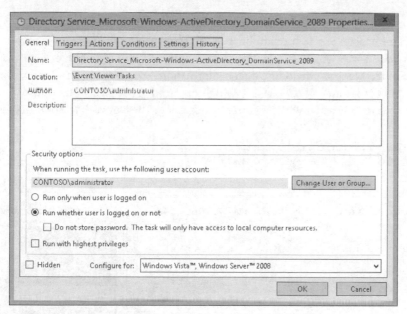

FIGURE 10-18 Run your task if the user is logged on or off

> **REAL WORLD** **IT'S NOT ABOUT SENDING EMAIL, IT'S ABOUT SENDING A MESSAGE**
>
> Even though the Send An Email task is deprecated, you can use the Start A Program option to execute a Windows PowerShell script that sends an email. In many cases, however, instead of sending a message to an administrator so the administrator can perform a task, it's better to have the task directly called wherever possible. Creating automated tasks that resolve problems without requiring direct intervention saves time and money. You should send email messages only when you need to notify yourself about an issue that cannot be resolved by running a script.

Performing network monitoring

Network monitoring enables you to track how a computer interacts with the network. Through network monitoring, you can determine which services and applications are using specific network interfaces, which services are listening on specific ports, and the volume of traffic that exists. There are two primary tools through which you can perform network monitoring on computers running Windows Server 2012 and Windows Server 2012 R2:

- Resource Monitor
- Message Analyzer

Resource Monitor

Resource Monitor enables you to monitor how a computer running the Windows Server 2012 and Windows Server 2012 R2 operating system uses CPU, memory, disk, and network resources. Resource Monitor provides real time information. You can't use Resource Monitor to perform a traffic capture and review activity that occurred in the past. You can use Resource Monitor to view activity that is currently occurring. The Network tab of Resource Monitor is shown in Figure 10-19.

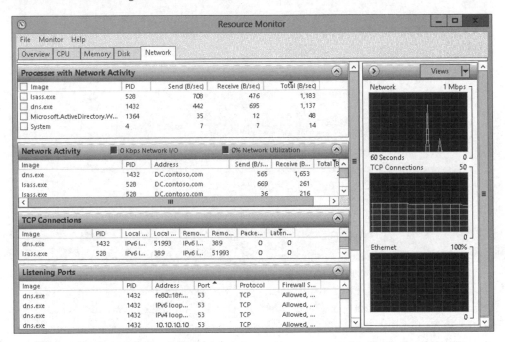

FIGURE 10-19 Resource Monitor Network tab

Resource Monitor provides the following information that is relevant to network monitoring:

- **Processes With Network Activity**   This view lists processes by name and ID; and provides information on bits sent per second, bits received per second, and total bits per second.

- **Network Activity**   Lists network activity on a per-process basis, but also lists the destination address, sent bits per second, received bits per second, and total bits per second.

- **TCP Connections**   Provides information on connections on the basis of local address, port, and remote address and port.

- **Listening Ports**   Lists the ports and addresses that services and applications are listening on. Also provides information about the firewall status for these roles and services.

Message Analyzer

Microsoft Message Analyzer is the successor to Network Monitor. You can use Message Analyzer to perform network traffic capture and analysis. Message Analyzer also functions as a replacement for LogParser, which enables you to manage system messages, events, and log files. When performing a capture, you select the scenario that best represents the type of event about which you are interested in capturing traffic. For example, the LAN scenario, shown in Figure 10-20, enables you to capture traffic on local area network (LAN) interfaces.

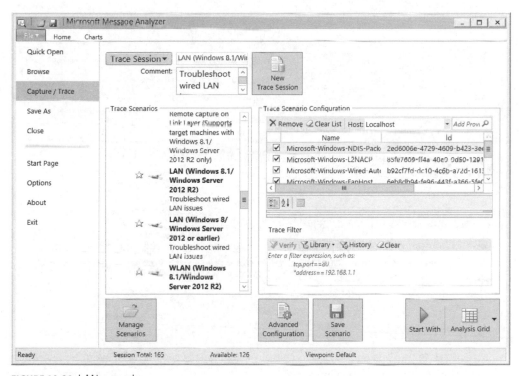

FIGURE 10-20 LAN scenario

When performing certain types of network traffic capture, you need to run Message Analyzer using an account that is a member of the local Administrators group. After the capture has been performed, you can analyze the content of each message, as shown in Figure 10-21. By applying appropriate filters, you can locate network traffic that has specific characteristics, such as using a particular TCP port, source, or destination address.

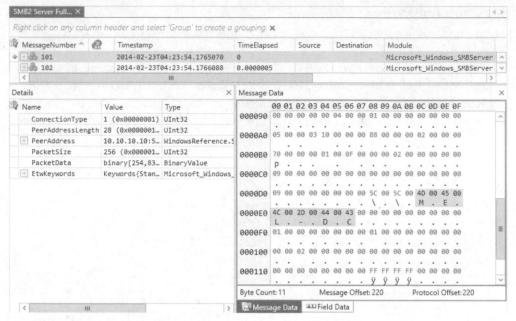

FIGURE 10-21 Message Analyzer

> **MORE INFO** **MESSAGE ANALYZER**
>
> You can find out more about Microsoft Message Analyzer by consulting the Microsoft Message Analyzer Operating Guide at *http://technet.microsoft.com/en-us/library/jj649776. aspx.*

Lesson summary

- Data collector sets enable you to collect performance counter data, event trace data, and system configuration information.
- Performance counter alerts enable an event to be written to the event log and a command to be run when a specified performance counter exceeds or falls below a configured value.
- Event log filters apply to a single event log and are not persistent.
- Event log views are persistent, can include items from multiple event logs, and can be imported and exported.
- Event subscriptions enable you to configure one computer to consolidate the event logs of multiple computers.
- Event-driven tasks enable you to configure a program or script to be run when a specific event is written to the event log.

- Message Analyzer, which is the successor to Network Monitor, enables you to capture and analyze network traffic.

Lesson review

Answer the following questions to test your knowledge of the information in this lesson. You can find the answers to these questions and explanations of why each answer choice is correct or incorrect in the "Answers" section at the end of this chapter.

1. You want to collect processor, memory, and network interface utilization data over the course of several hours. You need to be able to review the data at a later period in time. Which of the following tools should you use to accomplish this goal?

   A. Resource Monitor

   B. Task Manager

   C. Data collector set

   D. Message Analyzer

2. A particular network service on a computer running Windows Server 2012 R2 that you are responsible for managing is not functioning correctly. You suspect that the service is listening on a TCP port that Windows Firewall is configured to block, but you don't know which TCP port the service uses. Which of the following tools should you use to determine this information?

   A. Task Manager

   B. Resource Monitor

   C. Message Analyzer

   D. Data collector set

3. Which of the following tools can you use to capture and analyze network traffic?

   A. Data collector set

   B. Message Analyzer

   C. Resource Monitor

   D. Task Manager

4. You are configuring event log subscriptions. Computer MEL-DC will function as the event log collector, and computers MEL-A, MEL-B, and MEL-C will function as the event log sources. You want MEL-DC to collect events from the security logs on computers MEL-A, MEL-B, and MEL-C. To which of the following security groups on MEL-A, MEL-B, and MEL-C should you add the computer account of MEL-DC?

   A. Backup operators

   B. Power users

   C. Event log readers

   D. Administrators

Lesson 2: Advanced audit policies

Auditing enables you to track both actual and attempted access and changes to objects and policies. Auditing enables you to verify that the policies that you've put in place to secure your organization's network infrastructure are actually being enforced, from tracking modifications to sensitive user accounts through to access to sensitive files and folders. In this lesson, you will learn about advanced audit policy, how to configure expression-based audit policies, and how you can use auditpol.exe to manage auditing.

> **After this lesson, you will be able to:**
> - Understand advanced audit policies.
> - Configure auditing using Group Policy.
> - Use auditpol.exe to manage auditing.
>
> **Estimated lesson time: 45 minutes**

Configuring advanced auditing

There are two sets of audit policies in a Group Policy Object (GPO): *traditional audit policies* and *advanced audit policies*. The traditional audit policies are located in the Computer Configuration\Policies\Windows Settings\Security Settings\Local Policies\Audit Policies node and are shown in Figure 10-22. They are the audit policies that have been available with the Windows Server operating system since Windows 2000. The drawback of these policies is that they are general, and you can't be specific in the way you configure auditing. When you use these policies, you'll not only audit the events that you're interested in but you'll also end up auditing many events that you don't need to know about.

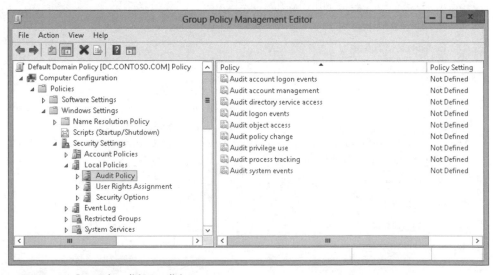

FIGURE 10-22 General auditing policies

The advanced audit policies enable you to be more specific in the types of activity you audit. The advanced audit policies are located under the Computer Configuration\Policies\ Windows Settings\Security Settings\Advanced Audit Policy Configuration node, as shown in Figure 10-23.

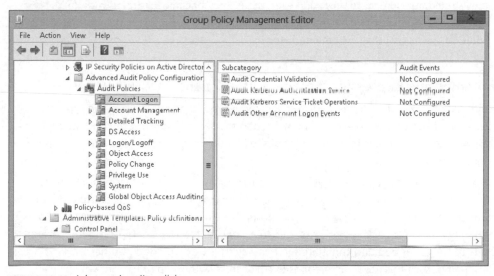

FIGURE 10-23 Advanced audit policies

There are 10 groups of audit policy settings and 58 individual audit policies available through Advanced Audit Policy Configuration. The audit policy groups contain the following settings:

- **Account Logon**   You can audit credential validation and Kerberos-specific operations.
- **Account Management**   You can audit account management operations, such as changes to computer accounts, user accounts, and group accounts.
- **Detailed Tracking**   You can audit encryption events, process creation, process termination, and RPC events.
- **DS Access**   You can audit Active Directory access and functionality.
- **Logon/Logoff**   You can audit logon, logoff, and other account activity events, including IPsec and Network Policy Server (NPS) events.
- **Object Access**   You can audit access to objects including files, folders, applications, and the registry.

- **Policy Change**   You can audit changes to audit policy.

- **Privilege Use**   You can audit the use of privileges.

- **System**   You can audit changes to the security subsystem.

- **Global Object Access Auditing**   You can configure expression-based audit policies for files and the registry.

> **REAL WORLD**   **CONFIGURE AN AUDIT POLICY**
>
> Determine what you want to audit first and then enable the policies to audit that type of activity. A mistake that many administrators make is that they aren't entirely sure what they should be auditing, so they audit everything. They become frustrated with the process because the auditing events that they might be interested in get lost in the vast sea of auditing events that they are not interested in.

Implementing expression-based audit policies

Traditional object audit policies involve specifying a group and configuring the type of activities that will trigger an event to be written to the security log. Specifying that an audit event will be written each time a member of the Managers group accesses a file in a specific folder is a good example.

Expression-based audit policies enable you to go further. These policies enable you to put conditions as to when auditing might occur. For example, you might want to configure auditing so that members of the Managers group have access to sensitive files tracked only when they access files from computers that aren't part of the Managers_Computers group. Figure 10-24 shows auditing configured in this way. This way, you don't bother tracking access when members of this group access sensitive files from within the office, but you do track all access to those sensitive files when members of this group are accessing them from an unusual location.

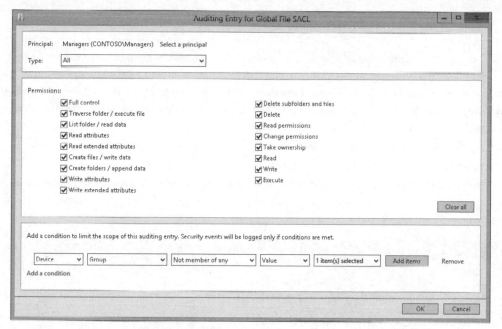

FIGURE 10-24 Expression-based audit policies

You can integrate expression-based audit policies with Dynamic Access Control (DAC) to create targeted audit policies that are based on user, computer, and resource claims. Instead of just adding claims based on user or device group membership, the claim can be based on document metadata such as confidentiality settings and site location. You can configure expression-based audit policies at the file or folder level, or apply them through Group Policy using policies in the Global Object Access Auditing node of Advanced Audit Policy Configuration.

✔ **Quick check**

- What type of auditing should you configure if you want to audit file access by a specific group of people only when they aren't signed on to a specific group of computers?

Quick check answer

- You configure an expression-based audit policy to audit file access by a specific group of people who are accessing files from computers other than those in a specific group.

Configuring file and folder auditing

After you configure auditing of object access, either through the traditional or advanced audit policies, you can configure auditing at the file and folder level. The simplest way to configure auditing is at the folder level because you can then configure all folders and subfolders to inherit those auditing settings. If you change the auditing settings at the folder level, you can use the Replace All Child Object Auditing Entries option to apply the new auditing settings to the folder's child files and folders.

You can configure auditing for a specific file and folder through the Advanced button on the Security tab of the object's properties. You can configure basic success and failure auditing, as shown in Figure 10-25. You can also configure expression-based auditing so that activity by members of a specific security group are audited only if other conditions, such as membership of other security groups, are also met.

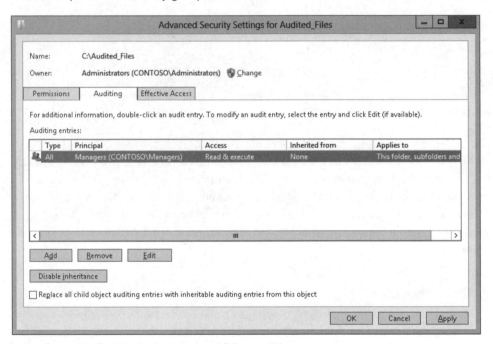

FIGURE 10-25 Configuring basic success and failure auditing

The advantage of using Global Object Access Auditing is that when you have it configured, you can use file classification to apply metadata to files and then automatically have auditing enabled for those files. For example, using file classification and DAC, you can configure a Windows Server 2012 R2 file server so that all files that contain the phrase "code secret" are marked as Sensitive. You can then configure Global Object Access Auditing so that all access to files marked as Sensitive are automatically audited. Instead of having an administrator track down all the files that are sensitive and configuring auditing on those files, the process is automatic. All that needs to happen to trigger it is the inclusion of the phrase "code secret" in the file.

Using auditpol with auditing

Auditpol.exe is a command-line utility that you can use to configure and manage audit policy settings from an elevated command prompt. You can use auditpol.exe to perform the following tasks.

- View the current audit policy settings with the /Get subcommand
- Set audit policy settings with the /Set subcommand
- Display selectable policy elements with the /List subcommand
- Back up and restore audit policies using the /Backup and /Restore subcommands
- Delete all per-user audit policy settings and reset the system policy settings using the /Clear subcommand
- Remove all per-user audit policy settings and disable all system policy settings using the /Remove subcommand

For example, to enable success and failure auditing for the File System subcategory of Object Access, execute this command.

```
Auditpol.exe /set /subcategory:"File System" /success:Enable /failure:Enable
```

To view the current audit policy settings for all audit policies, issue this command.

```
Auditpol.exe /get /category:*
```

To view the current audit policy settings for a specific category, such as Object Access, issue this command.

```
Auditpol.exe /get /category:"Object Access"
```

> **MORE INFO** **AUDITPOL.EXE**
>
> To learn more about auditpol.exe, consult the following TechNet article at *http://technet .microsoft.com/en-us/library/cc731451(v=ws.10).aspx*.

Lesson summary

- Advanced audit policies enable you to perform more granular auditing than is possible with the traditional auditing policies available in earlier versions of Windows server.
- Expression-based audit policies enable you to configure auditing based on object metadata. You can also use expression-based audit policies to perform conditional auditing.
- After you have enabled the auditing of object access, you can configure auditing at the file and folder level. File-level and folder-level auditing supports expression-based audit policies.
- You can use the auditpol.exe command-line utility from an elevated command prompt to configure and manage audit policy settings.

Lesson review

Answer the following questions to test your knowledge of the information in this lesson. You can find the answers to these questions and explanations of why each answer choice is correct or incorrect in the "Answers" section at the end of this chapter.

1. Which of the following commands should you use to enable success and failure auditing for all audit policies under the Object Access category on a computer running Windows Server 2012 R2?

   A. Auditpol.exe /set /subcategory:"File System" /success:Enable /failure:Enable

   B. Auditpol.exe /set /Category:"Object Access" /success:Enable /Failure:Enable

   C. Auditpol.exe /get /Category:"Object Access" /success:Disable /Failure:Disable

   D. Auditpol.exe /get /Category:"Object Access" /success:Disable /Failure:Enable

2. You want to enable failure auditing, but not success auditing, for all audit policies under the Object Access category on a computer running Windows Server 2012 R2. Which of the following commands should you use to accomplish this goal?

   A. Auditpol.exe /get /Category:"Object Access" /success:Disable /Failure:Enable

   B. Auditpol.exe /get /Category:"Object Access" /success:Disable /Failure:Disable

   C. Auditpol.exe /set /Category:"Object Access" /success:Enable /Failure:Enable

   D. Auditpol.exe /set /subcategory:"File System" /success:Enable /failure:Enable

3. You want to enable success and failure auditing only for the File System subcategory. Which of the following commands should you use to accomplish this goal?

   A. Auditpol.exe /set /Category:"Object Access" /success:Enable /Failure:Enable

   B. Auditpol.exe /get /Category:"Object Access" /success:Disable /Failure:Enable

   C. Auditpol.exe /set /subcategory:"File System" /success:Enable /failure:Enable

   D. Auditpol.exe /get /Category:"Object Access" /success:Disable /Failure:Disable

4. You want to disable all success and failure auditing on all auditing subcategories under the Object Access category. Which of the following commands should you use to accomplish this goal?

   A. Auditpol.exe /get /Category:"Object Access" /success:Disable /Failure:Disable

   B. Auditpol.exe /get /Category:"Object Access" /success:Disable /Failure:Enable

   C. Auditpol.exe /set /Category:"Object Access" /success:Enable /Failure:Enable

   D. Auditpol.exe /set /subcategory:"File System" /success:Enable /failure:Enable

Practice exercises

The goal of this section is to provide you with hands-on practice with the following:

- Configure data collector sets
- Configure alerts
- Manage event subscriptions
- Perform network monitoring
- Configure removable device auditing
- Configure logon auditing
- Configure expression-based audit policies
- Enable folder auditing

To perform the exercises in this section, you need access to an evaluation version of Windows Server 2012 R2. You should also have access to virtual machines SYD-DC, MEL-DC, CBR-DC, and ADL-DC, the setup instructions for which are described in the Introduction. You should ensure that you have a checkpoint of these virtual machines that you can revert to at the end of the practice exercises. You should revert the Virtual Machines (VMs) to this initial state prior to beginning these exercises.

Exercise 1: Configure data collector sets

In this exercise, you configure data collector sets. To complete this exercise, perform the following steps:

1. Start SYD-DC, and sign on as CONTOSO\Don_Funk.
2. On SYD-DC, click Performance Monitor in the Tools menu of Server Manager.
3. In the Performance Monitor console, expand the Performance\Data Collector Sets\User Defined, as shown in Figure 10-26.

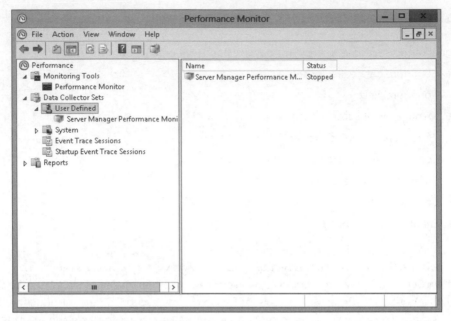

FIGURE 10-26 Accessing data collector sets

4. On the Action menu, click New, and click Data Collector Set.

5. In the Create New Data Collector Set dialog box, type the name **SYD-DC-Performance-Measurement** and click Create Manually (Advanced), as shown in Figure 10-27. Click Next.

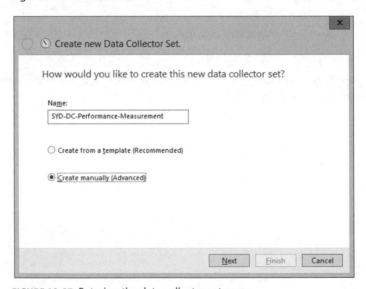

FIGURE 10-27 Entering the data collector set name

6. On the What Type Of Date Do You Want To Include? page, click Performance Counter, as shown in Figure 10-28, and click Finish.

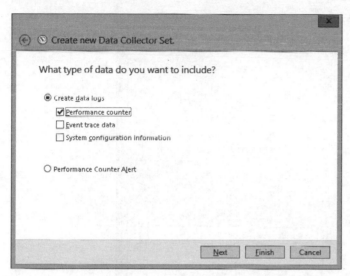

FIGURE 10-28 Selecting Performance Counter

7. In the Performance Monitor console, click SYD-DC-Performance-Measurement.

8. In the details pane, click DataCollector01.

9. On the Action menu, click Properties.

10. In the DataCollector01 Properties dialog box, shown in Figure 10-29, click Add.

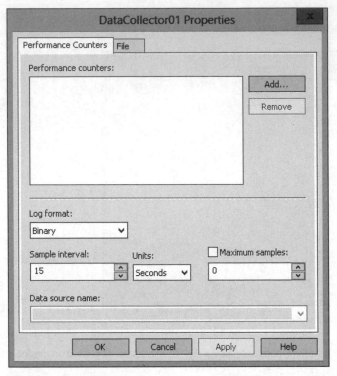

FIGURE 10-29 Performance counters

11. In the Available Counters dialog box, click Logical Disk, and click Add.

12. Click Memory, click the arrow, click Available Mbytes, and click Add.

13. Click Network Interface, and click Add.

14. Click Processor, and click Add.

15. Verify that the list of added counters matches Figure 10-30, and click OK.

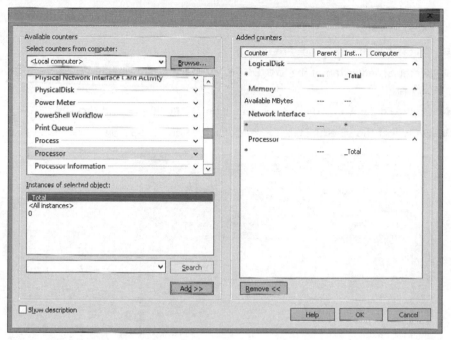

FIGURE 10-30 Matching added counters

16. In the DataCollector01 Properties dialog box, set the Sample Interval to 15 seconds (see Figure 10-31), and click OK.

FIGURE 10-31 Setting the interval

17. In Performance Monitor, click Data Collector Sets\User Defined\SYD-DC-Performance-Measurement.

18. On the Action menu, click Properties.

19. On the Schedule tab of the SYD-DC-Performance-Measurement Properties dialog box, click Add.

20. On the Folder Action dialog box, set a time of 3:00:00 AM, and click OK.

21. Verify that the Schedule tab appear similar to Figure 10-32, and click OK

FIGURE 10-32 Configure data collector set schedule

Exercise 2: Collect data

In this exercise, you collect data from the data collector set. To complete this exercise, perform the following steps:

1. In Performance Monitor, click Data Collector Sets\User Defined\SYD-DC-Performance-Measurement.

2. On the Action menu, click Start.

3. After 2 minutes, on the Action menu, click Stop.

4. Expand Reports, expand User Defined, and click SYD-DC-Performance-Measurement.

5. Double-click the report listed in the details pane, as shown in Figure 10-33.

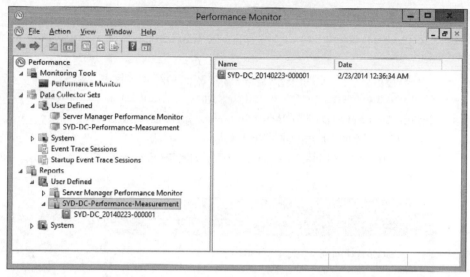

FIGURE 10-33 Selecting a report

6. Click Change Graph Type, and click Report.

7. View the report, as shown in Figure 10-34.

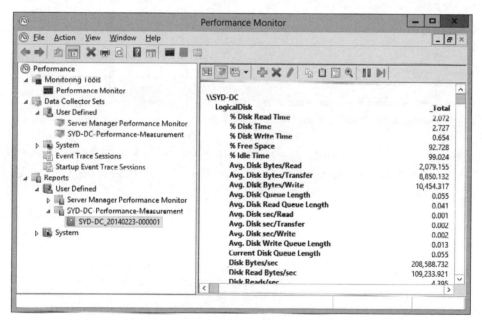

FIGURE 10-34 Viewing the report

Exercise 3: Configure alerts

In this exercise, you configure a free disk space alert. To complete this exercise, perform the following steps:

1. In Performance Monitor, click User Defined under Data Collector Sets.

2. On the Action menu, click New, and click Data Collector Set.

3. On the Create New Data Collector Set page, type **Disk Space Alert**, click Create Manually (Advanced), and click Next.

4. On the Create New Data Collector Set page, click Performance Counter Alert, as shown in Figure 10-35, and click Next.

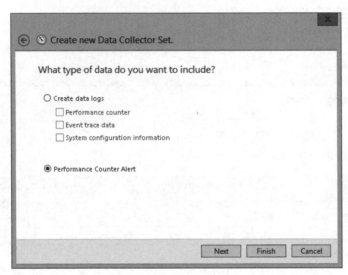

FIGURE 10-35 Choosing Performance Counter Alert

5. On the Which Performance Counters Would You Like To Monitor? page, click Add.

6. In the Available Counters dialog box, click LogicalDisk, click %Free Space, click C:, and click Add, as shown in Figure 10-36. Click OK.

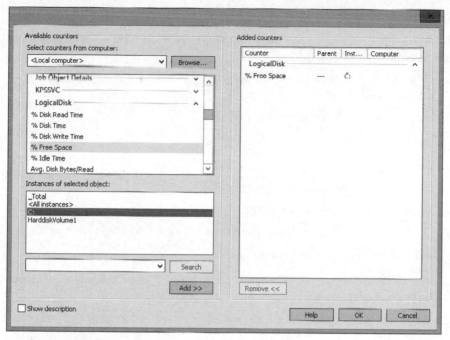

FIGURE 10-36 Selecting LogicalDisk

7. Set the Alert When menu to Below.

8. Set the Limit value to 5, as shown in Figure 10-37, and click Next.

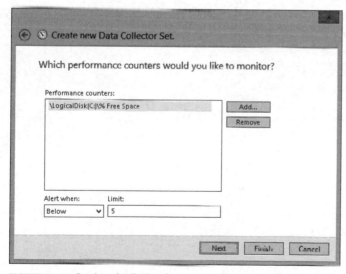

FIGURE 10-37 Setting the limit value

9. Click Finish.

Exercise 4: Prepare computers for event subscriptions

In this exercise, you configure computers to support event log subscriptions. To complete this exercise, perform the following steps:

1. On SYD-DC, right-click Windows PowerShell on the task bar, and click Run As Administrator.

2. Enter the following command and press Enter.

   ```
   Wecutil qc
   ```

3. When prompted, press Y, and press Enter.

4. Close the Windows PowerShell prompt.

5. Sign on to MEL-DC as Administrator.

6. Open the Windows PowerShell prompt and type the following commands.

   ```
   Add-Computer -DomainName contoso.com
   ```

7. In the Windows PowerShell Credentials dialog box, type **don_funk@contoso.com** and **Pa$$w0rd**, and click OK.

8. Type the following command at the Windows PowerShell prompt to restart the computer.

   ```
   Restart-Computer
   ```

9. Sign on to MEL-DC as Contoso\don_funk.

10. On the Tools menu on Server Manager, click Computer Management.

11. In the Computer Management console, expand Local Users And Groups, click Groups, and then click Administrators, as shown in Figure 10-38.

FIGURE 10-38 Accessing Administrators

12. On the Actions pane, click More Actions, and click Properties under Administrator.

13. In the Administrators Properties dialog box, click Add.

14. In the Select Users, Computers, Service Accounts, Or Groups dialog box, click Object Types.

15. In the Object Types dialog box, enable the Computers check box, as shown in Figure 10-39, and click OK.

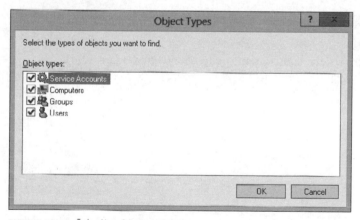

FIGURE 10-39 Selecting Computers

16. In the Select Users, Computers, Service Accounts, Or Groups dialog box, type **SYD-DC**, click Check Names, and click OK.

17. Verify that the Administrators Properties dialog box matches Figure 10-40 and click OK.

FIGURE 10-40 Administrators Properties dialog box

18. Restart MEL-DC.

Exercise 5: Configure event subscriptions

In this exercise, you configure event subscriptions. To complete this exercise, perform the following steps:

1. In the Server Manager console on SYD-DC, open the Tools menu, and click Event Viewer.

2. In Event Viewer, click the Subscriptions node, as shown in Figure 10-41.

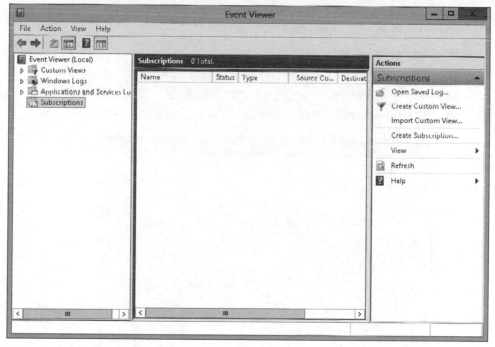

FIGURE 10-41 Clicking the Subscriptions node

3. On the Actions pane, click Create Subscription.

4. In the Subscription Properties dialog box, type the name as **Subscription-Alpha**, click Collector Initiated, and click Select Computers.

5. In the Computers dialog box, click Add Domain Computers.

6. In the Select Computer dialog box, type **MEL-DC**, click Check Names, and click OK.

7. Verify that the Computers dialog box matches Figure 10-42, and click Test.

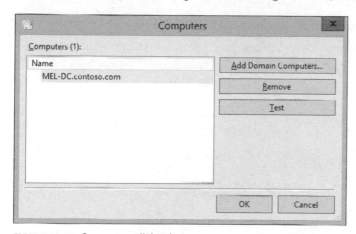

FIGURE 10-42 Computers dialog box

8. In the Event Viewer dialog box, click OK.

9. In the Computers dialog box, click OK.

10. Click Select Events.

11. In the Query Filter dialog box, select Critical, Error, Warning, and Information.

12. Click the Event Logs menu, and click Windows Logs.

13. Verify that the Query Filter appears the same as Figure 10-43, and click OK.

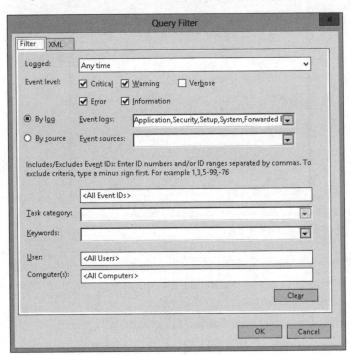

FIGURE 10-43 The Query Filter dialog box

14. In the Subscription Properties dialog box, click Advanced.

15. In the Advanced Subscription Settings dialog box, click Minimize Latency, as shown in Figure 10-44, and click OK.

FIGURE 10-44 Advanced Subscription Settings dialog box

16. Verify that the Subscription Properties – Subscription-Alpha dialog box matches Figure 10-45, and then click OK.

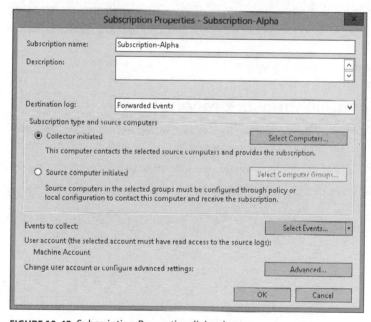

FIGURE 10-45 Subscription Properties dialog box

17. Restart server MEL-DC.

18. Expand the Windows Logs node, and click Forwarded Events.

19. Verify the presence of items in the event log, as shown in Figure 10-46.

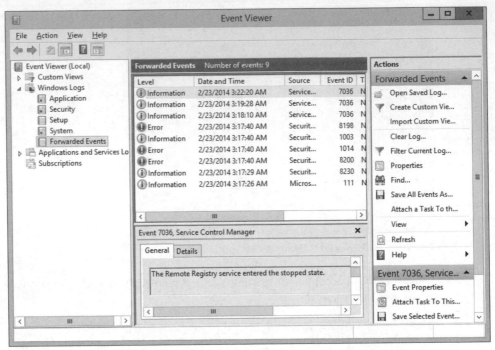

FIGURE 10-46 Event log

20. Close Event Viewer.

Exercise 6: Configure network monitoring

In this exercise, you monitor the processes and services that use network interfaces. To complete this exercise, perform the following steps:

1. On the Tools menu of the Server Manager console on SYD-DC, click Resource Monitor.

2. On the Network tab, click the arrow next to TCP Connections, as shown in Figure 10-47.

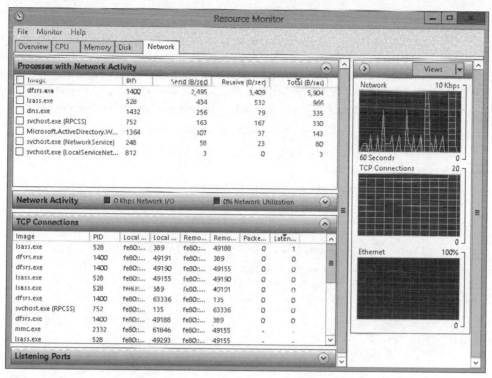

FIGURE 10-47 Network tab of the Resource Monitor

3. Click the arrow next to Listening Ports to list the ports on which different services are listening (see Figure 10-48).

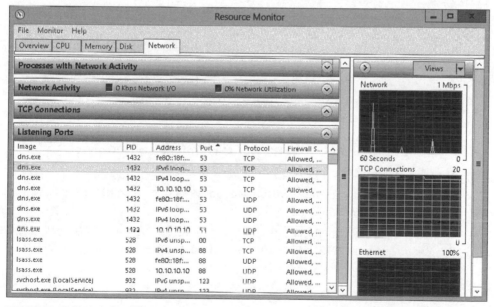

FIGURE 10-48 Listing the different ports.

Exercise 7: Using Message Analyzer

In this exercise, you use Message Analyzer to perform network monitoring. To perform this exercise, you need to download Message Analyzer from the following website: *http://www.microsoft.com/en-au/download/details.aspx?id=40308* (or just use a search engine to locate the installer) and then install it on MEL-DC. Ensure that you do not run the program and that you sign off after installation. To complete this exercise, perform the following steps:

1. Ensure that you are signed on to MEL-DC as contoso\don_funk.

2. In the Server Manager on MEL-DC, click Local Server, and then select IE Enhanced Security Configuration.

3. In the Internet Explorer Enhanced Security Configuration dialog box, set the Administrators setting to Off, as shown in Figure 10-49, and click OK.

FIGURE 10-49 Internet Explorer security

4. In the Search charm on MEL-DC, type **Microsoft Message Analyzer**.

5. Click Microsoft Message Analyzer in the results list.

6. On the Welcome To The Microsoft Message Analyzer dialog box, click Do Not Update Items, and click OK.

7. On the File menu, click Capture Trace, and click SMB2 Server Full PDU (Windows 8/ Windows Server 2012 or later) as shown in Figure 10-50, and click Start With.

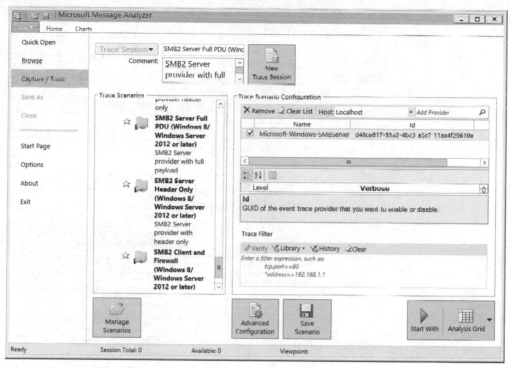

FIGURE 10-50 SMB Server Full PDU

8. On the taskbar, click File Explorer.

9. In File Explorer, click Computer, and then double-click Local Disk (C:).

10. On the title bar, click New Folder. Name the new folder **TEST**.

11. Right-click the TEST folder, click Share With, and click Specific People.

12. In the File Sharing dialog box, click Share, and then click Done.

13. In Microsoft Message Analyzer, click Analysis Grid, and verify that messages have been recorded, and click the final message, as shown in Figure 10-51.

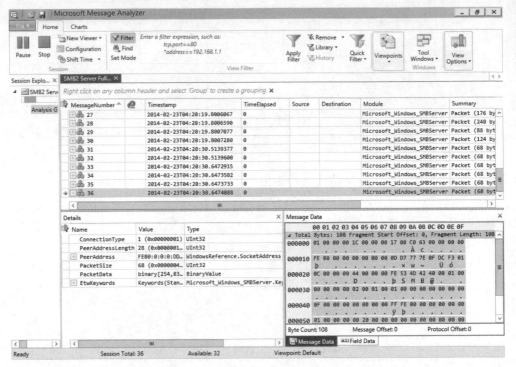

FIGURE 10-51 Verifying that messages have been recorded

14. Use File Explorer to navigate to C:\TEST.

15. Create a text file in C:\TEST named **secretfile.txt**. The content of the file should be the words "secret secret."Switch to SYD-DC.

16. On SYD-DC, in the Search charm, type **\\MEL-DC\TEST\secretfile.txt** and click Secretfile.txt in the Results pane.

17. Switch to MEL-DC.

18. Verify that additional traffic has been recorded.

19. Examine the message data for network addresses, such as server MEL-DC (see Figure 10-52).

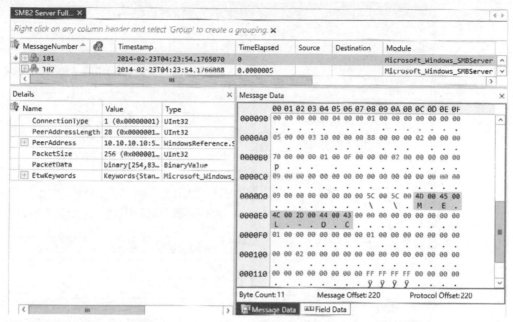

FIGURE 10-52 Examining message data

20. Close Microsoft Message Analyzer.

21. When prompted to save the captured trace, click No.

Exercise 8: Configure removable device auditing

In this exercise, you configure a GPO so that removable device usage is audited. To complete this exercise, perform the following steps:

1. On SYD-DC, click Group Policy Management on the Tools menu of Server Manager.

2. Expand Forest: Contoso.com\Domains\contoso.com\Group Policy Objects, and click Default Domain Policy, as shown in Figure 10-53.

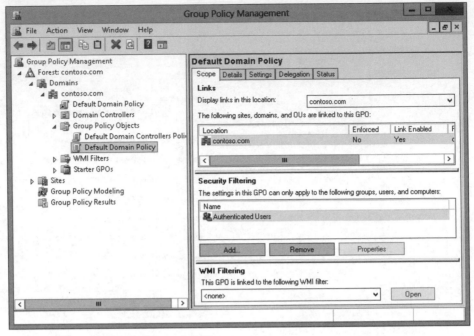

FIGURE 10-53 Clicking Default Domain Policy

3. On the Action menu, click Edit.

4. In the Group Policy Management Editor, navigate to the Computer Configuration\
   Policies\Windows Settings\Security Settings\Advanced Audit Policy Configuration\
   Audit Policies\Object Access node and click Audit Removable Storage, as shown in
   Figure 10-54.

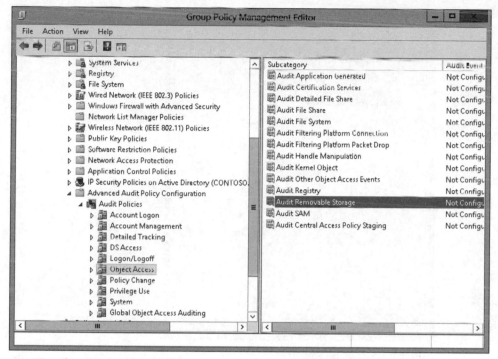

FIGURE 10-54 Clicking Audit Removable Storage

5. Double-click Audit Removable Storage.

6. In the Audit Removable Storage Properties dialog box, select Configure The Following Audit Events, Success, and Failure; then click OK (see Figure 10-55).

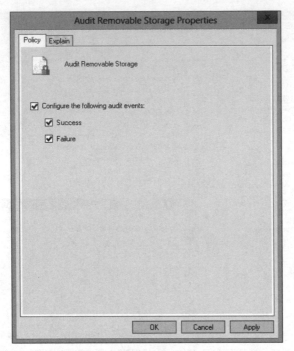

FIGURE 10-55 Auditing properties

7. Close the Group Policy Management Editor.

8. On the taskbar, right-click Windows PowerShell, and click Run As Administrator.

9. In the Windows PowerShell window, type the following command and press Enter.

   `Gpupdate /force`

10. In the Windows PowerShell window, type the following command and press Enter.

    `Auditpol /get /category:"Object Access"`

11. Verify that Removable Storage is configured for Success And Failure auditing, as shown in Figure 10-56.

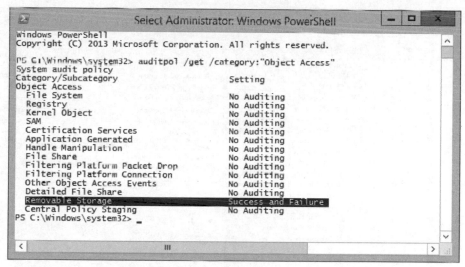

FIGURE 10-56 Configuring Removable Storage

Exercise 9: Configure logon auditing

In this exercise, you configure logon auditing. To complete this exercise, perform the following steps:

1. In the Group Policy Management Console (GPMC) on SYD-DC, right-click the Default Domain Policy, and click Edit.

2. In the Group Policy Management Editor, navigate to the Computer Configuration\Policies\Windows Settings\Security Settings\Advanced Audit Policy Configuration\Audit Policies\Logon/Logoff, and click Audit Logon, as shown in Figure 10-57.

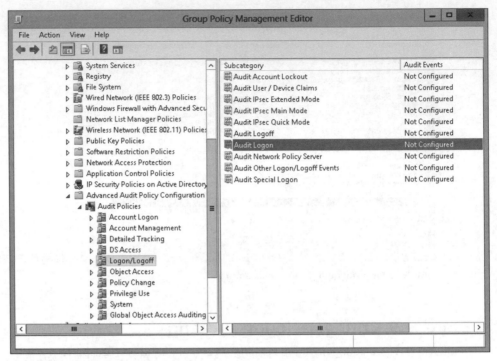

FIGURE 10-57 Selecting Audit Logon

3. On the Action menu, click Properties.

4. In the Audit Logon Properties dialog box, select Configure The Following Audit Events, Success, and Failure (see Figure 10-58). Click OK.

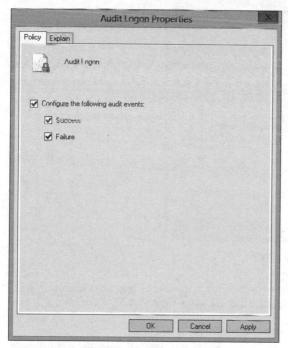

FIGURE 10-58 Setting audit properties

5. Close the Group Policy Management Editor.

6. On the Tools menu of the Server Manager console, click Active Directory Users And Computers.

7. In Active Directory Users And Computers, select Users, and then click Administrator.

8. On the Action menu, click Copy.

9. In the Copy Object – User dialog box, configure the following information, as shown in Figure 10-59, and click Next.

- First Name: **Gabe**
- Last Name: **Frost**
- User Logon Name: **Gabe_Frost**

FIGURE 10-59 Setting copy object data

10. Type **Pa$$w0rd** in the Password and Confirm Password text boxes, ensure User Must Change Password At Next Logon is not selected, click Next, and click Finish.

11. Close Active Directory Users And Computers.

12. In Windows PowerShell, type the following command and press Enter.

    ```
    Gpupdate /force
    ```

13. In Windows PowerShell, type the following command and press Enter.

    ```
    Auditpol /get /category:"Logon/Logoff"
    ```

14. Verify that Logon is configured for Success And Failure auditing, as shown in Figure 10-60.

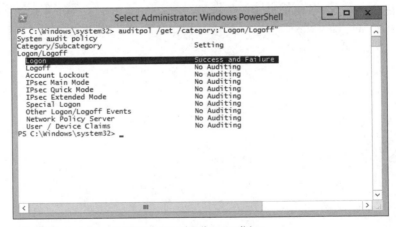

FIGURE 10-60 Logon for Success And Failure auditing

15. Switch to MEL-DC.

16. Sign out and sign on as contoso\gabe_frost with the password **Pa$$w0rd**.

17. Switch to SYD-DC.

18. On the Tools menu of the Server Manager console, click Event Viewer.

19. Expand Windows Logs\Security Logs and click the most recent event with Event ID 4624.

20. Click the Details pane and verify that the TargetUserName Gabe_Frost is listed, as shown in Figure 10-61. You may need to scroll through several events to find this TargetUserName.

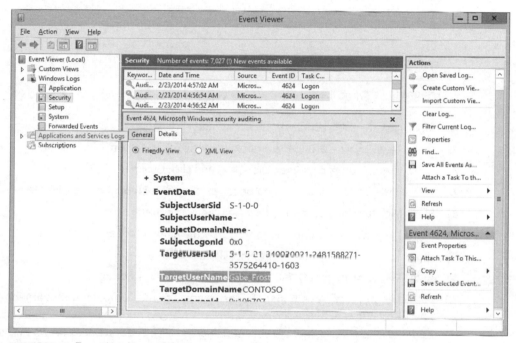

FIGURE 10-61 TargetUserName Gabe Frost

Exercise 10: Configure expression-based audit policies

In this exercise, you configure expression-based audit policies in Group Policy. To complete this exercise, perform the following steps:

1. On SYD-DC, open Active Directory Users And Computers from the Tools menu of the Server Manager console.

2. Right-click the Users container, click New, and click Group.

3. In the New Object – Group dialog box, type the name **Jupiter**, as shown in Figure 10-62, and click OK.

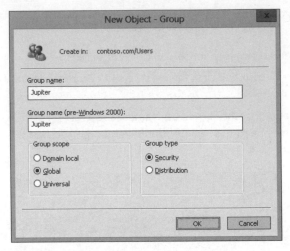

FIGURE 10-62 Typing the group name

4. Right-click the Users container, click New, and click Group.

5. In the New Object – Group dialog box, type the name **Saturn** and click OK.

6. Right-click the Users container, click New, and click Group.

7. In the New Object – Group dialog box, type the name **Neptune** and click OK.

8. Right-click the Users container, click New, and click Group.

9. In the New Object – Group dialog box, type the name **Mars** and click OK.

10. Close Active Directory Users And Computers.

11. In the GPMC, right-click Default Domain Policy, and click Edit.

12. In the Group Policy Management Editor, navigate to the Computer Configuration\
    Policies\Windows Settings\Security Settings\Advanced Audit Policy Configuration\
    Audit Policies\Global Object Access Auditing and click File System, as shown in Figure
    10-63.

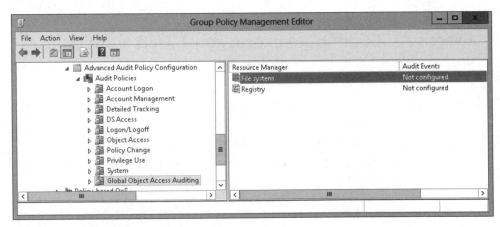

FIGURE 10-63 Selecting File System

13. On the Action menu, click Properties.

14. In the File System Properties dialog box, click Define This Policy Setting, and click Configure.

15. In the Advanced Security Settings For Global File SACL dialog box, click Add.

16. In the Auditing Entry For Global File SACL dialog box, click Select A Principal Link.

17. In the Select User, Computer, Service Account, Or Group dialog box, type **Jupiter**, click Check Names, and click OK.

18. On the Type drop-down menu, click All.

19. Click the Add A Condition link.

20. Click the Add Items button.

21. In the Select User, Computer, Service Account, Or Group dialog box, type **Saturn**, click Check Names, and click OK.

22. Verify that the Auditing Entry For Global File SACL dialog box matches Figure 10-64 and click OK.

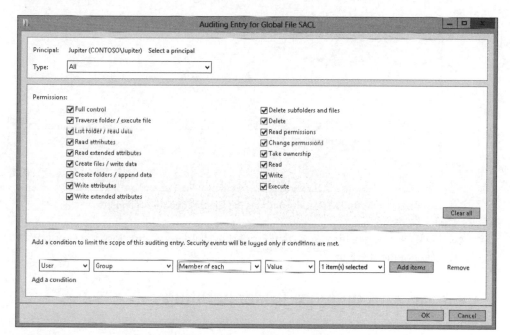

FIGURE 10-64 Auditing the Entry For Global File SACL dialog box

23. In the Advanced Security Settings For Global File SACL dialog box, click Add.

24. In the Auditing Entry For Global File SACL dialog box, click Select A Principal link.

25. In the Select User, Computer, Service Account, Or Group dialog box, type **Mars**, click Check Names, and click OK.

26. Set the Type drop-down menu to Fail.

27. Click the Add A Condition link.

28. Click the Member Of Each drop-down menu, and select Not Member Of Any.

29. Click the Add Items button.

30. In the Select User, Computer, Service Account, Or Group dialog box, type **Neptune**, click Check Names, and click OK twice.

31. Verify that the Advanced Security Settings For Global File SACL dialog box matches Figure 10-65, and click OK.

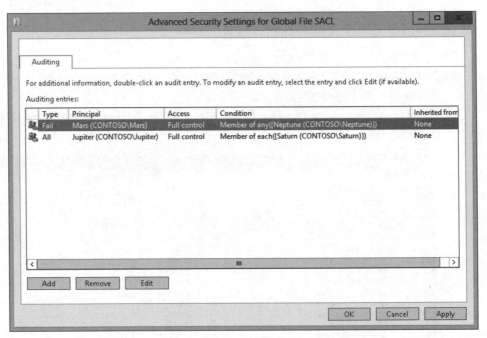

FIGURE 10-65 Advanced Security Settings For Global File SACL dialog box

32. Click OK to close the File System Properties dialog box and close the Group Policy Management Editor.

Exercise 11: Configure folder auditing

In this exercise, you configure expression-based audit policies at the folder level. To complete this exercise, perform the following steps:

1. Click File Explorer on the taskbar.

2. Click Computer and double-click Local Disk (C:).

3. On the title bar, click the New Folder icon.

4. Name the new folder **Audited_Files**.

5. Right-click the Audited_Files folder, and click Properties.

6. On the Security tab, click Advanced.

7. On the Auditing tab of the Advanced Security Settings For Audited_Files dialog box, shown in Figure 10-66, click Add.

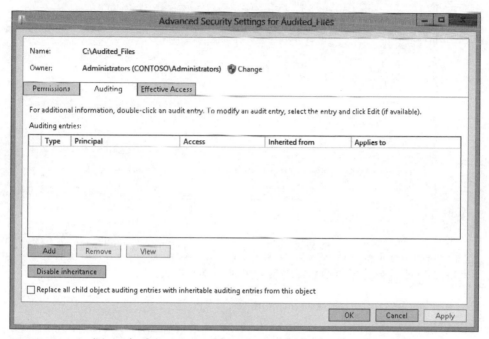

FIGURE 10-66 Auditing tab of the Advanced Security Settings For Audited_Files dialog box

8. In the Auditing Entry For Audited_Files dialog box, click Select A Principal link.

9. In the Select User, Computer, Service Account, Or Group dialog box, type **Neptune**, click Check Names, and click OK.

10. Change the type from Success to Fail.

11. Click the Add A Condition link.

12. Click the Add Items button.

13. In the Select User, Computer, Service Account, Or Group dialog box, type **Saturn**, click Check Names, and click OK.

14. Verify that the Auditing Entry For Audited Files dialog box matches Figure 10-67, and click OK.

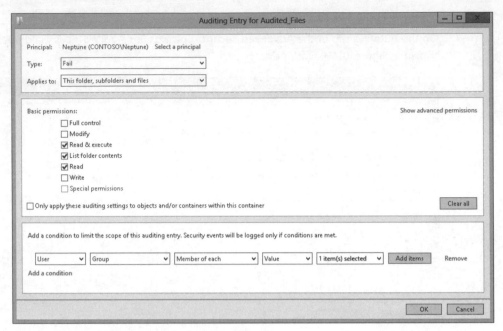

FIGURE 10-67 Auditing Entry For Audited Files dialog box

15. Click OK twice to close all dialog boxes.

Suggested practice exercises

The following additional practice exercises are designed to give you more opportunities to practice what you've learned and to help you successfully master the lessons presented in this chapter.

- **Exercise 1**   Use auditpol.exe to enable File System, Registry, and File Share Success And Failure auditing on MEL-DC.

- **Exercise 2**   Create a test share on SYD-DC and populate it with text files. Add user accounts to the Mars, Jupiter, Saturn, and Neptune groups. Sign on to MEL-DC and access the files across the network using different accounts. Verify that the expression-based audit policies record auditing information appropriately.

Answers

This section contains the answers to the lesson review questions in this chapter.

Lesson 1

1. **Correct answer: C**

    A. **Incorrect.** Resource Monitor enables you to view point-in-time resource utilization information. You can't use this tool to record resource utilization information for later review.

    B. **Incorrect.** Task Manager does enable you to view resource utilization information, but you can't record that data for later review.

    C. **Correct.** A data collector set can be used to capture performance counters and trace information related to resource utilization for later review.

    D. **Incorrect.** Message Analyzer, the successor to Network Monitor, enables you to capture and analyze network traffic. Although it can capture and record network traffic, you can't use this tool to record processor and memory utilization information.

2. **Correct answer: B**

    A. **Incorrect.** Task Manager provides real-time information about network utilization, but doesn't provide information about port utilization and firewall configuration.

    B. **Correct.** Resource Monitor provides information about services, the ports that they listen on, and firewall configuration.

    C. **Incorrect.** Message Analyzer enables you to capture and analyze network traffic, but it can't be used to determine port utilization and associated firewall configuration.

    D. **Incorrect.** A data collector set can record performance information and system trace information, but it can't be used to determine port utilization and associated firewall configuration.

3. **Correct answer: B**

    A. **Incorrect.** A data collector set can be used to capture performance counters and trace information related to network traffic, but it can't be used to capture network traffic.

    B. **Correct.** Message Analyzer, the successor to Network Monitor, enables you to capture and analyze network traffic.

    C. **Incorrect.** Resource Monitor enables you to view point-in-time network utilization information. You can't use Resource Monitor to capture and analyze network traffic.

D. **Incorrect.** Task Manager does enable you to view network traffic, but doesn't enable you to capture and analyze that traffic.

4. **Correct answer: D**

   A. **Incorrect.** Members of the Backup Operators group are enabled to perform backups; they do not have access to the Security event log.

   B. **Incorrect.** The Power Users group is included for backward compatibility; members of this group do not have access to the Security event log.

   C. **Incorrect.** Although members of the Event Log Readers group have access to the other event logs, they don't have access to the Security event log. Only members of the local Administrators group have access to the Security event log.

   D. **Correct.** When configuring event log subscriptions involving events in the Security event log, it is necessary to add the account of the collector computer to the local Administrators group on the source computer.

Lesson 2

1. **Correct answer: B**

   A. **Incorrect.** This command enables success and failure auditing for the File System subcategory.

   B. **Correct.** This command enables success and failure auditing for all subcategories under the Object Access category.

   C. **Incorrect.** This command disables success and failure auditing for all subcategories under the Object Access category.

   D. **Incorrect.** This command enables only failure auditing, not success auditing, for all subcategories under the Object Access category.

2. **Correct answer: A**

   A. **Correct.** This command enables only failure auditing, not success auditing, for all subcategories under the Object Access category.

   B. **Incorrect.** This command disables success and failure auditing for all subcategories under the Object Access category.

   C. **Incorrect.** This command enables success and failure auditing for all subcategories under the Object Access category.

   D. **Incorrect.** This command enables success and failure auditing for the File System subcategory.

3. **Correct answer: C**

   A. **Incorrect.** This command enables success and failure auditing for all subcategories under the Object Access category.

   B. **Incorrect.** This command enables only failure auditing, not success auditing, for all subcategories under the Object Access category.

C. **Correct.** This command enables success and failure auditing for the File System subcategory.

D. **Incorrect** This command disables success and failure auditing for all subcategories under the Object Access category.

4. **Correct answer: A**

A. **Correct.** This command disables success and failure auditing for all subcategories under the Object Access category.

B. **Incorrect.** This command enables only failure auditing, not success auditing, for all subcategories under the Object Access category.

C. **Incorrect.** This command enables success and failure auditing for all subcategories under the Object Access category.

D. **Incorrect.** This command enables success and failure auditing for the File System subcategory.

Index

Symbols

802.1X enforcement, configuring for NAP 382–385
802.1X group policies, cconfiguring authentication
363–367

A

A records 148
AAAA records 148
access-based enumeration 513
accidental deletion of objects, protecting from 212
accounting, RADIUS 429–432
Account Lockout Duration policy 71
  practice exercise 101
account lockout policies 70, 74
  practice exercise for configuring 101–104
Account Lockout Threshold policy 71
  practice exercise 102
account management tasks 71–75
Active Directory
  backing up 210–212
  database optimization 200–203
  defragmenting the database 200–203
  domain naming master 184
  metadata cleanup 203
  operations masters
    managing 182–187
    practice exercise 230–234
  recovering deleted objects 208–215
  snapshots 204–206, 215
Active Directory Administrative Center
  deploying an RODC 193
  domain functional level, configuring 80
  enabling Recycle Bin 208
  fine-grained password policies
    managing 81

practice exercise 110–113
non-expiring passwords, locating 72
  practice exercise 107–110
password settings, determining 84
practice exercise 234
Active Directory BitLocker recovery 526
Active Directory Domain Services (AD DS) 66
Active Directory Domain Services Configuration Wizard
  configuring a Global Catalog server 188
  deploying an RODC 191–193
  practice exercise 221–225
  removing domain controllers 203
Active Directory integrated zones 124–126
  practice exercise 159
Active Directory Recycle Bin 208–210
  practice exercise 234
Active Directory Schema 183
Active Directory Schema snap-in 183
  practice exercise 232
Active Directory Users And Computers
  accessing snapshots 205
  cleaning up metadata 204
  operations masters, managing 182–186
  practice exercise 230–232
Add-ADDSReadOnlyDomainControllerAccount cmdlet
  193
Add-DnsServerConditionalForwarderZone PowerShell
  cmdlet 134
Add-DNSServerDirectoryPartition cmdlet 125
Add-DnsServerForwarder cmdlet 132
Add-DnsServerPrimaryZone cmdlet 127
Add-DnsServerResourceRecordA cmdlet 148
Add-DnsServerResourceRecordCName cmdlet 148
Add-DnsServerResourceRecordMX PowerShell cmdlet
  149
Add-DnsServerResourceRecordPtr cmdlet 150
Add-DnsServerStubZone cmdlet 136

Add-DnsServerZoneDelegation cmdlet 130
/Add-Driver switch 6
Add-KDSRootKey cmdlet 88–90
/Add-Package switch 7
/Add-ProvisionedAppxPackage switch 8
Add Roles And Features Wizard 139
    deploying an RODC 191
    installing Windows Server Backup 210
    practice exercise 218–221, 226
AD DS (Active Directory Domain Services) 66
Add-WsusComputer command 31
Administrative Events custom view 601
administrative templates 296–302
    central store 297
        practice exercise 330
    filtering 300
        practice exercise 330
    importing in ADM format 299
ADMX format 296–300
ADMX Migrator tool 299
advanced audit policies 614–620
    practice exercises 641–654
Advanced Encryption Services (AES). *See* AES
aging and scavenging DNS zones 151
alerts, for monitoring servers 597–599
    practice exercise 628
alias (CNAME) records 148
    in GlobalNames zones 143
answer files 12–14
application directory partitions, creating 125
applications
    assigning 287
    publishing 288
    upgrading existing 290
/Apply-Image switch 10
app packages, adding to Server images 8
Approve-WsusUpdate command 31
assigning applications using Group Policy 287
auditpol.exe utility 619
audit policies, advanced 614–620
    practice exercises 641–654
authentication methods 357–359
    configuring with 802.1X group policies 363–367
    for network policies 372
authentication protocols for VPN 443–446
Authentication Requirements, configuring for HRA 349
authoritative restore for Active Directory objects
        212–214
autoenrollment, enabling using EFS 531

automatic approval rules for WSUS 36–38
    practice exercise for 58
Automatic Update Detection Frequency policy 34
automating server operating system deployment 12–14
autonomous mode, configuring WSUS 30
Autounattend.xml file 12

B

backing up Active Directory 210–212
backing up GPOs 243
    practice exercise 269–271
Backup-GPO cmdlet 242
BitLocker 522–529
    DRA (data recovery agent) 527
    modes, configuring 523–525
    Network Unlock feature 528
    practice exercise 566–571
    recovering data 525–528
    TPM (Trusted Platform Module) 523–525
BitLocker, protecting RODC virtual machines 196
BitLocker To Go 525
blocking Group Policies 254
Block Inheritance function 255
    practice exercise 275
block-level replication, used by DFS 514–516
boot environment, protecting with BitLocker 522–529
boot images, used by WDS 17
boot options for WDS 21
Boot.wim file 2
build and capture process 9
BYOD (Bring Your Own Device) scenarios 388

C

caching Group Policies 260
capture images, used by WDS 18
/Capture-Image switch 10
capturing traffic using Message Analyzer 611–613
centralized deployment 12
central store
    creating 297
    practice exercise 330
certificate enrollment practice exercise 574–578
Certification Authority (CA)
    choosing 348
    practice exercise 484, 566–571
    using with an HRA 397

CHAP (Challenge Handshake Authentication Protocol) 444
Cisco Network Access Control (Cisco NAC) 346
client naming policy 20
cloning DFS replication databases 519
cloning domain controllers 197
CNAME records 148
   in GlobalNames zones 143
collector-initiated event subscription, configuring 604
Computer Configuration settings 258–260
conditional forwarders, DNS 131–133
conditions
   for connection request policies 353–356
   for network policies 370–372
Configure Automatic Updates policy 34
Configure Forwarder Resource Usage policy 605
Configure Target Subscription Manager policy 605
connection request policies 350–363
   adding conditions 353–356
   creating 361–363
   default policy 360
   forwarding 356
   network access servers, specifying type 351
   realm name, applying 359
constraints, configuring for network policies 372
Control Panel settings, configuring with Group Policy
      preferences 319–321
Copy-GPO cmdlet 243
copying GPOs 246
corrupted DFS databases, recovering 520
counter alerts, for monitoring servers 597–599
   practice exercise 628
Create Multicast Transmission Wizard 24
creating GPOs 249
credential roaming, enabling using EFS 531
cryptographic policies of an HRA 397

D

data collector sets, for monitoring servers 592–596
   practice exercise 621–626
DCCloneConfig.xml file 198
DCGPOFix.exe command 246
Default Domain Policy GPO 67
defragmenting Active Directory database 200–203
delegating GPO management 248–251
delegating password settings permissions 78–80
Delegation Of Control Wizard 79

deleted Active Directory objects, recovering 208–215
Deny-WsusUpdate command 32
deployed servers, servicing and updating 27–39
deploying scripts to users and computers 291–293
   practice exercise 329–332
deploying software using Group Policy 285–291
deploying Windows Server images 11–27
   practice exercise for 43–47
Deployment Image Servicing and Management (DISM)
      tool 3
deployment topologies supported by DirectAccess 456
device drivers
   adding to Server images 6
   importing packages into WDS 25
DFS (Distributed File System)
   cloning replication databases 519
   configuring 511–521
   domain-based namespaces 512
   namespaces 511–513
      practice exercise 558–560
   practice exercise 555–558
   recovering databases 520
   remote differential compression 514–516
   replication 514–520
      practice exercise 560–566
      targets, adding 516
   staging folders 515
   stand-alone namespaces 512
DHCP enforcement, configuring for NAP 377–380
   practice exercise 401, 406–412
DirectAccess 454–473
   application servers, configuring 473
   benefits of 455
   client requirements 461
   configuring a DirectAccess server 457–460
   DNS, configuring for 463
   firewall rules, configuring 464
   infrastructure 455–460
   infrastructure servers, configuring 470–472
   Network Location Server (NLS) 460, 463, 470
   network topologies supported 456
   remote access servers, configuring 469
   Remote Access Setup diagram, configuring with
      465–473
   remote clients, configuring 467–469
Directory Services Restore Mode. See DSRM
discover images, used by WDS 15, 18
Dism.exe command-line utility 3–10

DISM tool. *See* Deployment Image Servicing and Management tool
Distributed File System (DFS). *See* DFS
DNS (Domain Name System)
   configuring, for DirectAccess 463
   preparing servers for DirectAccess 459
DNSKEY record 155
DNSSEC. *See* Domain Name System Security Extensions
DNSSEC Key Master 155
DNS zones 123–136
   Active Directory integrated zones 124–126
   aging and scavenging 151
   GlobalNames zones 142–144
   host records in 148
   mail exchanger (MX) records in 149
   pointer (PTR) records in 150
   practice exercise 159
   primary zones 127
   resource records in 147
   reverse lookup zones 128–130
   secondary zones 127
      practice exercise 168–170
   signing a zone 153
   split DNS 131
   stub zones 134
   supporting dynamic updates 126
   types of 124–130
   using DNSSEC with 153–157
   zone delegation 129
      practice exercise 163–168
domain-based namespaces 512
domain controllers
   cloning 197
   Global Catalog servers 187–189
   maintaining 200–207
   managing 181–200
   non-authoritative restore 214
   operations masters 182–187
   practice exercise 217–225
   removing 203
   RODC (read-only domain controller) 190–197
   snapshots, managing 204–206
   universal group membership caching (UGMC) 189
domain functional level
   fine-grained password policies and 80
   for GMSAs 88
Domain Name System (DNS). *See* DNS
Domain Name System Security Extensions (DNSSEC)
      147, 153–157

practice exercise 173–175
domain naming master 184
domain user password policies 66–70
   fine-grained 80–82
downloading software updates, practice exercise for
      40–42
DRA (data recovery agent)
   using with BitLocker 527
   using with EFS 533
driver packages, importing into WDS 25
   practice exercise for 52–54
dsamain command 205
DSRM (Directory Services Restore Mode)
   and the Active Directory Recycle Bin 208
   configuring domain controller as RODC 192
   performing authoritative restore 212–214
Dynamic Host Configuration Protocol (DHCP). *See* DHCP
dynamic update options for DNS zones 126
   practice exercise 159

E

EAP-MD5 CHAP (Extensible Authentication Protocol-
      Message Digest 5 Challenge Handshake Authen-
      tication) 443
EAP Quarantine Enforcement Client policy 383, 386
EAPs (Extensible Authentication Protocols) 357
EAP-TLS (Extensible Authentication Protocol-Transport
      Level Security) 443
EFS (Encrypting File System) 530–533
   certificates, configuring 531–533
      practice exercise 571–574
   practice exercise 566–571, 578–582
   recovering data 532
Enable Client-Side Targeting policy 34
/Enable-Feature switch 8
Encrypting File System (EFS). *See* EFS
encryption
   using BitLocker 522–529
   using EFS (Encrypting File System) 530–533
encryption, selecting types of 368
Enforce password history policy 68
   practice exercise 96
Enforce User Logon Restrictions policy 93
enforcing Group Policies 254
event-driven tasks 606–609
event log filters 600
event log forwarding 603–606

event log views 601–603
event subscriptions 603–606
  practice exercise 630–635
event trace providers 595
Event Viewer 599–609
EXE format, deploying files in 286
Export-DfsrClone Windows PowerShell cmdlet 519
expression-based audit policies 616
  practice exercise 649–652
Extensible Authentication Protocols. *See* EAPs

F

file classification, FSRM 505
file expiration, practice exercise 549–552
file integrity check, performing 200
file-level auditing 618
  practice exercise 652–654
file management tasks, FSRM 506
file quotas, FSRM 502
  practice exercise 541–545
file screens, FSRM 504–506
  practice exercise 545–549
File Server Resource Manager. *See* FSRM
filtering administrative templates 300
  practice exercise 330
filtering policies for GPOs 255–257
filters for event logs 600
fine-grained password policies 66, 77–85
  practice exercise 110–113
Flexible Single Master Operations. *See* FSMO
folder-level auditing 618
  practice exercise 652–654
folder redirection 282–285
  practice exercise 324–328
folder replication, DFS 514–520
forwarders, DNS 132
forwarding connection requests 356
forwarding event logs 603–606
FSRM (File Server Resource Manager)
  configuring 501–508
    practice exercise 536–541
  file classification 505
  file expiration, practice exercise 549–552
  file management tasks 506
  file screens 504–506
    practice exercise 545–549
  quotas 502
    practice exercise 541–545

storage reports 507
  practice exercise 552–556
Full Mesh topology 516
fully qualified domain names (FQDNs)
  host records and 148
  pointer (PTR) records and 150
  resource record maps and 147
  reverse lookup zones and 128

G

Get-ADDCCloningExcludedApplicationsList cmdlet 198
Get-ADDomain cmdlet 182
Get-ADForest cmdlet 182
Get-DfsrCloneState cmdlet 519
/Get-Features switch 8
Get-GPO cmdlet 242
/Get-ProvisionedAppxPackage switch 8
Get-Service cmdlet 91
/Get-wiminfo switch 5
Get-WsusClassification command 32
Get-WsusComputer command 32
Get-WsusProduct command 32
Get-WsusServer command 32
Global Catalog servers 187–189
global clouds 145
GlobalNames zones 142–144
Global Object Access Auditing node 617
Global Search function, Active Directory Administrative
      Center 84
GMSAs. *See* Group Managed Service Accounts
GPFixup.exe command 247
GPOs (Group Policy Objects) 66
Group Managed Service Accounts (GMSAs) 87–90
  practice exercise 114
  requirements 88
Group Policy Management Console (GPMC) 242
  configuring password policies 96–100
  delegating permissions 248–251
  linking GPOs 250
  policy processing precedence 253
  practice exercise 268–271
  practice exercise, using Group Policy Modeling
      104–107
  remote Group Policy update 262
Group Policy Modeling
  delegating permissions 251
  practice exercise 275
Group Policy Objects (GPOs) 66
  administrative templates 296–302

advanced audit policies 614–620
    practice exercise 641–645
assigning applications 287
backing up 243
    practice exercise 269–271
BitLocker, configuring 525
    practice exercise 582–584
block inheritance 254
    practice exercise 275
caching 260
copying 246
creating 249
delegating management of 248–251
deploying applications 285–291
editing 249
enforcing 254
fixing problems 246
importing 245
linking 250
loopback processing 258–260
    practice exercise 271
maintaining 241–251
migrating 247
.msi files, installing applications from 286
permissions, delegating 248–251
practice exercise 265–268
processing precedence 253
publishing applications 288
redirecting folders 282–285
    practice exercise 324–328
restoring 244
scripts, deploying to users 291–293
    practice exercise 329–332
security filtering 255–257
    practice exercise 273
slow-link processing 260
upgrading deployed packages 290
.zap files, deploying installations with 286
Group Policy preferences 303–321
  Control Panel settings 319–321
  Internet Explorer, configuring 314
  item-level targeting 305
    power options, configuring 309
    practice exercise 336–338
  Local Users and Groups option 315
  mapping network drives 306–308
  mapping network printers 308
  power options, configuring 309–313
  practice exercise 331–338

registry, configuring 314
settings commonly used 303
Windows settings 317–319
Group Policy Results, delegating permissions 251
Group Policy, using with WSUS 33

H

HCAP (Host Credential Authorization Protocol), installing
    346–350
health policies, configuring for NAP 395
Health Registration Authority (HRA). *See* HRA
health validators, configuring for Network Access Protec-
    tion 392–399
Host Credential Authorization Protocol (HCAP).
    See HCAP
host records in DNS zones 148
HRA (Health Registration Authority) 397
  installing 346–350
Hub And Spoke topology 516

I

IKEv2 tunneling protocol 444
Import-DfsrClone cmdlet 519
Import-GPO cmdlet 242
importing GPOs 245
inactive user accounts 75
-IncludeManagementTools switch 17
infrastructure master 186
Install-ADServiceAccount cmdlet 89
install images, used by WDS 17
Install.wim file 2
Install-WindowsFeatureWINS command 139
Internet Explorer, configuring with Group Policy prefer-
    ences 314
Invoke-GPUpdate Windows PowerShell cmdlet 262
Invoke-WsusServerCleanup command 32
IP filters, configuring for Network Policy Server 367
IPsec enforcement, configuring for NAP 380–382
IP settings, configuring 368
item-level targeting 305
  power options, configuring 309
  practice exercise 336–338

K

Kerberos constrained delegation 91–94
key distribution services root key, creating 88–90
Key Signing Key (KSK) 156
KRA (key recovery agent), using with EFS 533

L

L2TP/IPsec tunneling protocol 445
linking GPOs 250
link-local clouds 145
Local Users and Groups option 315
    practice exercise 333
lockout policies. *See* account lockout policies
logoff scripts 291
logon auditing practice exercise 645–649
logon scripts 291
    mapping network drives 306–308
loopback processing 258–260
    practice exercise 271

M

mail exchanger (MX) records in DNS zones 149
mail gateways, locating 149
Managed Service Accounts 87
mapping network drives 306–308
mapping network printers 308
Maximum Lifetime For Service Ticket policy 93
Maximum Lifetime For User Ticket policy 93
Maximum Lifetime For User Ticket Renewal policy 93
Maximum password age policy 68
    practice exercise 97
Maximum Tolerance For Computer Clock Synchroniza-
    tion policy 93
Merge (loopback processing) 259
Message Analyzer tool 611–613
    practice exercise 638–641
metadata cleanup, Active Directory 203
migrating GPOs 247
Migration Table Editor (MTE) 247
Minimum password age policy 68
    practice exercise 98
Minimum password length policy 69
    practice exercise 99
monitoring servers 591–611
    using data collector sets 592–596
    practice exercise 621–626
    using Event Viewer 599–609
    using network monitoring 609–612
        practice exercise 636–641
    using performance counter alerts 597–599
/Mount-image switch 6
mounting Windows Server images 5
Move-ADDirectoryServerOperationMasterRole cmdlet
    187
MS-CHAPv2 (Microsoft Challenge Handshake Authenti-
    cation Protocol version 2) 443
.msi files, installing applications from 286
multicast transmissions 14
    configuring settings for 22, 24

N

Name Resolution Policy Table (NRPT), creating 156
namespaces, DFS 511–513
    practice exercise 558–560
NAP. *See* Network Access Protection
NAT (network address translation) 448–451
Network Access Protection (NAP)
    802.1X enforcement, configuring 382–385
    DHCP enforcement, configuring 377–380
        practice exercise 401, 406–412
    enforcement methods 376–390
    health policies, configuring 395
    health validators, configuring 392–399
    IPsec enforcement, configuring 380–382
    network policies, creating 369–373
    RD Gateway enforcement, configuring 387–390
    remediation server groups 398
        practice exercise 405, 410
    SHAs and SHVs, configuring 395
    VPN enforcement, configuring 385–387
    WSHV, configuring 392–394
        practice exercise 403
network address translation (NAT) 448–451
Network Connectivity Assistant (NCA) 469
network drives, mapping 306–308
Network Location Server (NLS) 460, 463, 470
network monitoring, for monitoring servers 609–612
    practice exercise 636–641
Network Policy Server (NPS) 345 376
    authentication methods 357–359
        configuring with 802.1X group policies 363–367
    client configuration 363–367
    connection request policies 350–363

      adding conditions 353–356
      creating 361–363
      default policy 360
      forwarding 356
      network access servers, specifying type 351
      realm name, applying 359
   deploying 346–350
   encryption, selecting types of 368
   IP filters, configuring 367
   IP settings, configuring 368
   network policies
      adding conditions 370–372
      creating 369–373
   practice exercise 402
   RADIUS proxy and server 346
   templates 374–376
Network Policy Service (NPS)
   RADIUS accounting 429–432
      practice exercise 480
   RADIUS clients 426–429
      practice exercise 479
   RADIUS proxies 421–425
   RADIUS servers 418–421
      practice exercise 475–478
network printers, mapping 308
network topologies supported by DirectAccess 456
network traffic, capturing using Message Analyzer
   611–613
Network Unlock feature, BitLocker 528
New-ADDCCloneConfig Windows PowerShell cmdlet
   198
New-ADServiceAccount cmdlet 89
New Delegation Wizard 130
New-GPO cmdlet 243
New Zone Wizard 124, 135, 143
Next Secure (NSEC/NSEC3) record 155
non-authoritative restore for Active Directory objects
   214
non-expiring passwords 71–73
   practice exercise 107–110
NPS. *See* Network Policy Server
ntdsutil.exe command
   creating Active Directory snapshots 204–206
   defragmenting Active DIrectory database 200–203
   performing authoritative restore 213
   seizing FSMO roles 187

O

operations master
   domain naming master 184
   practice exercise 230–234
   RID master 186
   schema master 183
   seizing FSMO roles 187
operations masters
   managing 182–187
   practice exercise 230–234

P

packages, upgrading using Group Policy 290
PAP (Password Authentication Protocol) 444
pass-through mode, Web Application Proxy in 451
Password must meet complexity requirements policy 69
   practice exercise 100
Password Never Expires option 71
password policies
   domain-based 66–70
   fine-grained 76–84, 77–85
      practice exercise 110–113
   non-expiring passwords 71–73
      practice exercise 107–110
   practice exercise for configuring 96–100
Password Replication Policy for RODCs 194–196
Password Settings Container (PSC) 81
Password Settings Object (PSO)
   configuring 82–84
   creating 81
PDC emulator 185
Peer Name Resolution Protocol (PNRP) 144
performance counter alerts, for monitoring servers
   597–599
   practice exercise 628
Performance Monitor 592–595
   practice exercise 621–626
permissions
   setting for folder redirection 284
(PNRP) Peer Name Resolution Protocol 144
pointer (PTR) records in DNS zones 150
policy processing precedence 253
power options, configuring 309–313
Power Options (Windows XP) 309–311
Power Plans 312
Power Scheme (Windows XP) 311

PPTP tunneling protocol 445
Pre-boot Execution Environment. *See* PXE
precedence, Group Policy processing 253
prestaging an RODC account 193
primary zones 127
PSO. *See* Password Settings Object
publishing applications 288
push partners and pull partners, configuring WINS servers 140
PXE-compliant network adapters 14–16
PXE response settings, configuring WDS with 19

Q

quotas, FSRM 502
   practice exercise 541–545

R

RADIUS accounting 429–432
   practice exercise 480
RADIUS clients 426–429
   practice exercise 479
RADIUS, configuring 417–434
RADIUS proxies 421–425
RADIUS proxy 346
   connection request policies and 359
RADIUS server 346
   connection request policies and 359
RADIUS servers 418–421
   practice exercise 475–478
RD Gateway enforcement, configuring for NAP 387–390
read-only domain controller. *See* RODC
realm name, applying to connection request policies 359
recovering Active Directory objects 208–215
recovering data
   from BitLocker-protected volumes 525–528
   from corrupted DFS databases 520
   from EFS-encrypted files 532
Recycle Bin, Active Directory 208–210
   practice exercise 234
redirecting folders 282–285
   practice exercise 324–328
registry keys, selecting to monitor 595
registry settings, configuring with Group Policy preferences 314
relative identifiers (RIDs) 186

remediation server groups 398
   practice exercise 405, 410
Remote Access role service
   configuring on VPN server 438–443
   installing 435–437
   Web Application Proxy 451
      practice exercise 483–489
Remote Access Setup diagram 465–473
   configuring application servers 473
   configuring infrastructure servers 470–472
   configuring remote access servers 469
   configuring remote clients 467–469
Remote Authentication Dial-In User Service. *See* RADIUS
Remote Desktop Services. *See* RDS
remote differential compression, used by DFS 514–516
remote Group Policy update 261
Remote Server Administration Tools (RSAT) 89
   managing WDS with 16
removable device auditing practice exercise 641–645
Remove-GPO cmdlet 243
/Remove-ProvisionedAppxPackage switch 8
Rename-GPO cmdlet 243
Replace (loopback processing) 259
replica mode, configuring WSUS 30
replication, DFS 514–520
   cloning databases 519
   practice exercise 560–566
   targets, adding 516
replication partners, configuring WINS servers 140
replication scope
   configuring 125–127
   practice exercise 161–163
Reset Account Lockout Counter After policy 71
   practice exercise 103
resetting password permissions 78–80
Resource Monitor tool 610
Resource Record Signature (RRSIG) records 154
resource records in DNS zones 147
Restore-GPO cmdlet 243
restoring Active Directory objects 208–215
restoring GPOs 244
reverse lookup zones 128–130
RID (relative identifier) master 186
RODC (read-only domain controller) 190–197
   Password Replication Policy 194–196
   practice exercise 225–230

Routing and Remote Access
   configuring server routing 446–448
   configuring VPN server 439–443
   deploying 435–437
   NAT (network address translation) 448–451
Routing Information Protocol v2 (RIP) 446
RSAT. *See* Remote Server Administration Tools

S

schedules, replication 517
schema master 183
scripts, deploying to users and computers 291–293
   practice exercise 328–331, 329–332
secondary zones 127
   practice exercise 168–170
security filtering for GPOs 255–257
   practice exercise 273
security identifiers (SIDs) 186
security roles in WSUS 32
seizing FSMO roles 187
self-service password reset 79
semantic integrity check, performing 200
Server Core version of Windows Server
   installing WDS on computers with 16
   installing WSUS on computers with 28
Server images. *See* Windows Server images
servers, monitoring. *See* monitoring servers
service principal names (SPNs) 94
service tickets, determined by Kerberos policies 92
servicing Windows Server images 4–11
   practice exercise for 42
Set-ADComputer cmdlet 92
Set-ADDomainMode Windows PowerShell cmdlet 80
Set-ADObject cmdlet 209
Set-ADObject Windows PowerShell cmdlet 213
Set-ADServiceAccount cmdlet 89, 92
Set-ADUser cmdlet 92
Set-DnsServerScavenging cmdlet 152
SetSPN command-line utility 94
Set-WsusClassification command 32
Set-WsusProduct command 32
Set-WsusServerSynchronization command 32
shared folders, locating with DFS 511, 516
shared secret, configuring 424, 427
SHA (System Health Agent), configuring for NAP 395
shutdown scripts 291
SHV (System Health Validator), configuring for NAP 395

signing DNS zones 153
single-label name resolution solutions
   GlobalNames zones 142–144
   practice exercise 171
   WINS 138–142
slow-link processing 260
snapshots, Active Directory 204–206
software deployment using Group Policy 285–291
SPAP (Shiva Password Authentication Protocol) 444
Specify Intranet Microsoft Update Service Location
      policy 34
split DNS 131
SQL Server logging, configuring 430–432
SSL certificate, obtaining for DirectAccess server 459,
      463
SSTP tunneling protocol 445
staging folder, DFS 515
stale resource records in DNS zones 151
stand-alone namespaces 512
startup scripts 291
storage reports, FSRM 507
   practice exercise 552–556
Store Passwords Using Reversible Encryption policy 69
stub zones 134
subscriptions, event 603–606
   practice exercise 630–635
success and failure auditing, configuring 618–620
Sysprep.exe utility 9
System Health Agent (SHA), configuring for NAP 395
System Health Validator (SHV), configuring for NAP 395

T

targeting categories when applying Group Policy prefer-
      ences 305, 309
   practice exercise 336–338
tasks, event-driven 606–609
templates for Network Policy Server (NPS) 374–376
Ticket Granting Ticket (TGT) 93
time synchronization, performed by PDC emulator 185
tombstone lifetime setting 212
tombstone reanimation 214
topologies supported by DirectAccess 456
topology, replication 516
TPM (Trusted Platform Module), using with BitLocker
      523–525
transport agent policies, configuring for an HRA 398
Trust anchors 155

tunneling protocols, VPN 444–446
two-factor authentication, configuring 458

U

Uninstall-ADDSDomainController cmdlet 203
universal group membership caching (UGMC) 189
/Unmount-Wim switch 9
update deployment using WSUS 28
update files, downloading 40–42
upgrading deployed packages 290
User Configuration settings 258–260
user password policies, domain-based 66–70
user tickets, determined by Kerberos policies 92

V

views of event logs 601–603
virtual service accounts 90
VPN authentication protocols 443–446
VPN enforcement, configuring for NAP 385–387
VPN servers
   configuring Remote Access role service on 438–443
   practice exercise 481–483
VPN settings, configuring 437–446
VPN tunneling protocols 444–446

W

WDS. *See* Windows Deployment Services
Web Application Proxy 451
   practice exercise 483–495
wecsvc (Windows Event Collector) 604
Windows Assessment and Deployment Kit (Windows
      ADK) 12
Windows Deployment Services (WDS) 14–27
   client naming policy for 20
   configuring 19–23
      practice exercise for 47–51
   driver packages, importing into 25
      practice exercise for 52–54
   images, importing into 17–19
   installing on Server Core versions 16
   multicast transmissions 14, 22
   practice exercise for 43–47
   requirements for 15
   transmissions, configuring 24
Windows Imaging (WIM) files 2
   practice exercise for servicing 42

Windows PE 17
Windows PowerShell
   importing 16
   support in WSUS 28, 31
Windows Security Health Validator (WSHV), configuring
      for NAP 392–394
Windows Server Backup, installing 210
Windows Server images
   adding device drivers to 6
   answer files and 12
   automating deployment of 12–14
   build and capture process 9
   committing 9
   configuring 3
   deploying automatically 11–27
   mounting 5
   payload-removed features of 8
   servicing 4–11
   software updates to 6
   understanding 2
Windows Server Update Services (WSUS) 27–39
   automatic approval rules for 36–38
   configuring, practice exercise for 56–58
   deploying 28–32
      practice exercise for 54–56
   deploying updates 35
   groups
      creating 33
      practice exercise for 58
   installing on Server Core versions 28
   new features of 28
   policies 33
   replica mode, configuring 30
   security roles in 32
   updating files 30
   Windows PowerShell support in 28, 31
Windows settings, configuring with Group Policy prefer-
      ences 317–319
Windows System Image Manager (Windows SIM) 12
WinRM (Windows Remote Management) 604
WINS, configuring 138–142
wired network policies, configuring 363–367
wired networks, configuring 802.1X enforcement for 383
wireless network policies, configuring 363
wireless networks, configuring 802.1X enforcement for
      384

WMI filters
  and Group Policies 257
  delegating ability to create 251
WSHV (Windows Security Health Validator), configuring
     for NAP 392–394
  practice exercise 403
WSUS. *See* Windows Server Update Services

Z

.zap files, deploying applications with 286
zone delegation 129
  practice exercise 163–168
Zone Signing Key (ZSK) 156
zone transfers
  managing 127
  practice exercise 168

About the author

ORIN THOMAS is an MVP, an MCT and has a string of Microsoft MCSE and MCITP certifications. He has written more than 25 books for Microsoft Press and is a contributing editor at Windows IT Pro magazine. He has been working in IT since the early 1990's. He regularly speaks at events like TechED in Australia and around the world on Windows Server, Windows Client, System Center and security topics. Orin founded and runs the Melbourne System Center, Security, and Infrastructure Group. You can follow him on twitter at http://twitter.com/orinthomas.

Training Guide: Administering Windows Server 2012 R2 and Exam 70-411

This book is designed to help build and advance your job-role expertise. In addition, it covers some of the topics and skills related to Microsoft Certification Exam 70-411, and may be useful as a complementary study resource. Note: This book is not designed to cover all exam topics; see chart below. If you are preparing for the exam, use additional materials to help bolster your readiness, in conjunction with real-world experience.

DEPLOY, MANAGE, AND MAINTAIN SERVERS	
Deploy and manage server images	Chapter 1, Lessons 1 and 2
Implement patch management	Chapter 1, Lesson 3
Monitor servers	Chapter 10, Lesson 1
CONFIGURE FILE AND PRINT SERVICES	
Configure Distributed File System (DFS)	Chapter 9, Lesson 2
Configure File Server Resource Manager (FSRM)	Chapter 9, Lesson 1
Configure file and disk encryption	Chapter 9, Lesson 3
Configure advanced audit policies	Chapter 10, Lesson 2
CONFIGURE NETWORK SERVICES AND ACCESS	
Configure DNS zones	Chapter 3, Lesson 2
Configure DNS records	Chapter 3, Lesson 3
Configure VPN and routing	Chapter 8, Lesson 2
Configure DirectAccess	Chapter 8, Lesson 3
CONFIGURE A NETWORK POLICY SERVER INFRASTRUCTURE	
Configure Network Policy Server (NPS)	Chapter 8, Lesson 1
Configure NPS policies	Chapter 7, Lesson 1
Configure Network Access Protection (NAP)	Chapter 7, Lessons 2 and 3
CONFIGURE AND MANAGE ACTIVE DIRECTORY	
Configure service authentication	Chapter 2, Lesson 3
Configure domain controllers	Chapter 4, Lesson 1
Maintain Active Directory	Chapter 4, Lessons 2 and 3
Configure account policies	Chapter 2, Lesson 2

CONFIGURE AND MANAGE GROUP POLICY	
Configure Group Policy processing	Chapter 5, Lesson 2
Configure Group Policy settings	Chapter 6, Lesson 1
Manage Group Policy objects (GPOs) .	Chapter 5, Lesson 1
Configure Group Policy preferences	Chapter 6, Lesson 3

Exam Objectives   The exam objectives listed here are current as of this book's publication date. Exam objectives are subject to change at any time without prior notice and at Microsoft's sole discretion. Please visit the Microsoft Learning website for the most current listing of exam objectives: *http://www.microsoft.com/learning/en/us/exam-70-411.aspx.*

Free ebooks

From technical overviews to drilldowns on special topics, get
free ebooks from Microsoft Press at:

www.microsoftvirtualacademy.com/ebooks

Download your free ebooks in PDF, EPUB, and/or Mobi for
Kindle formats.

Look for other great resources at Microsoft Virtual Academy,
where you can learn new skills and help advance your career
with free Microsoft training delivered by experts.

Now that you've read the book...

Tell us what you think!

Was it useful?
Did it teach you what you wanted to learn?
Was there room for improvement?

Let us know at http://aka.ms/tellpress

Your feedback goes directly to the staff at Microsoft Press,
and we read every one of your responses. Thanks in advance!